LEAVENWORTH
TRAIN

LEAVENWORTH TRAIN

TRAIN

A FUGITIVE'S SEARCH FOR JUSTICE
IN THE VANISHING WEST

JOE JACKSON

CARROLL & GRAF PUBLISHERS
NEW YORK

As always,
to Kathy and Nick
and
to the memory of my father,
who dreamed of new frontiers

LEAVENWORTH TRAIN
A Fugitive's Search for Justice in the Vanishing West

Copyright © 2001 by Joe Jackson

Carroll & Graf Publishers
A Division of Avalon Publishing Group Incorporated
161 William St., 16th Floor
New York, NY 10038

First Carroll & Graf edition 2001

Library of Congress Cataloging-in-Publication Data is available.

ISBN 0-7867-0897-2

9 8 7 6 5 4 3 2 1

Printed in the United States of America
Distributed by Publishers Group West

Contents

Preface

AT FIRST GLANCE, the highway leading to the United States Penitentiary at Leavenworth, Kansas, seems like many rural American roads. Metropolitan Avenue, also called U.S. Highway 73, runs straight as a ruler west from the steel arch bridge spanning the Missouri River to the turnoff for the prison's parking lot; beyond this, the highway curves northwest to follow the first leg of what was once the Santa Fe Trail. The land immediately north of the blacktop is undeveloped and open, a vision as peaceful and rolling as any Kansas farmland, thanks to federal oversight, for this is the southern entrance of the Fort Leavenworth Military Reservation, approximately 6,000 acres of prime bottomland located on a high bluff overlooking the muddy river below. It is "as a pretty a spot as you can find on God's green earth," one observer said in 1895, and the same applies today. The southern side of the highway is much different. The town of Leavenworth itself, named after the army base, has pushed to the edge of the asphalt, the relentless amoebic advance of unplanned development checked by the government land. Nevertheless, the highway feels just like home. Like almost anywhere else in America, a visitor can eat at a Pizza Hut, bed down for the night at a cinder block motel, bargain for a new home at a real estate office, worship in a "full gospel" church, roller skate at the Wheel Thing Skate Center, and shop for provisions in a 7-Eleven, where prison guards stop on the way to their shifts to load up on crullers and steaming cups of French roast coffee.

People here are good to prison guards. The city of Leavenworth calls itself Prison City, U.S.A., and with seven jails, prisons, and work camps comprising the employment base, law and order is not taken lightly. A visitor can have his photo snapped in prison stripes; the Chamber of Commerce invites him to "do time" in town. It's all a joke, of course, but the roots of humor can be deadly serious, a fact that becomes quite evident when one turns off Metropolitan Avenue into the penitentiary. Suddenly, all pretense for humor ends.

At least it did for me. I couldn't help feeling dwarfed by the huge limestone walls rearing out of the prairie to form Leavenworth's famous front facade. An American flag fluttered in the central grass island of the prison's horseshoe-shaped entrance; aligned behind it in perfect ascending order rose a gun tower, marble steps, and the dome-capped rotunda for which the "Big Top" got one of its many names. Past that, my eye tracked up to the blue Kansas sky. All seemed very ordered here, without a hint of chaos, yet also intimidating, and I wondered if every visitor imagined eyes, cameras, or guns invisibly trained on him as he stopped to snap a photo. I certainly did, so I didn't stay long.

Such are the works of man. The spirit of an era is preserved, like amber, in its public shrines; the challenge comes in translating what they memorialize. Leavenworth was built in the early years of the twentieth century, the same period during which the Panama Canal became President Theodore Roosevelt's legacy to manifest destiny and imperial dreams. The New Deal faith in government's good works left behind massive dams and power lines coursing through otherwise deserted landscapes; the Eisenhower administration had its interstate highway system, tying the nation together in a different type of grid. Lyndon Johnson's Great Society raised small cities of public housing to the failed hope of eradicating poverty. The symbol for America's new millennium is the prison.

As writer Eric Schlosser observed in the December 1998 *Atlantic Monthly*, corrections is now the greatest area of growth in the public sector, turning prisons into ubiquitous and unintended monuments for our current age. *Correctional Building News*, a monthly newsletter devoted to the business of prison construction, listed a few of the projects: "a 3,100-bed jail in Harris County, Texas; a 500-bed medium-security prison in Redgranite, Wisconsin . . . two 200-bed housing pods at the Fort Dodge Correctional Facility in Iowa . . . and dozens more." Unlike previous public shrines, these works are neither grandiose nor inspiring, but they are in demand and seem to pop up everywhere. They fill the rural landscape at a time when, according to an October 2000 analysis by Washington's nonprofit Sentencing Project, America's rate of imprisonment has become the highest on the planet. Our era is one in which roughly 14 million Americans face the likelihood of imprisonment at some point in their lives, with some 2 million Americans already behind bars. Never before could the United States honestly be styled a prison nation, a sobering thought in a place that still calls itself the Land of the Free.

Leavenworth brackets this age. The edges of America's expanding wilderness—first in the New England colonies, then later in the seemingly limitless West—have always been "given up to the dreams of fancy, and the unrestricted experiments of innovators," Alexis de Tocqueville observed, in *Democracy in America*. Leavenworth was an expression of a particular moral vision—a utopia of benign social control. Begun in 1897 as America's largest and most progressive prison, by March 2001 it was still the nation's largest maximum-security compound, according to government sources. Along with Alcatraz, Sing Sing, and Attica, its name is synonymous with the historical violence committed within its walls. If the United States is the international leader for incarceration, Leavenworth is one of the largest, meanest, and most famous prisons in the world.

In the summer of 1999, I was following the route of one man who tried to escape this legacy. In some ways, the story of Frank Grigware, Leavenworth's most famous fugitive, has roots in three centuries. Born in 1886 to immigrant parents, he traveled with them in 1900 in hopes of achieving the well-advertised American Dream. As a young man he headed into the vanishing West, hoping to strike it rich, but instead was convicted in one of the West's last train robberies. He insisted on his innocence, but the weight of evidence, resources, and opinion was against him, and in 1909 he was sentenced to life in the Big Top. He didn't stay long, and even today he remains one of the prison's legends.

At first I didn't want to write Frank's tale. I had stumbled upon it while researching a previous prison book, *Dead Run*, and I didn't want to devote more years to another prison saga. Yet writing *Dead Run* had generated more questions for me than it had answered, and Grigware's flight and fate seemed one way to answer them. *Dead Run* was the story of Dennis Stockton, a man sentenced to Virginia's Death Row for a crime of which he was probably innocent; I'd discovered, as a former justice reporter for the Norfolk *Virginian-Pilot*, strong evidence of that innocence, but ultimately the state and federal courts were not interested and Stockton asked me to be a witness at his execution. In many ways, the act of witnessing changed my life. How had we as a people come to the point where we no longer cared about innocence, once thought the heart of justice? Is there a collective guilt that overshadows us all? Obviously, other nations think so, or are at least greatly troubled and baffled by us, given their vehement response to our continued use of the death penalty. The deadly misuse of power was perhaps *the* prime concern for the crafters of the U.S. Constitution, and we revere them for that. Yet more than two hundred years later, our actions diverge radically from that source of national pride. How did things change?

Frank Grigware, like Dennis Stockton, tried to escape the injustice around him, and vengeance was his reward. The societies in which the two men lived, separated by a hundred years, were similar in surprising and remarkable ways. Perhaps America has never fundamentally changed; perhaps that is why de Tocqueville's classic is still an accurate and prescient guidebook to the American soul. Both men lived in times of expansion, when America flexed her political and economic muscle yet seemed genuinely naive concerning international opinion. They lived in times marked by waves of immigrants drawn to the dream of America, who found the gap between rich and poor reaching record highs. They lived in times of fear when, despite phenomenal prosperity, Americans were haunted by visions of an underlying chaos and so turned to their police and courts to keep them safe and secure. More than ever before, prisons became the nexus where the harsh realities and strange chimeras of American justice came together; where crime and punishment, guilt and innocence, vengeance and penitence played out a kind of dumb show. Built to solve problems, the prisons nurtured them instead, incubating fear and violence, helping it to grow.

Interesting for me was the fact that Frank's story came at the dawn of the twentieth century, when the federal government decided to enter the prison business in hopes of somehow checking the nation's growing crime rate. This seemed one of those moments when opportunities were seen, yet abandoned, as the violence inside and outside the prisons grew unabated and exponentially. What part did prisons play in this growth? What went wrong?

I have been hypnotized by violence as long as I can remember, which probably makes me quintessentially American. I remember my grandfather's tales of labor violence in the Kentucky mining camps, of his brother's dash across no-man's land as a squad leader during World War I, and of another brother's desperate hours in an inmate riot as a prison guard. I learned of two murderers in the family. I thrilled to the cataclysmic force of the missiles my father helped launch as a NASA engineer in the 1960s and 1970s, awed when they exploded in a pinwheel of burning light and flame. I myself became a police reporter, describing the parade of bodies to Virginia readers at a time when murder records were being set across America. I watched as a tank rolled over a freedom fighter in Lithuania, watched the electrocutions and fatal injections of guilty and innocent men. Sometimes I wondered what witnessing so many deaths did to me; it almost seemed that nothing could surprise me anymore. It could, of course, but deep beneath the surface, where I couldn't see.

Maybe there were answers in a story like Frank Grigware's. I followed Frank's tracks to Omaha, Nebraska, where he was accused of train robbery; to Leavenworth, where he and five others hijacked a prison train; to the Coeur d'Alenes in Idaho, where he panned for gold and dug for silver; to the tiny town in the Canadian Rockies where he found some peace before the world crashed in. And to Spokane, Washington, where he said goodbye to his mother before all this happened, innocently giving her a locket with his picture inside and promising to return a success from his western foray. He vowed to make her proud.

The West is a beautiful place, but that beauty has nothing to do with man. I remember standing on a hilltop in Montana and watching as, far off in the distance, a funnel cloud dipped closer and closer to the earth until it finally touched and kicked up a plume of dirt and small trees. How beautiful, I thought. How inexplicably lethal. Why was I hypnotized by something so deadly? A man could disappear out here, sucked up to the heavens, and no one would know the difference. The funnel looked pencil thin at that distance and seemed so very fragile, more like a dangling string, a graceful filigree.

Although this is a reconstruction of the past, every event is true, gleaned from the records of Leavenworth, the FBI, the Pinkertons, the Union Pacific Railroad, newspapers, and other periodicals. No character is made up, no action contrived. There are times when I have had to speculate on the players' conversations and thoughts, but that is to make sense of their choices and delve into their minds. When I do this, I say as much, basing my conclusions on the documented evidence. Frank and his contemporaries are gone now, all dead, and cannot be interviewed. Some vanished as quickly and permanently from the records as if sucked up by the funnel cloud. They were unknowns, taking their individual missteps, bestowing occasional mercies, caught in a changing and confusing world greater than all of them, doing what they could to survive. They learned, like condemned prisoners, the difference between private mercy and public justice. Like every one of us, they tried to understand the walls around them. As does every generation, they reexperienced and tried to reconcile the ancient words of the Roman writer Plautus:

Homo homini lupus.

Man is a wolf to man.

Such . . . are the names of virtues and vices: for one man calleth wisdom what another calleth fear; and one cruelty what another justice.

—Thomas Hobbes, *Leviathan*

The Stuff of Dreams

THE PRISON RIDING on the sea of love grass was built to transform men. Legions of prisoners swarmed about its unfinished base like ants; it rose from the prairie soil like a stone island. For its planners, it was the stuff of dreams. For the prisoners, it formed the core of nightmares.

Although its official designation was the United States Penitentiary at Leavenworth, Kansas, or USP Leavenworth, it went by many names, as if the world's most famous prison could switch aliases as often and easily as the men locked up inside. While its architect proclaimed it as a twenty-two-acre "city within a city," members of the growing criminal underworld called it the "hard joint," the roughest cooler of all. Inmates dubbed it the Big Top, a brutal kind of circus, distinguished from the Little Top, the smaller U.S. Military Prison two and a half miles away. They called it the Wall, a shared moniker for prisons; the Hot House, after its lack of ventilation; 1300 Metropolitan Avenue, for its postal address. An ex-congressman who served two years for conspiracy there called it "the house of whispering hate" where "whispered group jealousies . . . filled every minute with peril." A prisoner once described his first sight of Leavenworth as "a giant mausoleum adrift in a great sea of nothingness."

Frank Grigware knew the feeling. Each night, as the barred doors slid shut on his and his neighbors' small cages, he felt like nothing too. Maybe this was like death—a yellowing necropolis filled with gray-clad bodies. Frank had no name in this correctional mausoleum, just a number signifying his date of internment and his slot in the records. He had no past before the day of what officials called his "delivery" into this alternate world. He had no future, for a future implies change. There was only an eternal present, every day basically the same as the one before. That monolithic present loomed before him the day the Leavenworth train took him through the gates. When they closed, he too felt buried.

Frank's name for Leavenworth was the Big House, inmate slang for all penal warehouses built in the first decades of the twentieth century. Years later he would sit in a dark theater and watch a prison movie of the same name. He stared in shock and recollection as the main character was photographed, fingerprinted, measured, and numbered; he remembered in every nerve and muscle how a man could be dwarfed by the size of the place, by the multitudes of convicts who marched in lockstep, their identities stripped away. Convicts from the Indian Territory said Big House was the name of a longhouse adopted by several Indian nations, a large dwelling in which a tribe's most important rituals were held. Its walls were the four sides of the earth; its door in the east, the symbol of all beginnings; the door to the west, a portal to the end of days. The White Path between the doors was the trail taken by all braves. Leavenworth followed the same plan. A new convict entered through the gaping portals of the east wall, called the Railroad Gate; his prison train rolled down tracks through the heart of the prison, called Railroad Avenue. From then until the end of his sentence or his life, the four walls formed the scope of his world. The tracks exited through the west gate, passed Government Hill, and vanished into the plains. As the train steamed out, prisoners glimpsed for an instant the prison cemetery half a mile off. Officials named it Mount Hope, but inmates called it Peckerwood Hill.

Symbols attached readily to the prison, both by chance and design. Leavenworth was built as a statement of something new. Situated 180 miles due east of the nation's geographical center, it rose like a monument to continental opposites: East vs. West, freedom vs. constraint, enclosure vs. open sky. Even the prison's setting in the southwest corner of the huge Fort Leavenworth military post had meaning. The land was once peopled by the vanished Kansa nation, the "people of the south wind." Now they were gone, replaced by a nation of completely different character. The fort, originally established in 1827 to protect Santa Fe Trail traders from Indians, became by 1850 the main supply depot for the conquest of the West and jumping-off point for the Oregon Trail. The fort and the settlement immediately to its south were filled with history: Abraham Lincoln came to town in 1859 seeking the Republican nomination for president; Generals George A. Custer and Philip Sheridan once walked the streets; in the early 1860s, Wild Bill Hickok and Buffalo Bill Cody lived there when they worked for the firm of Russell, Majors and Waddell, originators of the Pony Express.

The period of Leavenworth's conception had meaning, too. The old century of westward expansion was ending; the new century of science and technology, control and consolidation, would soon begin. The prison was a true child of the Progressive Era, that period of extraordinary growth and unprecedented social problems when Americans prided themselves on their growing world presence yet worried about bloody labor violence and the endless waves of immigrants arriving in search of better lives. Then, as now, some in power responded with exclusionary policies like restricting immigration, while others shared a faith in the state's capacity to resolve poverty, conflict, and disease. One means to that solution was by improving human character, and the road to that improvement was the law.

Progressives embraced a therapeutic model of criminality, and of social ills in general: since criminals were "sick," they could be "cured." This was Leavenworth's mandate when in 1897 its plans were unveiled. "This prison when completed will be one of the finest, one of the most secure, one of the most unique, and one of the most convenient in the United States," said James W. French, the prison's first warden. "The reformative idea in prison management will be given free scope. . . . No such arrangement of chapel, library, and school facilities can be found in any prison in the United States today." He later added, "A man may do in this prison what, as boy and man, he has failed to do outside—acquire the rudiments of an education, gain willpower and courage to do right, learn a trade, and leave the prison a reformed and useful citizen."

Though intended as a place of punishment and penance, Leavenworth would have "little of the forbidding appearance of a prison," promised the March 21, 1897, issue of the *Leavenworth Times*. The prison's main building was modeled after the U.S. Capitol Building; its two main cellhouses, each rising seven stories and stretching longer than a football field, were copied after the chambers of the Senate and the House of Representatives. These cellblocks formed the front wall of the prison, facing south toward town; they were joined in the center by a rotunda, a smaller version of the Capitol dome. The penitentiary's silver dome would rise 150 feet above the grass when completed and was planned at the time as the second-highest dome in America, surpassed only by the original in Washington, D.C. The prison's nine-room school, the first ever built in a penitentiary, attested to the nation's growing faith in education; three other wings—two smaller cellhouses and an administrative complex—radiated back from the rotunda like spokes of a wagon wheel. The prison's hospital, maintenance shop, industries, and factories were planned for the open area out back, a "yard" surrounded by a gun towers and a giant brick wall blocking all views out or in. Originally designed to hold 1,200 inmates, the penitentiary would be a world unto itself.

There was a cohesion here in the ends of government and of justice, as well as a convergence in seemingly disparate things. Turn-of-the-century pundits proclaimed the state as the new civil religion and America as a New Jerusalem, the highest expression of man. Leavenworth was a symbol of that state: of its power to rehabilitate as well as to punish; of its dominance of a wilderness that once seemed unconquerable. Its school and church, discipline, and training would finish what nature had started but failed. With hard work and effort, even the most unredeemable criminal could leave Leavenworth and reenter the Garden, a reengineered Adam ready to participate in the American Dream. The savage—in this case, the criminal—would be conquered again on the plains, and Leavenworth would lead the charge.

James French, the warden, was a dreamer himself. A former teacher, prosecutor, politician, and newspaper editor, French believed wholeheartedly in his new prison's power to reform and reshape lives. Because he had served as director of Indiana's state prison from 1889 until his 1891 appointment as warden of the nation's first federal prison, newspapers called him a "practical prison man." Contrary to prevailing practice, French tended to treat his prisoners like fellow humans. His first order of business was to give the men muslin pillows stuffed with straw and issue them a quarter-pound plug of chewing tobacco weekly. The centuries-old rule of silence was continued, but lights-out was moved from 8 to 9 P.M. The prison's first quarters in the old Quartermaster's Depot of the Fort Leavenworth military reservation sparked from him an angry letter to the U.S. Attorney General: the stockade, a series of iron cages in the rickety wood structure, would explode instantly into flames in the frequent and unstoppable prairie fires, roasting everyone inside. His lobbying proved effective. In 1896, the House Judiciary Committee recommended that the old facility be replaced, and on February 25, 1897, plans for the new prison were revealed.

The unveiling was the high-water mark of French's career. He still stares confidently from his century-old newspaper photo, ruddy, fit, his gaze as direct as the gunslingers he imprisoned. Even today, he strikes one as a man of strong opinions and high expectations, yet wise enough to temper such convictions with mercy. He was in the prime of life at age forty-five. Like most Americans of that era, French saw the West as the nation's future because of its seemingly limitless resources and the values it bred. "The majority of men sent to us come from Arkansas, Texas, and the Indian Territory," he told the *Leavenworth Times* on the day of the unveiling. "Criminals from this section are usually of the frontier type," men he considered "easier to reclaim" than Easterners. While eastern criminals had "chosen to become vicious," Westerners, a product of "the lax standards of the border settlements," made "more earnest efforts to reform." The Easterner, raised in the city, was corrupt; the Westerner, raised close to nature, was at heart a better man.

YET EVEN WITH such high hopes, things immediately went wrong. The problems were initially tied to a lack of funds. When Congress first authorized the prison on July 1, 1895, it somehow forgot to appropriate the money. Construction was delayed for two years. Since the Justice Department demanded cost savings in construction, the immediate solution was to use prison labor. According to convict legend unconfirmed by official reports, the first contingent of four hundred prisoners marched from the prison at Moundsville, West Virginia, to Leavenworth, a distance of 1,250 miles. Each man wore shackles and was handcuffed to fifty-foot chains. The prisoners hobbled in line behind chuck wagons driven by trusties, while armed guards on horseback kept the line moving. Old prisoners claimed that stragglers were whipped.

The marches didn't end once the men reached Leavenworth. Every morning, the inmates emerged from their temporary quarters in the military stockade and marched two and a half miles under armed guard. The prairie here was hilly and rough, with cottonwoods and swamp pine growing in the creeks and washes, and bluestem, galleta grass, and purple-flowered wild alfalfa growing on the crowns of the hills. The new prairie grass was still green that spring of 1897, spotted with the gold, lilac, and white of early-blooming wildflowers. The men marched southwest until they came to a small valley, 820 feet above sea level, nestled between two curving eminences. Here they were told to build the walls and cellblocks of their new home.

The first work crew that spring consisted of seventeen mule teams and three hundred prisoners, culled from inmates sentenced in the West and the healthiest of those who'd marched from Moundsville; their first order of business was construction of the giant wall. This would eventually be four feet thick in places, buttressed on the outside for support and rising 35 feet above the ground. It also sank 35 feet below ground level to prevent escapes by tunneling. Until this bulwark was finished, however, the workers were enclosed by a more modest palisade of wooden planks 12 feet high. Armed guards, many of them former infantry and cavalry soldiers, looked down from guard towers and sentry boxes; for security reasons, the guards down inside the compound with the prisoners were only issued clubs. The parsimony of the Justice Department affected everyone. Guards often complained of being short-staffed, they rarely received firearms training, and the Spencer repeating rifles they'd been promised were supplanted with aging frontier Winchesters. After the prisoners marched into the "bull pen," an enclosure in the southwest corner surrounded by barbed wire, the guards split them into work crews; they worked for twelve hours straight with a short break for lunch, served from pails. Food was another area affected by tightened purse strings. Trusties working in the kitchen told the men that prison officials typically bought the cheapest fare possible, thus coming under budget, though that meat and produce was sometimes already spoiled. Instead of recycling such savings back into the general funds, the corrupt officials, usually part of the quartermaster's staff, pocketed the difference to supplement their meager pay, a common form of graft the prisoners dubbed the "rebate system." Thus, the typical midday meal was beans flavored with chunks of hog jowl, to which bristles still clung. The only recourse was to stir the beans before eating in hopes of digging out the floating hairs.

Like the daily marches, the work at the construction site went forward through snow and sun. The wall started as a trench, dug by pick and shovel down to 35 or 40 feet; huge blocks of native limestone chiseled out by inmates were then lowered into the trench by a steam-powered winch and wrestled into place by prisoner gangs. Native clay was fired into bricks at the rate of a quarter-million units a month; during the harsh Kansas winters, bonfires were lit to prevent the mortar from freezing in the walls. Many injuries and illnesses were seasonal. Men lost fingers and toes to frostbite during that first winter of work; an outbreak of meningitis slowed progress during the second winter. In 1899, a smallpox outbreak stopped work completely while inmates and guards alike were vaccinated and burned their clothes. Pneumonia usually arrived with the fall, malaria with the summer. A doctor complained that every Indian and southern black who entered Leavenworth as an inmate contracted tuberculosis: admission to Leavenworth for them was a death sentence, regardless of the court's intended ruling. Laggards were clubbed, while those directly disobeying orders were forced to "carry the baby," chained for weeks or months to a 25- or 30-pound cannonball which they had to lift in order to move. As prisoners sickened, they were replaced by others from Arkansas and California, but turnover among the guards was also high. "The wall got me," one guard said, when asked why he resigned.

To no one's surprise, escape attempts began almost immediately. The first recorded death during an escape came in July 1896, during the early days of site preparation. George East was a cowboy who fancied himself a dandy, waxing his mustache into points. In 1895, he stole a horse in Indian Territory, for which he received a sentence of three years. He asked for a pardon and was refused and soon afterward became "insolent and abusive," his record said. One day he started running and was dropped by a shotgun blast from a hundred yards. He lingered a few days in the hospital and then died.

The first mass escape occurred on June 1, 1898, when seventeen prisoners led by badlands gunman William Pierce suddenly attacked two guards. All but Pierce were quickly recaptured, and he stayed free until July 1903, when he was arrested during a post office robbery. Three weeks after this escape, a second group of inmates crawled through a wire fence and ran for the woods. Two of the runaways were immediately captured, and the others were caught soon afterward. The only casualty, in fact, was Warden French, whose career never survived the back-to-back mutinies. Political foes called for his ouster, blaming construction delays and the escapes on his incompetence. He held out for a year. But in 1899, long before completion of his dream of an uplifting place of penance, James French resigned.

Leavenworth's second warden took over on July 1, 1899. Robert W. McLaughry, a sixty-year-old bristle-bearded Scotsman, was the former police chief of Chicago, superintendent of the state reformatory in Pontiac, Illinois, and twice warden of the Illinois state penitentiary. The papers portrayed him as well read in the classics and the Bible, tough but fair, punitive but not unkind. With these credentials, he also brought to Leavenworth a harsher style. Instead of muslin pillows and plugs of tobacco, he issued orders. One of the first was for guards at the worksite to shoot any prisoner who stepped closer to them than six paces or moved farther off than twenty. Silence was once again enforced at meals and at work; it was a serious offense to be found with anything not issued by officials, even a pencil. More serious offenses called for beatings, cuffing to the cell door, or getting thrown in "the Hole."

Left unspoken was the understanding that there'd be no more escapes like the one that sank his predecessor. At first, McLaughry's will prevailed. The prisoners marched to the worksite in the early morning and marched back to their cells at the end of the day. For several weeks during the winter of 1900–1901, the men worked on railroad tracks to the west of the prison. These skirted the north of Mount Hope and ran west into the Salt Creek Valley. The mercury hovered around zero during those weeks and the men seemed ready to riot, so McLaughry reassigned guards from the military stockade to the work gangs, thus heading off trouble.

In the end, the new warden saved the Justice Department $50,000 in wages by substituting prison workers for hired laborers. Although records do not indicate how many of these inmates fell victim to the cold, McLaughry's masters in Washington were pleased.

By January 1901, the outline of the prison had taken shape and work had started on two small cellhouses joining the rear of the rotunda. McLaughry worried about escapes but thought they would occur during the march across the prairie. In fall 1901, Deputy Warden Frank Lemon called thirty known troublemakers into his office and accused them of planning a breakout. "I have a bucketful of notes from other inmates, so I know what you're up to," Lemon said. He looked at the men and said that if they started anything, "I'll have every damn one of you shot, even if I have to come out and do it myself." Some of these men were indeed plotting something, but no one let on.

The second mass escape was set in motion on the night of November 6, 1901. That day, newspapers were filled with dispatches from the Boer War in South Africa and from American troops fighting Philippine *insurrectos*. Town residents worried about a "dog poisoning fiend" who had already killed a Great Dane named Brandy and a pet bulldog with strychnine. The worksite lay unguarded. The captain of the watch, Arthur Trelford, and Deputy Warden Lemon both warned McLaughry that guards should be posted around the clock. McLaughry reportedly told them not to worry about plans made by any "Territory bums."

That night, a recently released inmate returned to the worksite alone. By now, two sides were enclosed by stone walls, the other two by the high palisade. Barbed wire was strung across the top of the planks, while sentry boxes were raised around the walls at intervals. The west gate was open. The ex-convict buried two loaded Colt .45-caliber revolvers in a pile of coal beside the steam winch and left by the open gate, unseen.

Thursday, November 7, passed normally until the evening whistle summoned inmates to the march back to their cells. One conspirator, a machinist who operated the winch, dug up the pistols, keeping one for himself and passing the other to a friend. A third man grabbed an iron bar while a fourth man took a hammer. They slipped into the construction superintendent's shack, cut the wire and smashed the phone linking the worksite to the fort, and took Superintendent F. E. Hinds, two assistant foremen, and Captain Trelford hostage.

The plan was simple. They'd gather other inmates to them while using the hostages as shields, then leave by the west gate and flee into the prairie. The guards stationed in the sentry boxes could not fire without killing the hostages. At first the plan went smoothly. As the mutineers pushed their hostages before them and walked the hundred yards to the west gate, more inmates joined until a small crowd had formed. The sentry in the tower overlooking the gate raised his Winchester, but Hinds cried, "Don't shoot, it would be murder." As the sentry lowered his rifle, the convicts swarmed up the ladder. They added the sentry to the line of hostages and grabbed his rifle, two shotguns, and three more Colt revolvers.

Although the gate was open, the plan hit an unexpected snag. About two hundred yards to the west, three guards covered a gang of sixty-eight inmates who were grading a railroad switch. The tower guards had already shouted warnings and they'd formed into a line, kneeling with their rifles to their shoulders. The convicts hesitated. A silence descended on all.

If no one started shooting, Superintendent Hinds and the foremen were probably safe; they played square with their laborers and were known for treating them decently. Although Hinds complained loudly and frequently about getting a day's decent work from the inmates, he watched at the end of the day as they marched back to the stockade along the parallel paths worn into the grass and felt sorry for the poor devils. Hinds had seen many things on the prairie, but Leavenworth was downright brutal. Some days so many of the men's heads were wrapped in bloody bandages that he'd ask Trelford how he was supposed to stay on schedule if his workers had concussions. When the beatings slackened off for a couple of days, some inmates managed to mumble their thanks to Hinds as they passed by.

Not so with Captain Trelford. Of all the hostages, he was in the most danger. The inmates hated him with a passion. It was said among the prisoners that he'd killed three inmates, including cowboy George East. He'd allowed a guard in his command to shoot a man who bolted from a work gang, then shoot him again "for luck" as the man pleaded for his life. It didn't matter whether the stories were true: What mattered was that the inmates believed them. Trelford knew that once they were out of rifle range, his captors would release the others and shoot him "for luck" before they fled. So Trelford decided to run. A wooden passageway extended forty feet west of the gate, a long chute being built as a railroad entrance, and everyone had to pass through it to enter or exit. Trelford saw a chance and bolted down this passageway. The inmates fired and hit him in the leg, but

Trelford staggered on and dropped behind a corner. No one followed, knowing they'd be cut down by the line of guards if they tried.

If anything, Trelford's flight broke the spell. The inmates dropped into a trench hugging the inside west wall; shielded from sentry fire, they pushed their hostages ahead toward the stockade's southwest corner. Warning shouts flew from tower to tower; bullets thwacked harmlessly into the planks above the heads of the mutineers. The southwest sentry box was manned by C. E. Burrows, at fifty one of the oldest guards and a former police chief of Wichita, Kansas. He saw the crowd approaching but held his fire. The convicts were less kind. Once in range they started firing; when Burrows fired back, his Winchester jammed. The convicts ran beneath the box and shot up through the floor; a bullet clipped Burrows's ear and another struck him behind the neck, furrowing his skin. Burrows dropped to the floor and threw out his rifle; the prisoners climbed the ladder, grabbed more weapons, and left Burrows alone.

A "perfect pandemonium" ruled the stockade, witnesses later said. Twenty-seven convicts had now joined in the escape, and while the greater mass of 340 inmates refused to break out, they still cheered wildly. Gunfire erupted from half a dozen towers and the rioters fired back: witnesses later estimated that about a hundred shots were fired in five minutes, most never finding a target. One inmate was so excited that he cried while repeatedly pulling the trigger.

Suddenly, among the chaos, a strange drama unfolded. While the battle at the southwest tower was raging, Guard Andy Leonard jumped from a scaffold near the center of the yard to warn guards in the north and east, who were still uncertain what was happening. Leonard was well liked by other guards, possibly because he tended bar at a local resort; events suggest that some inmates liked him too. Instead of landing safely, however, he dropped on a pile of bricks and broke his right leg. If that wasn't bad enough, three escapees rounded the corner near him. The man in the lead was Frank Thompson, number 2064, one of the few black inmates in the escape. Blacks and whites were not yet segregated at Leavenworth; they worked side by side, respected and hated the same guards, ate the same swill. But the similarities ended when it came to discipline. While white inmates were routinely brutalized, black inmates endured a special kind of hell. Thompson, twenty-four, had served three terms in the Ohio and New York state penitentiaries before coming to Leavenworth in

October 1900 to serve seven years for larceny. He was a strong man, standing 5 feet 8 inches and weighing 170 pounds, at times seemingly impervious to pain. His face and body were laced with scars: one connected his nose to his lip, while another traced from his right cheek to his ear. Some scars were apparently inflicted by the guards, who seemed both enraged and intimidated by the man. "A penitentiary never sheltered a more desperate character than 2064," an unidentified officer told the *Leavenworth Times*. "He is the worst type of bad Southern negro, a giant in strength, cunning and brutal, with absolutely not a bit of good in him. From one prison he goes to another and is scarcely out three months before taken again."

In the summer of 1901, when Thompson finally grew tired of this treatment and refused to work, the guards chained and shackled him to a stake in the middle of the yard. They ripped off his cap, ensuring heatstroke in the merciless Kansas sun. "This treatment had to be resorted to again and again before he could be brought into subjection," the officer claimed. Given this history, Thompson went a little mad on the day of the mutiny. He'd been given a gun at the onset, and now, seeing one of his tormentors lying helpless, ran up and "threw the gun down" on Andy Leonard. Just as he was about to pull the trigger, other prisoners grabbed his arm. "My God, the man is helpless!" a fellow inmate pleaded. One wonders if Thompson dwelt upon the mercy he'd received himself up to this point—or how much he'd get if captured after the breakout. There is no doubt he was tempted to pull the trigger. Instead, he hesitated for the briefest instant, then grunted in disgust and turned away.

By now the mutineers had advanced a hundred yards east of Burrows's tower, hugging the wall. A weakness in the fence, where a gate had been boarded up, lay in this direction, but the route was blocked by Guard John Waldrupe in the middle tower. Waldrupe was fairly new to the guard staff, having joined in October 1900, the same month Frank Thompson arrived. He'd come to Kansas from the mountain town of Greenback, Tennessee, and married Lena Kramer, a local woman, almost as soon as he arrived. He doted on his wife, and townspeople, often wary of outsiders, thought he and Lena made a handsome couple.

Like Guard Burrows, Waldrupe held his fire when he saw the hostages, but the inmates rushed in shooting. As their bullets passed through the wooden walls, Waldrupe fell, struck in the hip. Several inmates rushed the tower. They were led by inmate Quint Fort, sentenced to five years in prison for stealing horses in the Indian Territory. Fort, seventeen years old when he arrived in 1899, was nineteen now. As he heard the mob surge forward, Waldrupe struggled painfully to a crouch and aimed at the man in front, sending a bullet through Quint Fort's brain. Someone fired back, hitting Waldrupe between the eyes, yet still he kept on fighting, driven purely by adrenaline. He clubbed the first man up the ladder with his rifle, and the inmate dropped back through the trap door and fell to the ground. The second inmate up the ladder grabbed his rifle from him and knocked him back, but instead of killing Waldrupe, as would be expected, he closed the trap door and yelled that the guard inside was dying. He tended Waldrupe's wounds as best he could, then dropped to the ground and hurried after his companions.

A madness reigned inside the prison enclosure, a kind of madness never seen inside an American prison before. Older guards described it as closer to the bloodlust they'd experienced during the Spanish-American adventure, the Indian uprisings, or even the Civil War. Something brutal arose in the men, hard to describe to civilians but understood perfectly by old campaigners. Forget the fine words of improving character, this was war. Leavenworth had invented something more enduring than rehabilitation programs; it had created the first full-scale prison riot of the twentieth century. The inmates grabbed a timber and battered through the weakened fence, and twenty-six convicts streamed through the breach, as guards fired indiscriminately. Frank Thompson disappeared into a field of corn, blood streaming from his face and clutching two revolvers. Those covering the hostages released them as promised, then scattered into town or west across the prairie. Panic gripped the residents as word of the breakout spread. A farmer was knocked off his horse and forced to hand over his coat. A wagon was stolen outside a vinegar factory. A student was robbed of his horse, buggy, and $13. The jeering inmates who remained behind were surrounded by a detachment of mounted troops and marched back to Little Top, rifles leveled at them across the soldiers' saddle pommels. Posses of armed guards galloped after the fugitives and found confusion instead. The general direction of flight seemed south toward Indian Territory, the closest frontier left, about 140 miles away, but when darkness closed over the prairie the pursuit was delayed until morning.

That night, McLaughry posted a $60 reward for every fugitive, dead or alive, and the next morning the countryside filled with volunteer posses. The *Topeka State Journal* advised hoboes not to make sudden or jerky movements, since they were often being stopped and searched; the paper advised readers that the fugitives would resemble ordinary travelers since the prison practice of giving close haircuts had ended the previous year. On November 8, the day after the breakout, five prisoners were surrounded in a barn 20 miles west and a gun battle ensued. Three of the inmates were killed as they tried to escape, a fourth was injured, and the fifth wisely surrendered. Another escapee was captured in a basement in the town of Leavenworth, still wearing his shackles. A prisoner was spotted running across a field and shot through the lungs; he died immediately. That night, a blizzard swept through parts of Kansas, hindering pursuit but slowing the fugitives too. On November 9, four convicts were seen abandoning their horses on the north bank of the Kansas River above Lawrence and rowing across in a stolen boat. On November 10, two escapees, thought to be ringleaders, broke into a house in the farm village of Pauline, outside Topeka, held the elderly couple at gunpoint, and captured the local sheriff. Using their hostages as shields against an encircling posse, they waited for night and got away. By Sunday, November 10, nine of the inmates had been killed or captured. The others would make it as far as Alabama, Colorado, Wyoming, and the Indian Territory, yet by 1903 all had been recaptured and sent back to Leavenworth for reprisals.

If Waldrupe had not died, perhaps the revenge of McLaughry and his staff would not have been so protracted, considered, and brutal. At first it even seemed as if the young guard might pull through. On the day after the escape, Dr. Meige Thomas reported that he had probed unsuccessfully for the bullet from "the base of the forehead, halfway straight back through the head." That Waldrupe survived the doctor's ministrations was in itself a miracle. He even seemed to rally. On November 14, a week after the escape, he told his wife that he felt well enough to rise. The effort apparently killed him, for by the following morning he'd caught a fever and by that afternoon had sunk into a coma. The doctor announced that brain inflammation had set in and that "several ounces of fluid from the brain oozed down" from the base of Waldrupe's skull. Friends petitioned that he receive the Medal of Honor for his fight in the guardhouse but were told that civilian guards weren't eligible. Waldrupe died on November 16, the first Leavenworth guard to die in the line of duty.

In their grief and anger, the guards made an example of every fugitive as he was captured and returned. Each was thrown into the Hole at night and forced to "carry the baby" by day. Eight escapees, including the five suspected ringleaders, were tried for murder and sentenced to life in Leavenworth. The fate of Frank Thompson was both typical and atypical. On the second night of his escape, the blizzard blew across Kansas; a week later, a cowboy searching for a stray horse found the frozen bodies of a woman and her daughter huddled together in the tall grass near Emporia, eighty miles southwest of Leavenworth. It was exactly in this direction that Thompson and most of the remaining fugitives ran. On November 10, Thompson was seen stealing clothes from a farmhouse; by November 11, he'd traveled to Council Grove, 85 miles away. When two deputies stumbled upon him in a thicket, Thompson drew his pistol and pulled the trigger, but the cartridge misfired. He wheeled and fired at the second deputy, but the gun misfired again. It was later found that a piece of leaf had lodged beneath the hammer of the Colt .44 revolver, preventing it from exploding the cartridges. One of the lucky deputies fired his shotgun from fifty paces, taking off part of Thompson's ear. When the big man was brought back by train to the town depot, McLaughry personally drove the "jumper," the rig used to carry inmates outside prison. Since the shackles on Thompson's ankles prevented him from making the jumper's high step, the guards grabbed him by his feet and pants and threw him inside. "I can tell I is getting close to home," he was reported as saying. He was chained to his "baby" and assigned to break rocks in a rock pile. At night, he was chained to a metal staple in the floor of his solitary cell.

ALTHOUGH THE CIRCUMSTANCES and aftermath of what would forever be called the "mutiny of 1901" were more bloody and frightening than in previous mass escapes, McLaughry was not crucified like James French had been. Waldrupe's death seemed to redirect anger toward the prisoners; in addition, the warden's generous reward offer made him immensely popular, a lesson he always remembered. Although he had been warned of danger by both Lemon and Trelford, there is no record of a reprimand, even in the popular press. Instead, the papers asked why prisoners would be so foolish as to escape, since it was widely known that they lived better in prison than they had in the outside world—a theme that echoed through the rest of the century. The *Omaha Bee* wondered how jailers could be thwarted by men "whose natural place was in submission." The *Lawrence Eagle* said the hunt for the fugitives would continue until every man was caught: "It would seem that even these desperate men would prefer the prison to having hounds forever baying on their trail." Only the *Wichita Eagle* noticed problems at Leavenworth, and this in terms of weaponry. "Something is the matter with the firearms furnished the guards," an editorial observed. "Those stolen by the convicts in nearly every instance failed to go off when the trigger was pulled."

In the days immediately following the escape, a siren was installed that could be heard ten miles across the plains. Guards spent more time at target practice. More men were hired. A hundred-foot tower was planned for the center of the enclosure, with signal lights, Gatling guns, and a bulletproof floor. The prison changed overnight, even before it was finished. "Leavenworth is hell," McLaughry told a guest, "and I guess I'm the chief devil."

Eight years later, Frank Grigware, convicted of train robbery, arrived in this hell. By then, the massive wall had risen. Stone gun towers, their roofs shaped like the bowler hats worn by robbers in formal portraits, enfiladed the central yard. The smaller cellblocks were finished and the daily marches across the prairie ended, yet prison officials still made examples of the ringleaders. There was no way out except by legal means or in a box bound for Peckerwood Hill, claimed McLaughry and his guards. Like Frank, many men were sentenced here for life. They watched the Leavenworth train creep through the east gate, deposit new prisoners, blow the whistle, and exit to the west, toward the prairie. Like Frank, they'd plunged into the last days of the vanishing West, dreaming of fame and fortune. But instead of a cave of gold, they found a grimy cell, 5½ feet wide, 9 feet long, and 8 feet high.

The Leavenworth train gained speed. Like every other prisoner, Frank watched it roll off, certain his life was over, his youthful dreams a sham. But he was mistaken. He *would* be famous, finding fame twice, under two names and in two nations. In the worst possible way, Frank Grigware realized his dream.

❦ PART I ❧

The Boys from Spokane

In the beginning, all the world was America.

—John Locke, *Two Treatises of Government*

CHAPTER ONE

The Grand Tour

"MOTHER, I'M GOING to see the world."

The words sent a shock through the family, seated in the kitchen for the evening meal. Frank felt stunned himself. He'd hoped his announcement would sound like a mature, well-reasoned statement of intent; instead, because of his nervousness, it came out like a roar. The year was 1906 and Frank Grigware was twenty years old. Twilight and silence surrounded the small whitewashed house at the rural edge of Spokane in eastern Washington. There were eight of them seated around the table; among the working poor, or "producing classes," the kitchen was still the hub of activity, warmed by the heat of the black Acme Regal range. Frank's family studied his face like the map of his imagined travels: his father, Edward, a failed fisherman turned carpenter; his three brothers and two baby sisters with a touch of envy; and his mother, who perhaps had seen it coming. Jennie Priscilla Grigware's exact thoughts were not recorded, but twenty-eight years later she would tell an endless stream of reporters that she'd felt a chill, even then.

Frank addressed his leave-taking directly to his mother: After all, she'd been the force six years earlier behind their 2,200-mile move out west from Michigan. Like five million others from 1865 to 1900, they'd been lured by promises of a "virgin land." She needed no explanation of where he planned to go. "Seeing the world" meant a journey through what newspapers already called "the vanishing West," and Frank wanted to see it before it passed away. Ever since Major John Wesley Powell's 1878 *Report on the Lands of the Arid Region*, the West had generally been defined as that area starting at the 98th meridian of west longitude, about forty miles west of today's Wichita and Oklahoma City, and ending at the Pacific Ocean. Yet there had been many "Wests" in the nation's history: a desert to cross, an El Dorado of untapped riches, a land of Indians and death. His parents' West was a more sober one of work, but it too was framed in hyperbole, described as an agrarian Eden by railroad pitch-men. When Frank looked out one window he saw the red-brick busi-nesses and banks of the booming city; when he looked out another, the golden wheat fields of what came to be called the Inland Empire rolled toward a rain-shadow desert and the Columbia River gorge. The newest farming marvels appeared seasonally in those fields: the four-horse planters moving in serried ranks; the towering Harris har-vesters cutting swaths through the wheat; the steam-powered thresh-ermen, smoke trailing from their smokestacks like small locomotives, threshing up to 1,000 bushels of grain per day. To think, this land had just a few years earlier been Indian country. Not far from here the U.S. Army chased the Spokane, Coeur d'Alene, and Palouse tribes in a fourteen-mile pitched battle. More recently, they'd tracked Chief Joseph of the Nez Perce in his doomed flight to Canada.

Yet this version of the West was not what Frank had envisioned during his family's trip here. He wasn't sure he had a future in this cultivated world. He was a builder, not a granger, and had already left for days at a time on carpentry jobs with his father, from whom he learned the trade. Sometimes he went with Jack Golden, his best friend. He'd go as far as Walla Walla, 165 miles south, packing little besides a double-headed hammer and a leather sack of machine-cut rose nails, and was troubled by what he saw. The *Spokesman-Review* boasted in an April 5, 1903, editorial that the wheat districts ad-vanced steadily from "poverty to affluence, from depression to prosperity, from general despondency to universal hope, elation, and contentment," but on these trips he spied a different reality. There'd been a rise in failures among the small farmers. Squeezed between chronic overproduction and ever-rising railroad freight rates, they de-clared bankruptcy or sold out to the expanding corporate farms. On his jobs he saw empty spreads where the previous season there had been life, the only sound now a creaking slat or rattle of an old Aeromotor windmill. The newspapers told almost daily of one more man going mad and exterminating his family, one more farm wife committing suicide. Society could be as harsh as the elements in the Garden, and success and failure were moral judgments. A man's fate was a reflection of his soul.

He wanted to make something of himself but Spokane wasn't the place to do it, Frank told his family. Fifty-three miles to the east, men were discovering riches in the mountains of Idaho. He planned to do the same. If that went bust, carpenters were needed in Texas and Denver. Jennie realized as she listened that he pled for her blessing, as if they were in the room alone. She could put a stop to his ambitions simply by refusing to let him go, but she'd instilled the wanderlust in him herself and couldn't deny her son his dreams. She remembered her own visions of the West when she was a girl and the frontier was still filled with names like George Armstrong Custer, Wild Bill Hickok, and Sitting Bull. All were dead now. She loved Frank in the way parents reserve for only children or the one they feel most vulnerable—he was gentle and openhearted in a way few women saw in this hard country, but too trusting of the bad advice of other men. Her son was handsome and lean as an athlete, quiet and modest around strangers, yet kind and cheerful in a way that instantly made him friends. But in return for that friendship, Frank often took others at face value, a fatal mistake in an unforgiving world. Sometimes he was so quiet that Jennie couldn't tell what went on behind his eyes.

It is not hard to guess a mother's thoughts and feelings, even today. Jennie watched the yellow light of the kerosene lamps flicker off Frank's face and thought how he, like so many boys of his generation, had been raised on tales of violence and adventure, blood and destiny: Ned Buntline's Buffalo Bill stories; Charles Averill's *Kit Carson: The Prince of the Gold Hunters*; Frank Tousey's *James Boys* chronicles; Edward Wheeler's *Deadwood Dick, the Prince of the Road*. Her four sons passed the old copies from hand to hand until the covers were ripped and the pages dog-eared, but of all her boys, Frank had taken them most to heart. She'd noticed his rapt attention when "Buffalo Bill's Wild West" came to Spokane and the performers staged a swirl of gunfire and dust billed as "Custer's Last Fight." She knew he spent

his earnings to watch *The Great Train Robbery* in the new nickelodeon downtown; Edwin S. Porter's nine-minute epic was so successful
it inspired a score of imitators, including *The Great Bank Robbery*,
The Bold Bank Robbery, and *The Hold-Up of the Rocky Mountain
Express*, most of which Frank had seen. Frank's sisters, ages ten and
thirteen, giggled when he returned from jobs with a red bandanna
tied around his neck, as if the simple change of clothes turned him
into a cowboy. Jennie bid them hush, her eyes flaring when she said
it. They saw the Irish in her and quickly did as told.

She'd known he'd be the first to leave the family, sensing his restlessness as early as 1900. That was the year a letter came from her
mother, Mary Fahey, urging her to move to Spokane. Her mother's
life had been a constant journey west: over the sea from doomed
Ireland to escape the Great Famine; west again to escape the poverty
and prejudice surrounding Irish immigrants in eastern cities. The new
century was the time to move, she wrote Jennie. Farmhands were
making $25.10 a month in the Pacific states, the highest rate in the
nation, while a good carpenter brought home $480 or more a year.
Mary Fahey was right. The nation's "long-wave" depression, which
started with the Panic of 1873, was finally over. The short-term en-
vironmental crises that turned the West into a hell on earth—from
1887's big blizzard that wiped out half the cattle stock to the 1891
drought, the 1892 plague of locusts, and the drought of 1894–96
—had mercifully ended. The rains returned in 1896, and the farms
and businesses that survived the bad years saw profits again. Edito-
rialists once again chanted the mantra, "Go West, young man, go
West, and grow up with the country!" made famous by *New York
Tribune* editor Horace Greeley, himself an Irish farmer's son. In 1899,
an estimated 400,000 pilgrims heeded Greeley's call.

It was frightening for Jennie to leave her home. She'd lived in Michigan for seventeen years, since 1883, the year she married twenty-
three-year-old Edward Napoleon Grigware and moved with him to
Rush Lake in the state's "green thumb" on Saginaw Bay. Edward
came from a family of French-Canadian fishermen who changed their
name from Gregoire when settling in Oswego, New York, on Lake
Ontario before the Civil War. He was a proud man, with dark eyes
and hair, touchy about his big ears; he promised when they married
that he would succeed. They'd been lucky with their children: in an
age when mothers' deaths in childbirth ran to 20 percent and sixteen

out of every hundred infants died at birth, all six of her offspring would live to adulthood. Joseph, the oldest, was born on September 7, 1884, followed by Frank on February 27, 1886. She gave birth to him on Edward's fishing boat while trying to reach the doctor in nearby Caseville. He would never do well in school, as if his mind were as shifting as water, but was always smart in a practical way. After Frank came the responsible and tight-fisted James, born in August 1887, followed by Edward, the artist, in 1889. The boys all looked like their father: dark Gallic features, hair that shone like lacquer, ears sticking out like wings. The girls took after Jennie: Mary, born October 1893, and Genevieve, born April 1896, barely four when they moved.

Still, it was no secret that Rush Lake had been a punishing place to live. The Lake Huron fisheries at first seemed inexhaustible, the whitefish, salmon, lake trout, and chub glinting like copper and silver as they dropped from Edward's nets into the hold. Yet Rush Lake, incorporated in 1867 and named after a drained lake that once covered 1,500 acres, was barely settled when they arrived. The lake bottom was quicksand, the surrounding land swamp, and in spring and summer they were plagued by mosquitoes and biting flies. The closest *real* town was Caseville, easier to reach by water than by the mud bogs that went for roads. During the winter the wind came off the lake like a scythe, locking the boats in harbor for months. These times were so lean that Edward's brother Bill finally gave up and moved to Grand Rapids to work in the train yards. He urged Edward to follow, but railroads were brutal work and the odds of being crippled or killed ran high. In 1890, the first year such statistics were kept, 22,396 railroad workers were injured in job-related accidents, a rate that would jump to 39,643 in 1900 and 95,671 in 1910. If that didn't kill him, the labor violence might. Who would care for his family then? So Edward stayed a fisherman, supplementing his income with trapping and carpentry, teaching these skills to his boys. And always, they searched for some deliverance, a glimmer of better things.

The idea of starting fresh was one that gripped the entire nation in the new century. Indeed, it is a national myth that has never gone away. Newspapers in 1900 proclaimed that the next hundred years belonged to America: the signs were everywhere. The nation's agricultural and industrial output rivaled that of Europe's big powers; advances in medicine prolonged life; an entire house could be bought and built from the pages of the Sears, Roebuck catalog. Anything seemed possible. In 1900, Henry Ford unveiled his first Detroit-built automobile, Orville and Wilbur Wright began their first experiments in flight, and the world's tallest building, the thirty-two-story Park Row building, opened in New York City. Electricity promised to change every aspect of daily life, from the ground coffee one drank in the morning to the electric streetcar one rode home from work at night. Americans were filled with an optimism that saw them adopt the tapering ladder as the symbol of their society. As on a ladder, there was movement up and down. Slum dwellers and unskilled laborers filled the lowest and broadest steps of the tapered ladder, while multimillionaires occupied the narrow top. Everyone else—farmers, tradesmen, small businessmen, and professionals—occupied the middle rungs. In this ostensible meritocracy, each wanted to believe that progress up the ladder depended solely on personal initiative.

So it was that in the summer of 1900, Jennie and her family packed their belongings, boarded a westbound New York Central, sliced through lower Michigan, and then transferred in Chicago for the longest leg of their journey—a $12.50 per seat one-way ticket from St. Paul, Minnesota, to points west aboard the Northern Pacific Railroad's "emigrant service." Emigrant cars were uncomfortable rides, hooked like cattle cars to the end of the train. The upper berths rattled on flimsy copper hinges, threatening to swing down and brain them all. The arc of the oil lamp hanging from the ceiling made Jennie seasick. Every sudden lurch went straight up her spine. She understood perfectly why cowboys called these trains "rattlers." Nevertheless, she marveled that a trip that once took months now took little more than eight days.

The nation's railroads symbolized many things to Americans, both good and bad: speed, science, and power; death, violence, and greed. It was an ambiguity that reflected the railroad's immense scope, the "octopus" of Frank Norris's novel that was still being written and would be published in 1901. The railroad had tentacles stretching in every direction. By 1900, there were 258,784 miles of track across America, operated by 1,224 railroad companies. Four years later, most of these had been consolidated into six great combinations, each allied with the interests of J. P. Morgan or John D. Rockefeller. In February 1900, the Baltimore & Ohio tested the "Wind Splitter," clocking an amazing 102 mph, yet that very speed made the railroad the era's great killer. In 1900, 7,865 people died in train-related accidents and another 50,320 were injured, a rate that climbed for the next seventeen years. The most famous train wreck in memory, the May 1900 crash of the Illinois Central's Cannonball Express, killed engineer John Luther "Casey" Jones. The juggernaut that linked the nation had also caused its twenty-year depression, with business practices so transparently corrupt and inept that when bond buyers finally lost confidence the lines were plunged into bankruptcy, dragging with them the great banks who'd sunk nearly all their assets into the "marvel of the age."

The railroads had even shaped time, thus altering reality. As the miles of track spread into a national network, trains ran a crazy quilt of schedules based on mean local sun times. Noon in Chicago was 11:27 A.M. in Omaha, 11:50 in St. Louis, 12:17 in Toledo, and 12:31 in Pittsburgh. The Buffalo station had three clocks, each with a different railroad time. There were twenty-seven local times in Illinois and thirty-eight in Wisconsin. As early as 1870, the *Railroad Gazette* urged adoption of a single standard time for the entire nation, but this found little support until Professor C. F. Dowd, headmaster of a young ladies' seminary in Saratoga Springs, New York, suggested the creation of four or more broad time "belts," a solution seized upon by William F. Allen, managing editor of the *Official Guide of the Railways* and secretary of the General Time Convention. Allen convinced the railroads to adopt a plan that called for four time belts divided at the 75th, 90th, 105th and 120th meridians, a standard that went into effect at noon on Sunday, November 18, 1883, and remains in effect today. As the shift took place, people in the eastern half of each zone experienced a day with two noons, while people in the western half were thrown into the future. One newspaper editor complained that he'd rather set his clock according to "God's time" than railroad baron Cornelius Vanderbilt's, but the public easily adjusted—easier, in fact, than the government, which did not officially adopt standard time until 1918.

One thing was certain: Jennie and her family found plenty of time on their hands as they rode west. During the trip, she told the children of the journey of her own parents, who'd fled Ireland to survive. They'd landed in Quebec in 1850 and settled in Woodstock, Ontario, where Jennie was born on June 23, 1863, the same week that two opposing armies marched to Gettysburg. In 1872, they moved to upstate New York. A tailor and a dressmaker, they hoped to share in some of the prosperity of the industrializing "needle trades." Yet all the stories in the world could not hide the fact that this train ride seemed incredibly long. Like children today, Jennie's brood complained, fought, and asked repeatedly if they were almost there.

Only Frank seemed more engaged. He had a thousand questions about his grandparents' journey; as the others slept, he stared out the windows at the rolling plains. He seemed fit to burst as they passed through towns linked to the outside world only by the railroad, their grain elevators and water towers announcing their presence miles away. The engine shrieked three short blasts as they stopped at county seats in cattle country, lonely outposts that were little more than a dusty road emerging from the emptiness, passing through a brief strip of flimsy storefronts, and disappearing into the haze. Frank longed for the excitement of the West, just a glimpse of all the wonders of which he'd read and heard. He searched for the vast herds of buffalo that numbered 40 to 60 million in the years before 1840; by 1890, barely a thousand remained. He dreamed of Indians sweeping off the plains on horseback; the only pony raids these days occurred in Buffalo Bill shows. He prayed for a holdup by a gang of robbers—telling his brothers and sisters how just a year earlier, on June 2, 1899, the Wild Bunch robbed the Union Pacific's Overland Limited near Wilcox, Wyoming, uncoupling an express car and riding off with $30,000—but no such excitement came Frank's way.

The closest he approached his vision of the West was when he eyed cowboys hanging around the depot or main street of some isolated cow town. They were lean, taciturn bachelors in their twenties or early thirties, faces prematurely worn by the elements, eyes never missing a thing. Many were bowlegged, hip-sprung, or stooped from chronic saddle weariness; others wore wide leather belts to keep their kidneys in place during the long rides. Instead of leather holsters and guns, they probably packed plug and twist chewing tobacco with exotic brand names like Winesap, Rock Candy, Star of Virginia, and Henry Clay. They seemed forlorn and proud in the same instant, as vulnerable as the towns in which they lingered, as if the hand of God could sweep them off the map and no one would know or care.

Frank loved it anyway. He was fourteen, and it was different from anything he'd known. By the 98th meridian, about forty miles west of Grand Forks, North Dakota, his lips began to crack and his nostrils dried out. His estimates of distance were always wrong. Green was no longer the earth's prevailing color, replaced instead by gray, rust, dirty white, and a thousand shades of tan. Grass grew in isolated clumps, not as uninterrupted turf. Even the language was different. A hand-rolled smoke was a "quirly." To "slam a bullet" was to fire a shot from a pistol. A "henskin" was a tarpaulin. A prairie dog was not a dog, nor a horny toad a toad. He told his mother that he too planned to be a cowboy. She smiled and nodded, as mothers do when young sons make such claims.

Yet now, years later, his boyhood boasts were coming true. Frank was going away. Jennie Grigware recognized the glitter of excitement in her son's eyes and remembered her own impatience at his age. She thought of all the traps and temptations that could ruin a life, creeping up before one noticed their approach to damage entire families. At some point, she realized, she could no longer protect her children. The thought was far from comforting. "Please be careful, son," she told him. Frank deeply loved his mother, and would give her a little locket with his picture before he left. But at that moment, one wonders if he heard.

LET US MEASURE Francis John Grigware for a wanted poster, for that is what awaits him, clinging for the next quarter century like a second skin. In 1906, when he headed into the interior West, Frank was a pleasantly handsome young man of twenty; three years later, when his troubles started, the sun and prairie wind had hardened the edges, yet a boyishness still remained. That year in 1909, as he sat for prison photos, full face and right profile, jailers sensed a fellow who was not so much a hard case as still a bewildered boy. His pale blue eyes look tired; faint smile lines crease the corners of his lips; his dark brows arch in an expression of mild surprise. If anything, he gazed at the camera wistfully, odd since he'd just been sentenced to life at hard labor. His brown hair was trimmed and dipped below his collar; his wool tie hung knotted to the left. His bowler hat was too small, sitting atop his head like a toadstool. He tried to follow fashion but never got it right; though he was a perfectionist in his work, he let details slip outside that focus, resulting in acts and deliberations that could be called foolish. This seemed to elicit a protectiveness in his acquaintances, especially women; he learned to trust in the goodwill of others, a naive innocence that was perhaps more common before two world wars and several genocides. Though the trait would divert his life forever, it saved him several times.

But these were only first impressions, not the hard evidence favored by an emerging scientific age. The facts were these: Frank was fair complexioned, a Catholic, used tobacco in moderation, but took no alcohol. He was athletic, having once played for the Spokane baseball team. His height and weight were recorded by a records clerk at Leavenworth as 5 feet 8½ inches and 161 pounds, then an hour later by the prison doctor as 5 feet 9¾ inches and 166 pounds. Warden McLaughry described him as "a young man of fine appearance; a fluent talker; rather modest in action and appearance." His chest measured 38 inches. Small scars, one at the tip of his left ring finger, another at the base of his right thumb, were earned as a carpenter. A small "pit scar" lay beneath his right eye, and the second and third toes of each foot were webbed.

This last was the smallest defect, usually unnoticeable, but it would play a major role in his life. Jennie felt responsible, wondering what she'd done to herself in pregnancy to cause the flaw in her son. Frank was self-conscious of the webbing and rarely removed his shoes except for bed. When other children found out, as they always do, they made fun of him. At such times, when Frank came home from rough play with other boys, perhaps Jennie would be shelling beans. He'd stand beside her and snap off the ends, not saying a word. "What might be troublin' you, Frank?" she'd ask, watching his face.

"Am I really that different, Mama?" he finally said.

She feared for him then, though she couldn't say why. The injustice of it made her so mad she feared she might explode. What was it about this country that taught boys such cruelty? There was time enough for that in later life, wasn't there? She ran her fingers through his hair and straightened it, liking its silky feel, then turned him by the shoulders until he looked at her. "What does it matter if some toes are grown together? When you're in a foot race, don't you leave everyone behind?" The words made him grin. His mother was right; even with the defect, he ran as fast as a deer. As he tore across a field to prove it, she thought how no one ever caught him. But there was a loneliness to runners. In their moment of triumph, they were by themselves.

Edward said not to worry, but it was hard not to worry in this country, so judgmental of every fault, whether a misstep in the past or a mark on the skin. Every immigrant embraced the idea of America, the rights of average men, yet a harshness had risen with the hope of a better life and the two often seemed at war. Maybe the tension came with increased expectations, maybe from the fear that in a land that so trumpeted success there were so many ways to fail. Maybe it had a simpler source: worry over rising crime and violence, suggesting a greater chaos than anyone dared believe. Whatever the reason, an "anomaly" like Frank's was seen as more than just a physical trait. It was a corrosive truth that lurked within the skin.

Other than this hidden defect, Frank seemed little different from other young men of his class and age. Most of his life had been one of work. He dropped out of fourth grade in Michigan to tend his father's nets; he spent only one year of school in Washington before going to work again. His first job was as a "newsy," rising at 4 A.M. to throw the folded *Spokesman-Review* from horseback onto the porches of his neighbors. If nothing else, he developed a good pitching arm, and baseball was the national rage. In 1904 he drove wagons for one of Spokane's many freight companies and then worked as a handyman for the mayor, Dr. Patrick Byrne. He drove Mrs. Byrne to shopping and the children to school; later he worked in the office as Byrne's assistant, collecting payment on medical bills. "He's a good boy," Byrne told Jennie Grigware. "He can be trusted and he works hard."

There was a myth in the West that hard work defined a man and made him an equal to others. That men were judged by their abilities, not their connections or heritage. The myth had lured millions to the West since the Civil War. By 1876, the year of Custer's Last Stand, the New York *Irish World*, considered a Socialist organ by the upper crust, supported colonizing the frontier as the only refuge from prejudice and poverty. There were endless encomiums to work, from President Theodore Roosevelt, who said during his 1903 campaign tour of the Pacific Northwest that "all honorable work is noble and confers honor upon the one doing it," down to Dr. Byrne.

Yet notwithstanding the paeans, the myth had not proved true. The class differences that tore apart the country in the last decades of the nineteenth century were just as strong or stronger in the first decade of the twentieth. Labor violence in the East had spread to the timberlands of the Pacific Northwest and the deep-rock mines of Colorado, Montana, and Idaho. If anything, the violence was worse out here. Members of the underclass, usually regarded as Irish and Jewish immigrants and their children, were blamed for a whole host of ills. They were blamed for the crime rate: From 1870 to 1900, the number of prison inmates jumped 172 percent. They were blamed for vice: The majority of prostitutes in New York, New Orleans, and San Francisco, the three "wicked cities," were from overseas. They were blamed for sickness: By 1900, nearly one in 500 people died of tuberculosis, most notably the poor and the young, and the high numbers of deaths from tuberculosis in slums convinced Americans that the disease was caused by the "immorality" of the poor, not the crowded and unsanitary conditions in which they lived. Even those promoting humanitarian causes took up the cry. Suffragists criticized the fact that foreigners could vote while the mothers of the nation could not. Early proponents of birth control argued that condoms and sponges controlled the spread of human "weeds." It was a bad time to be poor in the Land of the Free.

If hard work was not the way out of this trap, Frank and others of his era understood instinctively that sudden wealth was. Striking it rich had always been the true American dream. The search for El Dorado goes back to the Spanish conquest of the Americas and flows through our veins like gold. By 1900, this dream had been legitimized as the Gospel of Wealth, a truth above debate set as firmly in the American mind as the right to certain liberties. If not the purpose of life, it certainly served as a guide. First coined in an 1889 magazine article, the term was the brainchild of Pittsburgh steel baron Andrew Carnegie, a call to riches raised to a spiritual plane. Individualism, private ownership, competition, and acquisition: These were the pillars of the Gospel of Wealth that produced the "best fruit . . . essential for the future progress" of mankind. The irony was that true wealth clung to the hands of so very few. The public didn't know whether to love or hate oil tycoon John D. Rockefeller, financier J. P. Morgan, rail barons Cornelius Vanderbilt and Edward H. Harriman, or Carnegie, but they were certainly wowed by their riches. While monopolists like Morgan and Carnegie blocked the access of others to the top rungs of the tapered ladder of success, they also represented the oft-repeated Horatio Alger dream that every boy could become a "captain of industry." The typical American esteemed success and took pride that his country was its embodiment. Success was personal, not abstract. "The Good Lord gave me money," John D.

Rockefeller claimed. Carnegie, Rockefeller, and the others might be envied, even hated, but they had proven superior in the Darwinian struggle for success, and that struggle gave their wealth a holy glow.

In Spokane, the route to instant wealth lay east in Idaho. These days, the so-called Inland Empire encompassed parts of Washington, Idaho, Montana, and lower British Columbia, a rich economy of lumber, mining, wheat, and apples that left local financiers hoping they could parlay that into the next Denver of the Pacific Northwest. It had all started with gold. One raucous night in August 1883, Andrew Prichard, a fifty-three-year-old sourdough who'd prospected in Colorado and Montana, strode into a saloon in the humble village of Spokane Falls. "I've hit paydirt, boys," he said, and threw his buckskin bag on the bar. Nearly two hundred men crowded close, eyeing the four pounds of gold dust and nuggets bulging within. When someone asked where he found it, Prichard pointed east to the Coeur d'Alenes Mountains of northern Idaho. Within weeks, thousands on the Pacific coast were rushing to "Prichard's Creek," and their jumping-off point was Spokane Falls, Washington, which turned overnight into a boomtown. Two years later, the first electric arc lamps twinkled downtown. On August 4, 1889, a grease fire, started by a cook tossing a pork chop into a skillet, spread until the conflagration leveled most of Main Street. No worry: The wooden banks and hotels rebuilt in brick and granite. By 1891, the city had dropped "Falls" from its name as sounding too countrified.

These days, undiscovered wealth still lay in the mountains, every schoolboy's dream. Yet schoolboys also knew that most miners went broke, forced to work in the deep-shaft mines as "muckers," or unskilled shovelers, and car men. The muckers slaved ten hours a day, seven days a week, for $3 a day, and their name quickly became slang for "nobody." While most Spokanites avoided this fate, a bonanza fever still gripped the town.

One day, perhaps at Jennie's or Mary Fahey's request, Mayor Byrne asked Frank what he really wanted to do. They were alone in his office at City Hall, for Byrne liked his young jack-of-all-trades and would not wish to embarrass him. Nevertheless, Frank froze. He stared at his benefactor's mahogany desk, at the rich redwood paneling on the walls. He'd heard how mahogany trees in South America were dragged by mules from the steaming jungle and floated down the Amazon, while in California redwood groves still existed with trees 200 feet high and 30 feet wide. The adults who entered this office saw the trappings of power, but for Frank they meant exotic places. "You'll think I'm foolish," Frank finally replied.

"Let me be the judge of that," Byrne said.

So Frank told him—how he wanted to travel and, as a start, do some prospecting in the Coeur d'Alenes. Byrne chuckled to himself; half the men of his generation had caught gold fever when they were Frank's age. Those few who'd struck it rich were called "self-made men." The best known locally was Jacob Goetz, once called Dutch Jake, who became one of the most respected businessmen in town. Goetz, a German immigrant, had arrived at Prichard's Creek in 1885, hauling his gear in a toboggan over the snow. He staked rich claims in the Potosi Gulch, then invested his wealth in real estate in Spokane. Now Goetz was fifty-five and lived in a sprawling Queen Anne mansion on the city's north side, one of the richest men in town.

Though Byrne was pleased that such wandering spirit hadn't faded entirely from young men like Frank, it was a different age. The frontier wasn't as ripe for picking anymore. Though the older generation fed their children on such dreams of adventure, in fact that time was gone. The Bureau of Census officially closed the frontier in 1893, the year the government opened the Cherokee Outlet, the last free land for homesteading. Every year since then, some writer or "expert" said the Old West was dying, though isolated parts, like the mining towns and the Indian Territory south of Kansas, still hung on tenaciously. Byrne paused wistfully, remembering his own youthful dreams. While it was naive of Frank to think he could still find that Old West, a young man had to work such things out of his system before he was ready to settle down.

"It's not foolish at all," Byrne told him, "but you have to be realistic. I can maybe get you an interview with Jake Goetz to give you some pointers, but you know as well as I do that most miners go bust. What then, Frank? What if that happens? It's not like you can drift around like a cowboy."

So Frank told him the second part of his dream. If he failed as a prospector, he'd head south, living off the carpentry skills he'd learned from his dad. Maybe he'd make it down to Denver or Dallas, where he heard they needed builders. "I like building houses," he said.

The mayor was impressed. The boy *did* have direction. If only vaguely sensed, it was still more pronounced than most people, young or old, ever had. Bryne cleared his throat, touched by his young assistant, and told him his mother worried that he had no ambition.

"I keep things to myself, sir," Frank replied.

The admission was true, though not completely. By late 1905 or 1906, Frank had mentioned his idea to one other person—his friend Jack Golden. Jack was the same age as Frank; they'd met in school and stayed close ever since. Photographs show that while Jack had full, sensual lips and Frank stood slightly taller, the two still looked so similar that people mistook them for brothers. There were other differences, too. Jack was averse to work while Frank was industrious. Jack was a natty dresser, while Frank's attire looked thrown together. Frank was amused by Jack's vanity and laziness, largely because his friend was so persistently good-natured it was hard to stay irritated. The girls liked Jack too, amused by his small stature and big words. They kidded him that, whenever he grew excited, he talked faster and faster, reminding folks of a runaway train.

By 1905, Frank had formed the rude outlines of a plan. Since Jack was always broke, from spending all his pay on women, Frank taught him what he knew of carpentry and convinced him to work with him in the wheat fields. They hired out on shingling jobs, paid by the thousand shingles; they'd climb atop a roof, the highest things for miles. The rhythm of work took hold—it always seemed a miracle to Frank what people could do with their hands. One of the farmers had a woodshop in his barn, where he assembled cabinets; Frank marveled how they held together with dove-tailed notches and not a single nail. Even the simple act of shingling could be an art, the shingles overlapping perfectly, protecting the roof, shielding the people inside. Jack usually lay on his back and talked, wondering how the two of them could get rich quick, but Frank liked having him around for company.

It was during one such monologue that Frank interrupted and mentioned his idea. Jack had been talking about something called the Grand Tour. He'd heard that the education of rich Europeans included a trip around their continent. Travel in Italy used to be enough, what with all the ruins and art, but nowadays wild places like the Alps were part of the package too. Rich Americans now did the same. As Jack saw it, the two of them had as much right to travel as any rich people.

Frank looked up from his hammering and said he agreed.

For once in his life, Jack Golden was speechless, amazed by the words of his usually no-nonsense friend, but Frank was dead serious. The seed had been planted by his first glimpse of the saddle tramps during his family's transcontinental journey six years earlier. They'd work their way from place to place and get an education, he said, maybe try their hand at prospecting, since it was right in their back-yard. In all honesty, Frank admitted, they probably wouldn't get rich, but what a waste it would be not to see the West while parts of it still remained wild. It would be an adventure.

Frank's mother didn't trust Jack Golden—or Lawrence, his Chris-tian name, which she insisted on using. He was a bad influence, all talk and no work, and from bad stock, she said. His father was a one-eyed fruit peddler named Thomas Golden; his sister, poor girl, died in a horrible wreck on the Coeur d'Alene & Spokane Inland Empire Railroad. Two older brothers owned a saloon in Everett, a lumber town of labor conflicts and shady characters 280 miles west on Puget Sound. The saloon was said to be the haunt of thugs and safe crackers, a reputation that grew worse each year. Thomas Golden worried that his wild older boys would influence Jack, his youngest son. Sometimes Jack bragged of meeting train robbers through these brothers; rumors floated that Jack had spent a brief stretch in state prison at Walla Walla for robbery, but Frank knew where his friend disappeared for days. He went to Walla Walla, all right, but only to see his girl, Lillian Stevenson. Jack kept her picture in his watch case. She was tall, with dark, merry eyes and luxurious brown hair. Though he said she came from a good family, it sounded like she'd fallen out of favor with them for being too wild. Jack also mentioned that she tended to throw things when she got mad. She sure sounded like a pistol. Jack craved excitement. No doubt he found it with her.

To Frank, the rumors of Jack's criminal past didn't matter. They'd always stick together, he thought. He could never imagine his best friend letting him down.

THE GOLD THEY sought that summer of 1906 was the residue of violence 1.2 billion years old. Geologists believe that the Coeur d'Alenes' mineral wealth resulted from the cataclysmic spewings of huge hot springs west of Spokane. Occurring in mass, the gold shone a lustrous yellow, but found in individual flakes, it could be black, purple, or even the color of blood. Though neither the rarest, strongest, nor most useful metal, gold's brilliance had made it the greatest object of worship. Its chemical symbol, Au, came from *aurum*, Latin for "shining dawn."

The place where Frank headed was a kind of residue itself. Originally bigger than Texas, the Idaho Territory had been whittled down to form parts of Montana, Wyoming, Washington, and Oregon until what finally applied for statehood in 1890 was a curious-looking leftover with a northern border 44 miles wide and a southern border 300 miles across. In between lay a barrier of mountains, rivers, forests, and canyons that defied civilization yet drew fortune hunters—who were themselves the residue of other busted hopes or failed economies. They included Scandinavians from the stripped timberlands of the Great Lakes; Serbs, Croatians, Poles, and other "hunkies" from the Pennsylvania coalfields; and Irish from mining camps like Leadville and Cripple Creek, Colorado. They funneled into a mining district that had grown from 300 square miles in 1885 to 1,800 square miles in 1906. Even with such growth, there was little room for some ethnic groups. By 1906, there were few blacks, fewer Indians (most of the Coeur d'Alene and Palouse Indians had died of smallpox after their 1858 surrender to the army), and almost no Chinese.

Frank and Jack traveled light, carrying little more than their grips, money from their savings, and a .38-caliber Colt that Frank had purchased for protection from cougars at the Holly-Mason Hardware store in downtown Spokane. He'd bought it from clerk James Shriver, whom he knew from playing baseball. He also carried two prospector's pans. In all likelihood he got them from Dutch Jake, to whom Dr. Byrne sent Frank for advice on panning gold. Goetz answered Frank's knock and shook his hand. He loved to talk about his mining days; there was nothing like challenging the odds and winning, and mining for silver and gold was just another word for gambling, he said. Life itself was a gamble, and very few won. He'd known plenty of stampeders who'd gone into the Coeur d'Alenes with him during the rush of '85, men full of spit and vinegar with the same high hopes and lack of sense. Many didn't make it out alive. Snowslides around Elk Creek buried entire camps. One prospector was chewed up by a wounded grizzly. When lightning struck the dry summer timber, wildfire swept the draws and canyons, and a man's only chance was to duck down the deep tunnel of a mine.

Goetz showed Frank what equipment he'd need and recommended an honest outfitter, then showed him how to pan for gold. A good pan had a slope of 45 degrees and was two or three inches deep; the first thing to do was heat it in a wood fire till the metal glowed dull red. That burned off all the oil or grease, both of which ruined a pan for gold. Next you dropped it in cold water, darkening the metal blue. There was nothing prettier than that first small nugget or thimbleful of gold flour shining against the blue. Goetz made him practice, half filling the pan with sand and river gravel, then dipping it in water and swirling counterclockwise. A little water and gravel spilled over the lip with each revolution, till all that remained at the bottom was a half cup of heavy concentrate. That's where you find the gold, Goetz said.

As Frank practiced, Dutch Jake talked about gold's nature. He'd given this a lot of thought; a fellow really had time to think while panning for gold. The yellow metal was just like people, bound by certain laws. Since it was a heavy metal, it was bound by gravity, working its way downhill, downstream, down into sands and gravels, into cracks and crevices, into the riffles of a sluice box or the bottom of a pan. Most folks were like that, too. People and gold were both assisted in their downward journeys by rough handling and agitation and tended to take the shortest route to the bottom. They hung up at the least obstruction, which in gold's case was where the flow of water lost speed. Both tended to act in a predictable manner, though odd nuggets could be tricky and disappear downstream. In fact, the only certainty was uncertainty with either one. A man could search a half a lifetime and never find an ounce of gold, then stumble on the mother lode in half a day. Either way, he was hooked. Gold fever was a kind of slavery, entirely of a man's own doing.

The first stage of their journey was a peaceful twenty-mile trip from Spokane to the resort town of Coeur d'Alene aboard the Inland Empire Railroad. Frank wondered if Jack thought about his sister's death on this, the railroad where she died; he wished he could reach into his head and know the whole Jack Golden, not just the part he showed his friends. He watched the scenery flash past his window like the flickering images at a nickelodeon. A sign at the ornate station reminded tourists that Coeur d'Alene was the home of Paul Bunyan and his blue ox, Babe. They boarded a steamboat to cross the lake, also called the Coeur d'Alene, then took a narrow-gauge railroad another thirty-three miles east to Wallace, the mining district's municipal seat and largest town. Though a telephone line followed the tracks, parts of the district wouldn't see phones or electric power until 1910. Shadowed gulches and lush forest alternated with acres scarred by wildfire, the larches and pines now flame-blackened poles called "snags." Fire scars showed a cycle of fire dating back to the 1600s, but the greatest fire on record would not occur until 1910. In that year, five million forest acres were incinerated in the Rockies, three million in Montana and Idaho alone. The inferno killed eighty-five people, destroyed one third of Wallace, and turned the sky black for days. Four years before that holocaust, people had already feared the worst and built fire towers on the ridges overlooking the mining towns.

Yet the worst scars were man-made. Like many, Frank thought of gold mining in idyllic terms. A prospector panned gravel from a stream, swirled it around in a pan, and dumped everything back in but the gold. He turned over a rock and found a nugget; the world's biggest nugget, the 156-pound Welcome Stranger, was discovered in 1869 when a passing wagon churned it from the dirt outside Victoria, Australia. In actual fact, dust and nuggets were the rarest forms of gold; most of the precious metal was found in ore. Serious miners ripped ore from the earth, leaving piles of waste behind. Frank rode past the scars of hydraulic mining, where water was forced at fantastic pressure through an eight-inch pipe, melting gold-bearing hills to sludge; as the dirt ran over a flume, gold sank to the bottom and collected in riffles. Floating platforms called "elevator dredges" lifted mud from a river bottom, washed it through a gold sluice, and left mounds of waste on the shore. Frank had thought the deep-shaft mines caused little damage, but the company towns surrounding them were a kind of scar themselves, gray cookie-cutter shacks piled one atop the other, each valley town covered in a haze of coal and sulfur fumes. Creeks running through the middle served as outdoor plumbing, the banks lined with the soggy pages of the mail order catalog that were used as toilet paper. In larger towns like Wardner, an aerial tram stretched overhead, carting thousands of tons of ore from an outcropping high in the mountain. Miners stood calmly in the buckets, riding to and from their shifts. When they lost their balance, they fell spread-eagled through the air. One time a bucket tipped and dumped a fatal load of ore onto a housewife in her kitchen.

It amazed Frank that something as beautiful as gold caused so many fatalities. The most common deaths were by powder blast and cave-in; poisonous gas and bad air came a close second. Something as benign as river panning could spell a horrible end. Dropping a bead of mercury into the pan was an easy way to separate gold from waste—the gold bonded to the liquid metal like cement, forming an amalgam that was then heated to vaporize the mercury and leave only the gold. Yet it was easy to inhale the mercury vapor, a mistake that killed in a number of ways. Inhaling small amounts brought abnormal excitement or fatigue, splitting headaches, drooling, and convulsions. A little more made one's teeth fall out. Larger doses meant kidney failure; death was guaranteed in ten days.

Some said work alone could kill a prospector, as was the fate of Gus Gullickson, whose obituary proclaimed OVERWORKED, SO BLOWS OFF HEAD after he committed suicide in his cabin by Big Creek. As his brother walked to a spring to draw water, he heard a gunshot and ran back. Gus was sprawled in the doorway, rifle by his side. The two had worked area mines for twenty-four years. "Of late years, constant concentration on hard work by Gus and his refusal to lay off at any time and take a rest resulted in an illness which was mental to a large degree," a reporter concluded. "The brother blames hard work for the act of the dead man."

The lure and lust for gold was unrelenting, an ocean of obsession with no beginning or end. A prospector succumbed to "mountain fever"; if he died in the quest, he "went over the range." In the Americas, death and precious metals were old friends. The total gold stock of Europe was worth less than $225 million when the New World was discovered by Columbus; in 1850, 358 years later, the world gold output had mushroomed to $55.5 *billion*, most of it from South America and Mexico. It came at the expense of the Aztecs, Incas, Mayans, and other native peoples, who paid in slavery, disease, and extermination. But the seekers paid as well. In 1541–42, Francisco Coronado and Hernando de Soto marched their separate armored columns through the Southwest and the Mississippi Valley chasing golden ghosts. Both left blasted hopes and buried men, including de Soto himself, his weighted corpse sunk in the Mississippi River to conceal it from natives, who'd been told he could never die. In 1604, the Jamestown settlers arrived, seeking gold, but found starvation. In 1830, the United States' first great gold rush brought 3,000 men to

Cherokee territory in north Georgia. Eight years later, 20,000 Cherokee were marched at gunpoint to what is now Oklahoma. Four thousand died en route along that Trail of Tears.

The Coeur d'Alenes did not break the mold. When Frank arrived in 1906, the mining district meant to most Americans the murder of former Idaho governor Frank Steunenberg. Six months earlier, on December 30, 1905, he'd been blown to shreds by a bomb planted in his yard. The assassin, Harry Orchard, was hired by the Western Federation of Miners, a key player in the decades-long violence between miners and mine owners in the Coeur d'Alenes. To save himself from the death penalty when caught and charged with murder, Orchard implicated several Federation officials, including President William "Big Bill" Haywood. Frank promised his mother when he left that he'd steer clear of the "troubles," yet it was a promise impossible to keep. Tension hung thick as coal smoke in these company towns. The townspeople in Wallace glanced sideways at Frank and Jack when the two stepped off the train; their words were clipped when Frank asked directions. The two left the station and walked along Bank Street, the city's main drag.

Notwithstanding the violence, mining had been good to this town. Wallace nearly filled a narrow valley, the green mountains crowding up to its edge. If fire swept this part of the Bitterroots, cinders would rain from above. In 1895, the town had been a cedar swamp, but now Bank Street was lined with ornate structures of carved timber and stone. The Samuels Hotel, the town's tallest building, opened that summer. A number of establishments advertised "rooms" with exotic names like the Lux, Jade, Arment, U&I, and Oasis, but Frank soon learned that these "rooms" were sporting houses, less politely known as cow yards. At the corner of 7th and Bank, the Shoshone County Courthouse filled up an entire city block, its two-story arched windows, parapets, and pilasters proclaiming the permanence of justice in Idaho, a justice presently being tested. The trial of Steve Adams, implicated by Orchard in the union-ordered murders, was scheduled for early next year. Even now, months before trial, detectives with the famous Pinkerton's National Detective Agency lingered on the courthouse steps, gun belts peeking from beneath their coats. As they watched Frank and Jack with unconcealed interest, Frank realized that no one here liked strangers. To lawmen, every newcomer was a potential assassin; to miners, he was an undercover man. "The sooner we're out of here and hunting gold, the better," said Jack, his usual confidence shaken by the unsettling gaze of the Pinkertons.

Even so, life in the Coeur d'Alenes was every bit as dazzling as Frank had dreamed. The mining district reeked with romance and every day brought a new brush with legend, as if Frank had finally found the West he'd missed during the train ride six years ago. The most famous legend Frank heard was that of Wyatt Earp, who had arrived with his brothers during the gold rush of 1884. Wyatt was thirty-five, three years past his shootout in Tombstone, a famous if damaged man. He settled north of Wallace in Eagle City, filing claims and opening the White Elephant Saloon, so named because a man was said to go "see the elephant" when prospecting for gold. For a short period he also served as deputy sheriff of Kootenai County. Old-timers remembered Wyatt as gaunt and loose-limbed, with a long pale face, drooping yellow mustache, and deep-set blue-gray eyes. Some called him death personified. To Wyatt Earp, violence was just another tool for securing one's ambitions. Of four claim-jumping suits filed against him in district court, at least one alleged he urged the plaintiff off his land at the point of a gun.

Frank noticed that most of the district's legends involved whores. The majority seemed to die from a "lingering illness"—probably syphilis, we know now. Frank heard tales of Nellie the Bilk, Terrible Edith, and Old Arkansas, names that were a far cry from their sentimental categorization as "soiled doves." Miners were a sentimental bunch, especially toward those they considered lost souls like themselves. When penniless gold miner "Stumpy" Wicks died of mountain fever, forty fellow prospectors chipped in to make a casket and buy a headstone. "They found a woman's picture, very old and quite worn out in Stumpy's pocket, and this was buried with him," wrote the *Coeur d'Alene Eagle* on May 30, 1884. One of the boys commented that it "was the mournfullest plantin' he ever had a hand in." While Frank had already suspected that the rest of the world held a heightened, romantic notion of the West, he was learning that Westerners held a heightened, romantic notion of themselves.

The district's most famous prostitute, and the standard for those who followed, was Molly Burdan, better known as Molly B'Damn. Molly arrived in the Coeur d'Alenes in 1884 with Martha Jane Canary, better known as Calamity Jane. When Jane got bored and returned to Deadwood in the Dakota Territory, Molly stayed behind.

She was blond, 5 feet 6 inches, 120 pounds, with a sharp nose and thin lips but an otherwise "pleasing" face, a woman said to drink her whiskey straight, ride her high-bred horse into saloons, and have a soft spot for those less fortunate than she. When she died, of a "lingering illness," her obituary said she was born in Dublin, Ireland, on November 26, 1853, another refugee of the great starvation. She died at 6 A.M. on January 17, 1888, at the age of thirty-five. As the writer eulogized, "She flashed like a diamond in her early life from coast to coast and was the mistress of a millionaire; but she drifted with the tide of events . . . and finally found herself in a humble cabin in the Coeur d'Alenes."

Frank mulled over these tales, told so often they took on a separate life, reaching from the past to set a code of conduct that one hesitated to ignore. A man's fate was tied to violence, like Earp's slaughter of the Clantons. A woman's fall from grace made her one of the boys. How did such standards apply to him and Jack? he wondered. The West—in fact, the whole country—seemed drunk on tales of death, sex, and rage.

Within a week they'd gathered their gear and were ready to go. They bought picks, shovels, bedrolls, food, and a waterproofed tent; they bought a secondhand .44-caliber Winchester rifle after veteran sourdoughs told them they stood as much chance of stopping a cougar with Frank's .38 Colt as by throwing rocks. Last but not least, they bought a donkey to carry their gear. Locals called them Spanish burros. In town the animals tended to wander in search of a handout, drawn to the cooking smells of restaurants, nosing open their back doors. Cooks chased them off with cleavers, while boys stuck their feet in empty tin cans. But in the mountains a burro was a godsend, tougher than a horse, which tended to wander off or die.

They headed north from Wallace about twenty miles until they hit Beaver Creek, which merged with a thousand streams and gulches on its course northwest toward the North Fork of the Coeur d'Alene River. They watched for black sand, where gold hid out, or small veins of white quartz that crisscrossed the bedrock, another good sign. They wandered through ghost towns with names like Last Chance and Lucky Boy, where the saloons and stores were left to lizards and porcupines chewed holes in the walls of houses and hotels. The surrounding forest crowded the ruins, creating a silence that mocked men's dreams. In the creeks and gorges where gold seemed likely, they also found other prospectors: a cabin like the Gullick-sons', a long sluice box surrounded by a gang of shovelers, or some lone fool digging at the bedrock with a long-handled scraper. These men were jealous of their isolation, unwelcoming of strangers who passed through their claim. They panned for gold in several unclai-med bends in the streams and rivers but always came up busted. All they got for their efforts were sore backs and thighs from squatting in one place too long. After a month of this, Frank and Jack admitted they wouldn't be finding gold, at least not here. These waterways were played out by the thousand other dreamers who'd already come and gone.

So they looked for silver instead. They followed the "silver belt" in the ridges south of Wallace, searching through canyons at the very limits of the mining district that hadn't been explored in years. There'd been fire in these ridges during the previous summer, burn-ing off underbrush and exposing the rock, a good way to discover previously unspotted veins. They looked for the hard luster silver gave off in the sun. Jack soured on the search, especially when the rains came in mid-October, but Frank pressed on. He dreaded to go home empty-handed, but more than that he discovered that he loved the life out here. They'd ride through a grove and he'd suddenly smell the tang of cedar, or they'd emerge into a mountain meadow where the burro stood withers deep in rabbitbrush, a shrub resem-bling goldenrod. Come evening, they'd pitch their tent, catch a few grasshoppers, and cut birch rods for poles. The trout flashed in the river, dashes of orange and rose among the silver, backs sprinkled with gold.

ONE DAY IN early December it happened, as Frank knew it must if there was any truth to the talk about hard work prevailing in an ordered world. As they checked a ridge by the treeline, they saw a glint and followed a pile of "float" uphill. As they climbed, a blue jay hopped among the branches, crying, "Jay! Jay!" On the rock face they saw a six-inch vein of quartz and inside that a line of silver-gray. Frank loosened the quartz with his pick; the ore split apart in nearly perfect cleavage, the leaden crystals forming into cubes. "A vein of pure galena," he told Jack excitedly. The jay kept squawking. "Let's call it the Blue Jay."

They worked fast, for this was the limbo between discovery and legal ownership, when fortune hunters who prowled the mountains tended to jump a claim. Frank returned to Wallace and filed their claim with the county recorder: The Blue Jay, located December 3, 1906, officially recorded December 21. By law, the standard lode claim was 1,500 feet long and 600 wide and only covered the mineral discovery, but experienced miners staked adjoining plots for protection, should the claim do well. Frank merely filed the standard claim. The recorder said that in a year he had to prove $100 worth of work at the mine to keep it active, but that seemed an eternity to Frank and right now he raced the winter winds. He bought axes and an adze to build a cabin and carve out tunnel supports, steel traps for furs to supplement their income, gads and drills to loosen the ore, extra provisions, and dynamite for blasting. He trudged back with the claim and the new supplies and the two built a one-room cabin, felling the straightest pines and cutting the trunks into logs. Frank joined the ends with the dovetailed notch preferred by Swedes, slanting the upper notch with the adze to drain out the rain. They made a fireplace and chimney out of river rock, built a shed for their donkey, piled firewood for the winter, and then started on the mine. Jack held the iron drill while Frank struck it with the eight-pound hammer: in an hour, they made a hole three feet deep and a few inches wide. They inserted a stick of dynamite, added two feet of fuse, packed the hole with dirt and gravel, put a match to the fuse, and ran. Dirt and smoke shot everywhere, followed by the boom. Surely the ridge couldn't withstand such a blast? They found their joy and congratulations premature when they saw that only a bushel basket of quartz had been jolted free. They hand-sorted the ore into a sack, loaded it onto a wooden "go-devil" sled they'd built for the purpose, and started again.

After a week, they were twelve feet into the mountain; after two weeks, little more than double that. The vein of ore wasn't getting any wider, yet neither did it disappear. They shored the roof with beams, listening as the wood creaked overhead. Their pile of ore grew slowly. The best thing about the work was that it got them out of the snow and the wind.

The winter of 1906–7 was the worst in twenty years. By March 1907, the snow was deeper in the Coeur d'Alenes than anywhere else in the nation; news photos show miners' cabins buried in white and eight-foot telephone poles barely poking through the drifts. The railroads were blocked; the huge lake iced over; a few roads stayed open for ore shipments, though barely. Horses starved for lack of feed.

In the mountains, Jack Golden thought he would go mad. Frank seemed to thrive on this stuff, turning before his eyes into a modern-day Jim Bridger, but to Jack the winter was a nightmare. Every motion and minute dragged past, slow and cold. One morning they opened the cabin door—fortunately, it swung inward—and were confronted by a six-foot wall of white; they burrowed up through the snow like moles. At night they listened to the wind howl outside. The donkey snorted softly in its shed beside the cabin as though wondering if anyone was still alive. Some days they worked in the mine, but their arms grew too heavy to lift the sledgehammer, fingers too numb to hold the drill. At least it was warmer in the tunnel than in the cabin, but that caused problems. When Jack closed his eyes he had the strangest dreams. Once he saw a cat walk through a wall; when he woke he remembered old tales of miners seeing dogs or cats before the roof caved in. In another dream a woman stood in the tunnel entrance, shrouded in white. Women were considered bad luck around the mines, portending disaster. This one beckoned him outside. He tried to escape but couldn't move. She scowled and the skin on her skull withered like parchment; she stepped inside the tunnel and grabbed his hand. He tried to scream but no sound came out. When he tried to run, Frank shook him awake, warning that if he fell asleep out here he'd die.

Then came a week when the cold was so absolute that nothing moved outside the cabin and little moved within. Some mornings they heard the earth-shaking rumbles of an avalanche on the ridge, sometimes so close it seemed they would be buried, and all they could do was hide beneath the skins and pray. One morning Jack woke and his fingers were white, with no feeling at all. Frank got a scared look on his face and quickly banked the fire. He sat Jack near it, wrapped him in skins, and forced him to keep his hands beneath his armpits. This saved Jack's fingers, but a fever set in, followed by a rattling in Jack's chest that Frank feared was pneumonia. Jack knew he was going to die. He said it often, with increasing resignation, and the acceptance in his voice scared Frank more than the avalanche or the sight of the frost-bitten fingers ever had. "Don't be a fool," he answered, but there were a few bad days when he wasn't so sure. All he knew to do was feed the fire and keep Jack warm, and finally the fever broke. Frank nursed him back to health on a broth made of salt pork and venison from a deer he shot in the woods. It made him proud when Jack looked up from his bundle of covers and said, "This is pretty good."

Frank loved his time alone in the forest; the entire world seemed muffled except for the rasping of his breath and beating of his heart. He learned to read the messages of animal tracks written in the snow. He took with him the rifle, knife, and some line. He checked his traps methodically, stopping at each in a prescribed order like the stations of the cross. Everything he'd done before this, in Spokane and Rush Lake, seemed like a game, but this was for his and Jack's survival and that made it real. His mind seemed honed to a clarity he'd never before experienced. Though he came back with snowshoe hare and the black-eared squirrels that came out during thaws, his favorite prey was pine marten, which thrived up high. He knew that storekeepers in Wallace paid good money for their fur, so exceptionally thick, a yellow-chestnut color with orange or white at the throat, as well as the long, sharp claws. As he set his steel-tooth traps near running water where they hunted, he wondered what it was like when a predator became the prey.

That winter, miners told how cougars came out of the mountains and circled their cabins, drawn by starvation and the cooking smells inside. Particularly vulnerable were their donkeys, tied in their sheds. Some nights a weird howling from the trees sounded like a woman on fire. Sometimes the cats broke into the stables and left burros in a lake of blood. We do not know today whether Frank waged a war that winter against a cougar, but one brief comment made years later suggested that he did. He'd been terrified of the creatures before his arrival in the mining district, but never after that winter. Perhaps they lost the burro to a cougar; perhaps they confronted one of the mountain lions and won. Some prospectors butchered the remains of their burros and used the meat to bait their steel-tooth traps. They'd hear the cougar scream in the night and in the morning expect to find it trapped in the teeth, but all they found was part of its leg where it gnawed through the bone to freedom.

One day Jack cleared his throat as they were eating and Frank looked up. "You saved my life," he said, between sips of broth. For a guy who usually talked nonstop, Jack seemed to stumble over the words. In fact, Frank realized, his friend had been unnaturally quiet ever since his sickness. Mortality had written a change across Jack's face. "Some day I'll repay you, I promise," Jack added. But right now he had to leave. He was desperate to see his girl Lillian, take a hot bath, get a meal of something other than wild game and beans. Frank was not surprised. He'd seen his friend's depression deepen. He understood, but he didn't want to give up on the mine yet, he said.

Sometime after the first thaw of 1907, the two piled the furs and bags of ore onto the go-devil and dragged it back to Wallace. They took the ore to the assay office and the furs to a buyer. Jack booked the first train from the mining district, promising to return. When he settled into the coach's high-backed seat, his relief was visible. Frank watched the slow train pull off and wondered if he'd see his friend again. He bought more supplies with their meager profits, set more traps for furs, slowly worked the claim. He could see that the vein was thinning out. The Blue Jay was a borasca, the opposite of a bonanza. It was a disappointment, but at least he'd given it a try.

And there was something else—something he didn't understand till later. One day he heard a familiar squawk and looked up. The jay was back from wherever it wintered. Frank smiled as it scolded him. They'd both disappeared into the wilderness and come out in one piece. He may not have been a whopping success as a miner, but at least he'd endured.

Jack returned in late spring or early summer, leading two horses. Frank emerged from the mine head, wiping his hands, relieved to see his pal. Jack said he'd run into some friends in Spokane who'd talked about moving south sometime in the vague future; this didn't sound like a bad idea to Jack and he told Frank he wanted to leave right now. He wanted to get as far away from these goddamn mountains as possible. He couldn't take another winter like the last; ever since his sickness he often felt tired and seemed saddled with a cough that wouldn't leave. He didn't feel like his old self anymore.

To Jack's surprise, it didn't seem to matter to Frank. After all, the mine was nearly played out, Frank said. They had some money left, but to keep throwing it at the Blue Jay would be the same as throwing it down a hole. When Frank asked a few questions about the friends Jack mentioned, his pal was evasive. Frank should have persisted, but he was relieved to see Jack again and not eager to press him. Besides, he was already thinking of moving on from the claim.

We do not know today exactly when they left the Blue Jay, but this much is certain: by December 21, 1907, the first anniversary of its recording, the claim was not renewed, becoming yet another abandoned mine in the hills. The slow weight of the earth splintered the supports; a fine dust filtered from the roof, softening the edges of stone; and eventually the entrance collapsed. A dimple in the rock was all that remained of their work. Man and nature both abhor a vacuum. Except for a single document in the county recorder's office, it was as if they'd never staked their fortunes in the land of silver and gold.

FOR THE NEXT year and a half, Frank and Jack knocked around the West on their own, Frank would later say. They probably left Wallace by the end of summer 1907, selling the rifle and prospecting equipment for cash, though Frank kept the Colt revolver. "Folks come easy, and they go easy," Owen Wister said in *The Virginian*, and this described their itinerary. They were guided by whim and rumor, the new best thing heard from other wanderers like them. They may have traveled east to the Masabi Range of northeastern Minnesota, but this is based upon a single remark later made in prison, and stronger evidence suggests they pushed south by horse and by train. According to Pinkerton and FBI records, the farthest south they got during this stage of their journey was Manitou Springs, Colorado, immediately west of Colorado Springs. Sometime in 1908, police there held the two of them briefly on a watch complaint, the equivalent of an all-points bulletin, for a hotel robbery. A general description was issued, followed by a roundup of usual suspects and of friendless strangers like them. Their mug shots were snapped, they spent the night in a holding cell with other vagrants and unknowns, and then were released the next morning for lack of evidence. Court records noted that Frank was processed as "E. E. Hollingshead," a booking error he later said he failed to correct for fear his family might learn of his night in jail.

Far from being unusual, roundups like the one in Colorado were the common lot of thousands of western vagabonds. Instant aliases filled police files; identities were changed as quickly as clothes. Every day, nameless drifters blew in like sagebrush, and authorities were at a loss as to how to respond. Roundups were one way to dislodge such tumbleweeds and let them blow to the next town. A tent city rose at the edge of Caldwell, Idaho; skid rows wormed into the hearts of Spokane and Denver; in Boise, police chased the undesirables away. It was a foreshadowing of the hobo nation that would grow until the end of the Depression, an army of the displaced and discontented who rode the freights, climbing into open boxcars or into the cramped space between a car's floor and its truss rods in a risky expedient called "riding the rods."

The Pinkertons, a mainstay of railroad security, saw this army as a dangerous if amorphous entity loosely organized around mobile thievery. In reality, it drifted without purpose, its ranks filled with unemployed miners, busted cowhands and sheepherders, and immigrants of all stripe and national origins, as well as army veterans cut loose from the Philippine insurrection of 1898–1903. The general direction of travel was out of the country and into the glittering city, which seemed to promise life without end. Influential historian Frederick Jackson Turner in 1896 had called the traditional West of prairie farms and wide open spaces a "safety valve for social danger . . . a magic fountain of youth in which America continually bathed," but between 1900 and 1920, 30 percent of those Americans living on farms left for urban areas. The bulk of that shift occurred in the West. The drifters were the vanguard of a movement that profoundly changed the nation. They'd seen something disturbing in the Garden. Their impulse was to flee.

Although some social scientists raised a warning, they were ignored by their peers; such observations ran counter to the era's prevailing faith in the West as representing what was best in the nation, yet these dismissals ignored the evidence. The 1890 census showed a West where people died of madness, suicide, and alcohol, not heroic gunfights at the OK Corral. The West, with the nation's highest rates of suicide and alcoholism and its second-highest rate of madness, was the very region that eastern aristocrats like Teddy Roosevelt and Owen Wister saw as the nation's salvation, a crucible molding heroes who were just, fair, and wise. "I instantly preferred the Rocky Mountain place," said Wister's eastern narrator in *The Virginian*:

> More of death it undoubtedly saw, but less of vice, than did its New York equivalents. And death is a thing much cleaner than vice. . . . In their flesh our natural passions ran tumultuous; but often in their spirit sat hidden a true nobility.

But it was hard in the West to be both noble and mad. The papers overflowed with stories of murder, failure, and suicide. In exchange for ambition and hard work, a man found debt and ruin. In exchange for having babies, a woman died in childbirth or watched her children fade away from disease. The suicide of miner Gus Gullickson was part of a larger pattern, yet his death seemed benign beside others. The July 12, 1900, *Badger State Bulletin* of Wisconsin, home of Frederick Jackson Turner, told about Abraham Zweekbaum of the town of Holland who "committed suicide by battering himself on the head with a hammer. . . . He attempted to take his life a few days [earlier] by cutting his head from his body with a sharp instrument, but was prevented from doing so." On the same day that the November 8, 1901, edition of the *Leavenworth Times* screamed of the breakout and flight of the twenty-six federal prisoners from the new penitentiary, there was also the story of Mrs. William Texter, who "retired to the kitchen and thoroughly saturated herself with coal oil and then ignited it. . . . The skin was charred and burned and the hair was burned entirely from her head." In 1897, sociologist Frank Blackmar wrote of a family he called the Smoky Pilgrims of Kansas, who started in the East as poor but hopeful and healthy, then dramatically changed when transplanted to the West. The mother became "a twisted old woman," the oldest daughter descended into "unapproachable silence," her two sisters "had become harlots," and the son sank into "the agreeable but thick-witted stupor of a lazy and idle man." Blackmar said his pilgrims were victims of "economic overcrowding": while those worth anything had already migrated to the city, the remainder were driven mad by the "morbid state" of the frontier.

Frank and Jack headed south into the morbidity, still sticking to their plan of making a Grand Tour. The easiest way was to skirt the Bitterroots, and the best way to do this was by the route of the buffalo, Indians, and cattlemen who'd come before them. They headed east to Billings, Montana, rounding the worst of the Rockies and the Absaroka Range. At Billings they dropped south along the Bighorn Mountains, heading for Sheridan, Wyoming, a route that took them past the stark white stones set in the hillsides that marked the remains of Custer and his men. South of Sheridan they came upon the sites of two earlier Indian battles. A lonely stone pillar marked the Fetterman Massacre, named after the arrogant army captain whose eighty officers and men were annihilated in 1866 by Red Cloud's Sioux near Fort Phil Kearny on the Bozeman Trail. A few miles west of that lay the site of the Wagon Box Fight, the grassy plateau where, one year later, Indians tried to repeat their Fetterman victory but were repulsed by the soldiers and civilians armed with new rapid-fire breech loading rifles. Frank thought of those who came before him, to whom mastering the West meant mastering the Indians. He thought about those Indians, less as they really were than as they were portrayed, a demonic representation of the wild. He and Jack passed through Crow territory, traditional enemies of the Oglala Sioux, and heard about a photographer named Edward S. Curtis who'd traveled into the Pryor Mountains south of Billings to shoot plates of forty Sun Dancers, painted white, their breast muscles pierced by claw and lanyard as they hung from a pole seeking visions inspired by pain. Now the great tribes were exiled to the reservations, their children sent to government schools. Like inmates in the federal prisons, they were out of sight and out of mind.

Frank found something sad and overwhelming about it all. America was huge, endless, and beautiful, but with a beauty excluding man. Frank felt small as they trekked south, smaller than in Washington or in the mining district, dwarfed by the mountains, mere specks beneath the sky. Wyoming was tough country, a giant upland mesa dotted with antelope and overrun with scrub and sage. Things happened here that had nothing to do with history. They watched spellbound from a hill as a low bulge in a cloud turned into the thin finger of a cyclone, weirdly peaceful until it tore up dirt like a dynamite explosion and flung trees aside. Black storm clouds boiled from the mountains so fast they couldn't take cover; the best they could do was duck their heads between their shoulders as lightning branched beneath the clouds like veins on an old man's arm. On their right the Rockies rose straight up, while on their left the badlands contained the bones of strange gigantic creatures, long dead. In the sides of these hills they saw ancient limestone quarries, mined first by Indians for the iron oxide, which made a durable war paint, then by the Union Pacific to use on their boxcars, and finally, in 1880, by the City of New York to paint the Brooklyn Bridge. They rode through Johnson County, site of the range war between cattle barons and the alliance of rustlers and homesteaders that gave birth to Butch Cassidy and the Wild Bunch, made famous the hired cattle-rustler "regulator" Tom Horn, and inspired *The Virginian*. Now the Wild Bunch was gone, Tom Horn was executed, and *The Virginian* was responsible for creating an unreal culture hero. Though real cattle barons were as democratic as feudal lords and the cowboy little more than a hireling, the cattle trade did have style. They came upon a small ranch on the day of cattle-naming: as fast as a calf was vaccinated and run down the chute, the farm wife cried out whatever name hit her and it was recorded that way. Bigger ranchers kept wolfhounds to kill coyotes, but the dogs grew so vicious that they attacked anything on foot and were known to chase down and kill children. Frank and Jack came upon a circle of cowpunchers at night, sitting around a fire. Half a mile off the night herders rode around the cattle, singing to calm them down. By now, many cattlemen had been replaced by sheepherders, their old nemeses. It was estimated that by 1905 there were three million sheep in Wyoming competing with 800,000 cattle for range land. The sheep were winning; they took better than cattle to the winters, their wool trapping heat and protecting them from the cold and wind. As Frank passed through the country, he saw sheepherders in the distance with thousands of sheep around them, their only companions the dogs watching their masters from opposite ends of the flock, paused in continual anticipation for the next command.

At Casper, Frank and Jack turned right for some sightseeing along the old settlers' trail. They followed the North Platte River to the hump of Independence Rock, then the Sweetwater as far as South Pass and the Continental Divide. They rode past prosperous little ranches, nestled between shelter belts of trees to stave off the wind. Here a man's wealth was not measured in acres or number of cattle but by the water rights he controlled. The common Texas houses— two houses connected by a long roof with an open space, or dog-trot—were built close to the rivers, for away from water the land turned immediately to desert, with nothing growing but sage and greasewood. Everything was built low, imitating nature, because the wind never ceased and was said to drive folks mad. On those rare occasions when it did drop off, the world grew silent, as if awaiting word of some momentous change.

By now great things were afoot, yet man's work and worry meant little out here. In 1907, as Frank and Jack disappeared into the wilderness, plastic was invented, called Bakelite. That year 1.28 million immigrants came to America, an all-time record; many of them immediately headed for the West. The Great White Fleet left the Naval Station at Norfolk, Virginia, for a worldwide cruise proclaiming America's might. The *Ziegfeld Follies* hit the stage.

People said the West was conquered, but it was still rough out there. Two years earlier, in 1905, Teddy Roosevelt offered Bat Masterson an appointment in the Oklahoma Territory as U.S. marshal, but Masterson turned him down. "I am not the man for the job," he wrote. "Oklahoma is still woolly, and if I were marshal some youngster would try to put me out because of my reputation. I would be a bait for grownup kids who had fed on dime novels. I would have to kill or be killed." On February 29, 1908, on a lonely dirt road outside Las Cruces, New Mexico, Pat Garrett stepped from a buckboard to take a piss and was shot in the back of the head.

By then Frank and Jack were nearly penniless, whatever proceeds they'd dug from the Blue Jay long gone. They wintered at one of the ranches on the Sweetwater and backtracked to Cheyenne, paying for their keep through carpentry. As Frank rode through Crooks Gap on the Sweetwater, he saw boulders as big as houses. He didn't know they contained jewelry-quality jade, or that buried beneath them was enough coal to heat the nation for generations. He rode over traps of oil and natural gas that lay undiscovered until the 1920s, past uranium deposits that were not tapped until 1955. The riches were there, but not for him.

By spring of 1908, Frank was exhausted by travel and overwhelmed by the land. He'd seen enough of the abandoned sod dugouts built against the cutbanks, the sunken eyes of Indian children in the reservations, the hoboes in their jungles pitched beside the railroad water towers. He'd ridden past too many cows and horses staggering blindly from poisonous growth like locoweed or Johnson grass, through the ruins of too many prairie towns burned to cinders by wildfire, which the Indians had called "red buffalo." This was not the West he had imagined. He'd dreamed of a place of life, not an empty place of death. There was nothing to eat and damn little to drink; you could freeze in a sudden snowstorm or get sucked off the earth by a cyclone. It was lonely in a way he'd never imagined, a loneliness so elemental that a man's life meant nothing and his brief passage did little more than help wear a smooth path on the ground. He'd never had thoughts like these in Spokane. Thank God Jack had been out here with him, he thought, or the loneliness might have made him crazy. Jack's cough was getting worse, and he needed to see a doctor. Frank missed his family, his mother especially, and though he wrote regularly he couldn't bear to straggle back with nothing to show after all his hopes and dreams. A soft bed would be nice, a change of clothes that wasn't half patched, maybe a night out with a pretty girl. He'd like to tell a girl what he'd seen out here. He'd never fallen in love, nothing beyond a crush, and maybe it was time.

"Haven't we seen enough of this damn wasteland?" Jack finally shouted one day, and Frank laughed in relief as he noticed how thin and hollowed out they looked, both of them shadows of their former selves. Goddammit, they were deserving of a little fun. They needed some high life quick before their surroundings became a kind of second nature and they turned out as desolate as the other lost souls they'd encountered out here.

"Bring on the bright lights and big city," Frank answered.

They turned their sights toward Denver, the Queen City of the Plains.

❦ CHAPTER TWO ❧

"When We Are Absent, One from Another"

AT FIRST, DENVER in 1908 seemed everything the doctor ordered for two men fresh off the prairie. Eccentric, exuberant, and outrageous, the Mile-High City, as it already called itself, took Frank's breath away. One thousand miles of the Great Plains ended here. To the east, deep-rooted prairie grasses rippled like waves on the ocean; to the west, the Front Range of the Rocky Mountains rose abruptly from foothills to snow-capped peaks. Like Spokane, the city was born of a gold rush; like Spokane, a river ran through town. There the similarities ended. Denver was a grid of spacious parks, tree-lined streets, and broad avenues boasting the largest hotel Frank had ever seen—the Windsor, with three hundred rooms, three restaurants, a library, and a bar with three thousand silver dollars embedded in the floor. It had the biggest saloon he'd ever entered—Ed's Arcade, with a mahogany bar that stretched forever and a row of chandeliers overhead. The state capitol building's gold-plated dome gleamed in the sun. Mayor Robert W. Speer called his town "the Paris of America"; more cynical citizens called her "the great braggart town."

If anything, Denver was bragging more than usual. The Democratic Party National Convention was opening here in July 1908, and the hue and cry of renovation, construction, and boosterism filled the air. The city was draped in red-white-and-blue bunting. Thousands wore

I LIVE IN DENVER—ASK ME buttons. A tribe of Arapaho Indians, streaked with war paint and whooping war cries, had been hired from the reservation to circle the business district in a streetcar, while black Model Ts, called "buzz carts" by the locals, backed up at the intersections waiting for the Arapaho-packed streetcar to pass. Men wore black silk neckties, linen collars, brown or black business suits with high lapels, and sensible black shoes; women boasted bright peacock colors and hourglass figures. There was life here and constant noise, not the deathly silence Frank had found on the plains. There was growth, due to the convention, which should also mean jobs. Frank and Jack rented rooms in the Charleston Hotel at the corner of 15th and Curtis streets, and every day Frank visited the labor office to read construction notices.

Yet despite these first impressions, Frank soon learned that Denver had fallen on hard times. There were jobs for carpenters, but the wages were low and he struggled to pay their room and board. The city had boomed in the 1880s, but that bubble burst with the Panic of 1893, and despite all the boosterism the good times had never completely returned. The markets for Colorado silver had contracted or dried up, plunging the state economy to a catastrophic low. In 1906, when Frank and Jack entered the Coeur d'Alenes in search of riches, 435 Colorado mines and 377 related businesses folded, throwing 45,000 people out of work. Though downtown Denver hung on gamely, it was hit hard too. Market Street became a red-light district, jammed with "club rooms," dance halls, rooming houses, and bordellos. Prostitutes and their "macs," local slang for pimps, seemed as plentiful as customers. Larimer Street, once the city's gilded strip, was now a skid row. Fifty-five saloons lined the street, as well as thirteen pawnshops. The Mission of Living Waters sat among them, hoping to reclaim the legions of destitutes and drifters who made Larimer Street their home. Several times a week, a paddy wagon backed up to a Larimer Street bar called the Aurora. Under the gilded sign, Greek for "golden dawn," police would haul a dozen drunks off to jail.

Rich or poor, Denver was a crossroads for the famous and infamous, a clearinghouse for money, news, and goods. The famous vaudevillian Eddie Foy played Denver; Sarah Bernhardt trod the boards. Doc Holliday was arrested here in 1882, on a warrant for murdering a Utah man, and then released by some legal sleight-of-

hand by his buddy Bat Masterson; he knocked around the state for
the last five years of his life in a legal limbo folks called "Holliday-
ing." Big Bill Haywood and his fellow union leaders, all co-
defendants in the Steunenberg murder, were headquartered in Denver,
as was Western Pinkerton chief James McParland, who maneuvered
for their arrest. Much that was legal, illegal, or extralegal seemed to
have a Pinkerton connection. In 1907, as Frank and Jack went broke
on the prairie, the Sundance Kid and his girlfriend Etta Place unexpectedly appeared downtown, emerging from their hideout in South
America because Etta needed her inflamed appendix removed. While
she was under anesthesia, the Kid got drunk and shot up a saloon.
They fled back to South America before the Pinkertons got word.

Yet as the summer of 1908 turned to autumn, all of Denver's glamour and novelty could not stop Jack's deepening gloom. There were
several reasons for this depression. The two of them were broke. Jack
hadn't seen his girl, Lillian Stevenson, for nearly a year. Popular stories of the era often described the lovelorn as "mooncalves," turned
into simpletons and struck blind by love. Frank had never seen a
mooncalf—nor had anyone else—but if such a thing ever existed, it
would probably have looked like Jack. Most serious, however, was
his health. Jack's cough had worsened monthly, and some days Frank
caught him peering at his handkerchief, checking for spots of blood.
Every afternoon his face glowed with pink patches and his temperature rose. At night, sweat soaked his underclothes. For long periods
he'd be felled by fatigue. This wasn't Jack's familiar, cheerful laziness
but something deeper and more frightening, a debilitating tremble
that left him weak in the limbs. Both feared it was tuberculosis, although they avoided the word. Those diagnosed with the illness believed they were doomed.

Frank finally told his friend to do something about his depression
and go see Lillian, back in Walla Walla. He watched as Jack's train
snaked from Union Station underneath the seventy-ton Welcome
Arch erected for the Democratic Convention. On one side of the arch
the word WELCOME was illuminated by 2,194 electric light bulbs; on
the other side glowed the word MIZPAH, which Denverites said was
Indian for "howdy, pardner." (Actually, *mizpah* is a Hebrew parting
found in Genesis 31:49: "The Lord watch between me and thee, when
we are absent one from another." Frank preferred "Howdy, Pardner," since the other sounded so forlorn.) Jack's train grew smaller

and smaller, finally disappearing entirely into the flat horizon. Frank wondered how many friends had parted like this in train stations, never to see each other again.

It was an old refrain, learned by each succeeding generation. Nothing was permanent in the New World. Nothing prepared you for life in the West, where people died for no apparent reason and the romance of sudden death was shattered by its reality. On March 6, 1900, bubonic plague hit San Francisco, the first time it was recorded in America. On September 8, 1900, a hurricane wiped Galveston, Texas, off the map, killing up to eight thousand residents and washing their corpses into the Gulf of Mexico. On April 14, 1906, a massive earthquake turned San Francisco to rubble and plague broke out once more, spreading as far as Seattle that year. Life ended quickly out here, whether or not your will was in order and all Last Unctions said. How could Frank blame Jack for seeking comfort, in the little time he thought he had left, in whatever arms he could?

Yet try as he might to act stoic and manly about it, Frank felt homesick after Jack's departure in a way he'd never felt over the last two years. In the mountains he'd led a solitary existence there, true, but that had been a test, his will against the wilderness, and even if the Blue Jay had gone bust he'd prevailed in a more important and fundamental way. Here in Denver he saw despair reflected in so many strangers' faces he couldn't help wondering if he was headed there, too. He wrote long letters to his mother and his younger brother, Jim. He told them all that happened with the silver mine, both his excitement when he filed the claim and the disappointment when the vein played out. He told about the trek across Montana and Wyoming, and how times were tough in Denver. He had money saved from his old shingling jobs in Spokane and asked Jim to forward some. Soon letters arrived from home. Mother sent her love and wished he'd visit; Father had given up carpentry and opened a small meat-packing business, a third career switch in eight years. Jim said he did most of the work at the shop and often ran the store, but it was hard for a small shop like theirs to compete against Spokane's railroad-financed meat-packers. The girls were in school, and Eddie had developed a wicked curve ball on the pitching mound.

Jim's letter also contained bad news. Their older brother Joe had been losing weight and appetite over the past few months, and the doctor finally diagnosed TB. The rod-shaped bacillus that caused man's oldest known disease had been discovered in 1882, but a cure would not be found until 1924. Joe had taken a room in town, so not to infect the family, and had started playing piano at one of the east side saloons. It wasn't considered respectable work, but what did that matter if he was going to die anyway? Jim had slipped in once, while away from the shop, and listened to Joe play. He was pretty good, Jim said. A New Orleans black man named Jelly Roll Morton had traveled throughout the West, and his jass, or "jazz," style of piano, as some called it, was knocking people dead. Personally, Jim didn't think the style would last, though from what Joe told him the style was passing from musician to musician faster than fire on the plains. Still, Joe didn't cough while playing, like his mind and body were at peace and part of him healed.

Frank stayed in Denver over the Christmas holidays, refusing to go home. He had enough money for the trip but not enough for presents, so he merely sent his love. He wondered if he'd ever make his family proud. He killed time by following the wire stories from Sydney, Australia, of black boxer Jack Johnson's December 26 win over Canadian Tommy Burns for heavyweight champion of the world. There was a riot during the fight and the bout was halted by police; even so, a referee's decision made Johnson the first black champion. Outraged fans already talked of a "Great White Hope." They placed a lot of stock on another young Canadian, Victor McLaughlin, scheduled to go against Johnson for his first title defense in Vancouver on March 10, 1909.

Before that, in early January, a telegram marked URGENT arrived. It was from Jack in Walla Walla, telling Frank to come quick, he was leaving Walla Walla for good. This was a mystery to Frank but, more important, a break from his blues. He packed his carpetbag and caught the earliest train out, arriving in Walla Walla on January 5, 1909, and setting in motion events that would change his entire life.

FRANK HAD BARELY said hello before Jack demanded help moving Lillian and her roommate Alice down to Denver. There'd been trouble, he said, but he refused to give details. It was the second time the records show that Jack was really evasive—the first had been during Jack's return to the Blue Jay, when he deferred Frank's questions about his acquaintances in Spokane—and the second time Frank failed to heed the warning. There are times when Frank seems incredibly dense, unable or unwilling to recognize approaching danger. We know from several sources that he had a keen practical intelligence, but at times like these you cannot help but want to pick him up and shake him, maybe knock some sense into his head. Sometimes the most likable people prove to be the most unwise. It was the very trait that had worried Frank's mother, his tendency for misplaced loyalty, his willful blindness when it came to friends.

Even so, Frank knew that all was not right. "Trouble," when paired with women in this era, usually had some sexual connotation and often meant pregnancy. But then Jack made a startling admission. He said he went by the name Jack Sherman around the girls, not Jack Golden. Though Lillian's roommate called herself Alice Kelly, her real name was Alice Evans. Frank asked if Jack's girl was really "Lillian Stevenson." Jack said he didn't know for certain, but he figured the name was assumed.

Frank couldn't help but be stunned. This was a Jack he'd never seen. What else didn't he know? In 1909, only prostitutes, actresses, and women on the run from something assumed false names. He came to a halt in the middle of the Walla Walla train station, and it took Jack's fastest talking to get him moving again.

A Pinkerton report later laid bare Lillian's history. Born Helen Sanders in 1882, "she has been a prostitute from the time she was a very young girl," the report claimed. "Her mother and sister were prostitutes: that the mother was at one time running a house in some part of Idaho," probably the Coeur d'Alenes during the gold rush of 1884–1885, was a certainty. In fact, her early history sounded more like that of Calamity Jane, aka Martha Jane Canary, than of the stylish and modern "Lillian Stevenson" that Jack had always described. Jane came to the mining district in 1884, the same time that Lillian's mother set up her brothel; like Lillian, Jane was raised in her mother's bordello in Blackfoot, Montana. Jane and Lillian both called themselves "independent"girls. The similarities ended there. Though both were prostitutes, Jane was more freewheeling, known as an army teamster, an expert with a bullwhip, and a crack shot with a rifle—she was said to have shot up the ground beneath cowboy "Darling" Bob McKay for his comments about her underwear— while Lillian tried for refinement. Yet for all that, they were two sides of the same coin.

The western marriage of gold and sex was as strong if not stronger than that of gold and blood. The 1848 discovery of gold in Sutter's Mill brought prostitutes to California from all over the world; by 1851, an estimated two thousand from New York, New Orleans, France, and England had arrived at San Francisco and spread through the goldfields. In larger cities like San Francisco and Denver, the business formed hierarchies—from the most elegant "sporting house" to the quick ministrations of the "ladies of the alley." The names of the sporting houses have lasted through history. In Spokane, the most famous was the Owl Saloon, habituated by none other than Pinkerton's chief William A. Pinkerton; in Wallace, the Oasis Room was known for its elegant French girls and "red-headed Jewesses." For the majority of frontier men, however, the most common place to meet women was in barrooms and dance halls. American and Irish "waiter girls" and "slingers" would offer a man a drink or cigar and a dance for two bits and arrange to meet afterward in the girl's cramped room, or crib. Lillian knew this world intimately, yet she reinvented herself after leaving the Coeur d'Alenes.

Exactly how closely Frank quizzed Jack is hard to tell. Probably not much, if latter events offer a clue. They took a streetcar to the edge of town, then walked through dirty snow to a rooming house in the shadow of the state prison. Frank could see the closest gun towers, and standing within them darker shadows that would be the armed guards. Each man carried an army issue Springfield .30-06 or an older .30-caliber U.S. Krag; both were high-powered rifles that could punch a fist-sized hole in a man at two thousand yards.

Jack knocked on the door and Lillian answered. She was tall and slim, her dark hair piled high on her head like the picture in Jack's watch case. Although her true age is not recorded, she was somewhere in her late twenties or early thirties. She smiled and said she'd heard so much of Frank; her grasp was firm and warm. Her dark eyes sparkled when she said that Jack had painted his friend as a hero. "Are you really a hero, Mr. Grigware?" Even as she spoke, a younger woman walked up behind her and smiled. She was blond to Lillian's brunette, shorter and less slim than her older friend. But her eyes were friendly as she came to Frank's defense. "I think you're embarrassing him, Lil," she said.

Enter Alice Evans, with whom Frank fell in love. By now he was ready for a friend. What little record remains of Alice suggests that she was ready too. One can imagine that as Frank shrugged off his overcoat, his eyes met hers and they stared like this until Lillian suggested something to ward off the chill. Alice asked Frank if he minded helping in the kitchen. She tucked a loose strand of hair behind her ear, smiled, and led the way.

There was something tragic about Alice, even then, something appealing and slightly vulnerable. Frank could be perceptive when not in denial, so he probably sensed it too. Within ten months, her testimony on a witness stand would seal his fate; her tears in the hushed courtroom reminded spectators of the fragility of love. Frank's father one day told the FBI that he thought she was merely a "dalliance," yet Frank's history with Alice suggests that she meant as much to him as he did to her. Yet very little remains known about her, her presence an enigma in the Pinkerton and FBI files. Three years after Frank's conviction, government agents tried to find her but failed, as if she existed for the short time it took to have her heart broken and then vanish without a trace, a brief rumor her epitaph, her disappearance as absolute as those poor souls in Galveston washed out to sea by the storm.

This much is known: Alice was about Frank's age, perhaps a little younger, existing in the shadow of Lillian, her flamboyant older friend. She did not seem to be a great beauty, for while admirers swirled about Lillian, only Frank had eyes for Alice. Her choice of Kelly as an alias suggested Irish roots, which also suggests light hair and fair skin. She had a stepfather in Waco, Texas, to whom she eventually returned. Before 1909, she lived in Spokane with relatives on Augusta Avenue, a working-class neighborhood north of downtown. On every day but Sunday, she caught a streetcar to her job as clerk in one of the large department stores. She and Frank lived at opposite ends of the city, so their lives did not intersect before Walla Walla, yet as they sat in the kitchen making coffee, the Inland Empire was a shared experience and they gossiped about old hangouts and friends.

Sometime in 1907 or 1908, as Frank worked his way south from the Blue Jay Mine to Denver, Alice began her own journey. During this time she met Lillian. Although the circumstances of that meeting are lost, the attraction of the lively and seemingly sophisticated older woman for the shopgirl is easy to understand. The lives of women like Alice were dead ends, their days a litany of long hours, boring work, little hope of advancement, and low pay. The end of that cul-de-sac promised loneliness and spinsterhood, the one way out romance and a husband. There were changes in the air, but in that first decade of the century a woman's lot was still primarily marriage or whoredom, to paraphrase Martin Luther. During this period, Alice was engaged to a young man back in Texas, but the attraction was tepid, probably more a perceived escape from the salesgirl's life than an all-consuming love. Then Lillian arrived, settling in Spokane for an undetermined period. She had married and divorced, scandalous for the time. Alice saw in her all the things she wasn't: independent, stylish, supported by a circle of admirers yet seemingly beholden to none. She learned quickly enough that Lillian was a prostitute, yet the rules of the world's oldest profession had begun to change.

Before World War I, prostitution in America was not illegal, yet by 1909 criminalization seemed inevitable. In the East and Midwest, urban red-light districts were under attack from "moral purity" campaigns by the press and the pulpit, bolstered by Progressive reformers and federal officials who sought to end "white slavery." In the West, an official ambivalence still prevailed. Sporting houses with their brushed veneer of worldly elegance still existed, as did the dance hall girls and their dingy cribs. Yet the traditional hierarchy had started to fray.

Lillian represented a third avenue open to the western prostitute: she did not work in a brothel or dance hall but was kept by a small circle of clients or "admirers," as she preferred to call her men. Some of the most famous prostitutes of the West followed this path: their ranks included Etta Place and Laura Bullion, romanced respectively by the Sundance Kid and Ben Kilpatrick of the Wild Bunch. Mary Katherine Horony, better known as Doc Holliday's companion "Big Nose" Kate or Kate Elder, also chose this life. It was a less sordid arrangement than the random encounters of the brothel or alley, yet claims of independence were still a sham. Lillian and the others like her depended on the continued goodwill of their admirers; in the process they became identified with these men in ways unlike any other prostitute, learning their secrets, sharing their fortunes and failures. It was a marriage in its own right, and if their admirers broke the law, the women could suddenly find themselves threatened with jail.

Alice, on the other hand, was an example of a new type of working girl. In the first two decades of the twentieth century, many prostitutes were women who reverted to the business temporarily as a way out of a dead-end job. It was estimated that during this time about five to ten percent of young women in the cities briefly turned to prostitution, earning double in a night what they earned in a week in the factory or shop. Most were single, in their teens or early twenties, and new to town. Instead of whole-scale brothels, two or three girls would room together, a setup encouraged by landlords, since prostitutes tended to pay their rent on time. In the unlikely event of arrest, the girls were charged with vagrancy, a simple misdemeanor. Nonetheless, there were still extralegal controls—petty officials like beat cops and health officials who, in concert with the landlord, took a cut of the proceeds in exchange for looking the other way. As the countryside emptied and the cities filled up, the numbers of prostitutes increased, yet their careers were usually brief, since most eventually married or found more socially acceptable jobs.

Many of these women became temporary prostitutes because of acquaintances and friends, and Alice apparently entered the trade with Lillian as her mentor. Sex wasn't talked about by respectable women, but in this age of new sexual awareness—when circus posters showed shapely "aerialists" in tights and how-to books for newlyweds contained line drawings of sexual positions—a straightforward prostitute was probably the last person to mince words. Lillian taught Alice that catnip stimulated menstrual flow and was thought to induce miscarriage. Though Alice would have heard of condoms, mass-produced since the mid-1800s, Lillian would have taught her about other birth control methods like the vaginal douche, an early diaphragm made of sponge, and the not-so-reliable rhythm method. A woman was on her own in this world, Lillian preached. Sex was not intrinsically evil. If it wasn't always enjoyable, at least it could be a means to an end.

Frank would learn the realities of Alice's life soon enough; at the moment, however, he sat with her in the kitchen and realized it was the longest he'd actually talked with a woman since leaving home. He knew he'd been lonely, but the full extent of that loneliness had not been evident until now. As he told her about his winter in the mountains, her eyes never left his face. When he told of their tunneling out of their snow-covered cabin like rats, she laughed and her fingers lightly brushed his. The pot gurgled and she poured the coffee; there was silence, but of a companionable kind. She sat and watched as he sipped from the cup. He'd been drinking his own coffee for so long that he'd forgotten how bad it tasted, Frank said.

"Jack really does admire you," Alice said unexpectedly. "He depends on you."

Frank studied her for a second, then quietly asked what was going on. Jack's urgent wire and this sudden plan to move—none of it made sense, he said. The question made Alice nervous: she stepped close to the door and listened to Jack and Lillian in the parlor. Her lively eyes and face grew serious. There were some things he had to understand, she said. Jack had fallen in love with Lillian, but the love was not reciprocated. Lillian thought Jack cute and sweet but considered him a child. If anything, she kept him around to get things done. If it meant sleeping with him occasionally, what was that to a whore?

Frank jumped in surprise at such bluntness from a woman, but Alice smiled sadly and said that if he hadn't figured it out already, it wouldn't take long. In this country, there weren't many holds that women had on men. Sex and sympathy were among the few. Alice watched Frank closely and was relieved when he didn't turn away. She'd planned to form an alliance with Jack's self-sufficient savior, but she hadn't planned on liking him so well.

The hard truth was that they were in trouble, Alice told him, and had to get out of town. Lillian was in trouble because of a mess caused by her "admirers"; Alice was in trouble for hanging out with Lillian. "What mess?" Frank asked, but Alice hesitated, placing her finger to his lips. Some things were best unsaid. But she did add this: Jack was convinced he was tubercular and believed he would die in a couple of years. He wanted everything life had to offer, and he wanted it yesterday. Tomorrow would be too late.

ONE THING WAS certain: Jack wasn't fooling when he said they were ready to go. Alice and Lillian were already packed; Jack wired the Charleston Hotel in Denver and reserved rooms near theirs. They booked space in a boxcar and the next day hired a wagon, moving to the station their steamer trunks, Lillian's Columbia disc graphophone with steel floral horn, and her eight-day Waterbury mantel clock topped with a bronze conquistador. She carried in her carpetbag the tools of her profession: bottles of White Lily Face Wash for Beautifying the Complexion, Famous Parisian Depilatory, Dr. Rose's Arsenous Tabules for producing a "clear, dainty, and transparent complexion," Dr. Worden's Female Pills for "female trouble," and a Celery Malt Compound for "improving and relaxing the nerves and brain." Jack also sent off a second wire, which Frank didn't know. On January 7, they boarded the Great Northern express for the 1,100-mile trip to Denver; they arrived, sore from the rattle of the tracks and the hard-backed wooden seats, in the early evening of January 9.

Two men were waiting at the hotel when the tired travelers arrived. Jack and Lillian were ecstatic, but Frank sensed tension in Alice. Jack introduced the men as the fellows he'd mentioned from Spokane, and Frank studied the newcomers carefully. Both were thirty-six years old, but the similarities ended there. Dan Downer was balding and stocky, with an ironic glint in his eye and a thick mustache covering his lips that looked like a cheap disguise. His companion was Fred Torgensen, whom everyone called Fritz. Torgensen was taller than Downer and lean and lanky, with limp blond hair and pale blue eyes. Downer appeared to do all the talking, while Torgensen seemed content to watch the passing show. There was something hungry in Torgensen's gaze. Dan said he was a stockman looking to buy cattle, while Fritz hoped to buy into a saloon. They'd been on the road forever when they got Jack's wire—it seemed like a perfect excuse to stop with friends. He added as an afterthought that they'd taken rooms at the Charleston too.

Thus began a whirlwind tour. For the next two weeks the six former Spokanites lived it up; since Dan and Fritz had plenty of money, they footed the bill. Any doubts Frank had about the two were drowned by their largesse and generosity. One night they took in vaudeville at Elitch Gardens, where kangaroo dancing alternated with Irish jokes; the next night they visited the Opera block, where a theater troupe performed George M. Cohan's hit *Little Johnny Jones*. As they left, Frank spotted the western offices of Pinkerton's, with its unblinking eye painted on the windows. They haunted gambling halls and ate sirloin steaks and potatoes O'Brien at a swank restaurant called the Manhattan. Lillian was always the center of attention, never going out without her high French hat with its black ostrich plume. Dan and Fritz spoke of a friend, Bill Matthews, who was also scouting Utah and Nebraska for "opportunities." Alice grew restless at this talk and pulled Frank with her to the dance floor.

Frank was new to dancing, so Alice led. She placed his hand on

her hip and took the other in her hand. They whirled around the
floor to "The Rosebud March," then danced more slowly to "Be-
thena," a softer tune. It was the closest Frank had ever been to a
female save his mother or sisters. He felt drunk, yet at the same time
his senses seemed more finely tuned. He smelled the cigar smoke in
her hair, the soap on her skin. Her eyes were closed as she hummed
to the music; she was somewhere else, Frank realized. It occurred to
him that it was how she endured her job. What would it be like to
be pawed by strangers? he wondered, and suddenly had a glimpse of
how these women survived. It was the first flash of almost paralyzing
empathy he'd ever experienced; he imagined the two of them dancing
in a deep silence in which he could read Alice's mind. There was a
sadness in life one could never escape, whether in the silence of the
prairie or the bright lights of the city. He squeezed her hand gently
as the music stopped. "That was nice," she whispered, as she opened
her eyes.

Afterward, Alice thought of that dance, how the sounds of the
crowd diminished and she and Frank seemed alone. Her skin tingled
where he'd touched her hand, as well as through her dress. Frank
hadn't groped her like the others. He'd held her lightly. Was it possible he cared for how she felt? That was silly. *Nobody* cared for the
feelings of a whore.

Frank often wondered what it would be like to sleep with Alice,
an image he could not escape, given her profession. The others slept
with Lillian; trouble already brewed between Jack and Fritz for her
affections, while Dan took what was offered as if it were his due. If
they slept with Alice, he didn't want to know. The thought of making
love to her sometimes overwhelmed him, but he couldn't just offer
her money and be another customer.

Life had certainly been less complicated back in Spokane. Sometimes it was a relief just to pick up his nails and hammer and go out
on a job. Some of the businesses on the Tabor block were renovating,
and he landed steady work. When he'd return at night, Jack would
tell how he and Downer had visited the Turkish baths in the Barclay
block, Denver's largest office building, where the rich and powerful
gathered in togas to take the waters and close million-dollar deals.
Dan also took him to the Cupola, a parlor house, with the "highest-
class whores" Jack had ever seen. Many nights, when Frank came

back late from work, the others were out. His muscles ached and he'd be asleep when they returned.

One night when he was alone someone knocked at his door. He opened it and Alice stood in the hall, dressed in her coat and hat, eyes smudged from tears. She looked scared. When Frank asked what was the matter, Alice closed the door behind her and started to cry. Frank sat beside her on the bed and again asked what had happened; she took a breath and said that the tension between Fritz and Jack over Lillian was turning into hatred. Someone was going to get hurt. Sometimes they argued in her and Lillian's rooms; their anger was reaching a flash point and Alice couldn't take it anymore. She'd rented a room down the block at the Crescent Hotel and wondered if Frank could help her move. She knew he was tired from work and didn't mean to trouble him, but there was no one else to ask for help.

The Crescent was a flophouse, nothing else could be said. The girl whose trunk Frank shouldered was no longer as funny and happy as she'd been in Walla Walla less than a month ago. Things were happening quickly that he didn't understand. Though Fritz and Dan never worked, they still had money; these days they continually spoke of scouting out more "opportunities." In fact, they'd been on such a scouting expedition for the last couple of days. Jack talked of "opportunities" too, he wanted so desperately to be like the older men. Frank knew that understanding the full story might mean making a choice about whether he wished to stay with them or leave. Despite his doubts, these people were fun to be with. It was easier to wear blinders.

But when the door opened in the Crescent to a room as tight as a coffin, he felt inexpressibly sad. The place smelled of whiskey and unwashed bodies. The bed was crumpled, the sheets stained. "You're leaving, aren't you?" he said to Alice. "You're moving out for good."

"I'm going back to Waco," Alice said. She nestled in Frank's arms and her shoulders started heaving. One of them closed the door for privacy. We know from detectives' notes that they became lovers. This was almost certainly the moment when their desire took hold.

Afterward, they lay in darkness. The twinkle of the arc lamps glimmered through the window; Frank heard the shouts of Denver's street rats through the wooden walls. For all the benevolent societies and Christian charities in the City Beautiful, scores of nameless children lived a Darwinian existence: predator and prey, acceptable losses in a hard world. Frank wondered what had become of their mothers and fathers, whether he'd passed their abandoned houses on the plains. What was it like not even to have a mother, someone who said you were all right and not strange or different? It would be a haunted life, where love faded even as you touched it, just another desert mirage. Even as he wondered, Alice's thigh brushed his. The sheet covered her breasts; one shoulder was bare. All the things that happened here tonight amazed him, yet he felt heartsick and sad. He lay as close to a naked girl as he'd ever thought possible; yet he still felt a million miles away. Without thinking, he put out his hand to touch her. She laced her fingers in his, then turned her face to his shoulder. She whispered that she loved him, as if love were redemptive, the old mistakes now washed clean, allowing a fresh start.

Next morning, Alice said she must go. When Frank asked why, she seemed on the brink of an explanation—something Alice feared was just about to happen—then her frightened look returned. Maybe she would tell him when she was home safe in Waco. Maybe not, for trains went everywhere. Distance, no matter how great, was no guarantee of safety in the modern age.

That afternoon Frank loaded Alice aboard the train for her 850-mile trip southeast to Waco. Come with me to Texas, she begged. Come and start again. He felt as if his heart and lungs were being torn from their securing threads. You said yourself that Jack was dying, he reminded her. How can I just leave? Alice looked sadly in his face, then scribbled her address on a piece of paper and pressed it in his hand. Come when you're ready, she told him, and kissed him on the lips. Then Alice said something that sounded like his mother. "Don't be so trusting of your friends."

Once again Frank watched a friend settle in a Pullman coach. Once again he watched a train pass beneath the MIZPAH sign and dwindle to a speck on the horizon. This was far, far worse than Jack's previous leavetakings, from the Blue Jay and then to Walla Walla. It was as if all human connections that meant anything to Frank would eventually get swallowed up in the goddamned prairie. Why in hell had he decided to go see the world?

He returned to the Crescent and settled Alice's account, walked up the block to the Charleston, and found Lillian in her room. When he told her of Alice's departure, her eyes moistened and he thought for a second that she too felt a loss. But then Lillian's jaw set firmly. If Alice felt she had to leave, that was her decision. Good riddance, Lillian said.

The next day, newsies hit the streets, screaming the headlines: BIG ROBBERY OF THE DENVER & RIO GRANDE SPECIAL AT MILITARY JUNCTION, outside of Denver! Frank had a moment of panic, thinking it was Alice's express, but then realized Military Junction was in the opposite direction. He read the news more closely: several mail sacks rifled, but not much taken; no one hurt, but several passengers robbed. Jack and Lillian grabbed the paper from him when he brought it back. They looked frightened, yet strangely exhilarated. Frank felt a little sick but also strangely thrilled, as if allowed a glimpse of something forbidden. As long as he didn't actually speak his growing suspicions, maybe he'd be lucky and they'd simply fade away.

Yet Frank's suspicions just got worse when Dan and Fritz returned. The two men seemed elated but were restless and somehow disappointed. They talked of moving on. Before leaving, however, they'd have one final blowout, Dan told Lillian. What do you want to do?

Lillian thought a moment and said she'd wanted to visit the Garden of the Gods outside Colorado Springs ever since arriving in Denver, so the next day, Jack, Lillian, Dan, Fritz, and Frank boarded a first-class Santa Fe coach for the 67-mile trip. They rolled into the depot with its high gabled roof around noon. Downtown Colorado Springs was a tourist trap long before the term was coined. Rail coach excursions to the Garden of the Gods and Pikes Peak were advertised in countless storefront windows; a marble fountain gurgled at the intersection of Tejon and Pikes Peak; a land office was placed across the street for those enchanted tourists who wanted to stay. Outside this center lay the industrial city, a gray cacophony of belching smelters and long ore trains from the Trinidad mining district over two hundred miles to the south. At the edge of town lay the loading docks for beef and produce, the stockyards with cattle bound for Denver or the Armour plant in Chicago, the ramps lined with wagons dumping loads of sugar beets into the open cars of the Atchison, Topeka & Santa Fe Railroad. Frank was fascinated by the machinery of riches. While Jack, Lillian, and Fritz went ahead to their hotel, Frank and Dan walked to a levee overlooking the loading docks and engine yards.

What happened next is speculation, gleaned from testimony and Pinkerton files. We know from the evidence that Frank and Dan almost certainly had a private talk, yet we do not know when it occurred. Now—with Jack, Fritz, and Lillian engaged in their endless amorous dance—would have been the perfect opportunity. By now, Frank had grown to like Dan Downer. He is consistently portrayed in later newspaper accounts as a likable, intelligent rogue. He was the calmest of Jack's friends and in his way the wisest; he watched the jockeying of Fritz and Jack for Lillian's affections, found them amusing, but had enough sense to steer clear.

Dan sat beside Frank on the levee and tossed some gravel down the slope. "A doctor told Jack that his condition is getting worse," he said. "I figure he already told you."

Frank answered that Jack didn't tell him much these days.

Downer watched the wagons and tossed more stones. "The doctor said Jack should move where it's warmer. We thought we'd go to Hot Springs and play the ponies. You want to come?"

Frank stiffened slightly, as if awaiting a blow. His suspicions about Jack's friends had mounted until he'd have to ask some questions if he continued to tag along. Yet doing so was risky. What if he didn't like the truth? What then?

It was a critical juncture for Downer too. He liked this young friend of Jack's, but the boy was smart and wouldn't stay in the dark forever. He probably already suspected something. Alice's sudden departure worried him too. What had she told him? Jack said himself that Frank was a straight arrow. They could always use another partner, but if Dan told Frank the truth and he refused to join up, he'd be a danger to them all. Torgensen had his own way of fixing such problems, and although Downer could normally reconcile himself to Fritz's solutions, this time it seemed unnecessarily brutal and cold.

So they avoided the question while still dancing around the subject, each trying to read the other's mind. Downer watched the sugar beet wagons roll up the ramp, one after the other, in a process that seemed to have no start or finish, and asked why Alice had left. Frank said he guessed she got homesick for Waco. There was a brief silence as they watched the rumbling wagons. "You could do worse than a woman like Alice," Downer finally said. Lillian had been born and raised a prostitute and didn't know nothing else—she'd do whatever it took to protect herself, even ratting on old friends. But Alice had taken up the life because of hard times. She could stop just as easily as she started. Still, settling for a life with Alice would be like one of those sugar beet wagons. They drove the same circle over and over, just to line someone else's pockets. What was the use of that? There was a lot of money floating around this country, and living the straight life just made honest men poor while the fat cats grew rich. That was a fool's game, Dan said.

Frank chuckled and told Dan he sounded like a Socialist. Dan looked at Frank in surprise, then his face crawled into a grin. "I never thought of it like that," Downer said, slapping his haunches and rising with a grunt. "But I have been talking of sharing the wealth, ain't I? Maybe I'm a Socialist, after all." The joke defused the tension. The next morning they bought tickets on the Rio Grande Southern to Manitou Springs, gateway to the Garden of the Gods.

By 1909, the valley near the base of Pikes Peak was a prefiguring of the postcard West, a Kodak image for the rest of the century. Suddenly, the entire West was a tourist mecca. In its growing desire for international recognition, America was turning its western landscape into a symbol of national pride. This was a garden not of flowers but of rocks: huge and freakish red sandstone formations whittled away by wind and rain. They'd been christened by stampeders in the 1850s Pikes Peak Gold Rush and now were known by such colorful appellations as the Tower of Babel, Cathedral Spires, Three Graces, Sleeping Indian, and Pig's Eye. The prospectors carved their own names into the soft rock; by the turn of the century, promoters mined new veins of gold by encouraging customers to mimic the original prospectors. Now tourists' names filled the base of every major rock formation in the Garden, an increasingly common practice in landmarks throughout the West. No doubt Frank and the others left their own marks behind.

Afterward the five companions returned to Manitou Springs, then back to Colorado Springs the next morning. Frank and Jack told the others about the night they'd spent in the Manitou Springs jail in 1908, so everyone minded their manners in town. Yet on reaching home, the rivalry between Jack and Fritz finally erupted in a Denver bar. There were harsh words and Fritz's hand went to his holster; Frank and Dan rose in one motion to separate the two. It was as if Frank suddenly glimpsed Torgensen's true nature and it frightened him badly. He started carrying his own gun for protection; from then on, Pinkerton records mention people who said they saw the Colt on Frank's hip.

After that face-off, the group agreed to split up, at least temporarily. While Lillian remained in Denver, Dan and Fritz would go straight to Hot Springs. Frank and Jack opted for a more southern route, passing through the Oklahoma panhandle and stopping at Fort Worth, where Jack would linger while Frank went on to see Alice. The decision seemed to calm frayed tempers. Shortly before they split apart, the five sat together for a "novelty photograph" in the United Photo Stores Company at 1513 Curtis, down the block from the Charleston Hotel.

Since the portrait became so important later, it is worth examining closely. It was one of the many formal portraits then in vogue, as if these friends knew their time together in the West could be cut short and a photo was the only proof that they had been together. Several prints would be made from wet plates, and people hung on to them with a sentimental tenacity that wasn't always wise. Such was the fate of the Wild Bunch, whose 1901 portrait taken in Fort Worth fell into the hands of Pinkerton agents, who until then had been unsure of the gang's identities.

In this instance, Frank and the others were placed behind a pasteboard automobile with the number 2313 painted on the headlights; behind that, a backdrop depicted the Garden of the Gods. All are wearing heavy coats and hats. Lillian is seated in front, wearing her ostrich plume hat, squeezed cozily between Torgensen on her left and Downer on her right. She is the still life's focal point, just as she was the group's, yet her face is drawn and white and she looks trapped by the men. Dan's hands rest on the pasteboard wheel: he is the driver, the man in charge. Jack stands behind Torgensen, the two rivals for Lillian's affections grouped together; he stares into the camera, lips clenched, jaw firm. Frank stands behind Downer, a little apart, face relaxed, gaze unfocused. Of them all, he seems the least engaged.

IN EARLY FEBRUARY 1909, as Jack waited in Fort Worth, home of a busy red light district, Frank took the train a hundred miles south to Waco. Alice waited at the station and threw herself into his arms. Some old matrons clucked, but their husbands smiled, remembering what it was like to be so in love. Alice noticed the holster and Frank told her what had happened. "I think it's time we talked," Alice said.

For the next few days, Alice and Frank rarely left each other's side. She introduced Frank to her stepfather, who made no bones of the fact that he saw Frank as a suitor. No one in Waco knew of Alice's past, apparently, not even the stepfather. If he did, he was happy to have her back and didn't let on. Waco was the kind of place where a young man who wanted to be a builder could sink roots, the stepfather said. By 1909, the town had grown from a trading post and Texas Ranger station to the state's sixth largest city, home to six banks and 163 factories. The Cotton Palace, under construction, would be the biggest agricultural showplace in the South, boosters claimed. A twenty-two-story building still in the planning stages would be the tallest building in Texas. As Frank and the old man sat on the stoop and talked, they heard Alice humming through the open kitchen window. "This is the happiest she's been since she got back," the old man said.

But a few days later a telegram arrived from Fort Worth. To Frank's surprise it was from Fritz, saying they'd finally heard from the mysterious Bill Matthews. Fritz had come to collect Jack and Frank. New plans, the telegram said.

"New plans?" asked Alice. "What does that mean?"

Frank didn't know himself, and his wires to Fort Worth didn't settle the mystery. He didn't like the idea of Jack and Fritz spending too much time together with no one around to referee; sooner or later they'd start fighting over Lillian, which would probably end with Jack getting killed. He left for Fort Worth but promised to come back, and three days later returned to Alice in Waco. He told her that Fritz and Jack were still cold to each other but at least hadn't been at each other's throats. Instead, they'd talked of opportunities in Kansas City or Omaha and had gone on to Hot Springs. He was to meet them there.

Again we must speculate, for no document records what Alice now revealed to Frank. This part of his life stays private, only hinted at in testimony and files. But Alice left some clues. Her hurried departure from both Walla Walla and Denver suggests she knew the truth about Lillian's admirers. More important than that, Frank's behavior changed after his stay with Alice in Waco. There was a sudden urgency in his travels, a peripatetic restlessness that centered around Jack. Alice sent a series of love letters to Frank after his departure, as if begging him to return; in an era when such vulnerable admissions by a woman could mean humiliation, she would later admit in court that the remains of one such letter had come from her. And after Frank was gone from her forever, she would remain loyal to him in the brief time for her that remained.

Therefore, it is reasonable to think that she did whatever it took to save the man she loved. When Frank mentioned "opportunities," she no doubt laughed cynically. She wanted to pick him up and shake some sense into him, as we do, helplessly, one hundred years later. But Alice was not a woman to ignore her feelings. She told Frank bluntly that he was either stupid or ignoring the truth. When Frank grew angry at the insult, she really lost her temper and finally told him about his friends.

They were members of an outlaw gang, she said. As early as 1906, when Alice had still been a clerk in the Spokane department store, she remembered reading in the *Spokesman-Review* about a "tough gang of train robbers" who reportedly hung out in a livery stable on the city's east side. Although they were suspects in holdups on the Great Northern, Northern Pacific, and Coeur d'Alene Inland Empire railroads, there seemed to be no proof, so they were never arrested and charged. Until 1906 the gang had gone through passengers' pockets and taken their jewelry, but they had never robbed the mails, a fact that probably accounted for their continued liberty. Mail robbery was a federal crime, punishable by life imprisonment; it raised the stakes, catching the eye of the U.S. government and bringing with it a world of discomfort for everyone. For the outlaw, it meant the sudden attention of all sorts of law enforcement agents, including but not limited to U.S. marshals, postal inspectors, railroad special detectives, and Pinkerton men, plus state and local law officers. For the railroad, it meant an obligation to stop the robberies, which could mean considerable sums of money. The Pinkerton agents who drove the Wild Bunch from Montana and Wyoming, for example, charged $8 a day plus expenses, a fee some considered legal robbery. In some ways, it was easier to leave small fry alone.

Despite its respectable front, Spokane actually made a good operations base for criminals. Fifty miles to the east lay the mining district, and in the Coeur d'Alenes there was little love for the law. Crime was such good business that two of America's largest private detective agencies had opened local branches in Spokane: the Pinkerton's National Detective Agency, with twenty offices across the nation, and the Thiel Detective Service, a close competitor with fourteen branches nationwide. Most of their business came from investigating employee embezzlement cases for the railroads and acting as spies against the miners' unions for the owners of the big Coeur d'Alene mines. For train robbers, there were opportunities too. The mining towns were laced together by miles of track that cut through deep canyons and dark forests; the long slow trains left town with open gondolas filled with ore and returned with empty gons and the company payroll. The profits could be phenomenal. The Hercules Mine, for example, reported on August 10, 1906, that it had disbursed dividends totaling more than $112 million since the first big strike in January 1901. In tiny towns throughout the mining district, it was the general opinion that the law existed for the benefit of the mine owner and his rich backers, not the lone prospector or hard-rock miner working and dying in a company mine. The law existed for the protection of the rich, taking the form of the army or state militia during the frequent strikes and undercover detectives the rest of the time. If a few crooks were going to plague mine owners by preying on their ore trains, the miners weren't going to turn them in.

Alice didn't actually meet the gang until she moved in with Lillian. Like Frank, she liked Dan Downer best, but he was still no solid citizen. Downer had grown up in Spokane and in his early career had been a contractor specializing in rock work on railroad construction jobs, where he became an expert "powder" man. After that, he turned to small-time cattle rustling with another Spokane resident, Bob Splain. He and Splain lived on a small ranch north of Hillyard. They were rumored to be involved in horse theft and cattle rustling in north Washington and Idaho and in Victoria in British Columbia, yet they were never caught. Around 1905 or 1906, Dan started using the name D. W. Woods; it was also during this period that Fred Torgensen appeared. Torgensen was Scandinavian by birth and had drifted west with the failure of the midwest lumber camps. At one point he'd been a locomotive fireman, so he knew his way around trains. Torgensen hung out in the saloons on Spokane's Front Street, where he was known to the barkeeps and snitches as Whitey because of his light hair. It was there that he and Downer apparently met and became friends.

Between 1906 and 1908, Downer, Torgensen, and Splain became known in whispers as the Spokane gang. The glue that bound them was Bill Matthews. A heavyset bear of a man who looked and sounded like an old-time fur trapper, the forty-three-year-old Matthews was said to be the brains behind the outfit and soon became its leader. He used his job as a stage driver through Colorado and Idaho as a front for scouting out robberies. It was said that Downer and Matthews met while serving a three-year stint in Walla Walla for horse theft, and that Lillian met Matthews in her mother's whorehouse in Idaho. Matthews's criminal career probably went back the farthest. In 1890, he and a partner, John Miles, got into a shootout with Sheriff Felix Pugh of Spokane. Pugh shot Matthews through the arm twice and Matthews plugged the sheriff through the leg. Miles wasn't so lucky and was buried on the spot, but Matthews got away. Pugh had been after him ever since and currently had a warrant to arrest him for cattle rustling.

The problem with crooks once they taste success is that they often grow careless, and in 1908 everything started to fall apart for the boys. Early in the summer, Downer was arrested in Spokane while trying to clean out a noodle joint on Front Street; he was taken into custody on suspicion of connection with several unsolved holdups but was soon released. Soon afterward, he, Splain, and Torgensen were arrested for horse stealing in Franklin County, west of Walla Walla, and held for trial in Pasco, on the Columbia River near Oregon. Downer and Torgensen jumped bond and escaped, while Splain stayed in town and was acquitted.

Downer and Torgensen drifted across the state until October 1908, sometimes appearing in Walla Walla for rest and relaxation with Lillian and Alice, sometimes showing up as far west as Everett, where they roomed in the saloon of Jack's brothers, whom Downer had known as a boy. They made ends meet through rustling and safeblowing; in the process, each became a strange amalgam of urban thief and western outlaw. Downer was a perfect gentleman when he came to visit, but Torgensen had a cold glint in his eyes and left bruises on Alice's skin. The only man or woman that Torgensen feared was Matthews, whom he called "the toughest man in all of northern Idaho."

That October the boys' luck finally ran out when they were spotted in Everett by two Spokane officers, Detective Alexander MacDonald and Officer Chester Edwards. The officers were in town to testify in the trial of J. Henry Jahn, charged with the murder of an Everett man during a postal robbery. When they spotted Downer and Torgensen on the street, they told Everett police, who then followed the fugitives back to Jack's brothers' saloon. A search of their upstairs room revealed two valises containing "two quarts of nitroglycerine (stored in black rubber bags), fulminating caps, 20 feet of fuse, several revolvers, masks, yeggmen's tools of various kinds, and 'billies,'" according to the *Spokesman-Review*.

The nitroglycerine was the most damning find. Known among safecrackers as "oil," it was stored by cautious burglars in rubber bags and by novices or the unwise in glass bottles. Oily colorless nitro, also called "soup," was so chemically unstable that the slightest bump could cause spontaneous detonation; sad experience taught burglars that rubber bags gave them some protection, since their flexible sides absorbed more of the shock of an accidental impact than the rigid glass. Safecrackers sealed the cracks in a safe with softened soap, leaving a slight pocket in the top through which they poured the oil. As it oozed down the soap, a fuse and detonator were attached, and the explosion blew off the door.

Though Downer and Torgensen said the grips had been left in the room by two unknown men, police didn't buy the story and held them on the outstanding warrants from Pasco. Then the court released them on a technicality. Once out, the two jumped bail again and disappeared into the Columbia River basin. Soon afterward, a Great Northern express was robbed in the rocky hills surrounding the Columbia River, and police suspected the fugitives.

One day in late November, Lillian answered a knock and a Walla Walla municipal detective stood at the door. He understood she, Downer, and Torgensen were old friends and wondered if she'd heard from them. A uniformed officer standing behind the detective touched his hat and smiled. Lillian replied haughtily that she'd heard nothing; the municipal cop said they were checking, just in case, and would probably drop by occasionally to see if things changed. It would be a shame if the boys were seen visiting and Lillian failed to tell police, he added. That would make her look like an accessory, you know. The policemen doffed their hats and said goodbye. As soon as she closed the door Lillian knew she had to leave Walla Walla, and by December she had hatched the plan with Jack in which Frank was now involved.

Alice laid out the evidence for Frank, clue by clue. The Denver & Rio Grande had been robbed outside Denver in the very same month that Dan and Fritz had shown up in town. Immediately after the robbery, they said it was time to leave. Now they were hooking up in Hot Springs or Kansas City with Bill Matthews, who been scouting for "opportunities." Didn't it look suspicious? Alice asked.

"Jack wouldn't do something like that," Frank pleaded.

Alice finally erupted with the fury of a woman who could see all her hopes vanishing owing to some boneheaded masculine code. "How do you suppose Jack came to know Downer and Torgensen?" she asked. "Through his brothers in Everett," she answered. "How did he come to meet Lillian? Through the boys from Spokane.

"They're train robbers," she said. Frank was hanging out with train robbers. In the eyes of the law, that made him one too.

❧ CHAPTER THREE ❧

The Mud Cut

FRANK STOOD STUNNED as Alice's words sank in.

Could she be right? Of course she was right! It was the only explanation that made any sense of all his worries and suspicions. Alice and Lillian's sudden flight to Denver, Dan and Fritz's money flowing like water, the two men's absence during the train robbery. Frank had known the truth but hadn't wanted to face it, hoping that if he ignored it long enough his doubts would fade away.

How could he have been so naive? A trip that had started with a simple wish to see the West had suddenly grown quite complicated. Was he stupid, like Alice hinted? Too trusting of others, like his mother said? Whatever the explanation, he'd gone overnight from Frank Grigware, journeyman carpenter, to Dead-Eye Frank, member of an outlaw gang.

Yet hadn't he also gotten what he wanted? Hadn't he found the Old West of his dreams? He'd gone into the goldfields but come out empty-handed, ridden across the High Plains and come out homesick, and then, when he'd grown convinced that the Wild West was nothing but a fiction, found himself in league with desperadoes. The world moved in mysterious ways.

By 1909, there was certainly an air of glamour to the *idea* of the train robber, if not to the reality. The reality was that since the 1890s, it had grown increasingly difficult to be an outlaw in the traditional mold. Not only did the bandit contend against growing armies of public and private lawmen, but science and technology were aligned against him too. An outlaw's description flew by telephone and telegraph faster than he could flee on horseback; he was hunted by armed flying squads riding in trains, their horses stabled in freight cars for the chase across the last rough miles. The most famous such squad was the Union Pacific's hundred-man mobile posse composed of the railroad's men and hired Pinkerton agents who were kept in permanent readiness to chase the Wild Bunch. At the time, the Union Pacific was the nation's premier railroad and had money to burn to enforce its will. When the Wild Bunch held up the Great Northern Railroad on July 3, 1901, the special posse rode to the site in its own train, outfitted with rolling stables and a loading ramp, and chased the bandits from Montana to Texas. In the end they lost them, but others weren't so lucky. Bitter Creek Newcomb and Charlie Pierce of the Doolin gang were chased until surrounded in a farmhouse near Guthrie in the Oklahoma Territory. According to the *Guthrie Daily Leader*, the May 1895 shootout left Pierce's chest perforated by bullets and transformed Newcomb "into a lead mine." Photos of their corpses were sold as souvenirs, grisly mementos featuring an almost sensual close-up of their stripped chests and dark bullet wounds.

Notwithstanding the implicit warning of such portraits, train robbers plagued the railroads throughout the first decade of the new century. Unlike other trademarks of the Old West, the train robber refused to go away. The Indian Wars ended in 1890 at Wounded Knee, South Dakota. The last recorded stagecoach robbery occurred in 1898. By 1900, the last gunfighters were dying out: John Wesley Hardin shot from behind in 1895; Black Jack Ketchum hanged in 1901; range enforcer Tom Horn executed in Wyoming in 1902. Only train robbers held on. The Wild Bunch's last job together took place on a summer afternoon, July 3, 1901; their robbery of the Great Northern express outside Malta, Montana, netted $40,000 in bank notes and unleashed the Union Pacific's special posse on their heels. Although the chase dissolved the gang as a functioning unit, the individuals hung on for several more years. In 1902, Butch Cassidy, Harry "The Sundance Kid" Longbaugh, and Longbaugh's girlfriend Etta Place fled to South America via New York City. Harvey "Kid Curry" Logan committed suicide in June 1904 after robbing the Denver & Rio Grande Railroad at Parachute, Colorado, and getting cornered by a posse forty-five miles away. The last active member, Ben "The Tall Texan" Kilpatrick, was killed with an icepick by a railroad employee while robbing the Southern Pacific Railroad outside Dryden, Texas, on March 14, 1912.

The Wild Bunch's defeat seemed the death knell of the western bandits, but then came the years 1906 through 1910. In 1906, there was a sudden gasp of activity in the Rocky Mountains and Pacific Northwest; by 1907, this had spread to the Great Plains. Robbers hit trains in Idaho, Montana, Washington, Colorado, and finally Nebraska, concentrating especially between Lincoln and Omaha, an insult to the Union Pacific officials headquartered there. The holdups were apparently not committed by one gang but by several, the modern equivalent of copycat crimes, as newspapers lingered on every detail. In the process, would-be robbers were reminded of the financial opportunities and apparent ease of preying on the rails.

Train robbery was an American invention, springing from the chaos following the Civil War. The great practitioners were not long gone, and certainly not forgotten: the notorious western robber bands—the Renos, Youngers, James boys, and Daltons—were exemplars of an American tradition: family enterprise. Eastern safecrackers of the same period were liberating six- or seven-figure hauls from bank vaults far exceeding the takes of train robbers, yet the eastern thief never caught the public imagination like his western counterpart. America's continuing fascination with the frontier was a major reason; the train robber emerged from the wilderness and faded back into it like the Indian, an expression of the wild. There was something brash and adventurous about holding up a locomotive, something appealing to the American love of showmanship. Even better, it was done by homegrown farm boys. Finally, politics and populism were involved. The "social bandit" of the West and Midwest, from Jesse James to John Dillinger, could present himself, honestly or otherwise, as being forced into banditry by the same inequities that plagued the little man. He could claim he'd been forced into crime by persecution from an increasingly controlling state or the rapaciousness of big business. The century's "new economy" meant untold wealth, but only for a few. If the social bandit plagued the unscrupulous rich, wasn't that justice, too?

The first known peacetime train robbery in the nation, and possibly the world, can be attributed to the Reno brothers—John, Frank, Simeon, and William—who flagged down a train in Seymour, Indiana, in 1866. Like others to follow, the Renos discovered several advantages: like banks, trains contained a lot of money; unlike banks, they were always on the move, an advantage for robbers, who could pick the time and place of the robbery. A survey of robberies committed by the James-Younger gang showed that train heists could be lucrative; of the twenty-five stickups blamed on the gang, from the Clay County Savings Association robbery in Liberty, Missouri, on February 13, 1866, to the Chicago & Alton Railroad robbery in Glendale, Missouri, on September 7, 1881, twelve were of banks and seven of railroads, with the remainder being of stagecoaches and the box office of the Kansas City Fair. They took $145,000 from railroads, or $20,714 per stickup, compared to $113,400 from banks, or $9,450 per robbery. Plainly, robbing trains made better business sense. The benefits were high, the risks relatively low.

Sticking up a train made good PR sense, too. No matter what citizens thought of banks, they still deposited their money in them. In the days before depositors' insurance, robbing the bank meant robbing the little man. It was a different matter with railroads. So widespread was the popular hatred of railways that thousands of otherwise law-abiding citizens saw train robbers as American Robin Hoods. When Frank and Jesse James robbed the Iron Mountain Railroad at Gad's Hill, Missouri, on January 31, 1874, one of the outlaws said he would examine each male passenger's hands before taking his money. "Hard-handed men have to work for their money—the soft-handed ones are capitalists, professors, and others that get easy money," the outlaw reportedly said. The instruction transformed the bandits into folk heroes.

Such western adulation of outlaws was not unusual. The notion that an antisocial savage was more noble than the society he opposed was the gift of Jean-Jacques Rousseau. By the late 1890s, the noble savage had even entered official policy, as seen by Warden French's assertion that the western criminal was morally superior to his eastern counterpart. They were seen by lawmen as equals in a manly, deadly game. They were dangerous, but dangerous in the sense of a cougar or grizzly, forces of nature adhering to some natural law. Besting such a force carried its own dignity. The average Westerner might lynch the desperado or shoot him on sight, but he also appreciated the danger of his life and exhibited a curious sympathy. After the robbery of the Kansas City Fair on September 26, 1872 (a robbery blamed on the James brothers), the *Kansas City Times* called the heist "so diabolically daring and so utterly in contempt of fear that we are bound to admire it and revere its perpetrators." Western lawmen were famous for calling their opponents the "cast-iron" breed. Even as zealous a lawman as Evett Dumas Nix, U.S. Marshal of Oklahoma in the 1890s, expressed his admiration in his 1929 autobiography, *Oklahombres*:

> As for the old time Oklahoma outlaw, I am reluctant to compare him with the highjacker and gunman of today. As one who fought him to extinction, I must admit that I admire his sportsmanship . . . when they fought they stood up to it and took defeat like the cast-iron breed they were.

The attitude was not confined to the West. Inspector Thomas Byrnes, Chief of Detectives of the New York City Police Department, expressed his admiration for criminals in his popular *Professional Criminals of America*, published in 1886. "Some of the criminals are really very clever in their own peculiar line," Byrnes said. "[I]n the place of the awkward and hang-dog-looking thief, we have today the thoughtful and intelligent rogue." The smartest became safecrackers, whose thefts put western bandits to shame. In June 1869, Jimmy "Old Man" Hope liberated $1.2 million from New York's Ocean National Bank; on January 25, 1876, Eddie Goodie took $720,000 from the Northampton National Bank in Northampton, Massachusetts. Byrnes listed the traits of the successful thief as "patience, intelligence, mechanical knowledge, industry, determination, fertility of resources, and courage," the same qualities found in that peculiar American hero, the self-made man.

By 1909, however, the moral landscape inhabited by lawmen and lawbreakers had experienced a seismic shift. To American law enforcement, the fight against crime was no longer an equal if deadly contest; it was war. The criminal was no longer a cast-iron opponent who mirrored the wildness of nature but part of a greater social cancer whose existence threatened order and spelled anarchy. In 1886, a bomb thrown into the ranks of police dispersing a workers' rally in Chicago's Haymarket Square killed seven police and seven civilians.

In Russia, dynamite bombs killed Czar Alexander II in 1881, Interior Minister Vyacheslav Pleve in July 1904, and Grand Duke Sergei Aleksandrovich in February 1905. Gunfire claimed President Sadi Carnot of France in 1894, Premier Antonio Cánovas del Castillo of Spain in 1897, Empress Elizabeth of Austria in 1898, and King Umberto I of Italy in 1900. In 1901, President William McKinley was shot by Leon Czolgosz, a doomed idealist from Cleveland, Ohio, who called himself Fred Nieman, or Fred Nobody. He told police after his arrest that he'd heard anarchist leader Emma Goldman say that "all leaders should be exterminated. [It] set me thinking so that my head nearly split with pain." Four years after McKinley's assassination, in 1905, former Idaho governor Frank Steunenberg was blown to bits by Harry Orchard. The forces of annihilation seemed everywhere, at least to the average lawman, and they were a hell of a lot more deadly now that they packed dynamite, the "proletariat's artillery." All of a sudden, the enemy seemed more determined, secretive, and well-organized than ever, a continuing theme that would echo through an entire century of crime-fighting. In time, anarchists would be replaced by white slavers, the Black Hand, organized crime, "Masters of Deceit," drug cartels, religious cults, and youth gangs. The names might change, but evil always lingered. Chaos lurked outside the doorstep, in the dark forest at the edge of town.

For the reemerging and anachronistic train robbers of the early 1900s, the spillover from this fear meant bad news. The newspaper headlines might be breathless, the reading public enthralled, but rail owners were not happy. The last thing they wanted was a resurgence of the tradition made famous by the Renos and the James boys. They wanted the robberies stopped, and they wanted them stopped immediately. When the Union Pacific was plagued by gunmen in and around Nebraska in 1906, officials brought in the Pinkertons. The next year, the ubiquitous Charley Siringo was sent in as a soldier in this budding war on crime. A longtime Pinkerton operative who found fame with his memoirs of cowboy life—*A Texas Cowboy* (1886), and *A Cowboy Detective* (1912)—Siringo was first hired as a range detective and then sent undercover into the Coeur d'Alenes during the mining "troubles" of 1891–92. Now his career came full circle as he was told to chase old-style badmen once again. Superintendent W. B. Coughman of the Omaha Pinkerton office briefed Siringo on rumors picked up by informants that "No. 41" from Lincoln to Omaha would be held up, and the Union Pacific offered Siringo and his partner sawed-off shotguns capable of cutting a man in half at close range. Though no stranger to bloodshed, one senses a moment of recoil. No, thank you, said Siringo, sticking with his Winchester and Colt .45.

For the first few trips, although the two detectives rode in the smoking car and watched out the windows, nothing much happened. Then they received word of a definite time and place when the robbers might board. That night, Union Pacific officials coupled an empty express car behind the engine, and Siringo and his partner, identified as operative V.L.S., climbed aboard. Their car was dark and they cracked the side doors six inches to watch for anything strange.

> About an hour and a half before daylight, No. 41 stopped to let off a passenger in Sweetwater station [Siringo wrote]. Just as our train pulled out, operative V.L.S. called me over to his side to point out three men hiding in some tall weeds about fifty yards from the track. We saw one of them stand up and then sit down again, and as soon as the train had got past them they all struck out towards the south. They were evidently holdup men who had smelled "mice" on seeing this extra express car attached to the train. . . . Operative V.L.S. and I had discussed the putting on of this extra express car and had decided it to be a mistake, as train robbers are not fools.

For Frank Grigware, events moved quickly now, accelerating to catastrophe just as Alice warned. Where it had seemed that from the summer of 1906 to February 1909 his life poked along from station to station, now he was barreling down the track without a clear idea of where the trip would end. On March 10, 1909, despite Alice's pleadings, he left Waco and joined the others in Hot Springs, Arkansas. Within a week, Frank and Jack took off for Little Rock and Memphis, a trip that seemed at Frank's insistence to get Jack alone from the others and sound him out about Alice's fears. The attempt obviously failed. Jack quelled Frank's worries. Sure the boys had had their scrapes with the law, he argued, but who didn't these days? We know nothing more about that trip, except that, by April 2, Frank and Jack had rejoined the others in Kansas City, Missouri. By May 17, they'd moved in separate waves to Omaha.

A peculiar lethargy characterized Frank's life after his return from Memphis that spring of 1909. Though he took shingling jobs in Kansas City and Omaha, he seemed to be going through the motions, simply spinning his wheels, while Jack hung out in pool halls, spending his time with a succession of prostitutes. Frank's old friend had grown angry and snappish; Alice's belief that Jack was convinced of his approaching death and hated the world seemed right on the money. Downer later said that during this time they were all sick and low on cash. For the first time, Torgensen succumbed to a hacking cough, and they believed he too had contracted consumption. It was as if time were running out, as if each and every one of them knew he was doomed.

Why didn't Frank leave? Had he thrown in his lot with the Spokane boys, as police would later say? The evidence, scant as it is, suggests otherwise. Instead, he seemed like a man stalled at a crossroads, confused about which way to turn. If he stayed, there was a chance he'd get in trouble—as Alice warned him, guilt by association was evidence enough these days to send a man to jail, especially if he was poor. But if he left, he'd be abandoning Jack, saying goodbye forever to his consumptive friend. Which was the better choice: common sense or guilt and loyalty? Sometimes he'd walk to the bridge in Kansas City that overlooked the sprawling train yard and stare at the tracks snaking off in every conceivable direction. He remembered his relatives back in Michigan, his family back in Spokane. Above all else, he remembered Alice in Waco. She was the one bright spot in the whole Grand Tour, the unexpected flash of gold piercing the gloom. If he went back to see her, his independence was ended. He'd never rejoin the others. If he returned to Waco, he knew sure as shooting that his traveling days were over.

He tried to tell this to Alice this in a long and rambling letter, but he was never very good at expressing himself in words. Nevertheless, she was thrilled. She poured out her love in a return letter dated April 5 and mailed it care of Kansas City General Delivery. Frank kept the letter, as lovers do, storing it in his carpetbag with other important papers and his Colt revolver. He looked at the gun and laughed, realizing it had never been pulled from its leather holster for anything but target practice. He thought of how this tour of the imagined West had turned into a bad joke, picking through piles of rock for instant wealth, drifting through cattle country like a lost cowboy. If Dan and the others really were train robbers, like Alice asserted, they sure were a sorry bunch: nothing like the James boys or the Youngers but lazy, sick, and bored. It was nothing like the dime novels he'd read as a youngster. Maybe reality was never as good as fiction. Still, it would be something to tell his kids.

Only snapshots remain of this period, supplied later by the Pinkertons. On April 2, 1910, when Frank and Jack rejoined the others in Kansas City, they found that the mysterious Bill Matthews had finally arrived by way of Ogden, Utah. Matthews was bearded, rough-hewn, and sloppy, but surprisingly soft-spoken for someone that a crazy man like Fritz so obviously feared. He appraised Frank quietly when they met, then said he was a horse dealer buying stud horses for a man named Rex Buck out of Twin Falls, Idaho. He watched Frank carefully as he said it, his dark eyes lighting with interest when he realized that Frank didn't believe a word. The next day, Saturday, April 3, Matthews took Frank with him to the shop of tailor Gus Bren in downtown Kansas City, where he bought himself a new suit of clothes. The little tailor ducked around the bearded giant as he measured his sleeve length and inseam; Matthews paid with a big wad of greenbacks he kept folded in his pocket. The suit was delivered to Matthews on April 7, a label with the tailor's address, customer's name, and date of order sewn inside the coat pocket.

The old rivalries returned. Fritz roomed with Jack and Frank after Matthews's arrival, staying clear of the man he feared. At first, Jack and Fritz seemed to forget their old tensions, but one evening Frank returned to the rooming house and heard raised voices from the floor above. Katie Snell, their landlady, listened at the bottom of the stairs. "You'd better go up there," she whispered. "They're arguing about some woman, and Mr. Torgensen is threatening to smoke up your young friend." Frank took the stairs two at a time. When he opened the door it was worse than he'd imagined: Jack and Fritz were in each other's face, Fritz's hand on his holster, an ice-cold look in his eyes. Frank grabbed Jack and told him to get out. Jack wisely packed his stuff and headed down the street to stay with Downer and Matthews.

One day in early May, Frank came home to find that Fritz and his bags were gone. He felt a sense of relief until he saw that Torgensen had rifled through his own luggage, too. The Swede had taken his Colt .38 and leather holster, his letters from home, and, worst of all, his letters from Alice. He stormed down the street and found Jack alone in his room. Downer and Matthews had also vanished, Jack said. They'd left a note saying they'd wire in a few days and Jack and Frank could catch up then. Jack was crushed that he'd been left out of their plans; he merely shrugged when Frank demanded to know what the hell was going on. It left Frank disgusted. What right did a man have to steal another's love letters? He'd call it quits with the lot of them once he got back what was rightfully his.

On Sunday, May 16, 1910, about a week after the three men's departure, Frank saw a story in the paper that gave him pause. At 11 P.M. on Saturday, May 15, the Great Northern Railroad's No. 3 express was robbed northwest of Spokane near Hillyard, Washington. Two men boarded the engine, covering the fireman and the engineer with their guns. Although they indicated that four others were in the holdup, no one else was actually seen. The man covering the engineer had a quick temper, and his partner called him John. "You have heard of me before and will probably hear of me again," John bragged. The other robber was called Bill. He was quieter and more businesslike, giving instructions that suggested he'd worked on trains. They separated the mail car from the rest of the express and ran it, the engine, and the tender two miles west. They rifled the mail sacks and found only a few hundred dollars, then reversed the engine and sent it back toward the rest of the train. Though the collision wasn't great, it rattled the passengers. The Great Northern offered $10,000 for each of the six men suspected in the heist; when the U.S. Post Office Department offered another $1,000 apiece, that raised the total to $66,000, equal to about $1.29 million in today's dollars. The reward poster promised, "If any of the guilty party are killed while resisting capture, the Great Northern Railway Company will pay the reward . . . upon proof that the party killed participated in the robbery."

Frank read the bandits' descriptions more closely. Their faces had been covered with bandannas and their hair with soft felt hats with slouching brims; both wore high-topped lumberjack boots, one tied with leather strips and the other with linen strings. "John," the one with a temper, was tall, slim, and pale—like Fritz. "Bill," who knew his way around engines, was short and dark—like Dan. When he remembered that Dan's ranch was outside Hillyard, where the robbery took place, he reread the article several times. Sometimes it proved his suspicions; sometimes it didn't prove a thing. The only way to clear this up was by asking, yet doing that would tie him to the gang. And if Alice's suspicions were indeed the truth, they wouldn't let him walk away. If he left right now without further explanation, Torgensen and Matthews might see his sudden flight as an attempt to contact the law. Alice was right. You couldn't run and hide anymore. The world was too small.

On the same day that Frank read the story of the Hillyard robbery, a telegram arrived for Jack. It was from Downer, with the others in Omaha. COME IMMEDIATELY, it said. NEW PROSPECTS. BRING FRANK TOO.

Frank and Jack arrived in Omaha on the morning of Monday, May 17. The smell of the stockyards hit them first, followed by the shriek of engines from the sprawling Union Pacific train yards. The business of Nebraska was large-scale agriculture, and this city was its hub. The Platte River Valley, once a fertile home for homesteaders, was now a chain of corporate farms pumping corn, potatoes, sugar beets, and beans to the rest of America. Huge ranches, some as big as 120,000 acres, shipped thousands of cattle to Omaha's massive packing plants, manned by black, Irish, and Czech workers slaving long hours for scant pay. The Union Pacific, headquartered here, seemed to have nearly limitless power and reach, but for all the big money and commerce, Omaha was still a dingy, smelly city.

Frank and Jack rented a room in South Omaha, a milling section of town where immigrants talked to each other in strange tongues that were unintelligible to the new arrivals. Jack went to find his old friends. In a couple of days, Fritz came to see Frank and apologized profusely, quite unlike himself. He said he'd scooped up everything in the sudden rush of leaving and only later realized that he'd taken Frank's letters and gun. He'd give them back once he got organized, he said. It seemed a lame excuse and Frank didn't believe a word of it, yet he was surprised by Fritz's apology, so out of character. Frank decided it was safer not to question Fritz too closely. If he kept a cool head and stayed patient, he might be able to leave the gang safely.

So Frank bided his time. By day, he hired out on construction sites; at night, he and Jack ate at the nearby Uneeda Restaurant, where they flirted with the waitresses. Sometimes they stopped in a soda fountain or took in a moving picture show. Jack was his old self

again, funny, relaxed, a big talker around girls. It was as if the last
few months had never existed—as if they were back on a roof amid
a sea of wheat, Frank hammering shingles while Jack stared at the
sky and made big plans. Jack laughed when Frank reminded him of
those days. It seemed the first time he'd heard Jack laugh in weeks.
Suddenly Jack's voice grew serious, and he asked Frank if he really
cared for Alice Evans. "Yeah, I think I do," Frank said, after a pause.
Jack looked away and his eyes seemed sad. "You've been the best
friend a guy could ever ask for," Jack finally muttered, staring out
the restaurant window at the strangers hurrying to their own desti-
nations, each the central sun in a private solar system, hero or heroine
in an untold epic of glory, adventure, or love. "Things will get better,
Frank, I promise. Everything will turn out for the best, you'll see."

Later Frank thought of that moment—as if it were the briefest hush
before a bullet struck, one last sigh before a storm. If only he'd been
wise enough to read and heed the signs. Afterward, Jack would beg
him to believe that nothing had been planned before Omaha, that he
hadn't led him up there knowing there would be trouble. But Frank
would always wonder. The timing was too convenient. The planning
was impeccable. The others acted so quickly. In five short days, by
Saturday, May 22, 1909, Frank's life had changed forever.

THE UNION PACIFIC'S Overland Limited was one of the crack
trains of the West. It was an eastbound express, en route from San
Francisco to Chicago, carrying registered mail from the Pacific to
New York, powered by a ten-wheeled steam locomotive built in the
1890s and called a "Harriman engine" after Edward H. Harriman,
who controlled the railroad until his death in 1909. Late on the night
of May 22, the Overland Limited No. 2 was nearing the end of that
part of its trip from Ogden, Utah, to Omaha, a 940-mile journey
through the red southern deserts of Wyoming, past the Medicine Bow
Mountains, and into the Platte River basin, with stops at Laramie,
Cheyenne, North Platte, and lesser places in between. It carried eighty
passengers, all but eight of them asleep in the rocking Pullman sleep-
ers. In addition to the dining car, observation car, boxcars with
freight, and an engine tender, the train included the Omaha and Ogden Railroad Post Office, the official designation for the car containing eight mail clerks and the U.S. mail.

When the Overland Limited pulled into Fremont station that night, it was two minutes behind schedule and twenty-five miles west of Omaha, where there would be a change of crew. Everyone was a little edgy: the Ogden-to-Omaha leg was long duty, requiring a double shift, and everyone was nervous about the recent train robberies, including the one the week before outside Spokane. Engineer A. R. Meikeljohn was beat, his only respite a puff on his corncob pipe as he rode on the engine's right side. Fireman Roy Prawl rode on the left, while "deadhead" engineer Ira Wright sat in the fireman's seat up front, partially obscured from view; although Wright was not on duty, he was available for relief. The train tarried four minutes at the deserted Fremont station to take on water and pulled out at 10:20 P.M. No one left the train and no one was seen to board it, at least with any certainty. The rear brakeman, John Kriss, was sitting at his post at the rear of the train when he saw three men walk around the back and toward the engine. He watched to see if they boarded, but it was too dark to tell.

It was a nearly straight shot from Fremont to Omaha, and for most of the way Meikeljohn kept the train at a steady 50 mph. The road was double-tracked, and the westbound No. 111 was scheduled to hurtle past soon. They were on a ten-mile tangent, straight as a ruler, ending in a curve between high clay banks that trainmen called the Lane Cut-Off but locals called the Mud Cut. Omaha's Union Station was two miles farther on. A stone bridge traversed the opening of the cut near the village of Seymour. As they drew close, Meikeljohn thought he spotted a torch or blaze. "What's that?" he asked his fireman. Roy Prawl leaned from the window on his side of the swaying locomotive. "Number One-Eleven," he said.

"Not on your life," Meikeljohn shot back. "That's up on that bank." They stared as the light waved up and down three times. Suddenly two men who'd been hiding atop the engine tender leapt from the darkness and tumbled over the coal gate separating the tender from the locomotive cab. Each man carried a gun. Meikeljohn saw in the front window the reflection of a man with a handkerchief over his face; when he turned, he stared down a pistol barrel. Prawl had already raised his hands. Wright, still seated up front, realized he hadn't been seen. It would have been easy to pick off the robbers like ducks, but engineers weren't issued guns.

"Don't move, this is a holdup," said the man covering Meikeljohn. "Stop the train where I say." Meikeljohn reached for the throttle, but the robber added, "Not yet . . . closer to the mouth of the cut. I'll tell you when." The engineer relaxed his grip and looked more closely at the two. Both wore long dark raincoats with slouch hats pulled low over their foreheads and blue polka-dot bandannas covering their faces except for holes cut for the eyes. "You don't want to kill any innocent people," Meikeljohn protested.

"No, I don't want to kill or hurt anybody," said the man at his back. "Just do as you're told, and you'll be all right."

Wright still hadn't been spotted. He kept still as stone, hoping to climb out once the train stopped and give the alarm. But the gunman covering Prawl saw his feet sticking out and yelled, "Hey, you, come down here to the middle of the deck or I'll shoot your damn head off!"

Wright scrambled from his seat. "I'm coming, I'm coming," he said. He got the idea that the man standing behind Meikeljohn was the leader, while the tall angular robber behind Prawl was more nervous and cruel.

As the Overland Limited drew near the point where the light had flashed, the man behind Meikeljohn calmly told him to slow the train. Meikeljohn notched in the throttle, lightly working the valve so that four pounds of air shuddered down the train's length and depressed the brakes in each car. "Faster," said the gunman, slapping his arm, causing Meikeljohn to accidentally slip the throttle into emergency. The sudden lurch threw the gunman off his feet and into the coal behind him, but he was up in an instant. His companion yelled in surprise and pointed his gun at Meikeljohn, but the fallen robber took the blame. "I did that," he said, and made a joke about his sure-footedness. As the tall robber calmed down, Roy Prawl considered the short robber more closely. He seemed the most self-possessed man he'd ever seen. Prawl was no longer afraid that the two would intentionally kill them, but if some trainman or passenger started shooting it would be a different matter. He felt the shorter man would kill every one of them with a smile and a joke if he thought it necessary for his own survival.

It was 11:15 P.M. They'd gone about a mile and a half since the robbers first crawled over the grate; the train hissed to a stop about three hundred feet from the bridge. They were near 42nd Street, at the edge of the city; the yellow glow of lights from the South Omaha stockyards could be seen in the sky. There was no moon, no other lights but the engine's electric headlamp and dim lights from inside the train.

"Get down," one robber ordered, and the three trainmen climbed from the cab. They were met at the bottom by two other bandits, dressed like their partners and similarly armed. As the two bandits in the engine descended, they ordered their prisoners to line up with their backs against the mail car, immediately behind the engine tender, and keep their hands in the air. The robbery was going perfectly, not a single move awry, when suddenly a voice sounded overhead. George Whitmore, chief mail clerk, stuck his head out the door of the mail car and saw the trainmen aligned beneath him. "What's going on there?" he shouted. There was a shot, and a bullet struck metal near his head. Whitmore ducked back inside the car and slammed the door.

So much for secrecy, thought Meikeljohn. To top it off, conductor Ned Wallace ran up from the caboose, asking what was up. This was the type of interruption the robbers didn't like. "You've come far enough," one yelled, shooting into the air. Conductor Wallace got the message and sprinted back to the passenger cars. Expecting the bandits to board the Pullman cars at any minute to rob the sleeping passengers, he ordered his porters to lock the doors. The few terrified passengers who were awake had gathered in the dining car. Wallace spotted the Pullman conductor and asked what he had done with the night's receipts. "I've already hid them," the man replied.

But Wallace and the passengers weren't in jeopardy. The gunmen wanted the contents of the mail car, and that alone. One bandit pounded on its metal door and told the clerks to open up. When they didn't answer, he shot out a window. "Don't shoot anymore, we're coming out," one clerk cried. As they hopped to the ground the clerks were lined up with the trainmen and everyone was patted down for weapons. When it came his turn, Meikeljohn said he only had his watch. "We don't want any watches or money," the gunman answered. "All we want is a little of Uncle Sam's money to tide us over for a week or two."

The gang leader took George Whitmore, the chief clerk, back in the car to select and throw out the bags of mail. As seven mail sacks flew out the door, rear brakeman John Kriss, unaware of what was happening, grabbed his red lantern, torpedo flares, and fuses and started down the track away from No. 2. His job was to flag down any train that might be headed their way. He got about two car lengths when someone up front hollered, "Hey, get back in there!" When he turned around, he saw the others standing in line with their hands in the air. What was going on? What should he do? Before he could think, one of the robbers fired three shots and Kriss heard bullets. They didn't whistle so much as *crack*, unlike the pulp stories he'd read. A story later circulated that his hand was wounded, but Kriss did not mention a wound in his statement to police, and this became the first of the night's many embellishments. Nevertheless, the close call made up Kriss's mind: he vaulted over the railing of the rear platform, doused every light in the observation car, and told the porter to lock all the doors.

By then, the bandits were ready to leave. They ordered the trainmen and clerks to carry the mail bags down the track to the bridge, but doing this was not easy. Each was shaped like a long heavy sausage and reached from one's shoulders to the ground. A robber picked one up, then dropped it and turned to Meikeljohn. "You carry that," he said. If it had been the angry fellow inside the engine cab, he wouldn't have argued, but this bandit, one of those waiting on the ground, seemed younger than the rest. Besides, Meikeljohn was feeling testy. He was tired, he'd somehow lost his corncob pipe, and his train was being robbed. After this he could expect hours of questions from railroad dicks. Damn if he'd carry these guys' loot for them too. "I don't want to carry it," he answered. "I doubled on the road today, and I'm tired."

"You carry that, goddamn you," the young guy snapped. "You made more money than I did today." It was funny, Meikeljohn thought, but the kid sounded almost as pissed off about life as at him. He didn't feel overly threatened by the youngster, but he knew better than to argue with a man holding a gun. He picked up the sack and draped it over his back; the tail end bumped along the ground. When they walked in front of the engine, they were both dazzled for a second by its electric headlight; the youngster cursed and fired three times at it, missing each time. The leader walked up and put his hand on the kid's shoulder. "To hell with the light," he said. "Let it go."

They walked slowly up the track until the stone bridge loomed overhead. "Is this far enough, Bill?" the young bandit said.

Meikeljohn stole a glance at the man. "Bill," one of the men on the ground, had been the quietest so far. Though the short bandit had conferred with him briefly, the man said little otherwise. He was heavy and lumbering and seemed darker than his partners. He started when his name was called, and, though apparently annoyed by the slip, he answered, "Just drop it here."

As Meikeljohn dropped his sack, he turned to the short bandit who'd covered him in the engine and said, "I would like a little out of this lump if we ever meet."

The bandit laughed and answered, "Brother, I'll buy you a drink if we meet again," then raised his voice and told the crew to return to the train and wait ten minutes before getting under way. His tall partner told them not to look back or they'd get plugged. Meikeljohn returned to the engine and checked his pocket watch. Though time had seemed to pass slowly, the holdup took only ten minutes, maybe fifteen.

It was 12:10 A.M. when the Overland Limited pulled into the station at Omaha. The train was fifteen minutes late, and officials soon learned why. Within minutes, Union Station was crawling with police officers, detectives, postal inspectors, railroad special agents, deputy sheriffs, and newspaper reporters. Most of the passengers slept through the excitement, only learning of the adventure next morning as the train sped through midwestern cornfields. One passenger did awaken and, on learning what happened, grabbed his bags, piled off the car, and ran, opting to end his journey early on the Overland Limited No. 2.

SUNDAY, MAY 23, dawned on a city in an uproar. By daybreak a small army of lawmen from various and sometimes competing jurisdictions had descended on the scene of the crime. They included most of the 130-man Omaha police force; Sheriff Edward Brailey of Douglas County, Nebraska, and all his deputies; the South Omaha Police Force under Chief John Briggs; eight U.S. Post Office inspectors, headed by Chief William J. Vickery of Kansas City; U.S. Marshal William D. Warner of Nebraska and several deputy marshals; the entire Union Pacific special agency force headed by Special Agent in Charge William T. Canada; and every newspaper reporter for fifty miles, or at least so it seemed. By noon, editorials screamed that it was high time train robbers be taught a much-needed lesson. There was too much train robbery in this modern age!

Brave talk, but no help to investigators. The trainmen could give little description of the two men who'd climbed into the engine save their stature, carriage, and the sound of their voices. Meikeljohn said he couldn't identify either man. Ira Wright said he got a good look at their foreheads and eyes. Fireman Prawl said he might recognize their voices, but that was all. As for the two bandits on the ground, even less could be said. Meikeljohn felt one of them might have been riding unseen atop the tender, then jumped off before the others and joined his companion, but Wright and Prawl thought otherwise. They all heard one robber addressed as "Bill." As for the postal clerks, George Whitmore seemed to speak for them all when he said it was so dark that "I could not tell whether the men who held up the train were white or negroes."

The lack of physical evidence was no less daunting, though there were some clues. Bill Canada of the Union Pacific had been at the scene of the holdup within an hour of the Overland Limited's arrival, but every trace of stolen mail had disappeared. He did find one empty mail sack that had been cut in two and the top flap of another. Postal inspectors determined that the bandits made off with only $700, but that was not immediately disclosed. The next morning, Canada found a heap of ashes on the high bank where the signal fire had burned. Among the ashes were fragments of the Spokane newspaper the *Spokesman-Review*, and near that lay a few used cartridges. A man's tracks led from the fire and down the bank; the fire site commanded a good view of the track back to where it curved near Seymour. A mail clerk thought he'd heard a bandit say the mail sacks were "a hell of a load to carry in an automobile," so railroad employees telegraphed stations around Omaha to watch out for suspicious cars.

One other piece of physical evidence was found—quite interesting, if not immediately useful. Two torn portions of an envelope had been used by someone as toilet paper in the weeds a short distance from the fire. The envelope was postmarked WACO, TEXAS, APR. 5, 1909. The address was nearly obliterated. All that remained resembled the children's game of Hangman, where one filled in the missing letters:

<pre>
        F----K ---------RE
        --------- CITY, MO.
        GEN'L DE-------Y
</pre>

That Sunday evening, the robbery was the talk of Omaha. While police searched hotels and boardinghouses for shady characters, a Union Pacific spokesman vowed that the railroad would "do everything in its power to get the bandits." They started with an offer of $5,000 for information leading to the arrest and conviction of each gunman. The federal government added $1,000 apiece of its own money. Since four robbers were involved, the reward totaled $24,000, equal to about $470,000 in today's dollars. With that incentive, authorities expected a break at any time.

But the reward unleashed an onslaught of greed, not leads. Monday, May 24, began in different ways for different people. While Downer, Torgensen, and Matthews rose late, Frank and Jack walked down the street for breakfast, where they read in the *Omaha World-Herald* that investigators had made "considerable strides." [The] "systematic and thorough manner in which the holdup was planned and executed leaves not the slightest doubt in the minds of the police that the deed was done by four of the most expert and hardened desperadoes who ever engaged in the game," the newspaper said. Union Pacific detectives were swamped by hundreds of callers intoxicated by the huge reward. Police described their clues as the products of "excited imaginations." One citizen, hearing that the bandits may have fled by auto, reported that he spotted a dark red car with four "tough looking individuals" speeding down 32nd Street on the night of the robbery. Henry Smith, a barkeeper at the South Omaha Stock Exchange, said that on the morning of Friday, May 21, a day before the robbery, three men and their chauffeur were standing at the bar. "One of the party done all the talking and I thought they were intoxicated, and one said, 'Who is going to pay for the drinks?' " Smith recalled. "One stepped to the end of the bar to get some Pop-Corn and he said, 'Don't worry about the drinks,' and he was not drunk but was putting it on." The chauffeur was a "slim, sickly looking fellow" with a dark complexion and black gloves; the man who offered to buy the drinks had red cheeks, showed his teeth "quite prominently when smiling," and was smooth-shaven. Smith was suspicious, he said, because they were too free with their money and "they were strangers to me."

Such was the caliber of the clues. Two local men were reported because they were "considered quite tough." A Dr. Turner was reported because his friend, a bookkeeper, had an "unsavory reputation," and the bookkeeper's brother "was connected with the Postal Department sometime ago." Even lawmen were not immune. The marshal at Papillion, Nebraska, said that on the Wednesday or

Thursday before the robbery he'd seen a stranger with "dark complected hair and mustache" who displayed "a roll of about six
[hundred-dollar] and about eight [fifty-] dollar bills, and as he seemed
to have no special business, close watch was made."

By Tuesday, May 25, the Union Pacific's Bill Canada could only
promise, with a hint of exhaustion, "to keep on working until we get
the men, no matter how long it takes." One ray of hope was the
arrival of "Pinkerton's shrewdest operatives," led by Asher Rosseter,
manager of Pinkerton's St. Louis branch and later the agency's general manager. More momentous was the arrival of William Pinkerton
himself, who took personal charge of the investigation.

IN MANY WAYS, the history of train robbers in America was the
history of the Pinkerton National Detective Agency. It has often been
said that the Pinkertons shaped the course of twentieth-century American law enforcement; if so, their war against the Renos, Jameses,
Youngers, Daltons, and the Wild Bunch shaped the Pinkertons. In
this way it can be said that the railroads shaped American justice,
too. The Pinkertons began as railroad dicks, were sidetracked into
the labor wars through railroad connections, and returned to these
roots when the taint of labor struggles left the organization in sham-
bles. By the early 1900s, the Pinkertons gloried in their identification
with the great western railroads—the Union Pacific, Santa Fe, Great
Northern, and others. They'd nearly eradicated the old and infamous
gangs with a one-two punch of old-fashioned diligence and newfan-
gled science. When the upstarts moved in, it was like a personal slap
in the face. Any threat to their clients was a threat to the Pinkertons.

Such hegemony was hard-won. Although the Pinkertons had made
a name for themselves in the labor wars, nowhere else could the
agency's successes and excesses be better seen than in its alliance with
the railroads. Ironically, Allan Pinkerton, founder of the dynasty and
working-class son of a part-time policeman, was a labor revolutionary in his Scottish youth. When his name appeared on royal arrest
warrants in the early 1840s, Pinkerton and his wife quickly set sail
from Glasgow and landed in Nova Scotia. By 1842, he had settled in
Dundee, forty miles northwest of Chicago, where he resumed his
trade as a barrelmaker. One day while cutting wood for barrel staves,
he stumbled upon some counterfeiters. He contrived their arrest, and
local merchants hired him to track down others. Pinkerton discovered

that he had a knack for law enforcement—especially undercover work—quickly advanced from deputy sheriff to Chicago's first municipal detective, and then went on to serve as an agent for the U.S. mails. In 1850, Pinkerton opened his fledgling agency.

Chicago proved the perfect place to make money fighting crime. The Windy City was home of the Meat Trust, the most successful, ruthless, technologically advanced, and criminally inclined of the giant monopolies; it was also becoming the nation's crime capital, laying the groundwork for its later fame during the Roaring Twenties as Murder Central.

Pinkerton's agency specialized in providing "cinder dicks" (hobo slang for railroad detectives, named after the sparks flying from locomotives' smokestacks) for half a dozen railroads in Illinois, Indiana, Wisconsin, and Michigan. One contract was a $10,000 retainer to protect the Illinois Central; he dealt with the railroad's vice president, George B. McClellan, and its lawyer, Abraham Lincoln. By the time war broke out and McClellan was named a Union general, Pinkerton had already saved Lincoln's life. While investigating threats against another railroad, Pinkerton uncovered a conspiracy to kill the newly elected president as he passed through Maryland en route to taking his presidential oath in Washington. Pinkerton foiled the plot by disguising Lincoln in a woman's shawl, and now the favor was returned: Pinkerton became chief of the Union's intelligence services. Though his performance of this service was at best spotty, after the war Pinkerton displayed in every agency office a framed Mathew Brady photograph of Lincoln, Pinkerton, and Major General John A. McClernand standing before a tent at Antietam.

The Civil War was the young agency's first real break, providing future contacts and profits totaling $40,000. The Founder, as Pinkerton now called himself, expanded business on a national scale. He installed his youngest and favorite son, Robert, in the newly opened New York office, while keeping oldest son William with him in the Chicago World Headquarters. William, whose reputation as a rake included a passion for sporting houses and musical theater, oversaw the western and midwestern operations, all the while being closely watched by his father.

At this point, a symbol arose that progressed from marketing ploy to corporate identity and finally to frightening reality: a godlike omnipotent watchfulness that French phenomenologist Michel Foucault more than a century later would call "the Gaze." The detective's "gaze" was all-important, the essence of his professional being; an unobservant detective was an unabashed failure. By paying underworld snitches for information, he had eyes everywhere. "The great myth of a pure Gaze that would be pure Language: a speaking eye . . . taking in and gathering together each of the singular events that occurred," Foucault said. As the Gaze's range widened and became more omniscient, "it would be turned into speech that states and teaches" the truth of the unknown and unseeable, the veritable Word of God.

Allan Pinkerton was no philosopher, but there is no doubt that he understood, at least instinctively, the power and fearsomeness of the Gaze. His agency's motto, WE NEVER SLEEP, was stripped across the front of the Chicago headquarters; its logo, the huge unblinking eye, watched the streets below. Pinkerton delighted in repeating a tale, perhaps apocryphal if not embellished, of the agency's early days. After the murder of a bank teller in 1856, he assigned a detective to shadow the suspect, whose name was Drysdale. The detective hauntingly resembled the murdered man and hounded Drysdale day and night, never speaking, always watching—a ghost with the gaze of all-knowing God. Unable to take it any longer, Drysdale broke down and confessed, then committed suicide. Over time the tale assumed a Darwinian slant. Suicide and scrutiny winnowed out the weak and corrupt, and the criminal was morally weak. By contrast, Pinkerton, the survivor, proved morally superior. In his later years, Pinkerton told his clients that criminals everywhere feared him and, as a superstitious mark of respect, had named him "The Eye." Whether true or not, the story was good marketing and in time entered the vernacular, tagging detectives and operatives everywhere with Pinkerton's logo. Henceforth, these men would be known as "private eyes."

Allan Pinkerton's role in the Civil War and the postwar success of his agency quickly went to his head. With his long unruly beard, dark brows, and ursine physique, he radiated power and intimidation; now he tried to live that role and, like many powerful men, fell prey to hubris and arrogance. In the 1870s, he churned out dime novels devoted to revamping the image of detectives: Operatives were methodical and scientific plodders who were "pure and above reproach"; a black caller was described as "my sable visitor"; a good night's sleep was dubbed "the refreshing companionship of Morpheus." According to one biographer, Pinkerton increasingly became "a rigid martinet, persnickety, obstinate, irascible, egocentric, self-willed, and dictatorial." He sent spies among his own operatives to ensure that they did not curse, drink, borrow money, gamble, or leave "soiled linen" on the office floor. At home he was just as bad. His twenty-one-year-old daughter, Pussy, left home for months after Pinkerton found her on a couch with a suitor and flew into a towering rage.

The Civil War changed Pinkerton and his agency in one other way. Great heroes demand great villains, and a new kind of villain roamed the Missouri Valley after the war, robbing banks and railroads, outwitting town and city constabularies. These were the great familial robber bands. To fight back, banks and railroads banded together to hire their own private law; with increasing regularity, they chose the Pinkertons. Yet Allan Pinkerton soon found that he was out of his element in the rural West and Midwest. His agency's oldest and best tactic, that of sending in spies, no longer worked when gangs were small and cemented by family ties. The era's grudging respect for badmen, seen in the words of western lawman Evett Dumas Nix and New York Chief of Detectives Thomas Byrnes, quickly turned for Pinkerton into a contempt and hatred born of frustration. The bitter tone was first heard during the campaign against the Reno brothers, shielded from the Pinkertons by the residents of Johnson County, Indiana, where they lived. The wall of silence that rose during the war against Frank and Jesse James became legendary. Farmers who believed they had been cheated by the railroads' discriminatory freight rates, or who lost their savings in wildcat railroad stocks and bonds, were not about to help the roads' hired guns track down and kill an American Robin Hood.

The James brothers' robbery of the Iron Mountain Railroad at Gad's Hill, Missouri, on January 31, 1874, showed another side of the conflict: the escalating war of words. It was said that during this robbery one of the bandits, most probably Jesse James, turned to the conductor and asked, "Where is Mr. Pinkerton?" The comment reportedly infuriated the Founder. Being bested by a band of backwoods robbers in front of important clients brought out the worst in him. In an early example of his anticrime rhetoric, he vowed, "I shall not give up the fight with these parties until the bitter end. . . . It must be war to the knife and knife to the hilt." In this way, Pinkerton predated and influenced American law enforcement's frequent declarations of "total war" on crime. And just as total war allows excess under the guise of divine or royal mandate, Allan Pinkerton's hatred for criminals shaped his agency's penchant for stretching and breaking the law.

There was a precedent for this before the war against the Jameses, and this was the fate of the Renos. After repeated tries, their headquarters in Johnson County, Indiana, was finally infiltrated by operatives posing as a barkeep, a gambler, and a railroad switchman. These agents reported that the Renos controlled the county courts, so Pinkerton decided to seek a change of venue. One night in 1867, an undercover man lured the leader, John Reno, to the depot, where the Founder and six sheriff's deputies rode up in a "special" and snatched him off the platform. They spirited him to Missouri, where he stood trial and was found guilty of robbery. "It was kidnapping," Pinkerton later admitted, "but the ends justified the means."

Thereafter, that phrase seemed to characterize Pinkerton justice— a form that favored the client and overlooked the law's inconvenient niceties. It also reflected a new style of enforcement arising after the Civil War. Vigilante justice asserted an extralegal right to violence that was above man's law and answered a higher calling, the will of society. The original vigilantes in California in the 1850s and Montana in the 1860s directed their violence against lawmen who'd been in league with criminals; the motives soon turned less creditable and became a convenient way to stamp out economic competition or ideological enemies. Opponents of Reconstruction spawned the Klan; large ranchers in Wyoming suppressed their smaller counterparts; local and state governments encouraged vigilantism to suppress the labor movement. The Pinkertons participated in the range wars and the labor wars, bringing with them skills they'd perfected while protecting the railroads. As did all vigilantes, the Founder identified the enemy as a tribelike entity devoted to conspiratorial codes and secret purposes and, in the process, turned his agency into their mirror image.

The same happened with the outlaw gangs. In 1868, the remaining Reno brothers were extradited from Canada and lynched by a masked posse in New Albany, Indiana. Many thought the lynching was instigated by the Pinkertons, who feared acquittal at the hands of sympathetic jurors. In 1874, after Jesse James's taunt at Gad's Hill, Allan Pinkerton again took the law into his own hands. This time it wasn't as easy. When he sent agents after the outlaws, three of his men were killed. The Founder vowed revenge. In January 1875, acting on mistaken information that Frank and Jesse were visiting their mother, Zerelda Samuel, Pinkerton agents surrounded her house in Kearney, Missouri, and tossed a bomb through the window. The explosion killed an eight-year-old half brother and ripped off Zerelda's right arm. It was the first time the Pinkertons were universally condemned in the press, though not the last. Jesse James vowed his own revenge, once traveling to Chicago to kill the Founder. He failed but told a friend, "I know God someday will deliver Allan Pinkerton into my hands." Neither man got his wish. Allan Pinkerton died in 1884, two years after Jesse was shot in the head by gang member Bob Ford.

The business passed to William Pinkerton and his younger brother, Robert. While William placed faith in his operatives and the new world of scientific detection, Robert carried the agency even farther in its identification with big business by creating the Pinkerton Protective Patrol, a branch providing "watchmen" for strike-plagued mines, factories, and railroads. Since Robert was Allan's favorite son, the balance of power shifted his way. Although Allan had established a uniformed guard force in 1850, Robert's Protective Patrol was truly a private army; it drilled with military precision in blue flannel uniforms and slouch hats with gold cord and tassel and was well-armed. For the next two decades, the Protective Patrol was involved in seventy strikes, yet none were as infamous and potentially ruinous as the July 1892 pitched battle between striking steelworkers and three hundred Pinkerton watchmen at the Carnegie steelworks at Homestead, Pennsylvania. When the smoke cleared, three Pinkertons and seven steelworkers lay dead and dozens more were wounded. This would be the Pinkertons' second great vilification in the press: they were accused of hiring "Hessians" and "Cossacks" and of starting a "war of extermination" against workingmen. Although there were congressional investigations, nothing came of them, yet within the agency itself the balance of power reverted to William. The company limited its role in labor disputes to espionage, and eliminated its industrial division entirely in 1937 after Congress outlawed industrial spying.

Long before this, the Pinkertons had returned to their roots: the railroads. By the 1890s, pursuing robbers had become a business staple, and by the turn of the century the Pinkertons had carved a place for themselves unlike that of any other other public or private detective agency. Their successes were so legendary that their failures almost passed from mind. A major part of that success was the agency's institutional memory. The Pinkertons simply outlasted criminals and would go almost anywhere to track them down. The Wild Bunch pursuit was most famous, but others got plenty of press. The year of the Mud Cut Robbery saw the arrest of "Old Bill" Miner, an ancient and amiable outlaw who'd been holding up trains and stage coaches since 1869. Miner—credited with coining the classic phrase "Hands up!"—was arrested in the woods outside Dahlonega, Georgia. He told the posse his name was John Anderson and he was only hunting deer, but when Henry W. Minster, assistant superintendent of Pinkerton's Philadelphia office, showed Miner his mug shot from an old Pinkerton wanted poster, the geriatric outlaw shrugged. "Well, you're right and I guess it's all up with me now," he said.

Another part of the Pinkertons' success was the hold of the "Great Detective" on the popular imagination. While Sherlock Holmes was its avatar and Edgar Allan Poe's Auguste Dupin his progenitor, a host of far less literary detectives—with names like Kent Keen the Crook-Crusher, the Old Sleuth, and Mephisto—plied their trade in dime novels and pulp magazines. As society grew chaotic, the detective arose in its midst to restore order. He was cool, implacable, and all-knowing. Though perhaps outnumbered, his alliance with science and reason kept the forces of terror at bay.

Crime was like society itself, mobile and far-reaching, yet few law enforcement agencies had jurisdiction outside their own city or town. The Pinkertons filled that void, incorporating science and a nation-wide organization that paralleled in scope the industries it served. The Pinkertons succeeded by being everywhere, or at least by making others believe they were. To say the least, law enforcement in the early 1900s was a meager affair. State police departments did not exist in the western states, while only a few had been established back east, in Connecticut, Massachusetts, and Pennsylvania. The federal government had no criminal investigative body except the Secret Service, whose duties were limited to protecting the president and tracking counterfeiters. The Bureau of Investigation, predecessor of the FBI, did not appear until 1909. U.S. marshals limited their activities to the territories and the Indian reservations, as well as to protecting government property like the U.S. mails. By filling the gap between such entities, the Pinkertons made themselves indispensable in ways no other law enforcement agency had or would until their shoes were filled and their style emulated by Hoover's FBI.

In the process, the Pinkertons, a nineteenth- and early twentieth-century for-profit law enforcement agency with all the private sector's stress on image and marketable results, presaged and shaped public-sector crime fighting for our time. Allan Pinkerton's early methods of infiltrating criminal groups was imitated and perfected by federal and metropolitan forces, yet the success of this method ultimately lay with the skill of the operative and was thus hard to predict and control. More successful and far-reaching was the work of Allan's older son. William Pinkerton decided in the 1890s to centralize criminal records within their own national bureau of identification, the basis for the FBI's enormous present-day files. It was an effort to "weave together the bits and pieces of crime," William Pinkerton said. Anything about anyone could be contained in a file.

The ultimate heart of the Pinkertons' continued success was this criminal file. Through contacts as varied as frontier sheriffs, city policemen, and underworld snitches, the Pinkertons collected all known data concerning criminals, including their origins, associates, methods of operation, meeting places, and known and suspected crimes. One constant source of information was the newspaper: As crimes and criminals were reported, field agents clipped and sent in the stories, along with extra notations, all stored diligently in the criminal's file. Photographs found among the effects of killed and arrested men were forwarded to the central offices, with as much information as could be obtained. The mug shot, a Pinkerton innovation, soon spread to police and other detective agencies, yet the Pinkertons didn't stop there but made efforts to get photographs from friends, families, and associates as well as from local photographers. The file of train robber Gratton Dalton, for instance, contained the following entry:

> Is an inveterate tobacco chewer, card player, and prides himself as being the best cribbage player in the country. Is passionately fond of whiskey. Brags of detective ability. When embarrassed picks his teeth and cleans his nails. Eyebrows meet, ears stand out from head. Is left handed and generally shoots from left shoulder, though can shoot equally good with right.

In addition, the files were international, virtually unheard of at the time. The Gaze extended to every corner of the world; there was nowhere to escape the Unblinking Eye. An entry on Butch Cassidy reached into South America: "As soon as Cassidy entered an Indian village he would begin playing with the children. When hard pressed by local authorities, he would always find a hideout among the native population," his file read.

By 1894, the Pinkerton gallery of criminals was the largest in the nation and one of the largest in the world. Yet that was not enough. William Pinkerton dreamed of a worldwide web of data and social control, dreams that later saw greater expression in the development of the FBI's fingerprint files and IBM's early punch-card technology.

Pinkerton made early efforts to link his agency to the great European police forces, like Scotland Yard and the Sûreté, in hopes of creating an international exchange of information and assistance, a forerunner of Interpol. In North America, he helped create an association of police chiefs in the big cities of the United States and Canada that came to be called the International Association of Chiefs of Police (IACP). Pinkerton, a governor of its board from 1898 to 1923, suggested that a central bureau be created, and in 1897 the National Bureau of Criminal Identification was born. First located in Chicago near Pinkerton headquarters, and later in Washington, this bureau served as a vast data bank of criminal information made available to subscribing members, who in turn provided copies of their own files. The data bank remained under IACP auspices until 1924, when it was transferred to young J. Edgar Hoover's Bureau of Investigation, one year after William Pinkerton's death.

If a single word describes Pinkerton operations, it has to be "control." Belief in control pervaded the agency, from founder Allan through sons William and Robert and down to the superintendents in the twenty branch offices coast to coast. Allan Pinkerton admitted he was a tyrant, both in the office and at home. "I rule my office with an iron hand," he wrote in a letter to a new employee. "I am self-willed and obstinate. . . . *I must have my own way of doing things.*" The emphasis was his, boldly underlined. His sons were just as vindictive, opinionated, and intolerant, but they were more amenable to scientific and technological change. Emerging technologies, especially those in communications, extended their control.

When a prospective client came to Pinkerton's, he entered this regulated realm. He met first with the branch superintendent, who after an interview prepared a "journal" describing the basic problem and requirements with a detailed plan of operation from which field men received their marching orders. Copies of the journal went up the chain daily, giving division managers immense power over the fates and lives of hundreds if not thousands of people caught, however innocently, in this web. Yet by 1908, when Frank Grigware was about to become ensnared, the web had begun to fray. Allan Pinkerton once wrote to an aide, "I do not know the meaning of the word 'fail.' Nothing in heaven and hell can influence me when I know I am right." In time, this translated into an organization-wide belief in its own infallibility—a certainty that once the Pinkertons set their unblinking eye on a man or group, no matter how scant the evidence, that party must be guilty. Mix with this a complete identification with their clients—the railroaders, mine owners, and other industrialists—and by the turn of the century the Pinkertons had developed a Bourbon cast of mind. They were ultraconservative and could do no wrong, true practitioners of Social Darwinism who resisted social reform and were dedicated to the rule of the status quo. "Never has the private detective been used to such an extent, or with such unscrupulousness," as during the first decade of the twentieth century, Samuel Gompers, president of the American Federation of Labor, later said. "They have been not only private soldiers, hired by capital to commit violence, and spies in the ranks of labor; they have been . . . used in the capacity of *agents provocateurs*—that is, in disguise, as union men, to provoke ill-advised action, or even violence, among workingmen."

Even storied operative Charley Siringo would turn on his former masters. In *Two Evil Isms: Pinkertonism and Anarchism* (1915), Siringo attacked the employers he once so admired. After the Pinkertons tried to suppress *A Cowboy Detective*, his 1912 book of reminiscences in which he detailed the way he and the agency overcame obstacles to get their men, including breaking the laws they were sworn to protect, Siringo said he came to realize that all groups and forces—cops and criminals, owners and union members, detectives and the anarchists they tried to suppress—were ruthless, corrupt, and venal. The lone detective was, at best, a morally independent alternative to "greedy capitalists and blood-thirsty labor union agitators" but at worst "a slave of capital treated as a piece of machinery."

Siringo portrayed himself as a simple cowboy lured by the wiles of the city and engulfed by a system against which any protest would fail:

> The question might be asked why I did not show my manhood by resigning and exposing this crooked agency in the beginning. Exposing it to whom, pray? Not to the officers of the law, I hope. In my cowboy simplicity I might have been persuaded to do so at that time. But I am glad I did not, for, with my twenty-two years behind the curtains, I can now see the outcome . . . many "sleeps" in the city bull pen, and a few doses of the "third-degree" to try and wring a confession for blackmailing this notorious institution.
>
> Up to the time of the Homestead Riot, and since the moral wave has been sweeping over the land, the Pinkerton National Detective Agency was above the law. A word from [William] Pinkerton or one of his officers would send any "scrub" citizen to the scrap heap or the penitentiary. This is no joke, for I have heard of many innocent men "railroaded" to prisons, and my information came from inside the circle.
>
> A man without wealth or influence trying to expose the dastardly work of the Pinkerton National Detective Agency would be like a two-year-old boy blowing his breath against a cyclone to stop its force.

It was no coincidence that the slang term *to railroad*, meaning to send to prison with summary speed or by means of false evidence, came into wide use at this time.

WILLIAM PINKERTON TOOK charge of the Mud Cut Robbery investigation. The local police and Union Pacific detectives could do their jobs here, yet the Spokane paper found in the ashes suggested a connection with the May 15 holdup of the Great Northern in Washington. And Pinkerton already had a sentimental attachment to Spokane. The agency's motto WE NEVER SLEEP! and the logo, the unblinking eye, were already part of American culture; a third trademark hailed directly from the Inland Empire: UP! This was a watercolor painting of a gun-toting bandit whose eyes and gun followed

the viewer from every angle. Pinkerton had spotted it in 1880 in a
noted Spokane brothel, the Owl Saloon; he liked UP! so much, he
bought it on the spot and hung it in the boardroom of the agency's
World Headquarters in Chicago.

Pinkerton remembered that the descriptions of the robbers in the
Great Northern holdup were similar to those of the Mud Cut robbers;
the repetition of the name "Bill" had to be more than coincidence.
He also saw similarities to the January robbery of the Denver & Rio
Grande Railroad in Colorado.

Pinkerton wired his branch offices in Denver, Seattle, and Spokane and told them to watch for clues, however small. Yet as the
week progressed, there were no new leads. Frank continued as before, looking for work by day, getting together with Jack at night
for supper at the Uneeda. The tips that came to Bill Canada were
worthless, people willing to rat on a neighbor for the reward. He
wondered privately who was worse, the outlaws or the fine citizens
of Omaha.

On Thursday, May 27, ten-year-old Johnnie Krowlik and a pal
were let out of class at Brown Park Public School in South Omaha
for noon recess. The school, a two-story brick box with an attic, lay
little more than a mile from the Mud Cut. The robbery was the biggest thing to happen to this crowded immigrant neighborhood for a
long time; Johnnie and his friends had been to the tracks earlier in
the week and watched as police and detectives searched each inch of
ground. When they asked if they could help, the police told them to
"Scat!" and "Get away!" For the rest of the week they played at
being train robbers. His friends were the Wild Bunch, but Johnnie
was a traditionalist and preferred Jesse James.

The best part of recess these days was playing in the deep gully
across 19th Street east of school. The banks were high, and a telegraph pole had fallen from the top during the last big storm. It rested
with one end on the bank and the other in the gully. Miss Elizabeth
Hayes, the principal, had warned her students not to play there. It
was dangerous, she said. The pole could slip and crush them, and
who knew what kind of power still coursed through the dangling
wires. The truant officer tried to tell her there was no danger since
they weren't electrically charged, but no one really understood the
forces being tapped in this new century. She could just see one of her

students fried to a crisp like the condemned men in the state penitentiary. All the boys secretly loved Miss Hayes, but after all she was of that same overprotective sex as their mothers, who never did appreciate what kids called fun.

The two boys shinnied down the pole to the bottom of the gully and were jumping over a pile of rubbish at the end of the pole when Johnnie caught his foot and fell spread-eagled. His friend started to laugh and Johnnie felt more angry than hurt, but when he glanced back he spotted something interesting. He'd tripped on a leather strap protruding from the rubbish. "Lookit!" Johnnie called, then grabbed the strap and pulled. Attached to the other end was a leather holster, and inside this a blue-steel automatic revolver, fully loaded.

Johnnie and his friend stared. The birds chirped. The hot breeze whispered. They came to their senses and dug like mad.

When they were finished, they'd uncovered two more revolvers, a flashlight, two blue polka-dot handkerchefs with eye holes cut out, a black slouch hat, and a number of cartridges. Then and only then did they notice that they were late for class and their teacher was yelling their names.

"I guess we should go back," the friend said in a worried voice.

Johnnie looked at their pile of loot and picked up the black slouch hat. "I guess we oughta tell Miss Elizabeth." He thought a second, and added, "I hope she don't get mad."

❧ CHAPTER FOUR ❧

The Sweatbox

THE WEEK WAS a peaceful one for Frank, if tinged with suspicion. Like everyone else in Omaha, he read the accounts of the Mud Cut Robbery and its investigation. That was all everybody talked about—that and the reward. His fellow roofers dreamed aloud of a life of leisure; the waitresses at the Uneeda Restaurant gossiped about shady characters they'd served on the day of the holdup. As Frank listened, he wondered if his friends had robbed the train.

Despite himself, Frank watched for shifts in behavior but spotted none. No wild spending, no sudden disappearances. Jack kept his old schedule as they roomed at 518 South 16th Street. Dan Downer and Fritz Torgensen stayed a quick streetcar ride away at a rooming house at 324 North 15th. Bill Matthews lived at 1814 Dodge, not far off. Sometimes they met at the end of the day in a billiard parlor on North 24th. They played pool, laughed, and talked, but Frank never heard anything suspicious. If anything, they seemed like the same old boys from Spokane.

On the night of Thursday, May 27, someone knocked on Frank's door. He was propped up in bed reading the paper, listening through the open window to the clatter of the streetcars and shouts of the newsboys. Fritz came in, his eyes scanning the room. Frank was surprised how pale he looked; his cough had deepened and he occasionally spit

111

into his handkerchief. Fritz said the others were in South Omaha, waiting to pick up a parcel, but after that they planned to hit some bars. You in? Frank thought it strange for Torgensen to drop by like this alone, but he was bored and glad for any excuse to paint the town. He buttoned his collar and straightened his tie, and they hopped a streetcar for several blocks through South Omaha.

Fritz seemed more preoccupied than usual, and Frank asked if he'd heard from Lillian. That cheered the Swede up briefly. "Some Denver cop walking his beat saw her set a pie out to cool and asked if it was for him," Fritz said. " 'Sure is,' she says, and hits him with it." He chuckled. "That girl is crazy."

They alighted in a part of town Frank didn't recognize. There were fewer streetlamps here, and off the main street the lanes were dark and narrow. Frank felt they were being watched, especially as they separated from the herd of nighttime revelers, but when he glanced back he saw no one. A clock hanging in a pawnshop read nearly eleven. Fritz navigated by the light of a half-moon and the eerie glow from the stockyards, until Frank finally asked about the parcel. Fritz shrugged and said Dan had asked for help. That's all he knew, he added, and kept walking.

They came to a sign that read 19th Street and followed it down an even darker street where crowded houses lined one side. On the other side was a gully and, beyond that, what looked like a school. Past the school lay the tangled ravines of the Missouri River bottoms and then a long bend in the river. It was desolate and spooky; if Frank held his breath he thought he could hear the river. When someone stepped from the shadows, he must have jumped ten feet.

"Relax," Jack said. "It's me."

"Dan with you?" Fritz asked.

"He's gone ahead already," Jack said.

"See anything?"

"Not really," Jack answered. "Kids in some windows, that's all."

Frank was spooked already, but listening to these two gave him his first real twinge of fear. "What's all this about?" he demanded. Both men told him to keep his voice down.

"You're in this now too," Fritz hissed, "so don't mess it up."

Frank turned to Jack and asked what they'd done. His friend's face was still in shadows, and he couldn't see his eyes.

"Just do this for us," Jack answered, "Then that's it, I promise.

You can go back to Waco with maybe a little extra for Alice. You won't have to play my big brother no more."

It *was* the train robbery, Frank realized, just as he'd feared! He thought of running, but his feet wouldn't budge. His panic must have shown. "Get a grip on yourself," Fritz hissed.

"C'mon, Frank, you've toughed out worse than this," Jack added. "Nothing will happen if you keep your head." Frank took a deep breath and peered around. Jack was right—no one seemed to have noticed them. If he kept his calm it would soon be over. Fritz told Jack to stay put and watch for anything suspicious while the two of them checked ahead. They walked down 19th Street, keeping to the shadows.

"If we get stopped, we don't know each other," Fritz warned. "Give a false name and say we met an hour earlier and arranged to meet some girls."

They came to a spot where, on the opposite bank, a telegraph pole had lost its mooring and fallen headfirst into the gully. Fritz stepped close to the edge.

"You down there?" he whispered.

Dan's voice rose from the gully. "It's me."

"Find anything?"

"Not yet. Go down the street to the bridge and come back on the other side. Sing out if you see anyone."

Frank glanced back at Jack, but he couldn't see him in the gloom. There were also others he didn't see. Officers from the South Omaha Police Department were scattered through the neighborhood, keeping to the shadows too. Captain Nels Turnquist was in charge. Turnquist was a stout Swedish policeman, partial to his beef and beer. His waxed walrus mustache drooped below his lip, sometimes muffling his words. From his hiding place in the shadows of Brown Park School, he'd seen the two men walk out of the darkness and pause on the other side of the gully. He sighed as they walked on. This was a once-in-a-lifetime case for Turnquist; he didn't want to ruin it by jumping the gun. He signaled patience to the three officers with him: Patrolmen Dan Mawhinney and P. H. Shields and Detective Henry Elsfelder. Ever since the boys' discovery of the masks and revolvers earlier that same day, other officers had lurked in surrounding streets, but Turnquist warned them not to get too close. The last thing he wanted was for the robbers to sense a trap and run.

He had some unconventional backup, too. Stationed as lookouts in the windows of the house closest to the gully were ten-year-old Johnnie Krowlik, the discoverer of the robbers' cache, and five of his pals from school. The house, belonging to sheep butcher John Kurdna, had a bird's-eye view of 19th Street. The Pinkertons and the Union Pacific had objected to this part of the trap; trusting the case to a bunch of immigrant street urchins seemed the height of folly. Maybe so, but Turnquist also knew South Omaha. No one knew these streets better than the kids who lived there. While an over-zealous officer might accidentally spring the trap when some late-night drunk staggered close to the gully, the local brats would know who belonged to the landscape and who was a stranger. Let the robbers spot a bull and they'd be off in the instant. But who'd suspect a bunch of boys?

Turnquist's instincts had already proven true. When the boys saw the first stranger drop into the gully farther up the street, they phoned the station house, resulting in a quick tightening of the net. They called again when a tall stranger and a younger companion paused almost beneath their windows. They could barely see the man moving in the gully, and Kurdna wanted to throw a rock and knock him out. Just as Kurdna took aim, one boy grabbed his arm, and then the whole pack attached to him like lampreys. "Don't do it, Mr. Kurdna," they begged. "If you miss, you'll spoil it." They didn't let Kurdna go until he released the stone.

By now it was 11 P.M., and in the gully beneath John Kurdna's windows Dan Downer was greatly confused. The night was quiet, no bulls, everything going as planned. So where were the guns? He dug through the rubbish at the foot of the pole but found nothing. Fritz arrived, nearly giving him a heart attack, and he sent him down the street and up the other side. He dug through the rubbish again. Could he have forgotten where he put them? He moved down the gully a few yards to where some old mattresses were dumped and scratched there. Nothing. He was getting worried. He'd seen kids bowling through the neighborhood when he checked earlier in the week. Had they found the cache? Shaken, he climbed from the gully and walked toward the school. He'd meet Fritz when he came back and they'd get the hell out of this place.

A policeman with a mustache as thick as a horsehair brush stepped from the shadows and asked, "What are you doing here?"

Downer's heart skipped again, but he tried to play it cool. He laughed and said he'd been out for a good time, then lowered his voice and said confidentially that he'd just taken a lady home. "Point out the house," Turnquist demanded. When Downer hesitated, the detective drew his gun and placed him under arrest. He told Mawhinney to escort the suspect to the station. On the way, they stopped at a corner bar for a couple of drinks and Downer paid the tab.

Meanwhile, Fritz and Frank walked down 19th to U Street, unaware of events at the school. Fritz pulled a clasp watch from his pocket and checked the time: eleven-fifteen. They crossed the gully at a small stone bridge and strolled back on the other side. Nothing looked out of place. Frank began breathing normally again. In a couple of minutes he saw a building and above the door a sign: BROWN PARK SCHOOL. He looked toward the gully and saw where the telegraph pole plunged out of sight. Beyond that was a house with darkened windows. "Dan should be finished by now," Fritz muttered. As soon as he said it, a fat policeman with a gun stepped from the shadows.

Frank whipped around and saw two more men, one in uniform, the other in plainclothes, emerge from the corner of the building behind him. They, too, pointed guns. "Put up your hands and don't make a move or I'll kill you," Turnquist snapped.

"Tell me what you're doing here."

"We have a date with a couple of girls," Fritz replied. Frank thought how strangely calm Fritz sounded, as if he'd been through this before.

"No girls here," Turnquist answered. "You're under arrest."

"We ain't done nothing!" Torgensen cried. Even as he said it there was a shout, and Frank looked down the street to see Jack bolt from the shadows and run down the steep embankment, heading for the river bottoms. A whistle shrilled. "Stop or we'll shoot!" a voice cried. More policemen appeared and started running, but Jack had the lead. A bunch of heads craned from the windows of the house immediately across the gully. One figure waved at Frank as the cuffs clamped upon his wrists. They looked like boys, no doubt dreaming of adventure. Like he had long ago.

BY 1909, NEWSPAPER readers across the country were used to seeing crime reports in which suspects were put "into the sweatbox" and "sweated" by police to extract confessions. The term was as old as the Civil War. The original sweatbox was a cramped interrogation cell, heated by a fire of old bones and rubber until the stench and temperature were so overpowering that enemy prisoners confessed to nearly anything to get out. After the war, police departments adopted the practice, and by the 1880s and 1890s "sweating" and the "third degree" both meant long, harsh, and often brutal questioning by John Law. By 1900, the public, grown queasy by muckrakers' accounts of the routine abuse of power, took a dim view of legal torture, at least the more blatant kinds. Sometimes the outrage was so strident that newspapers or even the police themselves felt moved to engage in early forms of PR. The *Idaho Statesman*, when reporting in 1905 that suspects in Frank Steunenberg's murder were "put in the sweatbox," felt compelled a day later to issue a clarification. The phrase had proved so inflammatory that many readers assumed it was "a place of torture . . . heated to an unbearable degree." The *Statesman* assured its readers that such techniques from a more barbarous past had been banished. The sweatbox, it said, was "any pleasant room, like the office of the chief of police or sheriff, and the 'sweating' is merely a process of close questioning" to determine guilt or innocence.

Yet the use of torture and coercion in extracting confessions was as old as the law itself, and it would take more than bad press to end a time-honored tradition. It was not until *The King v. Warickshall* in 1783 that an English court clearly expressed the importance of a confession in a trial: "A free and voluntary confession is deserving of the highest credit, because it is presumed to flow from the strongest sense of guilt, and therefore is admitted as proof of the crime." Confessions were important for convictions, but how freely were they given, and how were they obtained? Police practices in the interrogation room remained unregulated, unscrutinized, and virtually undocumented until the last half of the twentieth century, and only haphazardly then. In 1908, the Supreme Court put its imprimatur on legal torture when ruling in *Twining v. Jersey* that the Constitution did not protect against compulsory self-incrimination in state courts, sometimes with terrifying implications. For suspects in general, and black suspects in particular, this legally maintained the status quo. Beating and whippings were often authorized, or at least unofficially condoned, at all levels of law enforcement. In Beaufort, North Carolina, in 1914, for example, county authorities directed that the prison superintendent "keep in his possession a lash 18 inches long and more than two inches in diameter, [which] may be split three times one-half way from the end. No convict may be whipped more than once during two consecutive days, and none shall receive more than 25 lashes at more than one whipping." It was only in 1936, with *Brown v. Mississippi*, that the Supreme Court specifically outlawed torture when a deputy sheriff who'd presided over beatings conceded that a black suspect had been whipped, "but not too much for a Negro." That single admission seemed to outrage the Justices more than any other evidence, and they finally ruled legal torture unconstitutional.

White suspects were subject to fewer physical inducements but still tortured nonetheless, as shown in the 1946 *Ashcraft v. State of Tennessee*. That year, Mrs. Zelma Ashcraft was murdered in Shelby County, Tennessee. Nine days later, on a Saturday at 7 P.M., her husband was taken to a fifth-floor county jail room and held incommunicado without rest or sleep for thirty-six hours until 7 A.M. Monday. During that time, Ashcraft was subjected to a constant barrage of charges and questions. For twenty-eight hours he held out, denying any knowledge of the crime, but after 11 P.M. on Sunday he broke down, confessing that he knew who killed his wife, though still denying he murdered her. The alleged confession, neither written nor signed by Ashcraft himself, was used in court as evidence in his conviction.

This was the immediate future Frank faced as he and Torgensen were marched to the police station a few minutes behind Downer. Frank's hands were in cuffs, the officers' guns drawn. It was obvious from their comments that they'd already tried and sentenced him for robbing the train. A panic flew up and made him dizzy, but he told himself they had no real evidence and wrestled the fear back down. If he stuck to his story, they'd have to let him go.

At the station the police separated Frank and Fritz, took their measurements for the criminal files, and asked their names. When Fritz identified himself as Fred W. Derf, the detectives looked at each other and rolled their eyes—Fred backward and forward, huh?—but they entered the name anyway. A search revealed some crumpled bills in his pockets, which they kept as evidence. Frank identified himself as James Gordon; there was no money on him, nothing else incriminating, but he was the youngest of the three and police figured he'd be the easiest to break. They snapped his mug shot: bowler on his head, tie pulled to one side, a good-looking young man with worry in his eyes.

"Derf" and "Gordon" both said that they'd only met an hour earlier and had become acquainted after picking up two girls. They did not know the third man, who identified himself as "Woods." That man denied knowing them. The police led Frank to the sweatbox and locked the door, leaving him alone inside. This was a far cry from the *Idaho Statesman*'s "pleasant room": it was cramped, with no windows and thin walls and barely enough space for a table and chairs. From a nearby room he heard what sounded like Dan Downer's baritone. The bulls had been grilling him the longest, and Frank wondered how he fared.

Dan was having a rough time. He'd already made mistakes that would come back to haunt him; he tried to hide his worry beneath the old insouciance, but everything had happened so fast he'd been rattled. First the guns were missing from the gully, then Captain Turnquist popped up from nowhere. When the bulls first asked his identity, he'd said "Dan Downer," his real name. It was only as he was being marched off to the station that he realized his mistake, remembering that the cops, or at least the Pinkertons, would have his name on file. Maybe the officers hadn't heard what he said. When they asked his name again in the police station, he said "Donald W. Woods," but the look that passed between the officers told Dan they'd caught the lie. The detectives found some mutilated bills in his pocket, and he realized they might be traced. How could he be so sloppy? Everything was going wrong.

The essence of the sweatbox was control. Captain Turnquist had control of the situation now, but he wasn't sure how long that would last once the Union Pacific and the Pinks moved in. There was no way to stop them if it came down to turf: it didn't take a genius to know who ran Omaha. He also didn't know exactly what he had. He knew in his gut that Woods, or Downer, or whoever, was guilty, but the man seemed hard to rattle. The tall man named Derf had the sick look of a dope fiend and looked mean enough to spit in his eye and enjoy it, but the kid seemed new to the sweatbox and therefore most vulnerable. They'd work on all three, but they'd focus on the kid.

Turnquist and a detective entered Frank's room, locking the door behind them. The kid sat on the other side of the table, farthest from the door. They kept at him all night. What was he doing near the gully? Who was the fourth guy who escaped? Where did he live and what was his real name? The kid's story never changed. They'd gone to meet some girls, he said. He'd just met Derf and didn't know the other fellow. He had nothing to do with the Mud Cut Robbery. When he grew angry at being held, the detectives grew angrier. When he pleaded ignorance, they acted certain of his guilt. They said the others had confessed and named him as an accomplice, adding, "Save yourself, tell the truth, maybe we can cut a deal." All night long they kept it up, working in tandem and trading off with others so only the kid grew exhausted, not them. They watched for that moment before every man confessed when his entire body cried defeat: the back and shoulders slumped, jaw slackened, eyes glazed. Some people got dizzy and put their head on the table. Others got sick. That's when the detectives would pounce. "Quit the lying and the hiding, you'll only feel better when you tell us," they would croon, moving in for the kill.

But by morning nothing had changed. The kid pleaded, yelled, cried, and argued, but never once changed his tale. He was innocent of the robbery, that was God's truth, why couldn't they believe him? he said. If the others said different, they were the liars, not him. The doubt doubled back on the police. Maybe the kid *was* innocent, a couple of detectives said.

Turnquist didn't buy it, but he was frustrated as hell. Another few hours of this and the Pinkertons would take the case away from him. Goddamn if he'd let those cocksure bastards take his prize. But the two older suspects hadn't broken either, and it's uncertain today how far their interrogations had gone. A newspaper photo shows Torgensen, limp and greasy as if from a long night under the lights. Downer's eyes were swollen, even as he smiled. It could just be exhaustion, or maybe he'd been knocked around.

The break came the next morning, on Friday, May 28, a series of breaks that built to a flood. The first came from the Brown Park School. With all the excitement about the arrests, the janitor, A. R. Bentz, recalled that on the Monday after the robbery he'd found a window unlocked and signs that the building had been entered. Bentz had looked around that Monday, but since nothing had seemed taken or disturbed, he figured it was kids. But now, with the arrests, he

renewed his search, even into the attic, gained only by a ladder lowered by rope and pulley. That was where Bentz struck gold. In a
corner he found the missing mail sacks and three dark raincoats described by the robbery victims. The sacks had been cut open and the
mail rifled through. The robbers had taken everything of value, leaving only such things as an embroidered nightgown, some women's
underwear, and a package containing a dozen glass eyes. But a closer
look by postal inspectors revealed one other thing—a letter written
by one Roy A. Mason, assistant cashier of the First National Bank
of Kimmerer, Wyoming, transmitting for redemption certain mutilated bills, listed by letter and serial number, to the National Park
Bank of New York City. Three of the bills had been found on Fred
Derf, and one on Woods.

Downer was the first to cave in. Turnquist let him read the assistant
cashier's note, then spread out the mutilated bill taken from his
pocket with its matching serial number. The old ironic smile creased
Downer's face, like this was just a game and he'd lost, that's all.
Turnquist asked again about his room and was surprised when
Downer shrugged and said 324 North 15th Street in Omaha. Derf
stayed tight-lipped, even in the face of the cashier's note and money,
only admitting that his real name was Torgensen. Of the three, only
the youngster—the one they'd all thought would cave in first—
refused to say anything. As that day's editions of the *Omaha
World-Herald* and *Omaha Daily News* ran the first grainy photos of
the suspects, detectives descended on Downer's rooms.

They found a treasure trove. They took two leather grips, one of
which Downer identified as his. Inside they found a pair of greasy
overalls similar to those worn by the bandits, and a linen collar
marked F. GRIGWARE. Most important, they found what would forever be called "the automobile photograph": the portrait of Frank,
Lillian, and the others seated behind a pasteboard auto in the Denver photography studio. The photo seemed to fit the police's theory
that the gang used an automobile in their escape. The Union Pacific
and the Pinkertons immediately circulated copies in hopes of identifying the three men they held and of locating the woman and the
fourth man.

That Friday evening, the combined law enforcement agencies held
the modern equivalent of a press conference as rumors of the arrests
began to fly. Police said they had not yet charged the three with the

Mud Cut Robbery, but evidence was accumulating. They passed to reporters copies of the automobile photograph, which they said proved the three were associates, as well as copies of their mug shots. When they'd test-fired the guns found in the gully, they found that one had a defective firing pin, leaving a telltale indentation on the shell—the same mark found on shells at the robbery scene. Although they could not directly link the three to the guns or to the mail sacks, witnesses had come forward who said they'd seen the men around the school in the days after the robbery. They failed to mention that the witnesses invariably asked about the reward.

Saturday, May 29, opened with stories of growing certainty of their guilt. "They are now entirely at the mercy of Uncle Sam," said the *Omaha World-Herald*. The "circumstantial chain" against them was growing stronger, said the *Omaha Daily News*. Woods and Torgensen had money in their pockets from the robbery; the third, still identified as Gordon, was a suspect because he was caught with the other two. They all "looked guilty," and Gordon and Torgensen had "shifty eyes." One officer thought Torgensen was a "dope fiend," a belief bolstered by the observation that he had a "hacking cough and expectorates frequently," signs that also indicate tuberculosis. Gordon's personal habits, on the other hand, astonished police. He apparently did not smoke, "which is uncommon in most criminals," and was not considered a dope fiend. Though a couple of detectives expressed doubts about his guilt, they remained an unnamed minority.

On Sunday, May 30, Frank was led from his cell to the sweatbox, where Captain Turnquist waited with Bill Canada, the Union Pacific man. They had bad news, Turnquist said, then smiled, which could only mean bad news for him. His landlady at 518 South 16th Street, a Mrs. Sinhold, had seen his photo in the paper and identified him as Frank Grigware. Turnquist carefully watched Frank's face and added, "There was a collar with the same name in Woods's grip." He let the news sink in. "Who was your roommate, Frank?" he asked. "Who was the young guy standing in the back with you in the automobile photograph? You two look so much alike you could be brothers. Did your brother run down the embankment and get away?"

Frank laid his head on the table. "I don't know him," he mumbled bitterly. "I am innocent of the robbery." The captain unhooked the top button of his tunic in preparation for another long session in the sweatbox. *Ask Jack Golden,* Frank thought, his mind swirling. Just one last favor, Jack had begged, then we'll be set.

He was set, all right. *Jack, goddamn you,* Frank thought. *Where will you go? Who will take care of you now?*

THE NIGHT SPENT in the Missouri River bottoms was the worst Jack had ever spent alone. Every rustle in the underbrush meant encircling policemen, every tug on his clothing by a branch was a collar by a detective. He'd watched in disbelief as Fritz and Frank paused before the Brown Park School and police flowed from the shadows like wraiths; even more bulls materialized as Jack finally realized they'd stepped into a well planned and executed trap. He tried to stay calm, thinking at least he could follow at a distance and see where they were taken, but when the dark figures doubled and tripled in number, drawing closer to his observation post, he panicked and ran. "Stop or we'll shoot!" someone yelled behind him, but he lit off down the embankment and dove into the underbrush like a scared deer.

It was a mystery to him how, in his panic, he'd found his way back to their rooming house, but by the early hours of Friday, May 28, he crept unseen up the stairs of Mrs. Sinhold's place and unlocked the door to his room. He latched the door behind him and looked around. Nothing had been touched: Frank had held out so far. Outside, in the street, Jack could hear the newsboys yelling the story of the arrest at the top of their lungs. His mind went blank with apprehension. How much longer before the police released Frank's picture and someone made the connection and told them this address? Maybe it had already happened and the bulls were on their way. Jack threw everything he owned into his two grips, then turned to look at Frank's things. He remembered the time they'd been picked up on the watch complaint in Colorado: Frank said then that the last thing he wanted was for his mother to learn he'd spent the night in jail. Jack hoped he'd been smart enough to once again give a false name. He dug through Frank's possessions, destroying everything that might help with his identification or link him to Spokane. He hesitated at Alice's photo, then tore that up also and flushed the shreds down the hall toilet bowl. He left in the closet a hat and coat stitched with a Kansas City tailor's mark, hoping to lead detectives away from the Inland Empire, then grabbed his own suitcases and crept down the back stairs. As the city began to wake, he hurried the couple of blocks down back alleys to Bill Matthews's rooms.

Bill sounded worried when Jack knocked on the door. "Anybody see you?" he asked, then hustled him inside. Jack noticed a copy of the morning paper spread at the foot of the bed. He felt safer in Bill's presence: Matthews was good friends with Jack's older brothers, more like an older brother himself. Anybody else would have kicked him out, but not Bill. Matthews asked what the hell had happened and Jack told him; they hadn't seen anyone, he said. "It says in the paper some school kids found the guns around noon yesterday," Matthews answered. "The cops probably were in hiding long before you got there."

"What're we going to do?"

Matthews thought a minute in his slow, deliberate way. Though Dan and Fritz said he was one of the most dangerous men they'd ever met, Jack had never seen him in a rage. He coldly and calmly thought things out; maybe that was where the danger lay. "We have to get out of town, that's for certain," he finally said. "But not together. Stay away from your old rooming house. Lay low and spend the night here."

For the rest of that day—as the janitor found the mail sacks in the school attic, as detectives searched Downer's rooms and discovered the automobile photo, as the combined agencies held their first press conference—Jack remained in Matthews's rooms, wondering where to go. He couldn't stay with Bill; the older man wouldn't tolerate it, and besides, he'd eventually be seen. He couldn't go back to Spokane; the bulls no doubt had already mailed out Dan and Fritz's photos across the West, and sooner or later someone would make the connection. The only other friend he had in the world was Lillian. She'd be comforting when he needed it most. He'd stay with her while figuring out his next move.

Early on Saturday, May 29, Jack fled the city, arranging with Bill to send his luggage ahead under the name J. C. Kelley. He walked several miles to a small train station in the country and caught a Union Pacific local to Lincoln. He bought an Omaha paper from the porter: Staring up from the page were the photos of Frank, Dan, and Fritz, as well as the novelty photograph they'd taken with Lillian. His heart seemed to stop as he glanced around the Pullman coach and saw other travelers studying the same photo. He slouched in his seat, hoping to shrink down to nothingness; he brought the paper close to his face and stared at the page again. He'd hated the idea of a photo even then, but Lillian, Dan, and Fritz thought it would be fun. He loathed the way Lillian squeezed intimately between Dan and Fritz, while he was relegated to the back, over her left shoulder. More than all his illusions and all her sweet words, this photograph spoke the truth of his position in the group—the odd man out, assigned to the back row. While the smirk on his face seemed confident and knowing, in truth he knew little at all. On the other side of Lillian, behind Dan, stood Frank, a peaceful look on his face, a distant expression, divorced from the competition for Lillian. His mind was probably a few hundred miles away in Waco. How much, even then, did Frank suspect about the gang? Dan had said Frank seemed suspicious in Colorado Springs; Dan had talked around the subject of their real line of work, but he'd never actually told Frank the truth. Dan wanted Jack to be the one to tell him, and to do it when they were alone. That way, if Frank wanted out, he could simply pick up and leave, and it would seem like a rift between friends. So many times after that Frank had seemed on the verge of asking, especially after his return from Waco. During their trip to Little Rock and Memphis, Frank had begged Jack to come back to Texas with him, and though he'd expressed his doubts about the Spokane boys, he never came right out and asked if they were train robbers. Even then, Jack realized, he must have guessed the truth but didn't really want to know it. Knowing would have forced him to make a decision and take sides.

Frank had never been able to make that choice, Jack thought; his old friend wasn't built that way. All along, from Jack's frostbite in the mountains to his contracting tuberculosis, Frank had been there for him, nursing him through the brush with death, convincing him to go see Lillian when the blues had grown bad. He owed his life to Frank, who'd been a better brother than his own flesh and blood, and how had he repaid him? By keeping him from Alice. By landing him in jail and running away.

He remembered their conversation in the Uneeda Restaurant more than a week ago. He'd asked Frank if he really cared for Alice, and his old friend's longing was so apparent that it choked him up a little and he had to look out the window. *Things will get better, Frank*, he had promised. *Things will turn out for the best.* Good God, he thought, unable to turn off the thoughts, consumed with self-revulsion. Not only had he led the lamb to slaughter, he'd used the knife himself.

Jack transferred in Lincoln to a Denver express, and his train slipped beneath the WELCOME arch the next morning, Sunday, May 30, at 7:30 A.M. Though he'd gotten little sleep, he'd figured out his moves. He'd find Lillian and destroy all remaining evidence of the gang's association, then go with her into hiding. Before that, however, he had to do the right thing by his friend. He stopped at the station's Western Union office and wired Jim Grigware. FRANK NEEDS HELP, he said, and asked for money for Frank's defense. He signed the telegram FRANK TORGENSEN, a touch he must have realized was confusing and erratic, for he immediately followed up the wire with an equally confusing letter:

Denver, Col., May 30

Jim:

I wired you today to send $150 to Frank; now he is grabbed under another name and they don't know him, or I don't suppose they ever will. So you write to me. Never write to him under any circumstances. It is nothing more than a strong suspicion yet; so don't worry or mention this to your people or any one else. He will come out O.K. in the long run. They're trying to locate me. Will wire the $150 to him so he can get a lawyer. For Christ's sake don't tell anyone, it will only make it hard for him and be sure and destroy all the letters you get from me. You will have to raise $500. What I want is to get him out of the affair as soon as possible. He is liable to be held 60 days. They will never know his right name. Address me, Denver, Col., General Delivery, J. C. Kelley. Burn this up.

Jack

He posted the letter at the station and went to find Lillian.

Many people were interested in Lillian Stevenson that day. Her whims and impulses singled her out from the crowd. As Jack fled Omaha that Saturday, T. R. Porter, a reporter with the *Omaha World-Herald*, stared at the automobile photo and tried to guess its secrets. By 1909, photography was taken for granted by most Americans:

Daguerreotype and wet-plate photography were both introduced in 1839, while Mathew Brady's photographs brought the horrors of the Civil War into the parlor. The stern family photographs associated with the nineteenth century were almost as old as the medium itself, while the 1900 introduction of Kodak's dollar Brownie box camera single-handedly created the new century's biggest hobby. Yet few still understood the science of the image and automatically assumed the "truth" of what they saw. Thus with the automobile photo: The police saw the five friends riding in a "car" and used this as proof that an auto had been used in the Mud Cut Robbery, a mistake that echoes down to contemporary tellings. Yet the journalist, a hobbyist himself, knew that truth could be staged. Porter had never seen an auto with numbers painted across the headlights; he reasoned instead that it was a pasteboard fake kept in some studio for group sittings. He also recognized the background as the Garden of the Gods. This has to be a studio portrait, he told his editors, probably made at or near the Colorado attraction. The *World-Herald* telegraphed its correspondents in Colorado Springs, Denver, and as far south as Pueblo, Colorado, instructing them to check all local studios for the background and prop automobile. Within an hour, the Denver correspondent wired back. He'd found both in the United Photo Stores Company downtown. What should he do?

A sense of unreality, or perhaps enhanced reality, can now be glimpsed. Once again, as with the photo's "truth," technology outstripped understanding; while the telegraph was taken for granted, the fact that the Omaha editors were holding a conversation with their Denver correspondent, 540 miles distant, struck them as immensely strange. Just like the police and Pinkertons, the *World-Herald* was engaged in its own manhunt, and the tools of the chase gave some of them chills. No one could run fast enough in this modern age to escape the state. Even in the West, vast as they'd all grown up to see it, there was no place to hide. The editors wired the photo's description to their correspondent and in minutes he wired back that he'd found the negative. Copies were struck off and given to the Denver police. The chief of police called an all-hands meeting and asked the assembled officers and detectives whether any of them had ever seen these men.

None of them had. But one patrolman, an Officer Barry, remembered the woman. He said her name was Lillian Stevenson, and he wouldn't be forgetting her soon.

Barry's introduction to Lillian had occurred six weeks earlier, around early to mid-April. Lillian apparently moved from the Charleston Hotel to the Welton Rooming House at 18th and Welton streets soon after the departure of the Spokane gang. It was a fine spring day, the officer recalled, and he was walking his beat when he saw a woman place some fresh-baked pies on a ledge to cool. "My, your pies look good, madam," he quoted himself as saying. "Now, you know, I wouldn't mind having one of them." The quid pro quo was an old one, especially among "working girls": Be nice to the officer and he will be nice to you. Instead she cried, "All right, take it," and flung a pie in his face. After his initial shock, Barry arrested her for assault, but the magistrate, trying to keep from laughing, let her off with a warning. "I'd recognize that woman anywhere," Barry said.

So it was that detectives Coleman Bell and P. J. Carr were watching Lillian's apartment when Jack arrived in town. They'd watched without luck through Saturday night; their reports to the chief through most of Sunday were more of the same. The chief was growing testy. He was already bombarded with queries from U.S. postal inspectors, Union Pacific agents, and the Pinkertons. The last were especially demanding. There was no escaping them in Denver; the city was the Agency's western hub. All decisions affecting its ninety detectives and untold number of informants from Laredo to Seattle issued from its offices in Denver's Opera House block, the same offices Frank had glimpsed while doing the town with his friends. All tips and leads were fed into the meticulously indexed files of the western headquarters, then mailed in duplicate to World HQ in Chicago. The Pinkertons and the Union Pacific wanted arrests so badly they could taste them. Yet by midafternoon Sunday the only news that Bell and Carr could report was that the woman had taken a number of calls over the hall telephone.

Although telephone wiretaps were first used in 1895 in New York City, their widespread use remained uncommon throughout the nation until 1917, when the federal government set up a huge switchboard in New York's Custom House near the Battery to tap the lines of hundreds of aliens. In 1909, most local law enforcement agencies still didn't include wiretapping in their crime-fighting arsenal. If the Denver police had tapped the phone outside Lillian's room, they would have heard Jack calling from the Charleston. The boys had gotten into trouble, he said. Had she been contacted by police? Did she think she was being watched? When she answered no, Jack said he'd be over soon.

He arrived between four and five o'clock. The two detectives watching from across the street saw a young man enter the Welton but did not recognize him from the automobile photo and could not know he went straight to Lillian's room. He was nervous and asked for copies of the group portrait, which she kept in a valise along with all their letters, including three he'd written. All of this will have to be destroyed, he said. She listened as he rambled, realizing that all the fears she'd left behind in Walla Walla had found her again in Denver. She watched as he shredded the photos and letters, then flushed them down the toilet. He asked if there was anything else and she remembered the hat she'd worn in the portrait; she took it from its hatbox in the closet and watched sadly as Jack tore apart the black ostrich plume and untied the pretty ribbons. Anything else they can link to us? Jack asked. Nothing more, she said.

However, she forgot one thing, stored beneath the linen underwear in another drawer: a 1908 photo taken in Spokane. It too was an automobile photo, but this time of the real thing, parked beside the curb in the Inland Empire's downtown. Bob Splain, Downer's partner in horse theft and safecracking, sat behind the wheel, while Alice Evans sat beside him. Jack sat in the back behind Splain, with Lillian nestled by his side. All four smiled for the camera, not a care in the world.

The next two days were nerve-racking for Jack. He contacted a criminal lawyer in Denver, who gave him the name of a colleague in Omaha and advised him to stay silent should police pick him up for questioning. He received an answer from Jim Grigware, saying that all he could send at the moment was $90, but he was coming to Denver for a fuller story. He told Lillian that once he got the $90, he'd hand it to her and she was to mail it to the Omaha lawyer for Frank's defense. There was so much to do, yet Jack dreaded leaving his room for meals or for business. Every moment seemed like his last, every passing stranger a curious detective.

Finally he needed the kind of comfort that only Lillian could give.

He phoned her to come over, but only after dark. Around midnight on Tuesday, June 1, the two increasingly bored and frustrated detectives got a start when a hack pulled in front of the Welton Rooming House and Lillian piled in. They followed at a distance and watched as she got out at the Charleston Hotel. They watched through the window as she talked to the night clerk; they waited until she boarded the elevator, then charged through the doors and showed the startled clerk their shields. She'd asked about a guest and the clerk gave them the room. They waited until it was evident she was not leaving for the night; best to get them with their pants down, literally. That way there'd be less chance of trouble, plus a little bit of payback for the long hours they'd put in. About 2 A.M. they broke through Jack's door, guns drawn, but there proved to be little fear of concealed weapons since the two lay buck naked in bed.

Now the sweatbox opened its doors for Jack and Lillian. It didn't take long for Lillian to fold. The Denver detectives and their chief showed her the copy of the pasteboard-automobile photo, as well as souvenirs from their search of her apartment: the ostrich-plume hat, stripped of its finery; the Spokane photo of Jack, Alice, Bob Splain, and her, all seated in a car. She started to cry. It was obvious she was part of the gang, the police chief said. The only way to save herself was to turn state's evidence against her friends. He said that a considerable amount of jewelry had been taken from the mail sacks in Omaha—a bluff, but one that Lillian could not dispute. They'd figured out from the date of the automobile photo that her friends had been in Denver at the time of the Denver & Rio Grande robbery, and jewelry had been stolen in that holdup too. The police chief watched her closely as he said that if she'd been given any of that jewelry, she'd go to federal prison for being an accessory to robbery of the U.S. mails. She started sobbing and said she had no part in either robbery. She'd tell all, she said.

As well she did. Lillian told of her move from Walla Walla to Denver with Jack, Alice, and the man they knew as James Gordon, whose real name was Frank Grigware. Who is this Grigware fellow? the police chief asked, holding up the automobile photo. She pointed him out, standing behind her and Dan. Where is this Alice? added the chief. She moved to Waco, Lillian said. Alice and Frank had fallen in love. She told police of the good times they'd all had together in Denver and Colorado Springs, and of the letters she'd gotten from everyone except Frank from Hot Springs, Kansas City, and Omaha. She said she knew nothing of their plans to rob the Overland Limited, yet on the morning after the holdup, she read the account of the robbery in the Denver paper and thought to herself that her friends were responsible. Soon afterward, Jack showed up acting more scared than she'd ever seen him. She did not ask him questions about where he had been or what he had been doing, because knowing the truth would make her an accessory. But the moment he started destroying the old photographs and letters that tied them together, "I knew then it was all up with the boys," she said.

There was a pause, then the chief asked whether she was willing to tell this to a jury. Lillian hesitated. One hopes she had a pang of conscience, though it's more likely that she saw a chance to make a deal. She told the chief that her father was one of the oldest and most respected citizens in Walla Walla. If it got out that she was mixed up with train robbers, it would shame her family. The chief quietly answered that her only chance, and the only chance for her family, was if she aided prosecutors. He paused to let the point sink in. She was being given a choice, and she knew it: turn against her friends or be thrown to the wolves. "Will you help us?" the chief repeated.

"I will," she said.

Jack was proving a harder nut to crack. To begin with, he gave his last name as Shelton, and the fact that Lillian still knew him as Jack Sherman placed another level of confusion between the police and his real identity. A search after his arrest revealed $70 in his pockets and another $30 sewn into the lining of his coat. Denver postal inspectors said that a couple of the bills bore the same serial numbers as those taken in the holdup. The police asked about his fancy clothes. They asked where he'd bought his new tan shoes, made by the Tilt Shoe Company, but Jack refused to say. His soft brown hat was barely worn; his coat was made of good material, a dark blue-gray with a fine brown stripe, from which the maker's name had been removed. The same with his linen: all laundry marks and names removed. Why would he do such a thing unless he feared pursuit? Jack refused to say. He said he was twenty years old, but the police thought he was at least two years older. The man standing beside him in the automobile photo—was that his brother? Jack said he didn't know him. Where was he born? Jack refused to say.

On Wednesday, June 2, Jack had two visitors. The first was Spokane's postal inspector, Charles Riddiford, who'd grown up with Jack's brothers and had known Jack for years. He'd recognized Jack at once when he'd seen the automobile photo; when Riddiford heard that Jack had been arrested in Denver, he caught the fastest train from Spokane. Riddiford told the police Jack's real name, then was led to the cell of the boy he'd known so many years. "What have you done?" Riddiford asked, but Jack still denied having anything to do with the holdup. If he was taken back to Omaha, he could prove an alibi, he said.

The second visitor was the superintendent of the Denver Pinkerton office, only identified in Pinkerton reports as "Supt. E. E. P." He brought with him photographs of "Woods," Torgensen, and "Gordon," sent from the branch office in Omaha. When the police chief showed Jack the photos of "Woods" and Torgensen, "he said he did not know them," the superintendent wrote in his report. "But when the chief handed him the picture of Gordon, he looked at it for fully a minute and his eyes took on a peculiar look and his lips quivered perceptibly." The Pinkerton superintendent and the chief both thought this was the break they'd sought, but Jack regained his composure. "He maintained that he did not know him, but the exhibiting of the pictures . . . upset him materially."

The Pinkerton superintendent signed off on his report with one last observation: "I wish to say that the man Sheldon (sic) bears a striking resemblance to the man Gordon under arrest in Omaha, and could be taken for brothers." It was a confusion that rose throughout the investigation and into the trial, and eventually doomed both friends. No one got a clear look at the bandits on the night of the robbery, unless perhaps it was the upper face and eyes of the two in the locomotive. Neither Jack nor Frank was clearly seen during the heist, but each would be picked out by witnesses, based on bearing, stature, and the fact that two of the robbers were thought to be young. A witness positive that Frank was one of the bandits would change his identification when he saw a picture of Jack, and vice versa with a second witness, while others simply said they could not tell the difference between the two. Even the investigators were uncertain. Each man protested his innocence, and although it seemed unlikely that all were telling the truth, the investigators did admit to one another that perhaps not all of them were guilty. Some thought Frank was innocent due to his vehement protests and the fact that, of the four in the photo, he alone had no stolen money on him or any evidence of newly purchased clothes. If he was a robber, he was the poorest of the bunch. Others thought Jack innocent, because he seemed younger and more vulnerable.

In the end they decided to charge everyone and let God and the jury decide.

But the statements of Lillian and the superintendent both revealed something that did not come out in trial. Jack was stricken with guilt over what happened to Frank. He tried raising money for his friend's defense and failed, in the process succeeding only in drawing Jim Grigware into a web of official and legal suspicion that dogged him for the rest of his life. Jack's composure nearly broke when staring at Frank's picture, yet to admit what he knew of his friend's innocence would only reveal his own guilt. During the trial Jack tried one more time to save him, but failed. He would always live with the burden of what he could have done that June 2nd in the Denver police station—and what he failed to do.

ON THURSDAY, JUNE 3, the Pinkertons moved in on the interrogation of Jack.

The day started normally for him, at least by the standards of the last few days. Jack was brought from his cell to the chief's office for several hours of grilling. This was usually conducted by the chief himself and detectives Bell and Carr, but today's audience was a little larger. The Pinkerton superintendent and the Spokane postal inspector were in attendance, as well as two new faces—postal inspectors from Denver and Omaha. The two newcomers started the questions and Jack demanded their identities. They said they were Post Office inspectors, and he demanded to see their commissions. They pulled them out and he looked at them closely. "This is all right," he finally said.

The questions began with information they'd learned from Lillian. When they mentioned his letters to her from Omaha, his face grew hard. "Those were personal letters," he said. He acknowledged leaving Omaha on Saturday and arriving in Denver on Sunday. "Why did you leave?" asked the Pinkerton superintendent.

"On account of the large reward that was being offered. I was afraid of being jobbed."

"If you were innocent, why were you afraid of the large reward?"

"People tell lies for that kind of money," Jack said.

"If you were innocent, couldn't you prove it?" the Denver inspector asked.

"People were already saying my friends were guilty. Just by me knowing them, they'd say the same of me." The Pinkerton man paid closer attention. This was an about-face from yesterday, a tacit admission that Jack knew the three suspects in Omaha. Earlier—even in the face of the automobile photo—he insisted he'd never seen them before.

"Why would anyone offer a reward for you if you are innocent?" repeated the postal inspector, assuming the role of good friend.

"I don't know, but people do strange things at times."

The chief, never known for his tact or patience, suddenly exploded in frustration. This was nothing more than horseshit, he yelled. He leaned forward with his finger pointed in Jack's face and said he didn't believe a word. He said point blank that things would go badly for Jack if he didn't tell the truth about the robbery.

Jack leaned toward the chief and answered that he knew nothing about the damned train robbery and did not know why he was under arrest, but was ready at any time to go back to Omaha with or without extradition papers and prove his innocence. He'd tell his story at his trial, thanks, because anything he said here would just get twisted, like his attorney in Denver had said. The chief sputtered like a wet fuse. The Pinkerton man laid a calming hand upon the chief's forearm and asked Jack, "Who is this attorney whose advice you mention? Maybe we should talk to him." The kid wouldn't answer that either, because, he said, they'd use that against him too. The Pinkerton man smiled and didn't believe a word of it, positive finally that they had the right man. But the kid had grit, and he liked him for it. He might be staring a life sentence in the face, but at least he'd go down fighting.

The Pinkerton superintendent returned to his office and reported what he'd seen. That afternoon, the agency's big guns arrived at the station to have a tête-à-tête with the police chief. On one side of the desk sat William Pinkerton, "principal" of the Pinkertons and son of the Founder. Pinkerton had arrived from Omaha on Wednesday after receiving word of Jack's arrest and planned to leave Denver on

Saturday. Next to him sat James P. McParland, manager of all operations between the Mississippi and the Pacific, agency veteran since 1872 . . . and at one time the most famous detective in all America.

By 1909, James McParland had grown old, but that did little to diminish his stature in the annals of crime fighting. A photo in an 1894 issue of *McClure's Magazine* showed a young McParland, large head set atop a wiry frame, staring icily at the camera from wire-rimmed glasses. His hair had already formed a widow's peak and his lip was hidden by a handlebar mustache, yet his was the kind of face that could instantly change from soft-spoken clerk to boisterous ruffian. By this dry afternoon in July 1909, the frame had grown thick around the middle, he drank too much "red licker," and he suffered from rheumatism. He'd walked with a limp ever since the amputation of one heel from frostbite, but he added style to that handicap by using a gold-handled cane. A devout Catholic, he lived comfortably with his wife, Mary, on his $45 a week salary. Visitors to their tidy bungalow on Denver's Columbine Street were announced by pet bulldogs.

Every day McParland limped into his office on Denver's Opera House block and without great fanfare decided who lived and who died in the Pinkerton sphere. Dashiell Hammett modeled the Old Man, the boss in his *Continental Op* series, after McParland, who by the time of Hammett's writing was still a legend in branch offices everywhere. The Old Man "smiled pleasantly when he sent us out to be crucified in suicidal jobs," Hammett wrote. "He was a gentle, polite, elderly person with no more warmth in him than a hangman's rope."

William Pinkerton's visit to the Denver police station was both an honor and a signal of how badly the agency wanted to wring a confession from a suspect in this highly circumstantial case. This final crusade to stamp out the last wave of train robbers was important to both the railroads and the Pinkertons. McParland's presence had another meaning—a warning to the chief that if he ruined their case against the train robbers, McParland, with the full weight of the Pinkertons behind him, could ruin the chief's career.

In many ways McParland *was* the Pinkertons, living proof of the agency's crime-fighting ascendancy during the Gilded Age and the Progressive Era. He was appointed western manager in 1889 and in that role shaped the agency's substance and style. In 1891, he helped solve the Sherlock Holmes–style mystery of Mrs. Josephine Barnaby, a Providence, Rhode Island, dowager who took a fatal drink of whiskey, laced with arsenic, while on a trip to Denver. The murderer was her doctor, whom McParland lured out west with a fake request to testify against another man. In 1892, McParland sent Charley Siringo on his undercover adventure to the Coeur d'Alenes; in 1899, he sent gunman Tom Horn to Wyoming to work for the cattlemen. Horn, who once said, "Killing is my specialty . . . I have a corner on the market," was paid $600 for every suspected cattle rustler he killed. He was paid, no questions asked, whenever a corpse was found with a rock placed beneath its head for a pillow. When the corpse was that of fourteen-year-old Willie Nickell, whose murder authorities couldn't stomach, Horn was tried and hanged in Cheyenne in November 1903. It was a tragedy for McParland, but his spirits rose again with the pursuit, breakup, and flight of the Wild Bunch. He missed the Old West, and the Mud Cut investigation made him feel young again. McParland was the first to admit that labor matters filled too much of his time these days. The Denver-based Western Federation of Miners battled mine owners in Leadville in 1894, in Telluride in 1901, and in Cripple Creek from 1894 to 1904. Harry Orchard dynamited the Cripple Creek train station in 1904, killing thirteen strikebreakers, and then assassinated former governor Frank Steunenberg in December 1905. Yet Harry Orchard would be McParland's triumph, for on January 22, 1906, it was the old detective who coaxed a confession from him.

The confession was a masterpiece of style and timing, admired by detectives throughout the world. Orchard had been placed in a cell on death row in the Idaho State Penitentiary, next to two convicted murderers awaiting execution. When he was escorted to the warden's office, a corpulent man wearing a tweed suit and vest walked through the door. James McParland was already sixty-two, with a drooping gray mustache and thick-lensed spectacles. He sized up Orchard, later describing him as having "the most cold, cruel eyes I remember having seen," and launched into a twenty-five minute statement about the advantages of cooperating with prosecutors. Orchard heard him out, then answered, "I don't know what you're getting at. I have committed no crime." Though Orchard had heard of cases where nice speeches like McParland's "made innocent men confess to crimes that they never committed and to implicate others who were also innocent," such "square dealing" with the state only ended with one's own execution, he explained.

McParland had expected as much and informed Orchard that men who turned state's evidence weren't always condemned to death. Had he heard of the case of the Molly Maguires in eastern Pennsylvania some thirty years earlier, when several Mollies who testified for the state were spared the death penalty?

Yes, Orchard said, he'd heard of the Molly Maguires. Everyone in the labor movement had. McParland asked if he'd seen the photo of the Pinkerton detective, McParland, who'd gone undercover to assemble the evidence. No, Orchard said, he had not seen the man.

"I am that McParland," the old detective said.

The Molly Maguire saga of 1875–76 was probably *the* favorite detective story of the late nineteenth century, told again and again in newspapers, cheap tabloids like *The Police Gazette*, and respected magazines like *Harper's Weekly*. It had a hold on the popular imagination like few true police stories before or since. Allan Pinkerton shrewdly started the craze in the first in his series of dime novels: *The Molly Maguires and the Detectives* and *Strikers, Communists, Tramps, and Detectives*. In the process, he heightened the fear of immigrant anarchists while polishing the image of his agency. In 1894, *McClure's* retold the story in a series culled from Pinkerton archives. Sir Arthur Conan Doyle, who'd been told the saga by William Pinkerton during a long ocean voyage, used it as the centerpiece of his Sherlock Holmes novel *The Valley of Fear*. Every book written about the Pinkertons would retell the tale.

Historians are divided on how much of the Molly Maguires' legend was fact and how much myth, but in the popular literature of the day they were described as a secret society formed by Irish immigrant miners in eastern Pennsylvania and named after an Irish widow who led an anti-landlord revolt during the potato famine. From the mid-1860s to the 1870s they were accused of waging a campaign of violence against mine owners, superintendents, local police, and anyone else they considered their enemy. When they were blamed for a strike in 1873, Franklin B. Gowen, president of the Philadelphia & Reading Railroad, called on the Pinkertons for help. McParland was sent, his orders from Allan Pinkerton explicit: "You are to remain in the field until every cutthroat has paid with his life." McParland worked in the mines, befriended known Mollies, and by 1875 was appointed "body-master," or chief officer, of all Molly activities in the Shenandoah district. In this capacity he became privy to the assassinations of several mine superintendents who ignored Molly hiring dictates: several weeks before a killing, the body-master would send the victim a "coffin notice," a roughly written warning that bore crude drawings of knives, revolvers, and, in the center, a large coffin. "This is your hous [sic]," one notice read. McParland testified only when he was exposed and no longer useful undercover; in 1876 and 1877, that testimony resulted in a score of convictions and nineteen executions, breaking the organization's back in America once and for all.

All of McParland's fame, all his influence, clout, and success, could be traced back to his nearly single-handed overthrow of the Molly Maguires. The case assured his future with the Pinkertons and assured the Pinkertons' future with American industry. All Pinkerton propaganda linking organized labor to anarchist cabals could be traced back to this early success. As the Gilded Age became the modern age and all evil was portrayed as secretly linked, the Pinkertons claimed to be America's last line of defense against anarchy. Many believed them. And squarely in the forefront was the old campaigner, James McParland.

It was hard to stand up against such a legacy of fiction and fact, and faced with the double threat of James McParland and William Pinkerton, the Denver police chief grew flustered, barking importantly like one of McParland's bulldogs. He informed his visitors that since the arrest of Lillian Stevenson and the man who called himself James Sherman, he'd had no time to talk with either one alone, something he intended to correct within the next twenty-four hours. The Stevenson woman was weak-willed and unhealthy, but what they'd gotten from her had already proved valuable. McParland just smiled, while Pinkerton gently agreed. "But the young man has proved a challenge," the chief said. McParland and Pinkerton sympathetically nodded their heads. "I've allowed and will continue to allow the Post Office inspectors and anyone from your agency the full privilege of seeing the prisoners, and I fully realize the importance of getting a full confession from one or both," the chief said. "I'm trying to get that before turning Sherman over to the United States authorities." Most wise, said William Pinkerton. The chief warmed to the Principal, so cultured and easy to talk with; he tried not to glance at McParland, who did not make him feel quite so comfortable. "In my opinion, the young man wants to get to Omaha, as he thinks he would have a chance to confer with the other prisoners and learn what they have said." The Principal, who'd learned long ago that sugar worked best for soothing local egos, said he couldn't more fully agree. Just the same, could they see the young man, please?

Of course, said the chief, and brought Jack in to see the Pinkerton men.

McParland's impression of the interview was later recorded in a Pinkerton memo dated June 4, 1909. It began with William Pinkerton's "long fatherly talk" with Jack, in which he explained that "the only person who could do him any good was [the Denver police chief] and that by making a clean breast to him, he would certainly do himself good." McParland watched Jack closely during the talk, guessing that he was twenty or twenty-one and marveling how closely he resembled Frank Grigware. "While (Jack's) face is thin and he walks with his head down and in what might be called a sneaky manner, nevertheless he has got good broad shoulders," the old detective observed.

Jack listened politely but denied knowing anything about the Mud Cut Robbery. Pinkerton asked where he had been between the time of the Denver & Rio Grande train robbery and his arrest on Tuesday morning. Jack would not say.

Pinkerton asked where he bought the new tan shoes tagged as evidence on the chief's desk, and Jack admitted to buying them in Omaha. "That's not what you originally said," urged the Principal. "It doesn't matter, does it?" Jack answered. "My picture is published in every paper in the country and I'm ruined anyhow."

"But that is not a fact," McParland interjected. He told Jack about a Rio Grande train robbery many years ago when a young fellow involved in the robbery made a full statement to police. The judge discharged him at the suggestion of the U.S. Attorney; since then, the lad had been "filling a very honorable position." Today, claimed McParland, he was the only one to know of the young man's statement and of his role in bringing down his partners in crime.

Jack studied the old detective, and finally asked, "Exactly who are you?"

A dramatic pause leaps off the faded report, then William Pinkerton told him their names. Jack said he did not recognize the Principal, but he had seen McParland's picture several times in the papers during the Big Bill Haywood case in Boise. Pinkerton, who reportedly relished his fame, may have felt a twinge of jealousy; however, he was not known for sabotaging the careers of subordinates. There would be no retribution when Jack asked, "You are the McParland who convinced Harry Orchard to confess?"

"I am the man," McParland said.

No doubt Pinkerton and McParland held their breath. They knew what had happened in the past. They knew the power of reputation on men in the sweatbox—the promise of help, the tiniest chance of salvation held out just when a man seemed damned. Jack hesitated, and the two unconsciously craned forward. This was the high moment, the glory of the chase. But this time the promise did not work. Jack must have remembered how Orchard, after helping these men, was still sentenced to death. These very men made promises in the name of the state but, once the trial commenced, left defendants to their fates. Although Orchard's sentence was eventually commuted to life, it was only after a long and uncertain fight. Jack shook his head and said he had nothing to tell them. The two Pinkertons sighed. The chief returned Jack to his cell.

While they were alone, McParland and Pinkerton discussed strategy in light of this setback. How should they handle the Denver chief, the federal agents, and Lillian? In the uncertainty of the early investigation, a plan began to form. By now, they had received telegrams from Asher Rosseter in Omaha telling them that Spokane detectives had identified "Woods" as Dan Downer and "Derf" as Fred Torgensen. The Pinkertons already had long files in Spokane and Chicago on these two men. The engineer, the deadhead engineer, and the fireman on the Overland Limited believed that Downer and Torgensen were the two who jumped into the engine and held them up. With that and the stolen bills found upon them, their fates before a jury were almost certainly sealed.

But Grigware and Golden were another matter. If they couldn't be linked to the robbery, at least the automobile photo and Lillian Stevenson could link them to Downer and Torgensen. Guilt by association might seem insufficient evidence for sentencing men to life in prison. But right now, that was all the Pinkertons and the Union Pacific had.

❦ CHAPTER FIVE ❧

The Trial

FRANK AND THE others sat in the Omaha jail while the Pinkertons searched station to station in the great chain of randomness, forcing order out of chaos, running every clue to earth, and tying all threads together into a great web of crime.

Jack returned to Omaha a few days after his meeting with William Pinkerton and James McParland, eager to prove his alibi. The landlady of his rooming house could prove it: he'd come home at eleven o'clock on the night of the robbery, the same time as the holdup, when she jollied him about chasing the girls so late, he said. But when they found the woman, she denied seeing Jack that night. She hadn't been in the house after 6 P.M., she said. It must be a mistake, Jack explained. Instead of the landlady, he'd spoken to an actress, whose name he couldn't recall. There was also a man named Marion, whom they couldn't find. The detectives looked at each other with a certain disappointment. They liked Jack because of his youth and had even hoped his alibi might prove true. Instead it proved nonexistent, and they threw him in jail.

In early June, Spokane detective Alexander MacDonald arrived in Omaha and identified Downer, Torgensen, and Golden as "three well-known Spokane crooks and safe-blowers" who belonged to a gang that roamed the Pacific Northwest and was thought to be led by an Idaho man named Bill Matthews. MacDonald said Downer and Torgensen

140

were wanted as suspects in postal robberies in Everett, Washington, and Victoria, British Columbia; in addition, they were suspects in the robbery of the Great Northern express near Hillyard, notwithstanding the fact that two other men, A. O. Olmstead and John Billups, had been arrested for the job on May 28. Spokane's chief of police also denounced Jack, Dan, and Fritz as "three bad men." He added in a footnote that Frank had never been in trouble before.

Frank felt the wind knocked out of him when he learned of Jack's crimes. The rumors had been right after all, but he'd ignored them, even the warnings of his mother. He'd placed his faith in friends' assurances rather than his own doubts and intuition. Jack's boasts about knowing the Spokane gang had been more than just hot air; he'd met them through his older brothers. His crimes may have started even before he and Frank began their Grand Tour. Frank felt a profound sense of sadness that Jack had fooled him, an even greater anger and humiliation that he'd let himself be fooled. Such feelings wouldn't help him now that his fate was tied to theirs. An Omaha reporter called them "the James boys of the West," which soon turned into "the James boys of Spokane." A detective, presumably working for the Union Pacific, was quoted as saying that the railroad "never quits when it is after a fellow for a job like this, and neither does Uncle Sam. This whole bunch is going to be put away for keeps." The implication was clear. An example would be made of them. The recent spate of train robberies would stop in Omaha.

Downer and Torgensen were kept in single cells, while Frank and Jack were kept with the general population. "I don't care to say who I may be or who I know," Downer told a reporter, when asked why he'd given his name as Woods. The guards and reporters were starting to like Downer: he always kidded with them, even considering the odds against his release, while Torgensen only cursed them or scowled. With a characteristic grin, Downer tried to direct the conversation away from evidence that no doubt would hurt him at trial. "This is a fine turkey you're feeding us," he told a deputy sheriff who walked up carrying a tin plate, large tin spoon, cup of black coffee, and what a reporter called "rather untempting viands." The deputy grinned and answered, "Sure, that turkey was raised on the left flank of an antique pack mule." The reporters laughed, while Downer replied between mouthfuls that he looked forward to the beefsteak dinner they'd buy him once the court proved him innocent and released him from jail.

During this time, a new theory of the robbery arose. If, as Spokane detective MacDonald said, the gang was led by Bill Matthews, was it possible that five men had robbed the Overland Limited instead of four? The witnesses were reinterviewed. Although most stuck to their original stories, a couple switched and said yes, possibly there were five. George Whitmore, the chief clerk of the mail car, the fellow who originally said, "I could not tell whether the men who held up that train were white or negro," now claimed that when he got out of the car "there was a man there who was not Woods, Shelton, Grigware, or Torgensen." That man had to be Matthews. What else explained the recollection by Fireman Prawl and engineers Meikeljohn and Wright that they heard one of the robbers addressed as "Bill"?

On June 12, a federal grand jury indicted Frank, Jack, Downer, and Torgensen for robbing the U.S. mails and endangering the lives of the mail clerks; a fifth indictment for "John Doe" was also handed down. Even before the fifth indictment, the hunt for Bill Matthews was in full swing. All Pinkerton branches were told to examine their files and rogues' galleries; soon the Portland, Oregon, branch responded with a mug shot and file information listing Matthews as a suspected murderer and well-known thief who went by the aliases G. W. Marvin, William Davis, and William Marvin. Included in the file was a note that a letter carrier in Buhl, Idaho, owed him $1,000. On the hunch that a penniless fugitive might go back to collect his debt, the Pinkertons sent an operative to Buhl.

Matthews had been on the run since Jack's departure from Omaha on May 29. On that day he was seen by his landlady, Mrs. Wyckoff, carrying two grips down the street. He told her they belonged to the young fellow who'd stayed with him the night before. The poor young fellow had lost his job and gone to Lincoln for work, and he was sending them on, he said. In fact he lugged the bags to the Wells Fargo Express office and checked them to J. C. Kelley in Denver, just as Jack had asked. He left Omaha that night, telling Mrs. Wyckoff that he was headed to St. Joe. Two days later he mailed a letter from Minneapolis, Minnesota, to J. C. Kelley in Denver, telling Jack what to do to help the others and offering whatever aid he could.

For nearly three weeks, Matthews's whereabouts were unknown. By then the Pinkerton agent sent to Buhl had contacted the local sheriff, and for days afterward they covered the arrival of every train rolling into town. In the early morning of June 18, their vigilance finally paid off. They saw Matthews swing off a train and trailed him to Room 19 of the Buhl Hotel. City Marshal William E. May, Deputy Frank Clutas, and the unidentified Pinkerton agent gathered outside the room. The door was not fastened; they flung it open and rushed inside. Matthews sat in a chair in the middle of the room, facing the door. His suitcase was open in front of him, a suit of clothes inside. A .45 Colt and a partly finished letter lay on the suitcase; the letter was to J. C. Kelley in Denver, describing how he'd forwarded the luggage yet had still not heard from him. Matthews reached for his gun but Clutas covered him first and Matthews raised his hands. The lawmen cuffed his wrists, took the worrisome pistol, and told him to sit back down. Instead, Matthews fell across the suitcase and grabbed the letter, stuffing it into his mouth. Clutas, who seemed to be everywhere during the capture, grabbed him by the jaw and throat and forced him to spit it out. The "meanest man in Idaho" went quietly after that, his arrest officially hiking the total reward to $30,000— the equivalent of $590,000 in today's dollars.

THE TRIAL, ORIGINALLY scheduled for early July, was postponed until fall once Matthews was arrested. He was brought back to Omaha on July 11. During the remainder of the summer and early fall the district attorney, Charles A. Goss, gathered information about the accused and lined up witnesses. It looked as if the trial might be one of the last in Goss's term as chief prosecutor. It was certainly among the biggest, and Goss was making sure he won. Jim Grigware wrote to Frank that the family was trying to raise money for a lawyer, but in the end the court appointed a legal team for the defendants led by Attorney John MacFarland of Omaha. Their fate depended on MacFarland's skill and energy, the jury's open-mindedness, and the fairness of the judge.

Scant news is available today of Frank's pretrial wait in county jail; few clues remain of his state of mind. A sense of inevitability seems to have set in, a sense of bitterness that all his hopes had ended this way. Though Dan, Fritz, and Bill were kept in what Omaha jailers called "solitary," their cells were adjacent and Frank listened as they talked. It seemed as if they'd expected incarceration; it was part of the game they'd chosen to play. Jack, on the other hand, was terrified of the thought of life behind bars. His cough worsened in the damp cell, and in a place like the federal penitentiary he thought he would die. Frank's father wrote to say that the family was behind him and they were trying to raise the $500 for a separate lawyer, but $500 in 1909 was equal to $9,800 today. In the end, Edward Grigware had to tell his son that the amount was beyond their means. The few times the lawyer, Mac-Farland, visited, his best advice to Frank was to take the prosecution's offer of a lighter sentence: All Frank had to do was plead guilty and turn state's evidence against the other four. The feds offered the deal several times during the long wait, hoping Frank's resolve had weakened, yet each time his answer was the same. How could he be a witness against the others if he was not part of the robbery?

It's your funeral, his defense attorney said.

Frank tried to tell his mother that he was innocent, something barely hinted in a letter years later. What did Jennie think as Edward and Jim tried to raise the money for a lawyer but could not do it? What did she tell her younger children, who'd grown so much in the three years since Frank's departure? They'd seen him as a kind of western hero, mining for gold and silver, working his way from ranch to ranch, falling in love with an Irish girl from Texas. What should she tell them now—to stay at home and take no chances? That the Pinkertons were right and Frank had gone bad? She could believe he'd been too trusting of companions, but not that he'd held up a train. When a reporter came knocking from the Spokane newspaper, she told him, "I know that my son has done nothing wrong. He has been well raised and he is a good boy. I cannot believe that he has committed the crime of robbing a train. I did not see the picture in the newspaper, and I don't know whether it is Frank or not. There must be some terrible mistake." Yet even as the reporter left, she knew there was no mistake. Frank was in jail, and the federal government wanted to send him to prison for life. It was as if all the vague fears she'd felt for her son had finally coalesced, as if the sense of doom she'd always feared had found them. What should she tell her children, that theirs was a land where the poor were not forgiven for many things, but most especially for trying to break free of their poverty?

There were no speedy trial laws in those days, so Frank's wait dragged through August and September of 1909 and into October. The prosecution asked for delays on procedural matters, but it was easy for Frank, even with no legal experience, to see that the purpose was to follow more leads. The Pinkertons performed their well-paid magic: tracking down suspects, finding evidence, building a case that stuck like glue. Other than his lawyer, some reporters, and detectives, Frank was allowed no visitors, yet he still heard from the outside world. He knew of the case mounting against him, perhaps better than his own lawyer did. He heard from his brother Jim about the day the Pinkertons, accompanied by police and postal inspectors, had grilled him for hours about Jack's telegram from Denver begging for money. They called him "the banker for a yegg gang," and in the end Jim had little choice but to hand over Jack's letter if he hoped to save himself. Alice wrote that she too had been sweated in Waco, again by a bunch of city detectives accompanied by Pinkertons. It seemed to be the agency's style: co-opt the local police and thus give any abuses an official veneer. Lillian had told them Alice's name and address, as well as what she knew of the boys' whereabouts in Kansas City and Hot Springs. The Pinkertons threatened to make Alice's past life public to all of Waco if she didn't own up to sending Frank the letter found near the signal fire. In the end she admitted writing him a love letter, care of General Delivery in Kansas City. *Please forgive me*, her letter begged. On August 28, Frank's lawyer fought half-heartedly to separate his trial from the others', but U.S. District Judge Thomas C. Munger ruled that all five men would be tried together. Munger was in his fifties, a no-nonsense member of the bench. A photo in the *Omaha World-Herald* shows dark eyes, apple cheeks, and an almost boyish grin. His ruling assured that any evidence against one man would stand against all five; the state had a strong case against Downer and Torgensen, while the cases against Frank, Jack, and Bill Matthews were still guilt by association. Plead guilty while you've got a chance, Frank's lawyer repeated, now with a touch of desperation in his voice. Frank still refused. Surely the jury could see his innocence, he tried to assure himself. Surely the weight of circumstantial evidence wasn't that damning.

Frank had no idea. As Judge Learned Hand would later write, mental habits "indirectly determine our institutions," and despite all the words about a man's presumed innocence, few accused train robbers ever went free. People saw the law as all that stood between America and chaos; the law protected America from the mob. The law could not err; by definition, it was just and fair. When the trial opened in Omaha's federal court on Monday, October 25, 1909, no one in the courtroom, described as "crowded to capacity," thought it strange when Judge Munger again refused to separate the cases.

No one marked it strange that eighty witnesses would testify for the prosecution and only four for the defense. There was no outcry of unfairness. That was the way things were done.

THE TRIAL LASTED two and a half weeks, from Monday, October 25, to Wednesday, November 10, with four days off for weekends. U.S. marshals guarded the courtroom, courthouse, and the route from jail should friends try to free the accused. The proceedings received daily coverage in Omaha, Lincoln, Denver, Spokane, and smaller towns and cities, with intermittent coverage in other western papers and throughout the rest of the nation. Train robbers in this modern age were strange and romantic, thus making them major news. A party atmosphere existed outside the court. Munger often called for order within.

Prosecutor Goss opened the trial with an account of the Mud Cut Robbery. The state's case against the accused was substantial, he said, yet as the trial progressed he would admit to the difficulty of tying all of the defendants directly to the robbery. The night had been dark and the robbers wore masks. The eleven witnesses—three trainmen and eight mail clerks—came to the stand one by one. Most stuck to their stories of May 22, that only four bandits took part, but a couple now believed there had been five. Some remembered hearing a bandit addressed as "Bill," while a fifth man was probably needed at the signal light, they said. Defense attorney MacFarland objected that this was speculation and should not be entered as evidence, but Judge Munger let it stand. In fact, during the trial Munger allowed lots of speculation into evidence. Ira Wright, the deadhead engineer, insisted that although he never saw Frank's face or heard his voice, he knew he was one of the bandits by his "stature and carriage." One of the mail clerks, Fred Eastman, also pegged Frank as an outlaw. "How did you identify Grigware?" MacFarland asked in cross-examination.

"By his voice," Eastman said.

"Did he talk much?"

"No, not much, but I still recognized his voice."

"Did you see his face?"

"No, he wore a mask. All were masked."

"Any other points you recognized?"

"He had the same build as Grigware." After a few more questions from the defense, Eastman grew irritated. "My identification was positive and I stick to it," he said.

Nevertheless, most of the mail clerks remembered the night as Andrew J. Niles did. He did not testify against Frank, with good reason. It was too dark to see, he said. At the time of the robbery, he'd stood a few feet from Eastman, both of them backed against the train with their hands in the air. "It was so dark I couldn't identify Grigware from any of the others," he recalled. "It was too dark. There was a little light from the train window, but no other light. And in the main, we were too scared to [later] identify anyone. To be hauled out of the car, stood in line, searched for guns, and with a bandit at each end of the line threatening to kill us all if any one in the line opened an attack was just a little too much for our nerves."

In the end, the identifications were tallied: seven men positively identified Downer, and six identified Torgensen. Three or four doubtfully identified Frank, while a couple identified Jack, yet these identifications were dubious since the two looked so similar, a couple of witnesses said. No one identified Bill Matthews, though some had heard his first name.

The physical evidence was then described. About $700 was taken by the robbers, and $250 of that was recovered. Some of the bills were found on Downer and Torgensen—the same bills described in the letter from the cashier in Kimmerer, Wyoming, Exhibit 26 on the wooden table in front of the jury. The bills found on Jack and positively identified in a Pinkerton report as bearing the stolen currency's serial numbers were not used as evidence, no reason given. Goss continued methodically—the ballistics tests that matched the guns found in the gully with the spent cartridges near the fire; the articles found with the guns, (raincoats, masks, and leather holsters); the Spokane newspapers and mutilated envelope bearing part of Frank's name, Exhibits 7 and 7a. Alice was brought to the stand to testify that she had written the letter to Frank while he roomed in Kansas City. "Why did you write it?" the prosecutor asked.

"Because I loved him," she said softly.

The gallery grew quiet. Goss asked her to repeat that a little louder. Frank felt sick and looked away. There was silence as every eye in the courtroom stripped Alice bare. "Answer the question," Judge Munger warned her.

"*Because I love him!*" she cried.

"That is all I have for this witness," said the prosecutor.

"You may go," the judge said.

Next the state established that all five men were friends. The automobile photo, Exhibit 61, showed that all but Matthews had been together in Denver, while landladies in Kansas City and Omaha testified that they had seen the five men together at various times and in various combinations. The Pinkertons tracked down Gus Bren, the Kansas City tailor who sold a suit to Matthews and remembered that Frank had been present; they found James Shriver, the hardware clerk in Spokane from whom Frank bought his pistol. Since that gun was not one of those found in the gully, Shriver's testimony had nothing to do with the case, yet Judge Munger did not rule it immaterial, allowing him to continue. A hardware clerk named Williams from Ogden, Utah, also testified, a man whom Frank had never seen before. But Williams swore he'd seen Frank. He'd sold him a gun, he said. Although there was no invoice or any record of the serial number, Williams recognized one of the guns in the gully as the one he'd sold to Frank in Utah. He backtracked a little—actually, two men had bought it from him, and Frank had been along. Defense attorney MacFarland for once got riled. He vociferously objected to this kind of evidence being allowed in court, but Munger sternly overruled the objection. He advised MacFarland to keep his temper if he didn't want to be cited with contempt. By now a sense of unreality had wrapped Frank in its arms. It was as if anyone could walk in off the street and accuse him of anything, and the judge would permit it because this trial was not about justice but rather a warning to those who dared cross the Union Pacific and its skilled dogs of law.

Eighty witnesses paraded to the stand, an unbroken train of hard and circumstantial evidence, hearsay, innuendo, and outright lies. Several residents of Fremont, Nebraska, near the Mud Cut, said they'd seen some or all of the five in the area on the day of the robbery. Most said they saw them from a distance, though a couple of the witnesses said they talked to them up close. Other witnesses said they'd seen the five together in Omaha on the evening of the robbery. Frank's lawyer failed to emphasize that this was physically impossible, since Fremont and Omaha were twenty-three miles apart and by this point the police had conceded that the robbers never used an automobile. There was even disagreement about whether they used a horse and buggy or simply went on foot. Waitresses at the Uneeda Restaurant who'd kidded Frank and Jack linked the two together. Johnnie Krowlik and his school pals said they recognized Frank and the others, although they'd only seen three of them on the dark night of the arrest from a block and a half away. Their principal, Miss Elizabeth T. Hayes, said she had seen the men around Brown School the week before their arrest, again from a distance. She said she especially remembered Frank because he'd worn a new suit of clothes, something Jack—not Frank—had purchased, according to Pinkertons. Brown Park was a rough part of town, so she always noticed new clothes on men, she said. The point was not disputed by MacFarland. Of them all, only Miss Hayes was asked about applying for the reward money. She *had* applied, she snapped, but "didn't count her chickens before they hatched."

On November 9, the penultimate day of trial, Lillian was brought in. She placed her right hand on the Bible, promised to tell the truth and only the truth, and sat down. Lillian had not been charged after her Denver sweatbox treatment: she'd been booked on suspicion, brought to Omaha to talk to prosecutors and Union Pacific officials, and then released with the understanding that she would testify at trial. The newspapers had been prepped for her appearance by the prosecutor or the police and were kind to her that day. "Miss Stevenson is rather a pretty woman, stylishly yet modestly dressed," lyricized the *Spokesman-Review*. "She admits that Stevenson is not her right name and refuses to state what it is. None of the attorneys have insisted that she tell, as they do not care to bring her family into the affair." Lillian described how she came to know Jack and the others, omitting her frightened flight from Walla Walla and what she already knew of "the boys." She told in detail about the day Jack returned to Denver with news that "the boys were in trouble." She insisted that she knew nothing of their plans to rob the Union Pacific or that the boys had any sort of criminal record, but she also knew they were somehow involved when she read about the holdup in the Denver paper.

"How did you know that?" asked Mr. Goss.

"I heard them planning some job while I was with them in a Denver restaurant," she said.

Frank snapped alert at the lie, amazed that no one raised an objection. The inconsistency occurred within minutes of her first statement that she knew nothing of their plans. He looked at MacFarland, but by now his lawyer seemed numbed to inconsistencies. He looked at Goss. Wasn't it a prosecutor's job to bring untruths to the attention of the court, even when they came from his own witnesses? He looked at the judge, who smiled and nodded as Lillian talked, quite charmed. MacFarland cross-examined Lillian, but very gently, afraid an aggressive defense would turn the jury against him for assaulting such a delicate vision of womanhood.

So much for truth, thought Frank. He had no chances now.

Then it was MacFarland's turn, and he called five witnesses. Bob Splain, Dan Downer's old buddy, said he owned the gun found on Bill Matthews the day of his arrest; former horse dealer Rex Buck said Matthews carried a lot of money on him when he left Buhl for Kansas City, so had no need for robbery; an Omaha barber said he thought he shaved Matthews on the night of the robbery, while a waitress at the Uneeda said she thought she'd served Jack at around the same time. It all seemed incredibly weak and flaccid, Frank thought, a ludicrous excuse for a defense. Why even make a pretense? Then Mr. MacFarland put Frank's father on the stand.

Edward Grigware looked old and frail. He gazed at his son, smiled thinly, then glanced away. He said that his son had bought a gun in Spokane to protect himself while working on a mining claim. His boy had never been in trouble, he said. It was three years ago when he left home; he smiled as he recalled the night Frank announced that he was "going to see the world." He was twenty years old then, a young man who wanted to get out on his own and make something of himself, but even so he wasn't wild. He'd stayed home at nights, kept good hours, saved his money, didn't drink, smoke, chew, or indulge in any other bad habits. "We were proud of him," Edward added, his throat catching. He'd brought along a couple of testimonials and asked if it was all right to read them: one from the Spokane chief of police stating that Frank was a good boy who did not cause trouble; one from Dr. Byrne describing Frank as a young man of promise and good character. "He would never do anything like this," Edward Grigware ended, looking across the silent courtroom. The stares of strangers told him that no one believed a word he'd said.

Jack was called to the stand. He and Frank were the only ones to testify in their own defense; Dan, Fritz, and Matthews sat mum. Frank no longer hated Jack for what had happened; Jack could only be Jack, something he should have realized long ago. Like the others, Jack denied involvement in the holdup. He described how, on the night of the robbery, he'd eaten with Frank at the Uneeda Restaurant between six and seven o'clock, then the two of them had gone to a

soda fountain, hoping to meet some girls. He and Frank roomed together, he explained, and on the following morning they'd gone for
breakfast at a Greek's place in Omaha.

Then suddenly and surprisingly, Jack started to defend his friend.
Jack would be the only co-defendant to try to help one of the others,
insisting that he knew that Frank could not have committed the crime.
When Jack heard that Frank had been arrested, he went to their room
and cut his name and all evidence of Spokane from his clothing, hoping to save his family from disgrace, he said. He left signs on a hat
and overcoat to make police believe they'd been purchased in Kansas
City, leading lawmen away from Spokane. "I knew he hadn't been
in this," Jack insisted. "I knew he couldn't possibly be guilty of robbery without my knowledge." Frank clenched his fists and for the
briefest moment prayed for the impossible. *Say it*, he thought. *Tell
them why you know—because you were there!* He'd turned it over
in his mind a hundred times during the long wait in jail; it was the
only explanation that made any sense. The stolen money in Jack's
pockets; the new suit purchased after the robbery, where before Jack
had barely enough to buy lunch; his friendship with the Spokane gang
before they left to make their fortune; his connection with the gang,
revealed by Spokane lawmen. The witnesses who kept getting the two
of them mixed up. The young bandit at the robbery who'd seemed
mad at the world. He gazed at Jack hopefully, trying to bore his
thoughts straight into his skull. *Tell them the truth!* Maybe Jack
sensed his silent pleading, because his head sank in defeat when Goss
asked why he was so certain of Frank's innocence. Frank begged him
to say it: *Because I was there!*

Even the spectators held their breath, aware that some crossroads
had been reached. Instead, Jack meekly answered, "I just know he
can't be guilty."

"That's all I have, Your Honor," the prosecutor said.

And finally it was Frank's turn on the witness stand. He said he
was in Omaha the night of the robbery. He admitted being arrested
with Torgensen five days later, but thought he was helping him pick
up a parcel. Yes, he'd lied about knowing Fritz and Dan when first
arrested, he admitted. He should not have lied, but he was scared.

"I was not at Mud Cut the night of the holdup," Frank said to the
court, gazing at the wall of stares. He watched Prosecutor Goss as he
made a show of disbelief and looked at the jurors, several of whom

shook their heads. "I did not know anything about it before it took place. I was never arrested before in my life but once, and that was in Manitou [Springs], Colorado, where I was bound over on a watch complaint. I was innocent of the charge," he said.

Goss leapt on the fact that he'd used the name Hollingshead when arrested before; it looked as if he made a habit of giving false names, he said. Frank admitted that he did not dissent when the name was called out, but it was only to save his family from shame. He couldn't remember the details of the charge for which he'd been picked up but others were picked up too. When some flaw occurred in the preliminary hearing, they were all sent back to the jail and discharged. Goss asked if there was a similar mistake when he'd given his name as "Gordon" after his arrest at Brown Park School. Frank said that was a mistake, too, but his own mistake, for he'd been terrified.

Goss questioned him about the most damning piece of evidence against him, Alice's love letter found at Mud Cut, as well as the fact that a gun was seen in his luggage in Kansas City. "While in Kansas City, I lost my gun and some letters," Frank replied. He looked at Fritz, who stared back, seemingly daring him to say who'd taken them. It had crossed his mind that perhaps Fritz and even Dan had been trying to set him up. His was the only name found anywhere among the evidence: on the envelope near the signal fire, on the collar in Dan's luggage. It was too convenient, as if they'd considered making him the fall guy if anything went wrong. But Frank wasn't sure. His suspicions could just as easily be the result of his companions' characteristic sloppiness and apparent disorganization. He wouldn't make accusations based on half-formed theories—not like the police and prosecutors had done with him.

And so Frank said the letter and gun were taken from him in Kansas City, but he refused to say by whom. Even as he said it, he knew his explanations fell on deaf ears. "I never saw them since. There was a holster with the gun. I don't have the number of the gun, but I know the gun, holster, and strap there"—he pointed at the evidence spread on the wooden table—"are not mine."

"So the envelope just magically appeared at the Mud Cut on its own," Goss prodded.

"I don't know how this envelope got out on the bank south of the Union Pacific. I did not put it there." Frank sighed. It was such a cruel joke: Alice, who'd tried to warn him, had mailed the piece of evidence that damned him. "I had nothing to do with the holdup or the shooting or the robbery."

"That's all, Your Honor," Goss said, looking significantly at the jury. Some jurors met his gaze.

And that was all. The heavy shackles were unlocked from the table legs and the five defendants were chained together. Twenty-five deputies surrounded them for the lockstep march to the Black Maria that took them back to jail. How could anyone seeing this possibly think he was innocent? Frank thought. As the noises of the jail echoed around him, he spent the night preparing for the inevitable.

IF ANYONE IN Omaha doubted the men's guilt by the close of testimony on November 10, they probably abandoned those doubts when they opened their newspapers the next day. On the evening of November 9, deputies discovered that Downer had nearly finished sawing a three-foot hole through the roof of his solitary cell on the second floor. A search of his co-defendants' cells the next morning, before trial, uncovered six more saws, but it was unclear from newspaper accounts whether they had been put to use. Someone on the outside was evidently looking out for his friends. On top of Downer's cage were found two heavy iron bars, long enough to pry loose the jail's outer windows, as well as a long rope the men could use to shinny to the ground. Officials said they kept the attempted escape secret so as to not prejudice the jury, but their release of the information on the very day that deliberations started seemed to belie their words.

Frank and the others were marched into court on the morning of November 11, again shackled together with the heavy chains. They were seated inside the railing, a short distance from the judge. The space around them was filled with forty to fifty deputies and federal agents, all present in case a breakout was tried. The jury filed in to hear a day of closing arguments. Prosecutor Goss methodically outlined the evidence against the five men, emphasizing why *all* were guilty. Then it was MacFarland's turn. The defense attorney literally wrote off Downer and Torgensen by admitting that the stolen money found in their possession was "a strong point against them." On the other hand, he said, several Spokane residents had written depositions attesting to Frank and Jack's good character, and the cases against Frank, Jack, and Bill Matthews were highly circumstantial. MacFarland reminded the jury that there was no middle ground in mail robbery: by law, the sentence was life imprisonment. He reminded the jurors of Jack and Frank's youth. If convicted, the two young men—indeed, all the defendants—would spend the rest of their lives in a "living tomb."

MacFarland finished at 4:30 P.M. Judge Munger charged the jury, which retired at 4:50. The jurors deliberated until 7:15, at which time the marshal's office got word that they were ready. By 8 P.M., the judge, lawyers, officers, spectators, and prisoners had assembled back in the courtroom.

In the two hours and twenty-five minutes that the jurors had considered thirteen days of evidence, there were things they did not and could not know. They did not know that three prosecution witnesses who testified against Frank would themselves be convicted of robbery three years after their verdict, or that Williams, the store clerk from Ogden, Utah, who said Frank was present at the sale of one of the guns found in the gully, was himself later convicted of perjury. Shortly after the trial, Williams testified to identical facts in the trial of two other men in Utah state courts, claiming they had used the same gun in yet another robbery. The testimony was proven false and Williams was thrown in jail. In the Utah case, just as in Omaha, a sizable reward for information had been offered, and Williams had responded.

The jurors did not know that possibilities for perjury were rampant in Frank's trial. The rush of claimants for the huge reward had started soon after the robbery in May: the "better" someone's evidence, the better the chance of collecting and the greater their share. Soon after Frank's arrest, South Omaha Police Chief John Briggs declared that Union Pacific officials had promised he would have "practically the say of how the reward money shall be split." On hearing that, the parents of Johnnie Krowlik and his fellow classmates stormed Briggs's office, declaring they were first in line. In June, two South Omaha officers got into a fight over who was more involved in the arrest and who deserved a greater share of the reward.

The jurors could not know that on November 18, seven days after their verdict, the fight for the reward money officially began. On that day, the six boys who discovered the cache in the gully and served as lookouts in the sheep butcher's house filed separate claims in federal district court of $5,000 apiece. It was the opening salvo in what the *World-Herald* predicted would be a "long and bitter struggle for a division" of the spoils. They weren't far wrong. Soon afterward, Principal Elizabeth Hayes claimed $20,000, since she had called police about the boys' discovery and testified that she'd seen all five men around the school. South Omaha police demanded $15,000; another South Omaha youth claimed $5,000 because he'd found a flashlight hidden near the guns. An Omaha landlady who testified against Matthews demanded $5,000. The shady characters who testified against Frank, including the perjurious clerk from Utah, all demanded money. By the time it was over, forty people—half of those who testified—made claims totaling $200,000, or $3.9 million in today's dollars. The claims grew so complicated that Judge Munger, who no longer smiled for the newspapers, would not make a final ruling until October 1913, when he awarded $33,400 to only nine of the claimants—$3,400 more than the actual reward total, but the closest he could come to an equitable solution.

The jurors could not know that by then another decision had been made, one speaking to the quality of the evidence. In summer 1913, a four-year investigation by U.S. postal inspectors came to a close. They had been troubled by the holes in the case; they'd learned of the perjured testimony and sent their recommendations to President Woodrow Wilson. The evidence—and lack of evidence—against Jack Golden was basically the same as that against Frank. In August 1913, the President commuted Jack's sentence, declaring him innocent of all charges and releasing him from Leavenworth.

But on November 11, 1909, Frank could not know this—and neither could the jury. He watched as the fifty guards took their positions in the courtroom. He watched more closely as the twelve jurors filed back into the hushed room. The judge told the defendants to stand.

The verdict was passed to the court clerk and the five prisoners nervously shifted their feet. The clerk's voice cut through the murmur as he read the names and charges. After each, he said, "Guilty as charged." Frank knew that the sentence was automatically set at life even before Judge Munger spoke; the judge asked each defendant if there was any reason why the sentence should not be carried out. Except for Dan Downer, the accused repeated their claims of innocence. Dan's show of bravado gave way as the blood drained from his face, but he still remained silent, merely shaking his head. Bill Matthews dropped his head. Torgensen said his imprisonment would not be for long because he was "near death's door" thanks to tuberculosis. When Jack tried to answer, he started to cry.

Frank groaned deeply and nearly passed out; two deputies, standing close, caught him under the arms and lowered him into his chair. He closed his eyes, the darkness around him swirling like the cyclone he'd seen from afar in Wyoming, a whirling darkness with a roar like a runaway train. He seemed to listen from the bottom of a pit as his attorney leapt to his feet and demanded a new trial on the grounds that the jury had been biased by news of the attempted escape. He would "go to the limit in an endeavor to secure an acquittal, at least in the cases of Grigware and Golden," McFarland declared. A week later, Judge Munger refused a new trial and reiterated that his sentence would be imposed. By then Charles Goss's term had expired. He left office in triumph, leaving the drudgery of appellate work to his successor, Frank Howell.

When Howell looked at the evidence, he couldn't believe what he saw. The evidence against Frank was some of the slimmest he'd ever prosecuted; he knew that if he'd been on the jury, he would not have voted to send Grigware to prison. If he'd ever seen a case of guilt by association, this was it. Why had Goss not seen it? In those days, when prosecutors still saw themselves as gatekeepers of justice, Goss had gone ahead and prosecuted on evidence that was far from just. Yet that was Goss's business, not his. There were times when the law allowed and even aided the very ruthlessness against which it was supposed to guard. At times like that, Howell despaired. But his duty now was not to try the case based on his own definition of justice. He was too late for that—three weeks too late. His duty now was to adhere to his role and fight the appeal. He did his duty—and won.

It might have given Frank some small succor if he'd known of Howell's pangs of conscience, his brief lawyerly dilemma, yet by then it would have been too late for him. On November 19, 1909, Frank Grigware and the boys from Spokane were handcuffed in tandem, locked into heavy leg irons, and placed under armed guard on a one-way train ride to the place called the Big House, the United States Penitentiary at Leavenworth. He closed his eyes until nothing remained but his unsparing thoughts and blackness, just like his whole life ahead of him. He was guilty, all right, he thought. Guilty of misplaced loyalty, just as Alice had warned him. Guilty of stupidity. Guilty as hell.

The whistle gave two long blasts, the signal to release the brakes. The railroad car lurched once and moved forward. He was headed south to Kansas, and no stops were scheduled before the prison. There was no getting off this train.

❧ PART II ❧

The Hard Joint

Without cruelty, there is no festival.

—Friedrich Nietzsche

❦ CHAPTER SIX ❦

A Kind of Prophecy

FRANK'S 160-MILE journey from Omaha south to Leavenworth lasted the morning of November 19, 1909, and most of the afternoon. The trip was normally faster, but this day it happened to rain. It had rained all month in Kansas, making 1909 the wettest year in the state's recorded history. Frank watched the rain streak backward across his glass window and felt the wind buffet the train as it followed the Missouri River. It was uncommonly quiet inside the prison car, a silence broken only by the coughs of Fritz and Jack or the rustling of a newspaper.

Little is known today about the early prison rail cars. By 1933, they were elaborate, fitted with steel bars and mesh across the windows and boiler plate reinforcing the floor. While guards riding with the prisoners went unarmed, a man with a shotgun sat in a wire cage by each door. The air brake cord was strung overhead so it could only be reached by those two armed guards. In 1909, however, cars for prisoners were still much like regular passenger coaches, the main modifications being screened windows and iron rings on the floor to which the men were chained.

The car was stuffed with lawmen. Along with Frank and the four other Mud Cut lifers, the special carried U.S. Marshal William Warner and five deputy marshals, Bill Canada, chief of the Union Pacific detectives, and an unidentified Pinkerton man. The lawmen were nervous because of the train's slow rate of speed. It usually barreled along at a rapid clip, but the storm and lack of visibility worried the engineer. Prison trains had priority over passenger and freight trains, which were sidetracked as it passed; the absence of stops left few opportunities for hijackers to board. Yet once saws were found in Downer's cell in Omaha, the marshals were wary and the train's crawl made them warier. Warner put a man up front with the engineer and kept men with loaded shotguns in the front and rear of the car.

Frank believed no help was coming, not now or ever. He stared out the window at the rain-blurred Nebraska fields. This part of the country was situated at the end of a glacial moraine, so the soil was deep and fertile, the nutrients replenished by intermittent Missouri floods. In 1903 the river had leapt its banks and washed out several railroad trestles—another reason the engineer kept his hand on the throttle as they steamed across the state line. Once in Kansas, the unvarying flatlands changed to rolling hills and streams of tangled growth, the farms hidden by trees following the course of creeks and rivers. Frank spotted herds of Holstein cattle standing dumbly in the downpour; he'd heard the cattle here gained as much as two pounds a day eating grasses rooted in the limestone underneath. They grazed in fields separated by crumbling stone fences, which stood about chest high.

Lumber was scarce on the prairie, and barbed wire at that time was too expensive for most homesteaders, so farmers did the next best thing and picked exposed limestone off the ground or quarried it from their property. This was the same ashlar limestone used for the main cellblocks and rotunda of the penitentiary, a porous stone that, unlike the marble used to build the monuments in the nation's capital, tended to chip and yellow under the onslaught of the elements. The farmers could have pointed to their own disintegrating fences and told the prison planners that this limestone was a poor choice of building material. But then, no one asked. The locals liked the prison well enough and especially all the new jobs and markets that came with it; still, it was another example of how Easterners barged in thinking they had all the answers and in the process just made problems for themselves.

Kansans liked to think they represented what was best in the nation; they lived in a place that was "hardly a state but a kind of prophecy," according to a boast by famous Kansas newspaper editor William Allen White. "When anything is going to happen in this country it happens first in Kansas," and from the mid-1800s to the Great Depression that seemed to hold true. The state's nickname in the 1850s was "Bleeding Kansas," the slave-state versus free-state violence that bloodied the country around Leavenworth from 1854 to 1857 would introduce the nation to abolitionist John Brown and act as a preview of the Civil War. Carrie Nation lingered awhile in Kansas before storming the rest of the country, and bringing with her the first hints of Prohibition. The Populist party and bitter agrarian protest anticipated labor strife that continued well into the 1930s. A foretaste of the Depression blew across Kansas during the Dust Bowl years. Somehow the prophecy that White hailed was often tinged with violence, the best intentions subverted by neglect or corruption.

Leavenworth fit right in. Northeastern Kansas lay on the "border," that stretch of country starting near Omaha and Council Bluffs, Iowa, threading south along the Missouri River where Kansas and Missouri meet, and ending at the juncture of Arkansas and the Indian Territory. More than that, the "border" was a state of mind: the meeting place of East and West, a launching site for countless westward journeys along the Oregon and Santa Fe trails. Before the Civil War it had been the border between the North and South, a turbulent, bloody country where opposing values crashed together like tectonic plates and the politics of slavery determined one's friends. This was the heart of Bleeding Kansas, the land of border ruffians and Missouri redlegs, of Confederate guerrilla bands like Quantrill's Raiders, led by men like William Quantrill and "Bloody Bill" Anderson. The 1863 guerrilla raid on Lawrence, Kansas, was right outside Leavenworth's doorstep, an attack that left 150 citizens murdered, many in front of their families. It was where the James boys and other border outlaws roamed after the war. If anything, the "border" drew hard cases.

These days, however, the border seemed tame. The town of Leavenworth, the first town built in Kansas, was planned by an army engineer and shaped like a giant T. Metropolitan Avenue, which ran east and west, formed the crossbar, while the military reservation and prison sat immediately to the north of the T. So many soldiers stationed in the fort married local girls that the Leavenworth area was soon called "the mother-in-law of the army." By 1909, at least eight railroad lines ran through Leavenworth. The town was the showpiece of Kansas, a Victorian haven boasting two breweries, a Catholic college, a flower queen, an apple carnival, the National Cemetery, and the Old Soldiers' Home. Prisons were a major employer; in addition to the federal penitentiary, Leavenworth County was home to the military stockade, the Kansas State Penitentiary, and the city jail. In 1861, the Kansas legislature had offered Leavenworth a choice between the state university or the state penitentiary. City fathers chose the latter, and work had started two years later.

The track turned west and Frank craned forward, hoping to glimpse his new home. He noticed that Jack, seated a few rows ahead of him, peered forward too. In the rain nothing distant could be seen except a gray blur. The train slowed and Frank felt the *clack-clack* of a switch being crossed; he rubbed his eyes and heard Jack gasp and suddenly there it was. The prison's brick wall loomed overhead, looking as if it leaned out toward them, threatening to crash down. They sat outside the eastern Railroad Gate; from this position, he could see the gate's gun tower and a southeast tower close to town. The lights were switched on and raindrops seemed frozen in their beams.

Bill Canada leaned across the seat in front of Frank to get a better look. "Great Jesus," he whispered, glancing back at Frank with a look that almost seemed pitying. "Better get them ready," he told Marshal Warner. "It looks like we're here."

Although far from complete, Leavenworth in 1909 had nearly achieved its builders' dreams of total autonomy. By March 16, 1909, the architects told Washington that $1.5 million had been spent so far and another $700,000 would be needed, a total sum equaling $43 million in today's dollars. The brick wall was finished, enclosing the prison yard. The east and west main cellhouses, domed rotunda, and hospital were still under construction, but almost everything else was completed and functioning. The two smaller cellhouses radiating from the back of the rotunda were finished, as was most of the center hall that stretched back to the yard. The power plant, school, shops, factories, kitchen, bakery, and laundry were all finished by 1909. The chapel could hold 1,200 men and boasted a wall-sized mural of Jesus comforting prisoners. The same number of inmates could be fed at once in the dining room, all sitting on benches that faced the same way.

The houses of the warden, deputy warden, and chief clerk were completed by 1907; they needed only to walk a few yards from the prison and they were home. Leavenworth had its own electrical shop, steel shop, tin shop, paint shop, carpenter shop, brick plant, stone shop, armory, ice-making plant, and broom factory. A shoe shop was still being planned. The prison pumped out its own building materials: steps, pipes, nuts, bolts, bed frames, steel cells, manhole covers, big pipes for tunnels, small pipes for sewers, and myriad other workaday necessities. In 1908, the prison paid $3,126.25 for a small H. K. Porter switch engine used to haul small loads of lumber and steel, a savings over leasing a locomotive from the Union Pacific.

Warden Robert McLaughry saw himself more as a town manager than as a jailer those days, taking pride in his small municipality. He took particular pride in the prison farm. This covered 300 acres on the north, east, and west sides of the prison and included a farmhouse, greenhouse, hog house, chicken ranch, and cow barn for the dairy herd. The fifteen to twenty-two trusties who worked there grew apples, beets, beans, cherries, cabbage, cucumbers, corn, lettuce, onions, parsnips, peas, peppers, potatoes, pumpkins, peaches, radishes, squash, tomatoes, turnips, and watermelons, as well as alfalfa for feeding cattle and cow peas for use as fertilizer. During the fiscal year of 1909–10, the prison farm produced 15,340 pounds of beef, 19,060 pounds of pork, 8,000 gallons of milk, and 6,000 eggs. It was larger than the corporate farms Frank had seen in Spokane and often more efficient. That year, the prison spent $1,760 to run the farm and produced food worth $15,897. Thanks to the farm, it cost only 11.2 cents to feed a man daily, a detail appreciated by McLaughry's cost-conscious masters in Washington.

The greatest step toward autonomy came on February 21, 1903. On that day, enough work was done on the laundry building to allow 418 prisoners to be moved inside, eliminating the need for the long march across the prairie that had gone on for nearly six years. With it went McLaughry's fears of another mass escape like the one in November 1901. To inaugurate the occasion, the first prisoner admitted into the new prison was classified as Prisoner Number 1. All the first prisoners in America's first three federal prisons were minorities: the first in Washington state's McNeal Island was Abraham Gervais, an Indian, while the first in USP Atlanta was Handy Middlebrook, a black man. But the first federal prisoner in Leavenworth, and therefore in the United States, was John Grindstone, an Eastern Shawnee of the Quapaw Agency charged with murder in the Oklahoma Territory. Grindstone was released soon after achieving this status, but he was sent back to Leavenworth on November 20, 1903, for killing another man. His prison records described him as an unmarried farmer, age thirty-eight in 1903 but looking ten years older, probably from disease. On June 26, 1904, he died of tuberculosis and was buried on Peckerwood Hill.

By 1906, all prisoners were housed inside the high walls, and the old military stockade was returned to the U.S. Army. By Frank's arrival, two societies existed side by side. In the town of Leavenworth were 24,342 people, 1,712 dogs, 1,338 horses, 629 cows, and two sheep. In the prison lived at least 887 inmates of all races, with 119, or one-eighth, sentenced there for life. Frank and the other new arrivals of November 1909 upped the percentages.

The prison train entered the gate and stopped between two long rows of factories. The train door opened and a cold blast pierced the stale air of the closed car. The five Mud Cut defendants, convicted and sentenced for the "most daring holdup in the West," groaned and stirred. A prison official took Bill Canada, Marshal Warner, and the others to see Warden McLaughry, while a guard took Frank and his fellows in tow. His manacles jingling, Frank limped down the aisle to experience what criminologists later called the "degradation ceremonies" meant to teach new inmates their proper place in the prison machine.

As Frank left the train, he noticed that the shops and factories on both sides of the track seemed to bulge with men. The workers watched the newcomers with interest, since train robbers were rare these days. For his part, Frank had expected an army of close-cropped prisoners wearing black and white stripes, but the close haircuts had been abandoned nine years earlier and only the very worst inmates— those reduced to "third grade" for escaping, attacking a guard, or seriously flaunting the rules—wore stripes. Most shuffled along dully, their prisoner numbers stamped on the pants legs and oversized jackets of their gray uniforms. A few of the inmates wore light blue for good behavior, while even fewer, the trusties, wore a white star on their jackets that served as a pass between buildings. Frank saw more trusties as he entered the center hall, the long corridor lined with administrative offices connecting the kitchen, dining hall, and chapel in the back to the cellblocks and still-to-be-completed rotunda in the front. He noticed that the floor was covered with red and white tiles and that the prisoners walked only on the red. As he watched, an inmate paying more attention to the newcomers than to where he was going stepped on a white tile, and a guard immediately knocked him into place with his club. The inmate, rubbing his arm where he'd been struck, shuffled past, eyes averted.

Frank paid close attention to the men. They all moved in silence, no talking allowed, the brush of the rough uniform cloth making a weird abrasive sound. Sometimes there were whispers, followed by a stern rebuke from the guards. Some guards were "pencil artists," quick to write up violations, though most seemed content with a harsh word or a nudge with the club. When a prisoner talked to a guard, he took off his cap, stood at attention a few feet away with his arms folded across his chest, and stated his business quickly. Guards took their time in answering, if they answered at all, and there was no small talk between prisoners and guards. Every rule seemed designed to emphasize an inmate's servility and a guard's absolute power.

The exception seemed to be the trusties, who alone of all the prisoners did not move in groups or under guard. Although still subordinate to their masters, they were not treated with contempt, if the regular inmate was the antebellum field hand, the trusty was the privileged house slave. Frank noticed that some trusties entered office doors carrying stacks of papers. They must be clerks, he thought, another cost-saving measure. He guessed there were very few secrets in Leavenworth if inmates did all the filing and recording. Eyes and ears were everywhere. Everyone, even the warden, lived under a microscope, every action seen and catalogued.

Since Frank and the others arrived late in the afternoon, his admission may have stretched over two days, though it was otherwise routine. His clothes and personal possessions were taken from him and inventoried; he was told to strip and shower; he was deloused and subjected to a search of all body cavities. As he stood naked and shivering, an admissions clerk and the guards took what were called Bertillon measurements, the core of a nearly universal criminal identification system developed in 1879 by French criminologist Alphonse Bertillon. The Bertillon system recorded eye and hair color, scars, and deformations, followed by a series of painstaking physical measurements that included the body—height sitting and standing, reach from fingertips to fingertips, length of trunk and head; the head—length and width, length and width of right ear; and the limbs—length of the left foot, left middle finger, left little finger, and left forearm. The clerk marked on a rectangular card every scar on Frank's body; he noted and joked about the webbing between his toes. It was as if Frank were a new kind of animal he'd found on the prairie to be readied for a zoo or museum.

A guard handed him a gray uniform with his new number, 6768, stamped in black ink; all five new arrivals were numbered in sequence—Frank as 6768, Matthews as 6769, Jack as 6770, Fritz as 6771, and Dan as 6772. Frank pulled on the uniform. The cloth was coarse and he was nearly choked by the jacket's huge metal button at the throat. The thing was as big as a half dollar, stamped with U.S. on the top edge and PENITENTIARY curving along the bottom like a smile. The guard snapped that leaving it unbuttoned was a violation. Everything here seemed to be a violation, Frank thought, and did as he was ordered. The clerk took Frank's mug shot and told him that, once developed, it would be glued to the Bertillon card and added to his file.

Frank was taken to the physician's office and told to strip again. Dr. A. F. Yohe was still relatively new to the prison hierarchy, having only joined the staff in 1906. The son of one of the town's first settlers, he'd watched the walls go up, but like most townspeople he had no idea what life was like inside. During his first year as prison doctor, fourteen prisoners died, an average mortality rate from previous years. Yohe was a conscientious doctor, and the rate declined: there were eleven deaths in 1907, ten in 1908, and five in 1909, mostly from pneumonia or tuberculosis. Each year Yohe begged the government for a water filtration system, since drinking water was pumped straight from the Missouri River, and he believed this to be the source of the inmates' persistent dysentery. He pleaded for a hospital, but Congress would not appropriate funds. From 1909–10, he saw 199 cases of malaria, 72 cases of tuberculosis, 69 of rheumatism, 67 of dysentery, and 50 of flu, or the "grippe," as well as another 345 injuries and ailments. He especially feared epidemics brought from outside. Without a hospital or quarantine unit there would be little way to stop them, and he checked each new prisoner carefully. Frank seemed like a good physical specimen for a desperado, Yohe thought:

no communicable diseases, normal pulse and heart rhythm. For all the romance surrounding western outlaws, many came in sick as dogs. Look at the others that had come in with Grigware: though Downer and Matthews seemed fit enough, Golden and Torgensen showed signs of consumption. In fact, they could be contagious, but without a quarantine unit all he could do was schedule regular exams and release them to the cellblocks. Yohe vaccinated Frank for smallpox, told him he was healthy as a horse, and released him down the admissions chain.

The next stop was the office of the chaplain, whose job was to sketch a word portrait of the inner man. F. J. Leavitt had been at Leavenworth for thirteen years and sometimes thought he was the last idealist left from James French's days. He asked Frank about his religion, trade, and family; about his education, place of birth, and marital status. He told Frank that although there was a school at the prison, there was no money yet for teachers; fortunately, there *was* a 7,680-volume library, including enough Bibles for every cell. He gave Frank three tickets entitling him to receive one ration of chewing tobacco each week (wasted, since he didn't use tobacco), to write one letter every two weeks, and to have visitors once a month. He could see his visitors any day except Sundays and holidays, the chaplain said. Leavitt reminded Frank that it was his job to screen the mail, and his duty to inform the warden if he read anything suspicious that might affect security. If Frank broke any rules, he said, his privileges would be taken away. Leavitt tried to remain upbeat as he said this, both for himself and the prisoner. The poor boy was here for life, and his card said he was only twenty-three. The years had given Leavitt a "broader view of life and a deeper sympathy for those who have fallen by the way," he wrote in the prison's 1909–10 annual report. "Indeed, the work is Christlike. It was on account of fallen man that our Savior came down into this wicked world."

Frank was taken to the office of Deputy Warden Frank A. Lemon. While the warden sat in the front office and dealt with the press and politicians, the deputy warden ruled the inside of the prison from his office in the isolation building. This was separate from the main building and well inside the prison yard. He handled discipline, hired and fired guards, decided where inmates lived and worked, granted special privileges, and threw troublemakers in the Hole, punishment cells that were located in his building. Lemon was in the prison from the time the gates were unlocked in the morning to when all cells were locked at night. He held night-time surprise visits to the different cellblocks to see that all inmates were quiet and all guards alert; one of his duties was to check the town's saloons and gambling halls to keep tabs on his guards' off-duty morals. Lemon had been here since September 1899 and knew the name of every inmate and guard. He'd sniffed out the 1901 escape before it happened, yet the warden had chosen to ignore Lemon's warning to guard the old construction site at night. McLaughry never ignored him again. The way Lemon saw it, the world was divided between high hats who took the credit and those who did the work. Lemon was one of the latter, but that was okay because he knew who held the real power here. The inmates might have their grapevine, but Lemon's was just as extensive, a network of guards, stool pigeons, and trusties who left messages in a box outside his door. He, Frank Lemon, had ferreted out the real leaders of the 1901 escape, and he had taken a patient vengeance through the years. There would be no more escapes from *his* prison, Lemon vowed. He made sure of that with what he considered the skillful and judicious use of fear.

If anything, the 1901 mutiny had brought Lemon's brutality into full flower. After that disaster, he devised exacting means of discipline. Prisoners returned from the isolation building telling of how their hands were shackled to the top of a cell door and their feet to the bottom. Cables attached to an electric battery were run along their spine and belly. There was the tale of Prisoner 3701, who fell off a scaffold while laying bricks and broke his arm. He'd warned guards earlier that the scaffold was unsafe, and after the accident he was so angry that he threatened to sue the prison once he was released. The previous doctor had refused treatment after he made these threats, fearing inclusion in the suit, and soon gangrene set in 3701's arm. When he begged for help, Lemon reportedly laughed in his face; when 3701 was found dead in his cell on November 5, 1905, his arm had turned black and swollen twice its normal size.

There was the tale of Prisoner 4002, who went insane and was thrown into isolation when he became uncontrollable. Lemon entered his cell, kicked and beat 4002 until his arm and three ribs were broken, and then transferred him to the Washington state asylum on August 26, 1905, where he died. There was Prisoner 5846, who told friends he was "tromped on" by Lemon in isolation. His lungs hemorrhaged and he died within thirty days, on October 3, 1908.

The most famous tale was the death of nineteen-year-old Clarence Maitland, Prisoner 5657. Maitland was too high-spirited for prison life and continually broke the rules. He was warned by older prisoners that the officials would kill him if he persisted with such foolishness, but the boy was naive about such things and thought he could never die. "No, they won't kill me," Maitland said. "They may punish me, but they have no right to kill me." He didn't understand that he no longer had rights in Leavenworth, even to his life; when the guards finally grew sick of Maitland's antics, they threw him in the Hole. For sixteen days he was beaten, given bread and water, and kept chained to the door. Each day the guards asked Maitland whether he would straighten up, but the boy refused to back down. Each day Lemon and a guard pumped ammonia into his face for thirty minutes, and on the seventeenth day of this treatment Maitland went insane. He was put in a straitjacket and chained to his bed. During one of his beatings, the lining of his stomach ruptured, and on May 17, 1907, he died. When told of his death, Lemon remarked to other prisoners within hearing, "If he don't last any longer in hell than he lasted here, they will make damned short work of him."

One axiom of prison life is that cruelty breeds corruption, and by 1909 rumors of graft surrounded Deputy Lemon. Most of the black and Indian prisoners were illiterate, thus making them easy prey for legal scams. When they filed appeals for release or a mitigation of sentence, Lemon reportedly recommended that they hire local attorney William Bond. He didn't mention that Bond and he were friends. Bond would take the appeal for $1,000 or whatever the inmate could afford and, once paid, apparently did nothing. Instead, he kept the money and paid part of the amount to Lemon as a kickback.

Frank was sent to see Lemon after leaving the chaplain's office. The deputy warden addressed him as "Prisoner 6768" and informed him that for the rest of his life in Leavenworth he was neither Frank Grigware nor a hotshot train robber but merely that number. Lemon exuded menace, staring at Frank while he spoke as if daring him to disagree. He was a big man, thick-chested, with a big walrus mustache that slashed sharply across the corners of his lips like a dark frown. Lemon conceived of order in Leavenworth as a form of frontier justice—the men in here were dangerous, as proven by the courts, and when something was dangerous you shot it before it shot you.

All this talk of rehabilitation and rebirth was eastern claptrap uttered by fools. As if to advertise that creed, he wore a high-crowned Stetson cowboy hat everywhere he went—the only prison official so clad in photos of the time. All other officials and guards wore the standard pillbox hat except McLaughry, who favored a white Panama, as if he were a planter and Leavenworth his personal plantation.

Lemon waited for dissent from Frank, and when none came he told Prisoner 6768 he would work in the carpenter's shop and assigned him to a cell. He handed Frank a ninety-page rule book issued to guards and inmates alike and outlined what was expected of him. The list of offenses seemed beyond number. They included: answering to his prisoner number in an improper manner; not making his bed; creating disturbances in line, in his cell, or in the dining hall; not buttoning his coat to the top button; showing disrespect, insubordination, or disobedience; quarreling, fighting, stealing, lying, or creating any kind of malicious mischief; breaking silence in line, in the dining room, at work, at sick call, in the chapel, or between cells; laughing, loafing, malingering, or acting foolhardy; using profanity, smoking, or spitting on the floor; wasting food; injuring library books; injuring or killing guards or other prisoners; approaching too closely to guards; writing unauthorized letters; escaping from prison; trying to escape from prison; plotting to escape from prison; or any other unbecoming conduct not mentioned. Lemon smiled and asked Frank if he had any questions. Both men knew that since the list covered everything but breathing and sleeping, it was nearly impossible not to get thrown in the Hole. "If there are no questions, the warden wants to see you," Lemon said.

This was unusual, since Robert McLaughry rarely interviewed new prisoners. But train robbers were a rarity for Leavenworth in 1909, a holdover from the frontier West, and the seventy-year-old warden wanted to see these oddities for himself.

Frank was ushered to an office near the front of the central hall and through a glass door to the inner sanctum. By November 1909, McLaughry had been Leavenworth's warden for a full decade. He would last until 1913, longer than any other Big House warden until the 1930s. During his fourteen years in charge he had forced through the construction of the great wall and most of the cellblocks, but he did so at a price. By now, the Progressive Era dream of reshaping criminals into law-abiding citizens had virtually vanished at Leavenworth, its one remaining proponent Chaplain Leavitt, the prison official with the least power. McLaughry stood before Frank as he entered, tall, gray-bearded, and ramrod-straight, dressed in a starched white shirt and black frock coat and pants, looking for all the world like a Calvinist minister, the picture of moral authority in a sinful world. It was the kind of image Americans took comfort in, one cultivated by many wardens of the time. After ten years, the *Leavenworth Times* and the competing Kansas City newspapers still treated McLaughry as a kind of rough-hewn prison saint, an iron-willed father presiding over a colony of lost and wayward boys. After the 1901 mutiny, construction delays, and a decade of rough-and-tumble Kansas politics, this was an accomplishment in itself.

McLaughry looked at Frank and said he knew a life sentence was a burden, but it must be faced manfully and perhaps things would change. He and other wardens supported a parole bill up before Congress, and President William Howard Taft did not threaten a veto. Given patience and good behavior, "life in prison" might be considerably shortened, McLaughry said.

Perhaps the warden's words gave Frank hope, though later events suggest otherwise. The push by wardens for parole and early release, called an "indeterminate sentence law," went back to McLaughry's predecessor, James French. Warden French argued as early as 1897 that "the greatest reform in the management of convicts would be to make their terms of imprisonment indefinite, so that instead of serving a fixed time a man would be allowed freedom at the earliest moment he was capable of returning to society." For French, the bill (which would be passed by Congress long after his departure, on June 24, 1910) fit into his larger vision of Leavenworth as a place of self-improvement, since a man had more hope if he worked toward a goal. McLaughry adopted French's goal, but with a difference: the hope of release made an inmate more *pliable*, a big stick that could be used for control.

The heart of McLaughry's method was not an idealistic belief in the state's power to improve the fallen but a reliance on the efficient use of power, obedience, and control. It is a fine point, but critical in understanding the direction Leavenworth had taken over the previous ten years. Finishing the construction and meeting costs took priority in McLaughry's annual reports over improving the inmates' health or education; he left it to Dr. Yohe to argue, unsuccessfully, for a hospital, or to Chaplain Leavitt to plead, unsuccessfully, for teachers and funds for the nine-room school, once thought integral for the prison's purpose and design. McLaughry worried about credits and debits, not lofty ideals.

By 1909, rumors of corruption and cruelty swirled around Robert McLaughry, but they never quite touched him in the same way they did Frank Lemon. Where Deputy Lemon had become brutal by nature, McLaughry rose above this, apparently considering the brutality of Lemon and his lieutenants a necessity in a brutal world. Unlike Lemon, he could just as easily hold out the carrot of early parole. Yet there were already troubling undercurrents in these last years of McLaughry's reign. Rumors that he had been investigated for cruelty and graft in his previous jobs as Chicago's police chief, warden of the Illinois State Prison, and warden of the Boys' Reformatory at Huntington, Pennsylvania, ran rife among the guards and prisoners. A federal investigation of the kickback scheme involving Lemon and Attorney William Bond eventually resulted in Lemon's quiet dismissal but never touched McLaughry. In 1906, the warden recommended Arthur Trelford, the captain of the watch held hostage during the 1901 mutiny, as Superintendent of Territorial Prisons in Santa Fe, New Mexico. A few months later, Trelford was fired for cruelty. One inmate was chained to a cell door as a punishment. When he complained he could no longer stand, he was beaten with handcuffs by guards and left hanging by his wrists until he reportedly went insane and died. Trelford had learned his craft at Leavenworth, and though McLaughry was never implicated, this and other incidents suggest that such practices were common. In order to control his prison, he turned a blind eye to the kind of brutality that, as an ostensibly enlightened Progressive Era warden, he publicly disavowed.

Remarks made in the late 1890s before the National Prison Association (precursor of today's American Correctional Association) suggest that at one time McLaughry abhorred corporal punishment, yet if one event can be blamed for his later blindness, it would be the mutiny of 1901. On November 6, 1901, the day before the escape, McLaughry was in Kansas City, preparing for a keynote speech at the prison association's annual congress; on November 7, he was speaking before 85 dour fellow wardens from across America when a messenger brought word of the riot. "Gentlemen," he told his listeners, "I have just been informed of a mutiny at my prison. I'll conclude this talk some other time." The episode left a bitter stain. He forced the resignation of three guards who said there were so many bullets flying during the breakout that *they* could just as easily have shot and killed Guard Waldrupe by accident as the inmates by design. Charles Ennis, the man eventually convicted of burying the two revolvers at the unguarded worksite, was allegedly tortured with an electric battery when he arrived at Leavenworth. As Ennis screamed and begged the guards to stop, McLaughry said, "Turn it on him, men! I have handled electricity all my life—turn it on him!" For the ringleaders sentenced to life at Leavenworth for Waldrupe's murder, every day in prison became a new kind of hell.

Frank's last stop in his "receival" at Leavenworth was the most recent addition to the admissions routine. He was taken down the hall to the office of Records Clerk Matthew W. McLaughry, the warden's son. Frank stood in the office of the neatly groomed young man; the walls and corners were stacked with filing cabinets and wooden boxes containing an avalanche of paperwork that the younger McLaughry always seemed to be putting into order. "I'm going to take your fingerprints," the records clerk said, pressing the pad of Frank's right thumb against an ink pad, then gently but firmly rolling it within the marked box of a rectangular card. He did this separately with all ten fingers, then at once with all the fingers of each hand. Frank looked at the inked whorls and loops left by his fingers and for the first time that day found himself amused. What did the unassuming clerk think he was doing? Frank wondered. "Nice prints," said the records clerk, almost gratefully, as if Frank had done him a favor, and then said Frank could wash his hands. This place got stranger with each moment, Frank mused. Yet more than anything else that day, this single innovation would have far-reaching consequences for Frank, the prison, and the nation. Warden McLaughry's nepotism would be his greatest legacy.

Matthew McLaughry existed in his father's shadow, a quiet man then in his early thirties, considered by some a clerkish bookworm, forgotten in the Sturm und Drang of the elder's personality. But Matthew McLaughry, like James French, had a vision, though it may have been vaguely formed when he came to Leavenworth and only took shape through expediency. His father had appointed him prison records clerk while at the Joliet penitentiary, and in 1899 the son followed the father to the prison on the plains. Then in his twenties, he dreamt like many young men of striking out on his own, and the exciting new prison would be the means. Where the level-headed father saw Leavenworth as a daily contest of will, the son imagined it as a giant test tube. For Matthew McLaughry did not see himself as a mere records clerk. He saw himself as an explorer in one of the last frontiers, that of man's psyche and soul.

Social scientists in the late nineteenth and early twentieth centuries were obsessed with somehow equating physical traits with behavioral patterns; these were still the glory days of such pseudosciences as physiognomy, the belief that facial features provide the key to an individual's moral and spiritual character, and phrenology, the theory that a person's character and intelligence could be measured by feeling the lumps and depressions on his or her skull. Nowhere could this obsession be more easily detected than in the developing field of criminal identification. The new "science" sought a criminal "type," a constellation of physical markers thought to be based on race, that allowed police to determine not only which men had broken the law, but which ones would. This very search drove Alphonse Bertillon's system, but the difficult series of measurements required a uniform exactness that was practically impossible at the time. Nevertheless, police in the United States and Europe dutifully marked the Bertillon values by hand onto heavy stock and classed each card according to head length, believing like the French criminologist that science would eventually find a criminal standard based on racial characteristics, most notably cranial capacity and the size of the brain.

They were wrong; the standard was never found. But Bertillon's difficulties did not deter others but served instead to spur them on. One logical consequence would come years later, during the Nazi era, with the development of a discipline called racial social research, or *Rassenseelenforschung,* in which a person's facial expression and physical bearing revealed the true nature of the "racial soul." Well before that, on December 3, 1902, Arthur MacDonald, a specialist with the U.S. Bureau of Education, could comfortably and confidently ask Congress to fund a lab for the study of Criminal, Pauper, and Defective Classes. His accompanying paper, "Statistics of Crime, Suicide, Insanity, and Other Forms of Abnormality," brought together the streams of fear- and race-based science in a 107-page statistical stew. "It may be said, with few exceptions, that within the last thirty or forty years there has been an increase in crime, suicide, insanity, and other forms of abnormality," he began. Although the increase was due "more to the rapid development of the world in general, rather than to any specific cause," MacDonald still generalized. "Dark hair," he said, "is predominant among criminals in general. . . . [C]raniums of small volume exceed, and those of very large volume are rare. . . . The extremities of criminals are often deformed."

Not surprisingly, Matthew McLaughry studied Frank's Bertillon measurements and took special notice of his webbed toes. Such obsessive classification indicated another stream of thought, one more subtle and frightening that remained unexplored until the philosophical inquiries of French phenomenologist Michel Foucault later in the century. The beliefs of Bertillon and lesser lights like MacDonald were part of a gradual differentiation between the normal and the abnormal that Foucault saw beginning in the eighteenth century and reaching through the Industrial Revolution to its fullest realization in the latter decades of the twentieth century. During this time, Western society increasingly defined and categorized the difference between normal and abnormal, healthy and sick, criminal and law-abiding, sane and insane. It then used these definitions to institutionalize, hide, and exclude those outside the "norm." This separation took two general forms: in a clinic or institution, for the "good" of the patient, and in a prison or workhouse, for the "good" of society. In these settings, outsiders were more easily regulated; they were also more easily watched and examined. Authorities wondered why the residents were different and what this difference said about society and the soul. It seemed a responsible way of arriving at the truth, based on sound principles of detached observation, yet such officially sanctioned exclusion was not always the norm. Before the eighteenth century, criminals were publicly punished, the mad were part of town life, the sick, disfigured, and disabled were cared for at home. Although the criminal, the mad, and the sick were separated from society, their exclusion was never absolute; their continued presence shaped family ties and public affairs. Now, however, the norm was defined by the abnormality shunted to its borders. That which was unseen became fascinating, dark, and sinister. The extreme, which framed society, gained a new importance, becoming the key to creating a utopia where the abnormal could be observed, codified, and controlled.

What better place to study abnormality than in a controlled environment like Leavenworth, home of the nation's worst criminals? the younger McLaughry wondered. Yet the Bertillon system had proved extremely unwieldy when hundreds and thousands of men were being measured, photographed, and classified. In the 1890s, while still in his twenties, Matthew had met Bertillon when the criminologist visited his father's prison at Joliet; Bertillon had honored the young records clerk by allowing him to take measurements of criminals with him. The process was difficult, slow, and yielded different results depending on the measurer. There must be a better system, thought Matthew, but nothing else seemed practical.

In 1901, Matthew was charged by his father to make sense of Leavenworth's massive and disorganized collection of criminal files; that year the prison population increased to 902, and it seemed as if it would just keep growing. Matthew collected all the files, back to the prison's authorization in 1895, and ordered that Bertillon measurements be taken of all incoming prisoners. Yet even as he did so, the prospect of keeping the files in order seemed impossible. He recorded the charges of newcomers by year and judicial district, creating a criminal "snapshot" decades before the FBI's Uniform Justice Reports, and discovered in the process some interesting facts and trends. The number of cowboys and farmers sentenced for crimes was diminishing, while the numbers of bank tellers, clerks, and other predominantly urban white-collar workers grew. Two of the men recently admitted had been sentenced for shooting angrily at passenger trains. Yet details like this did nothing to solve Matthew McLaughry's dilemma, and in 1903 a mix-up occurred that convinced everyone, even his stubborn, conservative father, that something had to change.

That year, an incoming black prisoner named Will West arrived aboard one of the prison trains. He was a tall lanky man, and as an admissions officer affixed a card with West's new prisoner number to his chest in preparation for his mug shot, he said, "You're William West, I presume."

"That's me," the prisoner meekly replied.

"You've been here before," said the officer.

"You're mistaken, sir," West said. "This is the first time I've been in this place." It was an important point for West, since first offenders were afforded more privileges than recidivists. Yet a file card existed for a William West, and the man's Bertillon measurements seemed to match those written on the card. He even looked like the photo. The admissions officer called West a liar, which the man adamantly denied.

But there was another problem, even if West was lying, for a release from Leavenworth was not recorded on the card. Had they overlooked it? Had he escaped and no one noticed? West continued to deny what seemed so obvious, when suddenly a guard came forward and said that another William West was even then in prison. He was serving a life sentence for murder and had been received in Leavenworth in September 1901. The admissions clerk had been unable to tell the two black prisoners apart from a photograph. More important, the Bertillon measurements proved worse than unreliable and actually helped confuse their identities.

So Matthew McLaughry conducted an experiment. By then an alternate system of identification using fingerprints was making news, and, though Leavenworth had not yet incorporated the system, the young records clerk was intrigued. Using a stamp pad and some card stock, he took the fingerprints of the two Will Wests. The prints were different, the only observable difference in the entire battery of measurements the two inmates had endured. Later correspondence from immediate family members showed that not only were the two Wests related, contrary to their statements, but they were identical twins. The only way to tell them apart was through their fingerprints.

The incident helped fuel a controversy then raging within scientific and law enforcement circles: Which system was more reliable, fingerprinting or Bertillon measurements? Although the original theory behind Bertillon's system had never been proven, the accumulation of painstaking physical measurements appealed to the new scientific spirit of detecting and fighting crime. Fingerprinting, on the other hand, seemed too easy to detractors; it recorded nothing but prints, and the system's use was new and untested. On the plus side, however, the prints themselves were remarkably easy to take, file, classify, and use. In 1888, Sir Francis Galton, Charles Darwin's cousin and the founder of eugenics, began a study of fingerprints in the belief that they, not cranial capacity, were the key to determining race and heredity. Galton was not the first to notice the individuality of the ridges, spirals, and loops left behind by an impression of the finger-tips; in ancient Babylon, fingerprints were used on clay tablets for business transactions, while the ancient Chinese left thumbprints on clay seals. In fourteenth-century Persia, a doctor observed that no two fingerprints were exactly alike; in 1686, Marcello Malpighi, a professor of anatomy at the University of Bologna, noted the whirls and ridges; in 1823, John Evangelist Purkinje, an anatomy professor at the University of Breslau, identified nine fingerprint patterns. Other English and American researchers took up the study of "skin furrows," but none developed a workable classification system.

Galton's book *Fingerprints*, published in 1892, changed all that. Although, like Alphonse Bertillon, he never found proof of his original theory of a criminal "type," he did succeed in proving what others had suspected—that fingerprints do not change over one's lifetime. More important for law enforcement, he proved scientifically that no two fingerprints are exactly the same. In fact, he calculated the odds of two prints matching as one in 64 billion. Galton delineated the characteristics by which prints could be identified: these "minutia," often referred to as Galton's Details, are basically still in use today.

In 1892, the same year as the release of Galton's book, Juan Vuc-etich, an Argentine police official, made the first known criminal fin-gerprint identification in the world. A woman named Rojas had killed her two sons and then cut her own throat in an attempt to make it look as if she too had been attacked and place the blame on another. But she'd left her bloody print on a doorpost, and using Galton's method Vucetich proved her identity as the real murderer. The news was electric and worldwide. Mark Twain's *Tragedy of Pudd'nhead Wilson*, which ends with a dramatic courtroom scene based on a fingerprint revelation, was published two years later in 1894.

In 1901, prints were introduced as a basis for identification in England and Wales, and in 1902 the New York Civil Service Commission began taking prints as part of their files.

In 1904, the year after the Will West problem, Matthew Mc-Laughry went to visit an expert in the field, Sergeant John Kenneth Ferrier, Scotland Yard's expert on fingerprinting, was giving demonstrations of the new technique at the British Display of the St. Louis Exposition, and McLaughry was impressed. He invited Ferrier to Leavenworth, and on October 1, 1905, McLaughry began taking fingerprints of all newly arrived men. By 1906, the year McLaughry took his own Grand Tour of Europe to study continental methods, his file included 3,000 prints. By 1907, there were 20,000 prints in Leavenworth's files. In time, Leavenworth would be named the Identification Center of the United States. Their files became the core of the FBI's fingerprint system when 800,000 prints were sent in 1924 to Washington.

It was the germ of a technological revolution, a system that in years to come would keep tabs on millions of Americans. Even the older McLaughry saw the possibilities and was not loath to share credit with his son. As the warden wrote in his report of 1906:

> Many habitual criminals, who were trying to pass themselves off as first offenders, have been discovered by this system. The effect of reliable identification upon prisoners is shown by the fact that no successful escape has taken place from this institution for nearly five years past. . . . It is coming to be understood that the certainty of capture and identification is more potent even than bolts and bars, or prison walls, in keeping the criminal element in line with the law.

All of this was lost to Frank on November 19, 1909. It meant less than zero. He had no idea that the inky smudges on the card stock would follow him like a bloodhound for nearly twenty-five years. Right now he wanted to get all this over with. He was tired and hungry. He felt less than worthless, for he'd been turned into a number and could look forward to at least forty more years of this gray sameness unless he got lucky and died.

The guards gave Frank a Bible, cup, mirror, cuspidor, face bowl, one piece of hard soap, a comb and brush, blankets, sheets, a pillowcase, a nightshirt, a rule book, and a change of clothes. He watched as Jack and the others were led off under escort to separate cells. Jack glanced back and tried to raise his shackled hands in parting, but a guard tapped him on the thigh with his club and told him eyes front and no malingering. He walked away slowly, flanked by the blue-suited guards. There is a brief reference to *Jack Shelton* buried among other inmate names in the 1910 annual report: between November 19, 1909, and June 30, 1910, Jack was thrown three times in solitary, a high rate for a new prisoner. Other than that, there are few references to Jack in the prison chronicles. Frank watched him leave. If one can see his youth passing in a single instant, this may have been the moment for Frank. He felt drained by sadness. They'd both been so naive.

Then it was Frank's turn. Two guards flanked and led him through locked doors and down long halls to his cell. This was an open cage with a steel bedstead and a mattress, a camp stool and table, a small shelf for books, one electric light, a "night bucket," and flowing water "for all purposes." The cell was double-bunked, but for the moment no one else was assigned with him. Frank walked three paces from end to end until he stopped at the bars; he stretched out his arms and touched the walls on both sides. The voices of other inmates came to him in whispers. It seemed like the whispers never stopped, an undercurrent of sibilance that slackened only when a guard passed by.

A long bar slid over the top of his cell door, locking fifty cages at once. His cellblock rang like iron. "Lights out soon!" a guard yelled. Frank stripped to his shirt and shorts, crawled beneath the blanket, and closed his eyes.

CHAPTER SEVEN

The Rules of the Game

THE MORNING BELL pealed at 5:30 A.M., ringing off the steel cell walls. A muted shifting, shuffling, and swearing rose from the surrounding cells. Frank put on into his uniform, made his bed, swept his cell. Since he didn't chew tobacco, he didn't have to clean his cuspidor. He washed his face and hands. Until recently the plumbing had not worked; when that happened, prisoners had marched to a pit, each carrying his "night bucket." The buckets were still issued, but the toilets were more reliable, which meant the inmates spent more time in their cells.

Frank gazed out his bars. The cellblock was a box within a larger box, a giant stone rectangle five stories high enclosing two rows of cages. These were stacked in the building's center, one atop the other, back to back and side by side. Each tier of cells was fronted by a steel balcony; Frank figured that the open space between his cell and the wall was twenty feet wide. Square windows overlooked the railroad track and the prison's shops and factories. Steel for the unfinished east cellblock lay piled in the yard. As the prison train crept slowly on its east–west track, the factories and powerhouse belched a smoke as gray as the inmates' uniforms. It was said that the huge cathedral windows planned for the unfinished east and west cellblocks would overlook a spacious park and give the illusion of open space. There were no illusions in Frank's cell.

At 6:30 A.M. a second bell rang, and Frank marched to breakfast an arm's length behind the man in front of him. His tier marched in columns of two. If visitors passed, he dropped his gaze to the floor. His column marched through a locked door at the end of the building, curved through a locked gate, went down a long hall, and marched through a second gate into the dining room. Frank doffed his cap as he entered and followed the others down twenty rows of tables divided by four wide aisles. They sat on one-way benches. Frank sat with his back straight, arms folded, eyes in front, waiting in silence until every prisoner was seated and facing the same direction. Guards strolled down the aisles, clubs tucked under their arms, enforcing the no-talking rule. A bell rang and everyone started eating. As Frank ate, he saw men hunched over their plates like dogs guarding their food. He hunched protectively too.

Frank had thirty minutes to eat, no more or less, three times a day, a half hour for each meal. The dining hall was the one place in Leavenworth where a man found abundance, if not quality. His meal was based on the standard army garrison ration, set in 1901 after food spoilage in the Spanish-American War contributed to the high death rate; for every soldier who died in battle, fourteen died from illness and disease. Frank's standard meal included beef, flour, beans, potatoes, prunes, coffee, vinegar, salt, and pepper. Peas, rice, hominy, onions, canned tomatoes, and fresh vegetables were provided when available. Mutton was a treat, as were peaches and apples. Frank could fill his plate as often as he wanted, but he had to eat it all or be written up. Inmate waiters, food trays hanging by leather straps from their shoulders, ranged up and down the aisles. Frank raised his right hand if he wanted bread, his left hand if he wanted to speak to an officer about the service or food. If he wanted more coffee or water, he held up his cup; if he wanted more meat, he held up his fork; if he wanted more vegetables, he held up his knife; if he wanted more soup, he held up his spoon. Unused bread was placed to the left of his plate: leaving it anywhere else was a violation. Silverware went to the right. He sat erect when finished, arms folded.

A bell rang and Frank dropped his hands to his sides. A second bell rang and he rose, marching back to his cell for a rest. At 7:30 A.M., he left his cell again and marched to the yard. He stood in a row of prisoners to the south of the railroad tracks as an officer called their numbers from a roster. The switch engine hissed and creaked by the west gate, delivering supplies. They answered promptly. Anything less earned a dressing-down.

The captain of the Day Watch strolled behind the row of guards, eyeing the prisoners. Fred Zerbst was an ex-calvary man from Wisconsin with beetling brows and quick, jerky movements, a career officer who knew his prison backward and forward. "Number 6768," called the guard. "Present, sir," Frank said. Zerbst called him out of line, checked his own roster, and assigned him to the carpenter shop. Frank joined the line and listened as Zerbst went through the same ritual with Matthews, Jack, Fritz, and Dan. Zerbst announced that all five prisoners had arrived the previous day for train robbery and now were here for life. He made a joke that the only train around today was the switch engine, but there was nothing there worth robbing. He warned the newcomers to answer briskly each morning if they didn't want to visit the Hole.

"Pay no attention to Zerbst," whispered an inmate to Frank's right. "He'll do anything to break the monotony." Frank turned and glimpsed the man's number: 6624. "Keep your eyes straight," he hissed. "You wanna get us busted?" A guard yelled for quiet, but turned too late to see who broke the rules.

Frank worked in the carpenter shop from eight to noon, took thirty minutes for lunch, then worked until shortly before 5:30 P.M. A whistle blew and they marched to supper. Frank ate, sat straight, lined up, marched up the hall, reentered his cell. Mail was delivered, but there was none for Frank; he read his rule book and started a letter; lights-out was called at 9 P.M. The next day was the same, followed by the day after that. On Saturdays he showered and cleaned his cell. On Sundays he exchanged his clothes and linen and stripped to his underwear for inspection.

The unchanging routine numbed him, but anything was infinitely better than staying in his cell. He quickly understood why old-timers called Leavenworth a mausoleum. Each cell was like a dark slot where the dead were stacked and stored. The limestone walls smelled damp and fusty; the metal bars and walls smelled of gray paint and cold steel. He knew by heart the sixty rectangles formed by the crossbars at the front of his cell; his pillow was propped against them, and every morning on waking he felt them through the muslin. Most of his time in the cell was spent on the bunk, propped on his stomach, studying the sky outside the windows and listening to the steady ringing footsteps of the guards making their regular rounds on the tiers. There was barely room to sit up in his cage, no room to walk, just three steps from the stone wall in back to the bars in front. Men hung on their bars all night, peering out like monkeys in a zoo. He doubted he could ever visit a zoo again without sympathizing with the poor creatures—but what was he saying? He was in here for life, he was the monkey in the cage. There were times when the weight of the cellblocks seemed to press on his chest. If he went crazy from the weight, would he also hang from the bars and scream?

So getting out of the cage was a blessing, but even then everything was regimented. He was counted anywhere and everywhere he went. When he left his cell for breakfast, when he returned, when he started work, when he finished. Frank was counted when he left his cell on Saturdays for close order drill, when he went to bed at night, when he rose in the morning. The head counts were said to guard against escapes, but with the high walls and gun towers he could not imagine how escape was possible. He heard the counting when he went to sleep at night. He heard the counting in his dreams.

Thanksgiving came six days after his arrival, and even in that short time the day's change of routine seemed a kind of freedom. At 10 A.M. that day, the inmates marched to the chapel; the visiting preacher's sermon was titled "Sunshine and Awkwardness." Frank struggled to stay awake, since sleeping in chapel was a sure route to the Hole. After the sermon the prison orchestra played music normally heard in a concert hall. Frank spotted among the other musicians the same inmate who'd told him about Zerbst; 6624 played violin, his long sardonic face unusually peaceful as his bow glided across the strings. By now Frank knew that the man's name was Theodore Murdock, but that was all he knew. Murdock worked next to him in the carpenter shop, but Frank was too frightened of being caught by the guards to open his mouth and ask more. After chapel they filed to the dining hall, where they ate turkey and dressing, mashed potatoes, green peas, brown gravy, currant jelly, mince pie, pickles, oranges, apples, coconut cake, and coffee with milk and sugar. All work details were called off for Thanksgiving, and Frank marched back to his cell. The rest of the day he dozed fitfully, the best way to forget Alice and home. While other prisoners held on to their memories, counting the days to release, lifers tried to forget the past. They'd never go back, so memory was torture.

The Thanksgiving variations merely emphasized the backbreaking sameness of every other day. During his first couple of weeks, Frank fought the monotony by watching others. In the three years that he'd journeyed through the West, Leavenworth—and the society it mirrored—had undergone a change. In 1906, when Frank left Spokane, more than half of Leavenworth's inmates came from Indian Territory. In 1909, 59 percent were from the East and Midwest, with large numbers coming from Washington, D.C. In 1906, more than half the prisoners were ages twenty to thirty; by 1909, that number had dropped to 44 percent. In 1906, 42 percent of the men were convicted of property crimes and 28 percent of violent crimes. By 1909, the rate had flipflopped, with 41 percent jailed for violent crimes and 37 percent for theft. In 1906, when nearly half the inmates had previously lived and worked in rural locales, 431 prisoners called themselves farmers and 24 were cowboys. In 1909, there were 133 farmers and no cowboys. The vanishing West was also vanishing here.

In three short years, Leavenworth had become eastern, older, urban, and more violent, the opposite of that place James French had envisioned in 1897. In addition to horse thieves and train robbers, as well as the expected murderers, rapists, and stickup artists, Frank was surrounded by safe blowers, hotel sneaks, porch climbers, confidence men, sharpers, and other false pretenders. There were fifty women prisoners kept in a separate dorm, but few of the men ever saw them. Frank rubbed shoulders with former actors, artists, bankers, bartenders, druggists, embalmers, prizefighters, and wrestlers, as well as one pilot and a professor of languages. There were Italian Black Hand counterfeiters accused of passing fake bills and of killing an Italian detective in New York City. Somehow they all seemed to know about him and about each other, something he found amazing in a supposedly silent world. He too learned ways to break that silence without getting caught by the guards. Cellmates spoke in undertones; men whispered to those in adjoining cells between the bars or through the air vents above the beds. They knocked lightly on their steel walls, the messages tapped from cell to cell via inmate telegraph. Men talked from the sides of their mouths during meals so it looked like they were chewing; they passed notes everywhere, even down in the Hole. They swept messages crumpled as trash into each other's cells. There were ways to fish messages down the toilets to cells immediately underneath, but that was an art requiring a knowledge of water levels and air pressure that Frank never mastered.

Frank quickly saw that a social structure existed, built and maintained by thieves. Hard-core murderers tended to be loners while rapists were shunned, but thieves—maybe because their livelihood depended upon the exchange of reliable information—had established in Leavenworth a society similar to their own outside. They adhered to a rigid code of conduct based upon a prohibition against cooperating with the guards. The greatest sin was ratting on a fellow prisoner, or "snitching," about the only offense in this era that earned a man the death sentence from his fellow prisoners. This was usually exacted with home-made knives called shivs. Those who lived by the code were called "Johnsons," "right guys," or "regulars." There were prison "merchants," "gamblers," or "politicians," who controlled the flow of contraband; "rapos," the child sex abusers who were pariahs; and of course the snitches, or stool pigeons. The common enemy were the guards, or bulls. Everyone in here had at least one thing in common: all had been arrested, or "ditched," and sentenced, or "settled."

The cant grew strangest when Frank's neighbors described a violent interlude. In his first month, he heard at least eleven expressions for being knocked in the head. While he easily understood "I busted him on the cranium," "whiffed him on the skull," "cracked him on the nut," and "dinged him on the brain box," it was harder to recognize "I bammed him on the bean," "tapped him on the conk," "bumped him on the beezer," and "biffed him on the coco." "I nailed him on the knob" had nothing to do with carpentry; "I slugged him in the belfry" did not occur in church.

When Frank heard "I lammed him on the peak," he asked for a translation. The man he asked was Teddy Murdock, 6624. Murdock seemed puzzled by Frank and finally one day said so. It was easy to do in the carpenter shop, where voices faded into the pounding of hammers, swipe of planes, and whine of saws. In addition to planing beams for framework and cutting them to size, Frank had to make prison furniture, particularly small tables and frame-back side chairs. Though he knew how to build a house, furniture was a whole new game. One day Murdock was given permission by a guard to teach Frank the use of a felloe saw, a contraption with a handle that turned the thin blade at right angles, making it good for cutting curves in the wood. Murdock interspersed his lessons with questions of his own. The grapevine had figured out Downer, Torgensen, and Matthews; they had the look of ex-cons and seemed to fit right in. Golden, though new to prisons, was angry at everything and already getting into trouble with the guards. Only Frank had the look of a "fish," or prison virgin, and the inmates had a hard time believing he'd actually robbed a train. "I didn't rob any goddamn train," Frank spit back. Murdock laughed quietly and answered, "Everybody says that here."

Murdock was only three years older than Frank, but decades removed in the ways of prisons and crime. He was thinner than Frank and two inches shorter; like Frank, he was a carpenter, listing his profession as "builder and joiner." He mentioned that he'd done some cabinetmaking but his real love was counterfeiting. The production of counterfeit money required patience, education, and artistic talent, and Theodore Murdock had all three. Even his jailers conceded his intelligence, noting that he played violin like a master and subscribed to the *Kansas City Journal*, a rarity among inmates in that day. He was a skilled sketch artist, able to capture a guard or prisoner's likeness with amazing speed and accuracy. Early in his youth, he'd decided to use these talents to get rich quick, for he too believed in the Gospel of Wealth, he said. In 1907, under the name of Arthur Collins, he was arrested in Seattle for forgery and sentenced that June to serve two years in the Washington penitentiary. He was paroled a year and two months later, on August 1, 1908, the same summer that Frank and Jack moved to Denver. As Murdock worked his way east from city to city, he kept trying to get rich illegally. On April 10, 1909, the month that Frank and the others lingered in Kansas City, he was arrested in Milwaukee, Wisconsin, for passing bogus $10 gold Indian head eagles. He got lucky, convincing the judge that he hadn't known the coins were counterfeit, and was either released on bond or served a minimal amount of time in jail. The summer of 1909 found him in Chicago, married to a woman named Emma. There were suggestions that the marriage was not made in heaven and that Emma Murdock turned her talented mate in. On June 13, 1909, Theodore Murdock was convicted in Chicago of counterfeiting silver coins, fined $2,000, and sentenced to ten years in federal prison. Three days later, he arrived in Leavenworth.

As Frank watched Murdock cut a graceful curve for the chair seat, it struck him that this man could make almost anything. The creation of turn-of-the-century "wildcat," or counterfeit money, was an exacting if lucrative activity. The practice went back to colonial days, when notes issued by the colonies did not carry the complex engravings of later currency. It was assumed that the introduction of national paper currency in the 1860s and the establishment of the U.S. Secret Service would put an end to the practice, but just the opposite occurred; the amount of bogus money reaching circulation actually increased. Between June 1875 and June 1876, the federal government seized counterfeit coins and currency with a face value of $232,000, equivalent to $3.8 million today. Murdock's choice of coinage over notes, though unusual, was timely. The controversy over the gold standard and Roosevelt's own personal animus to coins led the U.S. Mint to start and stop new coin designs with disconcerting suddenness. The Secret Service and the Treasury Department actually aided counterfeiters by refusing to divulge details of bogus bills and coins to all but banks, believing that public disclosure would encourage new wildcatters to test their own skills. If anything, this created an atmosphere where the fake was as "real" as the real.

As Murdock worked, he pointed out a couple of other convicts in the carpenter shop. He motioned toward a man in his mid-thirties, with 5332 stamped on his pants and collar. "That's John Gideon," he said. Like Frank, Gideon was a lifer, and like Frank he was convicted of robbing the U.S. mail. Though not as talented as Murdock, John Gideon was acknowledged as one of the most cool-headed men in prison. In 1905, he'd single-handedly held up a Union Pacific express outside Moscow, Idaho, and taken $50,000 from the mail car, a small fortune equivalent to $980,000 today. He was not caught for several months, a testament to keeping his own counsel and working alone, but eventually was sent to Leavenworth on October 6, 1906. He'd stayed out of trouble since then, rarely getting written up, no record of being thrown in the Hole. He was seen but unnoticed by the guards, biding his time and watching the world around him. John Gideon didn't plan to stay in prison forever, Murdock said.

The other man that Murdock pointed out was thirty-seven-year-old Bob Clark, 4768, a wild-eyed man with a pasty complexion. Clark was built like a brick, standing 5 feet 5 inches and weighing 143 pounds; his head was square, his nose long and pointed, and he stared at men balefully with deep-set piercing blue eyes. The tip of his right little finger was missing, and he lacked a tooth in his lower jaw, adding to this gnarled, battered visage. Clark was dangerous and partly crazy, Murdock warned, but some people thought he was brilliant, including the warden. "He is capable of doing much good or much harm," McLaughry wrote. "He is one of the most thorough criminals that I have ever known—one of the most cold-blooded and cold-hearted, and he would not hesitate to take your life or mine, in an instant, if either stood in the way of his path to escape."

Bob Clark had let it be known that he planned to escape, and Murdock, though cautious and distrustful, admitted that if any prisoner in Leavenworth was capable of breaking out, it was 4768. Life at Leavenworth was a war for Bob Clark; he'd been one of the three main conspirators in the 1901 escape, along with Tom Kating, 5903, and Arthur Hewitt, 5956, and all three had been paying for eight years for their brief taste of freedom.

Clark was born in 1876 in Arkansas to a father from Georgia and a mother from Alabama, just two of the thousands of transplants from the Deep South escaping Reconstruction. He received from his parents a hatred for the federal government, a mechanical mind, and the ability to read and write. He inherited little else, for he left home in 1892 at age sixteen. Three years later he was arrested for robbery and sentenced to ten years in the penitentiary. Little was known about those missing three years except that by the time of his arrest in Texas he'd qualified as a machinist and was skilled in operating heavy machinery. His sentence started in 1895, the year the military stockade opened to federal prisoners in Fort Leavenworth; given these skills, he was assigned to the construction site, where he operated the steam-powered winch moving heavy limestone blocks into place for the cellblocks and walls.

The job determined his fate. Controlling the winch gave Clark a certain measure of independence. More importantly, he was not watched at every second. About a month before the 1901 mass breakout, Arthur Hewitt and Tom Kating approached him with a plan. A friend of theirs, Charles Ennis, had just been released from prison and gotten two pistols from Kating's brother in Kansas City. Though Ennis promised to creep back into the unguarded worksite at night, they said, the best place to hide the guns was in the winch's coal pile, protected from the elements in a shed. Clark's job gave him natural access to the hiding place. Was he in? Bob Clark smiled for one of the few times anyone could remember. Sure, he said, but only if he got a gun.

Though the mass escape succeeded, Clark was recaptured within a few days. By then, Guard John Waldrupe had died, shot between the eyes while defending the worksite's south wall from the rioting prisoners, and Clark was thrown in the Hole. The only light came from a high window overhead. In order to get full rations, he was required to break up a certain quantity of limestone rocks with a hammer. Doing the job meant breathing in rock dust and contracting a form of silicosis thought to be pneumonia. Refusal meant near-starvation, or at least it felt that way to the men. When he was let out, it was to face trial with seven other escapees for Waldrupe's murder. He was found guilty, sentenced to life at hard labor, dressed in black and white stripes, and told he'd stay in Leavenworth until he died.

For the next eight years, Clark's record was one of unrelenting hatred for the guards, which they returned in kind. He tried talking other prisoners into staging another mutiny, but never with success. In October 1905 he was caught sweeping a newspaper with hand-written notes into the cell of two men sentenced for murder and train robbery; on August 2, 1906, he was caught talking with another inmate about an escape plan. He was thrown in the Hole until October and almost immediately upon release was caught talking again. He was marked for constant surveillance by the warden, Deputy Lemon, Captain Zerbst, and all subordinate officers, watched so closely he barely had to open his mouth to be written up. The harassment drove him over the edge. On January 25, 1908, he was caught with letters containing plans for starting a riot; he hoped to escape in the confusion. McLaughry called him to his office and demanded to know for whom the letters were intended. Clark stared at the warden and refused to answer, an unrelenting stubbornness that raised McLaughry's Scottish ire. "You've been in isolation twice before, and I'll keep you there until you tell the truth!" McLaughry shouted. "I will not trifle with you again!"

Clark stared back at his old enemy. "I'll die in the Hole before I tell you."

"All right." McLaughry spat. "You can start working on that experiment now."

Clark stayed in the Hole for nearly a year. Sometimes McLaughry would visit and ask Clark if he was ready to talk. From the darkness of his cavern, Clark told him to go to hell. "Your destiny is in your hands," McLaughry replied.

In June of 1908, the warden learned that Clark had somehow

smuggled a letter outside the prison to Mrs. G. P. Black, a widowed evangelist, who asked to see the prisoner and talk to him about his immortal soul. McLaughry answered the widow in no uncertain terms. Clark was "a very shrewd and sharp villain" who was playing on her sympathies, he said, in refusing her request. The next month, Clark was found with a false key in his cell, made from the metal of a tooth powder can. For that, he stayed in the Hole for the rest of the year. When he came out, he talked to his old friends Hewitt and Kating. The details of the conversation are not recorded, but after it was over they agreed that Bob Clark had nearly been driven insane.

One way he kept his sanity during the long hours in solitary was by dreaming up an invention. There is a long history of prison inventors. A former inmate of the Colorado penitentiary patented an indoor toilet and cleared $2 million in royalties after his release. A man released from Sing Sing in New York patented a method for automatically rewinding motion picture reels, which had previously been rewound by hand. Clark dreamed up a device allowing livestock dealers to dip their cattle without danger of injury or loss as the cows and bulls crowded into the chemical bath designed to kill ticks and other parasites. In 1909, an inventor in Sheffield, Alabama—one S. M. Avery—wrote U.S. Attorney General George Wickersham that he thought Clark's idea was viable; in turn, Wickersham told McLaughry to let Clark draw up detailed plans. Wickersham seemed to sense the old hatred between the warden and the prisoner and apparently phrased his letter as diplomatically as possible. McLaughry still hit the roof and fired off a letter to Washington, objecting that giving Clark the time and material for plans and a model "would be considered as evidence that the authorities are afraid of him and have to favor him in order to keep out of danger." His main consolation was the hope that "the invention will not prove patentable."

Clark was not the only notorious prisoner. Frank Ledbetter, the "Oklahoma Badman," was sentenced to Leavenworth for life for a murder committed during his desperado days. Frank Thompson, the black inmate mistakenly called the leader of the 1901 escape, was still in Leavenworth, as were the true ringleaders, Arthur Hewitt and Tom Kating. Fred Robinson, sentenced to life for his part in the escape, had been shackled so tightly as punishment that he'd become a cripple for life. At one point the previous prison doctor broke Robinson's leg to reset it, remarking as he did so that he "guessed he would not run anymore."

Leavenworth had a way of entrapping everyone who set foot within its walls, and not just the inmates. As November crept into December, Frank began to see that the guards were prisoners too. Until 1908, they had worked seven days a week; now they worked six, but still in twelve-hour shifts, and if they wanted another day off they had to find a replacement. Even with the new shifts, their hours in 1909 stretched longer than they seemed. The guards were required to rise at 5 A.M. and be ready for duty when the gates opened at 6 A.M., a challenge, considering the unreliable trolley they rode that started three miles away in the heart of town. By 7 A.M., the prisoners had returned from breakfast and were soon marched to work; they were not locked back in their cells until after 6 P.M., which meant that a guard did not eat his own supper until 7 P.M. or later. It translated into a fourteen-hour workday.

For all his troubles, a guard in 1909 was paid $70 per month; from that he purchased his blue uniform and paid a $3 monthly trolley fee, among other expenses. Although no taxes were taken out in those days, there were no fringe benefits. If he died on the job, his widow and children were destitute. Both on the job and off, a guard was expected, according to the 1898 prison rule book, to refrain from "whistling, scuffling, immodest laughter, profanity, boisterous conversation, exciting discussion on politics, and other subjects calculated to disturb the harmony and good order of the penitentiary." He could not smoke at work; he could not talk with prisoners or other guards except in the performance of his duties. He could not discuss the penitentiary when off duty; Lemon reportedly had informers in the saloons to tell him when men complained. A guard was hired and fired at Lemon's pleasure. There was no appeal.

Not surprisingly, anger festered easily among the guards, most of it taken out on the prisoners. It was a common saying that no guard felt dressed without his nightstick, relinquished only when he drew wall duty and carried a gun. Eight years after the 1901 escape, bandages were still common sights on the split skulls of prisoners. Although there was no corroboration, a letter written by Tom Kating to President Woodrow Wilson in 1913 mentioned that only the most brutal guards were promoted. Even among lawmen there was acknowledgment of the problem. "A great deal depends upon the characters of the prison officials and guards, who in some instances are rough men," wrote F. H. Tyree, U.S. marshal of the Southern District of West Virginia, to R. V. LaDow, superintendent of Federal Prisons and Prisoners. "Bad treatment, together with dirt and bad food, do not tend to elevate."

But there were other means of control than beatings. These were all the little things that chipped away at Frank, making him more pliant for the guards: the reminders of his worthlessness, turning him into something without substance, a walking ghost; the prison haircut; the uniforms, all issued in the same size; the shuffling silence, day in, day out; the Prussian punctuality of daily schedules; the meaningless labor of moving wood from one pile to another, just to move it back. Then there was the near-total control of information, cutting off Frank and most other inmates from the outside world; the limit on the number of letters he could write, books he could read; the guards who disdained speaking or looking at inmates; the few possessions allowed, which could be taken away for any reason.

On December 4, 1909, Frank watched as McLaughry banned the matches that were issued to inmates for lighting their pipes after a couple of dropped matches started fires. Beforehand, the inmates could smoke after lunch and at the end of the day, one of their few pleasures. Now Frank listened as inmates called out for lights and guards brought oil lamps, then passed lighted tapers through the bars. The guards took their time or didn't come at all, one more small show of power. The contradictory rules assured violation; there were so many it was nearly impossible not to be found guilty of some offense at least weekly. If a man was accused of an infraction and admitted guilt, he was punished. If he denied his guilt, he was accused of calling the guard a liar and thrown in the Hole.

THE VERY ARCHITECTURE of Leavenworth served to oppress people, the opposite of its original intent. William Eames had visited the most innovative prisons in England and the Continent before building Leavenworth, insisting with James French that the new penitentiary must be as impressive as any national institution then existing. He wanted a huge gate that opened into a spacious park, but this was nixed by Congress and the Justice Department, both citing costs. His other design statements—rotunda and columns, huge cathedral windows and limestone facings—made it through government auditors because a tradition of parallel styling already existed between public places and prisons. The original and characteristic forms that inspired architects in the eighteenth and nineteenth centuries were radial plans like Leavenworth's, as well as circles and polygons, a classical formalism that found expression in such monumental arrays as Versailles and Washington. In fact, many of the architects steeped in this tradition had cut their teeth on prisons. The first public project in America of English engineer Benjamin Henry Latrobe, arguably the most famous of the United States' early civic architects, was the 1797 construction of the Virginia State Penitentiary in Richmond, later known as the Wall. Latrobe's design was inspired by English prison reformer Jeremy Bentham's circular "panopticon"; it featured a three-story horseshoe-shaped building in which exposed balconies allowed light and air into each cell, a design that so impressed Thomas Jefferson he commissioned Latrobe to design the Virginia state capitol and then made him surveyor of public buildings. In this capacity Latrobe designed the south wing of the U.S. Capitol and supervised its reconstruction and completion after the British burned it during the War of 1812. Elements of Latrobe's prison in Richmond inspired the Capitol, which in turn inspired the prison on the plains.

The principle that style must reflect purpose was a familiar one to jailers, but the original intent was usually the opposite of that planned for Leavenworth. A prison must inspire "darkness, threat, ruin, (and) terror" to control crime among the citizenry, wrote Francesco Milizia in his 1785 *Principi di architettura civile*. The truth was in the details, which should be terrifying. Prisons should be places of "high and thick walls with savage-like appendages which throw forth the most horrible shadows," of "uninviting and cavern-like entrances" and "frightful inscriptions," Milizia said. Through the end of the nineteenth century, state prisons were built to resemble medieval battlements: huge, gloomy, gothic fortifications, like Eastern State Penitentiary in Philadelphia and Sing Sing in New York, that weighed heavy on the criminal while frightening citizens outside into toeing the straight and narrow path of the law. The idea of individual "cells" had somber religious antecedents. Prior to the Enlightenment, jails and prisons were basically large cavernous lockups where men and women were dumped, regardless of age, crime, and sex, while awaiting trial and punishment. Many of these were underground cisterns accessible only through a grating covering a hole in the top, while others were large common rooms in reconverted manor houses, con-

Prisoners marched two and a half miles from the military stockade at Fort Leavenworth to the worksite where they completed the new federal penitentiary, circa 1900. Armed guards can be seen at the edges of the column. The cross-prairie marches continued from 1897 until the prison's walls were up and the first cellblock opened on February 21, 1903. *U. S. BUREAU OF PRISONS*

John Grindstone, Leavenworth's first prisoner. He was an Eastern Shawnee Indian, charged with murder in the Oklahoma Territory. He died of tuberculosis on June 26, 1904, and was buried in the prison cemetery, which inmates called Peckerwood Hill. *U.S. BUREAU OF PRISONS*

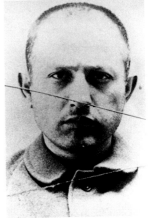

Prisoners dig a trench for Leavenworth's towering wall, circa 1900. A shack with an armed guard can be seen behind the prisoners. The worksite was surrounded by the 12-foot wooden palisade until the four stone and brick walls enclosed the 22-acre prison. *U.S. BUREAU OF PRISONS*

An artist's rendition of Leavenworth Penitentiary, circa the first decade of the twentieth century. The view looks north toward the U.S. Military Reservation. The rotunda, main cell blocks and factories can be seen, as can Railroad Avenue, running east to west. The east and west gates can also be seen. The "chute" through which Grigware and five other inmates escaped on April 21, 1910, can be seen by the west wall. *NATIONAL ARCHIVES*

A view of Leavenworth's dining hall. Inmates had thirty minutes in which to eat; they all faced the same direction, and ate in silence. The hall was said to hold 1,200 inmates; food was plentiful, but the prisoners were put on report if they failed to eat everything served on their plates. *NATIONAL ARCHIVES*

Leavenworth's uniformed guards with their rifles, 1910. Warden Robert McLaughry sits in the front, second from the right, holding his Panama hat; Deputy Warden Frank Lemon sits to his left, wearing a Stetson hat.
U. S. BUREAU OF PRISONS

Although each cell was originally intended to hold one man, Leavenworth soon grew overcrowded and double-bunking became common. A small table containing an inmate's few possessions can be dimly seen in the shadows of Cell 119. The toilet and other fixtures would have been by the back wall, at the foot of the beds. **NATIONAL ARCHIVES**

The eastern "Railroad Gate" into Leavenworth, one of the first sights new inmates had as they arrived aboard specially fitted prison trains. The towers with the derby-shaped roofs were manned by armed guards. **U.S. BUREAU OF PRISONS**

A modern photo of Leavenworth's west wall. The concrete section in the middle was the location of the west gate and "railroad chute" through which Grigware and his fellow prisoners hijacked the supply train on April 21, 1910. The west gate, chute and railroad tracks were torn out in later years. **AUTHOR'S COLLECTION**

Arthur Hewitt, Thomas Kating, Theodore Murdock, and Bob Clark escaped with Frank Grigware by hijacking a prison supply train on April 21, 1910. No photograph exists today of John Gideon, the sixth escapee.

Of Hewitt, Prisoner 5956 (wrongly labeled here with another number), Warden McLaughry wrote, "He is a large, good-natured prisoner, fairly well-behaved in the matter of industry, but always ready to take a chance or opportunity to stir up trouble, which may result in his escape."

These photos show the prisoners in stripes, reserved for "third-grade" inmates, whose infractions were considered so egregious that they were stripped of almost all privileges. Third-grade prisoners were often shackled with the Oregon boot, and spent their nights in solitary cells or in the Hole. **NATIONAL ARCHIVES**

Thomas Kating, Prisoner 5903, became a persistent letter writer, complaining about violations of his rights to lawyers, Department of Justice officials, the U.S. Attorney-General, and President Woodrow Wilson. In 1910, McLaughry declared in a letter to the Department of Justice that "the more (Kating's) character and conduct are investigated, the more thoroughly paced scoundrel and criminal he will be found to be." **NATIONAL ARCHIVES**

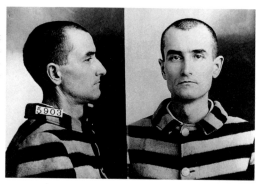

Theodore Murdock, Prisoner 6624, worked beside Grigware in the carpenters shop. A convicted counterfeiter, he played the violin, received a daily newspaper, and was the man who carved the fake Colt revolvers that allowed the escapees to fool their guards and hijack the supply train. His health suffered due to punishment after the escape, and he was released early on the recommendation of the prison doctor. **NATIONAL ARCHIVES**

Bob Clark, Prisoner 4768, was also a prison inventor, dreaming up a device that allowed livestock dealers to dip their cattle for parasites without danger of injury or loss. "He is capable of doing much good or much harm," McLaughry wrote. "He is one of the most thorough criminals that I have ever known—one of the most cold-blooded and cold-hearted, and he would not hesitate to take your life or mine, in an instant, if either stood in the way of his path to escape." **NATIONAL ARCHIVES**

$100 REWARD $100

FRANK GRIGWARE, No. 6768
Aliases James Gordon, E. E. Hollingshead

Escaped from the United States Penitentiary, Leavenworth, Kansas, April 21, 1910.

DESCRIPTION: White, age 23 (in 1909), height 5 feet 8½ inches in bare feet, weight 161 pounds, fair complexion, light brown hair, blue eyes, light brown beard. Scar ¼ inch oblique inner at 3d phalanx left 3d finger front. Small scar of ¼ inch vertical at 2d phalanx right thumb rear. Pit scar at ½ inch below right eye; 2d and 3d toes of each foot web.

RECEIVED November 19, 1909, from Omaha, Nebraska, under sentence of life for robbing U. S. mail train. Occupation, carpenter. Residence, Spokane, Washington.

BERTILLON	174.8, 182.0, 93.5, 19.7, 16.4, 14.0, 6.4, 25.7, 11.5, 9.3, 47.8.
Finger print classification:	25 10 14
	9 00

$100.00 Reward will be paid for his delivery, after identification has been made, to an authorized officer of this Penitentiary.

Arrest and wire:
A. V. ANDERSON, Warden
United States Penitentiary
Leavenworth, Kansas

A wanted poster for Frank Grigware, circa 1920, circulated by authorities. Thousands of these were mailed throughout the world. By the 1920s, Grigware was living peacefully in Canada under the name James Fahey; he was a husband, father, and had been elected mayor of Spirit River, a small frontier town in northern Alberta. He moved to Jasper in 1924. **NATIONAL ARCHIVES**

Frank Grigware's mother, Jennie Fahey Grigware, was in her 70s or 80s when this photograph was taken in the 1930s or 1940s. By then she was living in Seattle, Washington, and had grown ill after reuniting with Frank in Canada in 1934. She wanted to see her famous son once more, but a pardon had not been granted, and he would have been returned to Leavenworth, if he'd crossed the border. Jennie died in 1944 at the age of 81. **PHOTO COURTESY OF KAY WERNER**

Frank Grigware, November 19, 1909. This is the mug shot of Grigware taken upon his arrival at Leavenworth Penitentiary. The heavy wool jacket with big metal buttons, each stamped with U.S. PENITENTIARY, was the standard-issue uniform for new prisoners; it was also what he would have been wearing when he escaped five months later. **NATIONAL ARCHIVES**

Salt Creek, with the probable site of the old Shanghai bridge, looking north. Rotting pilings on the east bank are all that remain of the wooden trestle bridge crossing the creek. On the morning that Grigware and the others escaped from prison new pilings were being driven into the bank and the bridge was jacked up; if they had kept going, both the train and the bridge would have fallen into the creek. The photo gives a good idea of the heavy growth around Salt Creek. Away from the creek, in the valley, the escapees were hindered by scant cover and open fields.
AUTHOR'S COLLECTION

The main entrance to Leavenworth Penitentiary from Metropolitan Avenue. A visitor is greeted with a guard tower, Administration Building, and the dome-capped Rotunda, the structure that gave the prison its nickname, the "Big Top." The dome was modeled after the original atop the U.S. Capitol Building in Washington, D.C. ***AUTHOR'S COLLECTION***

A typical publicity photo of Jasper, Alberta, in the Canadian Rockies. The Chaba Theatre can be seen to the left, advertising "Broken Blossoms" with Lillian Gish and Richard Barthelmess. Frank Grigware arrived in Jasper in 1924, as James Lawrence Fahey. **PHOTO COURTESY OF DWAIN WACKO**

The interior of the Chaba Theatre from the stage beneath the movie screen. The auditorium looked like this until the early 1950s; it was where Frank Grigware watched "I am a Fugitive from a Chain Gang" with his family in 1932. **PHOTO COURTESY OF DWAIN WACKO**

Frank Grigware's home on Tonquin Street in Jasper, Alberta, where he lived when arrested in 1934. It was one of two homes in Jasper that he built for his family. The house stands today and is owned by Phyllis Jeffrey, daughter-in-law of William Jeffrey, the Jasper store owner who helped pay Grigware's bond after his arrest in 1934. **AUTHOR'S COLLECTION**

Forecast—Fair and mild
Since Midnight—Highest 48 at 12 Noon
Lowest 40, at 6:00 a.m.

Edmonton Journal
"ONE OF CANADA'S GREAT NEWSPAPERS"

Last Week's Net Paid
Daily Average Circulation 32,463

30TH YEAR, NO. 221   EDMONTON, ALBERTA, WEDNESDAY, APRIL 4, 1934.   SINGLE COPY, 5 CENTS   24 PAGES

U.S. MAY DROP FAHEY EXTRADITION CLAIM, PRESIDENTIAL PARDON ORDER IS HINTED

Case Becomes International Affair, Appeals for Aid Flood White House; Ex-Companion 'Lifer' Urges Mercy

FIRST PICTURES OF FAHEY CHILDREN

Waiting in Jasper for the final freedom of their beloved father, not on bail pending efforts of the United States government to extradite him as an escaped lifer from Leavenworth penitentiary, the three children of James Fahey and Mrs. Fahey are being cared for by friends in their beautiful mountain home. Here are the Fahey children to be published of the three children and were welcomed exclusively by the Journal. (1) is Louise Fahey, 13, with the dog that is favorite of the household. (5) is Jack Fahey, 15, born here the Fahey family was, 9 understanding near Spotts River, and (3) is Marie Fahey, eight born after the family had moved to Jasper.—(Copyright, 1934, by Edmonton Journal).

Travesty to Return Fahey to Cell, Says Ex-Convict Now in Congress, Declares U. S. Cannot Claim Man

Urges "Canadians" Fight Extradition of Former Fugitive

KEEP HOME SECURE

(Special to Edmonton Journal)
WASHINGTON, April 4.—"Canada, stand by your guns. Don't allow for one minute this man Fahey's Canadian home to be broken up by a travesty of justice. I really believe the United States has no case for extradition, if Canada really and truly fights on the issue, going to the mat on every point, both technically and from the standpoint of humanity."

This startling statement, given to the Journal here Wednesday, by a member of the congress of the United States, provides a new chapter development in the Dr. Jekyll-Mr. Hyde case of James Fahey, alias Frank Grigware. It personifies the immense amount of support rallying to the cause on this side of the border as an answer to the flood of wires, letters and reports from Canada to President and Mrs. Roosevelt and other leaders, asking official leniency for the former Leavenworth convict, whom the arm of the law would now pull from his...

Ottawa Officials Say American in Error on Extradition

TREATY IS CLEAR

(Special to Edmonton Journal)
congressman, who has volunteered to go the limit in fighting for Fahey on the floor of congress in the department of justice consideration in forcing the naturalized Canadian back to Leavenworth, is himself a fellow ex-convict who did time at the same Leavenworth penitentiary. He is Congressman Francis Henry Shoemaker of Red Wing, Minnesota, who is proud to recall he served seven months in Leavenworth during the Hoover regime on political principle rather than pay a fine for libel. While incarcerated he was elected representative-at-large in Minnesota and was pardoned about a year ago by President Roosevelt at the most sensational pardoning case of his administration up to the current Fahey-Grigware point.

Coming direct to congress, Congressman Shoemaker tried unsuccessfully to insert at his name in the congressional directory biography section, "the only man to get straight from the penitentiary to congress, not from congress to the penitentiary."

Interviewed at his office on Capitol hill, Congressman Shoemaker plunged at once into the human aspects of Fahey's case.

"How many children has he?" was the first question from the "stormy petrel" representative, whose hobby is exposing American prison conditions largely through personal case histories of the convicts themselves, some of whom were his friends in Leavenworth.

"Now frankly, I sincerely believe that Canada can stand against extradition of this man, and you can quote me on that, too. Canada can stand against it on the ground that Fahey is a naturalized Canadian, that he is a good respectable family man raising his family in Alberta, that he has never committed a crime against the Canadian federal government and that he is thoroughly entitled to the protection of the Canadian government.

"Fahey Has Gone Straight"

"Honest justice will not deny this man but be hounded to his death. He has gone straight. He has run out through 24 years. Besides our good Canadian friends are even now developing evidence which would seem to clear him in the first place. Plenty of men have been railroaded to Leavenworth on the flimsiest of evidence, third-degreed over and over on the officer of the law...

Ex-Kansas Governor Now To White House Ask To Man Who Fled Hom

An ex-governor of Kansas, from which state James Fahey escaped while serving a life sentence at Leavenworth penitentiary, has written to President Roosevelt, asking a full pardon for the man who for 24 years has lived a highly respected life and won a place of honor and esteem in the Canadian west. Hon. Jonathan M. Davis, 13th governor of the state of Kansas (1850-56) and for many years a resident of Edmonton, has written to President Roosevelt in earnest on Fahey's behalf.

Ex-Governor Leedy's letter to the president is in the following terms: "His excellency, Franklin D. Roosevelt, president of the United States of America. Honorable Sir:

Leedy Feels Ends of Justice Would Be Served by Move

KEENLY INTERESTED

Believing it to be in the interest of public welfare that men should be encouraged to abandon evil ways and, and ways, and as this man James Fahey, has and an example that should encourage others to follow, I would heartily recommend executive clemency in his case and respectfully yours, John W. Leedy, ex-governor of Kansas (1896-98)."

Mr. Leedy, despite his 85 years, has taken a keen interest in the case, especially in view of the fact...

Ex-Fugitive Faintly Recalls Acquaintance of Former Years

SILENT ON HOLDUP

Convicted With Grigware, Man Served Seven Years of Term

Case of James Fahey, Jasper resident held on bail as Frank Grigware, fugitive from Leavenworth penitentiary, Wednesday assumed proportions of a delicate international matter. Officials in Washington and Ottawa declined comment, but it was hinted in high circles that either a presidential pardon for the man might be issued or else the United States department of justice might drop the extradition proceedings it has instituted against Fahey. In any case, developments are expected almost within a few hours.

The White House Wednesday was feeling an ever-growing flood of written and telegraphed ap-
(Continued from Page 1, Col. 1)

Fahey Fails Recall Night Mail Robbery

Cannot Remember Exact Whereabouts on Fateful Evening

NOT WITH ROBBERS

James Fahey, convicted of robbing a mail train in the outskirts of Omaha in 1909, does not remember exactly where he was on the night of the robbery. He does know he was not at the scene of the robbery nor was he with the other four men who were convicted with him and sentenced to life terms at Leavenworth penitentiary.

These were statements of Fahey when interviewed by the Journal Wednesday on recent developments of the case.

"I knew I was in Omaha but I don't remember exactly where I was on the night of the robbery. I had chummed around with the men who were convicted but I wasn't with them on that night. I say sure of that." Fahey said.

The Journal learned that Mrs. Fahey was feeling much better since her husband's release on $10,000 bail pending extradition proceedings. Following the shock of husband's arrest as an escaped lifer and circumstanced acquaintances, Mrs. Fahey was on the verge of a nervous breakdown. Since her husband's release and the unprecedented manifestation of sympathy for thousands of persons, she has been greatly heartened and encouraged to hope for an early pardon.

What Happened 4 Other Lifers

(Special to Edmonton Journal)
WASHINGTON, D.C., April 4.—Here is what happened to the four men who were convicted with Fahey and sentenced to life imprisonment in 1909 and since:

JACK SHELTON—Pardoned by President Wilson, Aug. 4, 1912.

FRED TORGENSON, alias T. W. Davis—Life sentence commuted to 15 years, released July 1, 1918.

DONALD W. WOOD, alias Dan Downer—Released July 1, 1913.

WILLIAM MATTHEWS, alias William Morris—Life sentence commuted to 15 years, paroled Jan. 5, 1920.

CHARANK RESERVES DOWN ERLIN, April 4.—A Reichsbank in Wednesday showed in had used a decline during the last 5 of March of 15,900,000 marks to 64,900,000, but in gold and currency reserves.

vents, or fortresses in which a hundred or more prisoners might live, eat, sleep, work, age, sicken, and die.

The first "cellular" prison was built for youthful offenders by the Roman Catholic Church under Pope Clement IX and formed part of the Hospital of St. Michael in Rome. Completed in 1704 and designed by Carlo Fontano, this Vatican prison introduced the idea of cellular separation to allow each prisoner to reflect on his misdeeds in solitude. The cells were arranged so that they lined the outer walls of the prison and looked inward; there were ten cells per row, stacked three tiers high, for a total of sixty cells. The intent was that each prisoner was afforded a view of the altar in the center aisle, thus letting him join in religious services. The stacked cell arrangement with a large open hall imposed a discipline on architectural design that was never present before and has influenced prison architecture to the present.

It is hard to comprehend today the power that architectural form held over the eighteenth- and nineteenth-century imagination. Prisons, like other public buildings, could not be isolated from their social context, either in an aesthetic sense or in light of the belief in democracy and emancipation sweeping Europe and America. An open floor plan symbolized freedom and hope; towering columns, cathedral windows, resplendent parks, and huge domes spoke to the glory of man and of God. Opposed to this was the practical consideration of punishing the guilty and preventing the dangerous from escaping. Major prison reform movements walked this line like a tightrope, trying to find balance between the two.

Modern discussion of legal punishment—and of criminal law reform in general—truly began in 1764 with *Dei delitti e delle pene (An Essay on Crimes and Punishments)*, by Cesare Beccaria, a twenty-six-year-old Italian nobleman. Subsequent debates were restatements of the arguments and counterarguments Beccaria inspired. The purpose of punishment was not vengeance, he said, but rather the reformation of the criminal and the prevention of future crimes; it was a secular view of republican reform—that the human condition could be improved on earth—as opposed to the more theological view that man must atone on earth as he would in heaven or hell. To Beccaria, legal brutality reflected a more general political and social backwardness: "Countries notorious for the severity of punishments were also those in which the most bloody and inhuman actions . . . were committed."

Beccaria was immensely influential in British reforming circles, and not surprisingly the prison debate shifted to England in 1777, one year after America's Declaration of Independence caused ferocious debate about the rights of man. That same year, British reformer John Howard published *The State of the Prisons.* Howard believed unflinchingly in the power of environment to improve the minds and morals of felons. "In order to redress [the] various evils" of overcrowding, corruption, and continual backsliding among criminals, he wrote, "the first thing to be taken into consideration is the prison itself." Howard called for improvements in hygiene, health care, and sanitation, for the separation of inmates by sex, age, and nature of crime, and for the inclusion of open space for exercise and clean air. His ideal prison was one where cellblocks were surrounded by large open courtyards, with a chapel in the center. Though Howard's design was never turned into reality, his ideas were so influential that prisons sprang up in Britain and Europe with churches as their focal point, thus stressing the importance of moral and religious training. His book also influenced fellow reformer Jeremy Bentham, whose circular prison with a chapel on top led Benjamin Latrobe and others to come up with their own horseshoe and radial plans.

By the early 1800s the prison debate had shifted west again, this time to America, which became for about fifty years the world center of prison reform. Two opposing philosophies shared center stage, and bitter arguments erupted over the merits of each. The first system originated in 1817 at Auburn State Prison in New York. Prisoners worked together in total silence during the day, but were housed separately at night. Sing Sing, opened in 1828, had the characteristic design of prisons adopting this system, with five tiers of back-to-back cells stacked in the center of a sticklike building, the cells flanked by long dark corridors. The second model, called the Pennsylvania or monastic system, adopted cellblocks radiating from a central hub, like the spokes of a wheel, with the cells built on the outer wall facing in, a reflection of the inmate's inner meditations. Its best example, the Eastern State Penitentiary in Philadelphia, opened in 1829. Inmates there were kept in solitary confinement night and day. The prison itself had seven radiating spokes, its cells only one tier high. Europeans flocked to the United States to study the competing systems, including Frenchmen Alexis de Tocqueville and his friend Gustave de Beaumont in May 1831. From de Tocqueville's visit, made ostensibly to observe and analyze the mechanics of imprisonment, would come his classic *Democracy in America*, which observed and analyzed the mechanics of American democracy. At Auburn Prison, de Tocqueville saw hard-working prisoners in huge workshops, sneaking glances at each other and using every opportunity to talk with their neighbors. If caught, an inmate was hit with a rod or club. Eastern State, on the other hand, seemed as quiet as a church and reminded him of one. Guards at Eastern State wore slippers or socks over their shoes so not to break the silence; when a new inmate arrived at the prison, such care was taken that he not see other prisoners that he was hooded before being led to his cell. When a visitor like de Tocqueville peeked through a small observation glass in the door, called "the eye of Judas," he saw a silent man or woman working alone at some light task, like weaving, or reading a Bible. In theory, a felon left alone with his thoughts and the Scriptures would become penitent, thus the term *penitentiary*.

In actual practice, both systems were flawed. Proponents of the Auburn system stressed the activity of prisoners and the profits of their work—profits which, incidentally, made a prison self-supporting. Yet critics called it slavery, since state officials and private contractors who managed the inmates' labor grew rich. Meanwhile, in Eastern State, the enforced isolation caused an abnormally high death rate, both by suicide and disease. It was the problem of the prairie: Whatever benefits accrued there were lost since so many people went mad. Most states found the profits generated by the Auburn system irresistible and adopted that approach, while Europeans, influenced by de Tocqueville's report, chose the radial plan.

For 114 years the United States had gone without a federal prison system, choosing instead to pay county jails and state prisons to house those convicted of federal crimes. But the end of the Civil War changed everything. There was an increase in disorder, especially in the South and the West, and existing prisons became severely overcrowded, the inmate population climbing from 33,000 to 57,000 between 1870 and 1900. Worse, both the Pennsylvania and Auburn systems had failed. An 1867 *Report on the Prisons and Reformatories of the United States and Canada* commissioned by the New York Prison Association listed a litany of evils. States relied on the lash or on the yoke, a heavy flat bar of iron, five or six feet long, with a center ring for the neck and manacles for the wrists. The Auburn system had evolved into the lease system, a money-making scheme in which inmates dug railroad tunnels, built roads, and quarried stone, making profits for prison officials while surviving at most ten years. James French visited western jails and prisons where cells built for twenty men held two hundred. "I have seen men brought out . . . that when you ran the hair-clippers through their hair, the lice would run out the other side," he remembered. "I have seen men come with little or no clothing, who had so much dirt on their backs that they would have to have it scraped off by someone else."

By 1891, Congress had grown sufficiently uncomfortable with existing conditions to enter the prison business too. Americans could accept that their country was violent, but the taint of barbarism made them uneasy. That year, Congress passed the "Three Prisons" Act, which authorized the construction of two new federal penitentiaries, as well as the acquisition of a third. The second prison was planned for Atlanta, where construction started in 1902; the acquisition was of aging McNeil Island in cold and wet Steilacoom, Washington. But Leavenworth was the first and, as the government's premier prison, had to succeed. Instead of relying on the flawed Auburn or Pennsylvania systems as models, the planners adopted what they considered the better parts of both. While the tiered cellblocks emulated Auburn, the general radial outline mirrored Eastern State. The men would work in prison industries, but not for outside contractors. Though they did not live in monkish solitude, a centrally located church and school would allow them to do penance while improving their minds. Copying the design of the U.S. Capitol reminded all men, not just prisoners, that democracy survived only under the rule of law.

Yet by Frank's arrival, something was going seriously wrong. Like the farmers' fences on the prairie, the prison's limestone facade was crumbling before Leavenworth was even completed; the grand symbol did not inspire hope, as its designers intended, but hopelessness and gloom. As the grandeur faded, the crowding grew worse. Violence and corruption hidden behind the walls during the 1910s would burst forth in the 1920s and 1930s, giving Leavenworth the reputation of one of the most brutal prisons in the world.

FRANK HAD ALREADY glimpsed signs of its disease. How could he survive a year in this place, much less a lifetime? If he didn't get out soon, he feared he would go mad. Before that happened, however, he stood a good chance of dying from sickness or disease.

Early December saw the start of cold and wind that raged in a series of storms for the next three months, bringing the West and Midwest to a standstill. On December 5, 1909, freezing rain and ice cut off train and telegraph service between Leavenworth and surrounding cities; a thunderstorm rolled out of the west, its barbed lightning splitting the sky. The prison schedule slowed to a crawl since many guards couldn't make it to their shifts; the ice wreaked havoc on the trolleys, burning out more than $125 in steel wheels in less than a day. The rain froze instantly when it hit the overhead wires. The *Leavenworth Times* declared that the "worst storm in years was sweeping the entire country." Towns and cities became islands in the cold. In Denver, the temperature dropped 53 degrees in one day; in Wyoming it dropped 63. In the mountains, the wind blew 75 miles per hour, tearing off roofs and blowing in windows. Coal mines shut down, leaving homesteaders without heat. Huge losses were feared for unsheltered livestock. In Kansas City, St. Louis, Denver, and Omaha, hoboes crowded police stations, begging to be arrested so they'd have a warm meal and a roof above their heads.

In the prison, too, the cold was relentless. Frank put on all the clothing he was issued, wrapped himself in his jacket and two wool blankets, but still could not get warm. On the job, he could work up a little body heat, but at night the blizzard wind shook the bars of the windows and moaned down the corridors. He watched as older prisoners started dropping out of line around him for sick call, complaining of cold or the grippe. A rumor started that some of the sick were diagnosed with typhoid fever, but prison officials called it untrue. Typhoid came from bad water, they told the press, and Leavenworth's water was boiled.

There were occasional moments of reprieve. In early December, the Justice Department sent orders to Leavenworth appointing a third captain of the watch, which meant hiring new guards and changing shifts from twelve to eight hours a day. The guards were so elated that for a few days they forgot to be free with their clubs. On December 21, James and Lincoln Wolf, two Indian brothers from the Territory, received a pardon. They were given $5 apiece and a train ticket home. Both men had been sentenced in June 1906 to prison for life for killing another Indian in a drunken brawl. "Don't you dread to leave the warm prison where your clothes are furnished to go out into the cold wintry weather?" a reporter asked Lincoln Wolf.

The brothers laughed and said they planned to go to their farms and families in Stillwell, Oklahoma. "Sell hogs, buy clothes," Lincoln Wolf exulted. His further silence was telling. How could he answer a reporter who either knew nothing about prison life or was a fool?

Christmas came and went like Thanksgiving, a day of roast turkey and gravy and no work, a day when Frank stayed in his cell and froze. At 2 P.M., the manager of the People's Theater in town set up a projector in the back of the chapel, and for an hour and a half Frank sat in the dark watching celluloid dreams. There were a couple of comedy shorts by dapper Max Linder, predecessor of Charlie Chaplin and Buster Keaton; there were exhibition films of two trains crashing head on in a strange, silent orgy of destruction, of the Squires versus Burns prizefight of 1907, of the 1904 Great Toronto Fire, and the 1906 San Francisco earthquake. There was a more recent film, D. W. Griffith's *The Lonely Villa*, in which a mother and her children were menaced in a lonely house by bandits. Frank would remember it for two reasons: It introduced the last-minute rescue to movies, and Mary Pickford, not yet America's Sweetheart, cowered in a corner with the other besieged youngsters.

More than anything else, Frank remembered a two-minute short called "Electrocuting an Elephant." He watched as the pachyderm was chained to stakes in the ground. The beast weaved nervously, sensing bad news. Four puffs of smoke blossomed from the shackles on its hooves; the elephant shuddered, toppled over, shuddered again, then lay still. Men in the background waited for its throes to stop, and then the screen went black, the last image one of these watchers of death. The lights snapped on and he returned to his cell, the last image stuck in his mind.

The cold continued into 1910. On January 7, trains throughout Kansas nearly slowed to a stop; in Lansing the temperature was 17 above zero, while there were reports that the Missouri River froze. On January 20, a comet was visible one hour after sunset, but the skies were so overcast in Leavenworth it could not be seen. By January 28, there were reports that the cold was forcing coyotes and wolves off the prairie and into the small farming towns of Easton and Kickapoo, not far to the west. They crept into farmyards, raided poultry sheds, killed young pigs. On February 3, the prison finally announced what everyone already knew—that typhoid had indeed coursed among them despite official denials, killing one man and prostrating scores. The first to die was Richard Bruno, a black prisoner from Washington, D.C., sentenced to fifteen years for assault and buried on Peckerwood Hill. Others lay in the clinic with the fever, and at least one other man was not expected to live.

By then, Frank's body had already rebelled. Soon after Christmas he'd been hit by fever and diarrhea and felt himself grow weaker and weaker. Ted Murdock looked at Frank and told him to get on sick call; if he didn't go, there was a good chance he would die. On January 4, he gave his name and number to the guard after entering the dining hall for breakfast; he stood out of line until all the others started eating, then dragged slowly with other ailing inmates to the doctor's office in the central hall. He stood quietly in line, slumped against the wall, until a trusty called his number. "What's your complaint?" Dr. Yohe asked briskly, and Frank told him of the diarrhea. "Any blood in the stool?" Yohe snapped, and Frank said he didn't think so, he just felt mighty weak, was all. Yohe peered in his eyes and down his throat and listened to his heart and lungs. He turned to an orderly and said, "Place him on quarters for observation and tell me when he has a bowel movement." Frank was left in a small room with white tile walls, a bed, and a chamber pot. He lay down and tried to sleep. By early afternoon he had a regular bowel movement, and the trusty took away the chamber pot. In a few minutes Yohe came back with a guard. "There's nothing wrong with you," he said. "Let's see what the deputy says." He was sent to Deputy Lemon, who found him guilty of malingering, based on the evidence of his bowel movement. There'd been too much malingering lately and Lemon was making an example of people like him. At 2:30 P.M., Lemon sent Frank to isolation.

Frank was thrown in the Hole for two days. Triangular in shape, there were six "dark holes" located on the second floor of the isolation building. Frank was stripped of his wool uniform and handed a set of ragged cotton longjohns and cloth slippers. A guard escorted him to a vacant dungeon, pushed him inside, and closed the heavy wooden door, made of several thicknesses of flooring material and padlocked from outside. The only furnishings were a night bucket and a tin cup; there was icy water on the floor. If he was really being punished, he would have been chained to the door, but for something as common as malingering he was left unchained. The room was neither tall enough to stand in nor long enough to lie full length on the floor. At noon the door was opened and the guard poured water in his cup and brought a tin plate with a crust of bread. A small amount of light entered through an iron mesh in the ceiling; he could see radiator coils affixed to the ceiling for heat, and there were tales of guards turning the steam up or down, according to the season, to punish men who caused disturbances. There was no record that Frank caused problems, and since he hadn't been around long enough for any of the guards to hate him particularly, they left his steam heat alone. At night he was given a small woolen blanket, smaller than the one in his cell. He curled up in a fetal position, trying to get as much of himself as possible under the blanket. His teeth chattered through the night. "Sleep well?" the guard asked the next morning.

There were tales of men who spent years in the Hole. The most famous in America by 1910 was Jesse Harding Pomeroy, who was fourteen years old when a Massachusetts court sentenced him to "life in solitary confinement" for the murders of a young boy and girl. He served thirty-eight years alone, some of that in a "coke-oven" type of cell. Probably the longest solitary term served in federal prison was by Robert F. Stroud, "the Bird Man of Alcatraz." Stroud was kept in isolation in Leavenworth and Alcatraz from 1916, when he killed a Leavenworth guard, to 1959, when he was released from isolation at the age of seventy. The most notorious prisoners to spend extended time in Leavenworth's Hole during Frank's tenure were Tom Kating and Arthur Hewitt, who along with Bob Clark were the original conspirators in the 1901 mutiny. Kating and Hewitt were always thought of as a pair. They'd belonged to the same horse-theft ring in the Oklahoma Territory before their arrest; they'd approached Clark with the breakout plan. Once they escaped, they stayed free for two years, longer than any other fugitives in the mutiny. They both worked in the tailor shop and could often be seen together in the dining hall and in line.

Kating was the brains of the pair. It had been his brother, Lon Briscoe, who'd supplied the revolvers for the 1901 escape; Kating had been the one to talk Charles Ennis into burying the pistols in the empty worksite after his release. He was a slender man of about medium height, weighing 120 pounds; he was quick and alert, a trait that turned to nervousness under the constant strain of Leavenworth; he had a receding chin, and his Adam's apple bobbed in his throat whenever he grew excited. He'd come to Leavenworth on October 26, 1900, sentenced to five years for horse theft, and had just turned twenty-four a year later when he led the mutiny. He was educated and said to have experience around trains. The rumor was supported by the fact that his left thumb was amputated at the second joint and his right forefinger near the end, common sights among railroad switchmen, who often lost fingers when connecting cars with primitive link-and-pin couplings. Over the years he'd transformed himself into a persistent letter writer, on the theory that the squeaky wheel got grease, and in the process became the type of inmate jailers love to hate. He complained about violations of his rights to lawyers, Justice officials, and the U.S. Attorney General, and eventually to the President of the United States. In 1910, after nearly a decade of conflicts with Kating, Warden McLaughry declared in a letter to James Finch, parole attorney for the Department of Justice, that "the more his character and conduct are investigated, the more thoroughly paced a scoundrel and criminal he will be found to be."

Arthur Hewitt served as a foil to his more excitable friend. At 6 feet 1 inch and 200 pounds, he was described by Deputy Lemon as being of "phlegmatic temperament"; he was also prone to unexplained stomach ailments, for which Dr. Yohe prescribed frequent enemas. Unlike Clark or Kating, his best friends in the prison, his disruptions were more akin to schoolboy unruliness than the whinings of Kating or the more serious escape plots of Clark. The violations in his file sound almost like visits to the principal: "talking during breakfast," "placed arms along the backs of chair on both sides of him" in mess, "talking in mess hall," "snapping pieces of bread" at one of the dining hall guards. "He is a large, good-natured prisoner, fairly well-behaved in the matter of industry," McLaughry wrote, "but always ready to take a chance or opportunity to stir up trouble, which may result in his escape." To Hewitt's mother he wrote that Arthur "does not seem to be a bad-hearted man," yet he associated with "evil disposed prisoners" like Kating and Clark who got him into trouble.

Taken together, Arthur Hewitt and Tom Kating were greater than the sum of their parts. They came to Leavenworth together in late 1900 and almost immediately plotted to escape. They planned the Thursday, November 7, 1901, breakout almost to perfection, and unlike the other fugitives, who scattered to the winds, they stuck by each other while making their way across the plains. While Kating worked at ranches in the Indian Territory, Hewitt went to Texas, a common way to avoid the law. But by November 1903 both had been recaptured, the last of the 1901 escapees to be caught and re-turned. McLaughry immediately threw them in the Hole, beginning a cycle of release and return that continued over the next seven years. He took steps to have them charged with Waldrupe's murder, and in 1905 both were given life sentences.

At first it seemed that Hewitt would spend more time than Kating in solitary. He was in the adjoining cell in 1907 when nineteen-year-old Clarence Maitland was given his daily dose of ammonia; he listened as the boy was strapped in a straitjacket and screamed himself to death. "Well, I see the Maitland boy has crossed over the Big Divide," he said to Lemon, when guards carried out his body, to which Lemon an-swered that the devils in hell would make as short work of Maitland as had the guards in Leavenworth. Meanwhile, Kating was put to work in the rock shed in the basement of one of the new cell wings. The cells were damp and cold, the rock dust drifted in clouds around him, and finally he began spitting up blood. When he felt a stab in his right lung every time he breathed, he feared he had contracted tuberculosis and petitioned Yohe, Lemon, and McLaughry for relief, to no avail. On August 29, 1909, he petitioned U.S. Attorney General Wickersham for a transfer to another prison, pleading it was his only chance for sur-vival. This request was also denied, yet the letter apparently had some effect. Hewitt was released from the Hole and Kating from the rock shed, then both were called into Lemon's office. "If you get a foot out of line out here, I will throw you into solitary and let you stay there un-til you rot, goddamn you," Lemon screamed. "We are not through with you fellows yet. We are going to give every damned one of you hell, that is my orders from the warden."

Kating may have been in the Hole at the same time Frank was visit-ing; the records are unclear. On November 16, 1909, shortly before Frank's incarceration, Kating pushed open a window in the tailor shop "to suit himself" and was thrown into solitary for an unstated amount of time. Frank's stay in isolation would only have been a fraction of Kating's time. At 11 A.M. on January 6, Frank was returned to the gen-eral population after 44½ hours in the Hole. He was sicker than when he entered, chilled to his core from the cold stones and wet floor, but no longer experiencing diarrhea, since his diet of bread and water had flushed out his system. If he'd had the beginnings of typhoid fever, those two days in the Hole probably would have killed him. As it was, he survived and never went on sick call again.

Although he may not have known Hewitt and Kating, by then he would have heard about them. And now he had a taste of the anger that drove both men for all those years. "Good God, you look like shit," said Murdock, when he returned to the carpenter shop, and for the next few days Murdock and John Gideon helped him with his duties. The guards saw the assistance but looked the other way. Shop guards, considered more lenient than those in the cellblocks, were judged more by their shop's output than by slavish adherence to every rule; it was an unstated practice at work for other prisoners to help those who'd just returned from the Hole. As significantly, Frank discovered that he'd passed an unwritten test and had become accepted by the other prisoners.

Frank saw with clearer eyes the wheels that moved the prison and the grease that kept those wheels spinning. It was the same as on the outside—the rich and powerful got the breaks, while everyone else lived and died in powerless anonymity. On January 18, 1910, he watched with disgust as John Walsh, McLaughry's old friend of twenty-five years and former president of the Chicago National Bank, was escorted into prison by his son and lawyer to begin serving a five year sentence for embezzlement. Frank watched how, over the next two months, the convicted bankers sat apart in the dining hall at the "bankers' table," where they were served real milk, toast, beefsteak, eggs, pork chops, and other victuals that regular prisoners hadn't tasted in years. Walsh was given a desk job as identification clerk for Matthew McLaughry, scanning the papers for information to be clipped and placed in the criminal files. He was immediately made a trusty instead of earning the privilege slowly over months or years. As more convicted financiers arrived, Leavenworth got the name of a "bankers' colony."

Frank could understand when, on February 11, 1910, Kating stepped out of line in front of all the other prisoners at lunch and told the guards that he refused to go to work anymore. He was on strike, he said.

Deputy Lemon stormed from his regular post in the front of the dining hall to where Kating stood. "What do you mean by stepping out?" he shrieked, his hatred evident in every word.

"I can get no satisfaction from Dr. Yohe on my complaints about the pain in my lung," Kating answered. "I refuse to work until I do."

"Get back in line or you go back to Isolation," Lemon ordered.

"I refuse to go to work until I get satisfaction," Kating repeated coldly, his hatred for the deputy as evident as Lemon's for him.

Lemon turned to a guard, his face white with barely controlled rage. "Take this prisoner to a solitary cell," he said. The entire dining hall watched in silence as Kating was led away.

Frank listened in growing indignation one Saturday in March when he was called to the central hall for a records matter and overheard Warden McLaughry holding "court" in his office for the benefit of the press. McLaughry held these little exhibitions whenever he felt his image required burnishing: this time he'd invited a friendly reporter from the *Leavenworth Press* to sit in on the period he set aside each Saturday to hear inmate complaints. At one point Frank had considered petitioning McLaughry for relief, because his stomach pains and diarrhea continued, knowing full well that if he reported back on sick call he'd get thrown in the Hole again. McLaughry sat behind his desk with the prisoner's file spread before him. If the complaint came from a dispute with an officer, he explained to the journalist, he very rarely reversed a decision—only in about one in twenty-five cases, he estimated, and then only reluctantly. More like one in a thousand, Frank mused, as he listened through the door.

The prisoner sitting in front of McLaughry was a counterfeiter, a slim man with wire glasses and small, delicate hands. "What are you here for?" McLaughry asked. "Warden, I would like to have permission to write letters on plain paper," the inmate said.

McLaughry reared back in his seat like Solomon before the baby. "Why do you want to write on plain paper?" he demanded. "Why won't prison paper do?"

"It's this way, warden," the counterfeiter explained. "I have a sister who is an invalid and she does not know where I am. I don't want her to know I am in the penitentiary. If I write on plain paper, I could send the letter to my father, and he will transmit it to my sister."

Frank cracked the door an inch and watched the unfolding scene. McLaughry put on his reading glasses and looked down his nose at the counterfeiter's file. "Let me look at your record," he said, grunting in disapproval as he read. He looked up, took off the glasses, and fixed the man in his stare. "This does not look very good for you. You have broken two cups in the dining room, and then one morning at the breakfast table the deputy saw you gazing at some new prisoners and ordered you to stop. I also find that you are writing one letter a week now"—which was one more than the regular limit. McLaughry gazed sternly at the inmate, letting the man's sins and transgressions sink in. The inmate shifted nervously in his seat; as Frank watched, he could feel the man's discomfort and embarrassment. The counterfeiter pleaded again that his sister was sick and he feared she might be dying; she'd asked their father several times why he did not write. His sentence was for five years and she'd probably be dead by then. It broke his heart not to even be able to write, he said.

McLaughry nodded sympathetically as he listened, but there was a hard gleam in his eyes. This was what he wanted, Frank realized. It wasn't so much that he enjoyed the man's suffering, but making him beg like this, especially in front of the press, was just one more sign of control. This was the end result of the grand experiment called Leavenworth, he thought, making men bow before authority as if whipped, making them grovel like dogs. This was what the authorities called rehabilitation: slavish obedience to their masters' whims.

"Well," said McLaughry, clearing his throat magnanimously, "I will give you permission to write this letter on plain paper tomorrow, and future favors will be governed by your conduct. We have rules here at Leavenworth, and they must be obeyed." The counterfeiter twisted his hat in his hands as he thanked the warden. Frank noticed he avoided the next man's eyes as he hurried out the door.

One day Frank was working when Bob Clark stopped beside him at his bench and sat down. He watched Frank plane and sand a newel post for some stairs in one of the main cell buildings, then check it with the level. "I hear you made it through the Hole," Clark muttered.

Frank looked at Bob Clark and grinned in surprise, then bent back to his work. People didn't talk to Clark. He talked to them.

"I think—" Frank said, then hesitated, not sure exactly what he meant to say. "I think they'd kill every one of us if it didn't mean they'd be out of a job."

"Damn right," Clark said.

"I'll die before I spend my life here," Frank said. "But I don't know a way out."

Bob Clark chuckled. "Oh, there are ways out," he answered, rising from his seat. He stared as the switch engine uncoupled from a flatcar of lumber, whistled once, and moved slowly toward the west gate. "There's always a way out. You just gotta see it. Sometimes it's so obvious, you don't even know it's there."

❦ CHAPTER EIGHT ❦

The Clockwork Train

TWO TRAINS CAME to the prison, but the inmates called them both the Leavenworth train. The first was the prisoner express, which visited irregularly with its newest load of residents and chugged, heavily guarded, through the East Gate. Its arrival was always attended with a certain amount of fanfare: Guards lined up at the prison car's steps, a U.S. marshal got off and was greeted by Deputy Lemon or one of his subordinates, and the shackled passengers stepped into the yard. Work in the shops stopped to size up the new arrivals. For their part, the newcomers always stared, paralyzed by what they saw.

The second train arrived every Thursday morning, like clockwork, to deliver a load of lumber or other building materials to the yard. Rain or shine, hot or cold, one of two switch engines backed a flatcar through the West Gate, almost always at 8 A.M. and never attended by fanfare. Its arrival was a given of prison life, a ritual the inmates watched without seeing as the train crawled slowly between the factories until it stopped at the scales. Regular loads were brought in by the prison's H. K. Porter engine, an American 4-4-0 engine, a classification based on the layout of a locomotive's wheels. The Porter engine had four big driving wheels, two on a side, and a four-wheel pony truck up front. On days when the load was heavier than usual, the Porter engine would be replaced by a larger Union Pacific "mogul," used to pull freight trains. Moguls had six driving wheels, three to a side, and a front truck with two wheels, for a 2-6-0 configuration. American or mogul, the procedure was always the same. Shortly before eight, the engineer gave a short toot of his whistle, the signal to the guard. The West Gate was double-gated, each one made of heavy steel bars. It was an early example of the sally-port design now so common in modern prisons: The outer gate opened to admit the backing train, then closed as the engine waited in a forty-foot stone enclosure. When the inner gate opened, the train proceeded slowly into the yard.

An officer, linked by phone to the offices of the warden and deputy warden and armed with a high-powered rifle, kept watch in the tower overlooking the gate. On a normal day, Captain Zerbst gave the okay for the gate to swing open, then he and another guard, usually Harry Reed, hopped onto the side ladders and rode the train back to the scales by the powerhouse. When the train finally stopped, it was about four car lengths from the inner gate; the engineer and fireman remained inside the cabin while the two guards hopped off. As Zerbst walked to the scales, the cars were automatically uncoupled from the engine tender. Reed stood by the tender, club in hand should any inmates come near.

Ever since the walls had risen, the western train and its track had been acknowledged as a possible Achilles heel. This route was recognized as the way to freedom; some of the prisoners had laid those tracks themselves. The prison sidetrack switched into the main line under the shadow of Mount Hope, then curved northwest beneath Government and Sentinel hills until dropping into Salt Creek Valley. This was broken country, open fields alternating with woods and streams of heavy growth, but once the track passed Easton there was open prairie—the perfect terrain to pick up speed. Every prisoner knew you needed speed to escape Leavenworth; in one of the few snippets of information allowed to leak into prison, inmates learned how a posse of fifty men in motorcars left nearby Atchison, Fuller City, Troy, and Hiawatha and quickly surrounded a pair of horse thieves. The posse almost surely rode in Model Ts. The black four-cylinder Tin Lizzies had a top speed of 45 mph, and their sturdy wheels made them good for off-road pursuit. Yet a locomotive running with its steam up could outrace any Model T. By 1910, nearly 250,000 miles of track had been laid in America since the first 40 miles in 1830: that was ninety-one cross-country trips, or ten times around the earth at the equator, or once to the moon and partway back. Get the steam up and an escapee could go anywhere!

Sometimes it seemed to McLaughry that too many trains came here. In addition to the Porter engine, the mogul engine, and the intermittent prisoner specials, tourist trains arrived in the spring and summer packed with curiosity seekers drawn to see the amazing prison on the prairie. These specials were usually chartered from the Kansas City Railway Company, which specialized in booking church groups. In the summer of 1909, an average of 150 tourists arrived in each trip; McLaughry didn't like the excursions, but there was little he could do. Prisons were part of the tourist route, and trains came packed with women and children. The moms wanted to show their "kidlets" what would happen if they weren't good little boys and girls, Murdock and the other prisoners said. Tuesdays and weekends seemed the favorite days for visits, and on these days McLaughry felt dyspeptic, worrying what would happen if a woman or child fainted in the summer heat. The warm months were when prisoners grew "more nervous and excitable," he complained. There'd been a record day last summer when 190 visitors arrived. Several women in that group complimented McLaughry on the table he set for inmates, and one woman exulted, "Why, the things you serve them to eat are all that anybody could ask for." The guards always stood ready to scoop up any inmate they saw staring at the tourists. After the sightseers left, they'd throw him in the Hole.

Frank's first encounter with the tourists occurred on Tuesday, April 12, 1910, about two weeks after he'd listened in on McLaughry's "court." He'd been in a foul temper ever since, and the coed sociology class from Kansas University in Lawrence didn't improve his mood. It was a class in "remedial and corrective" sociology, and the students were brought to see what newspapers throughout the country now called "the finest penal institution in the United States" and "one of the strongest prisons in the world." He watched as the special pulled through the gates at 2:30 P.M. and then stood beside his workbench, eyes lowered, as a guard led the students through the carpenter shop. Frank peeked under his lids as they passed; they all looked his age, though obviously from more money. The young men wore ties and blazers. The girls wore white blouses with dark ribbons tied at the throat, bustles beneath long skirts, and high-topped blucher shoes. They walked past him and stared like he was a zoo animal. "I feel sorry for them," said a girl with light hair and fair skin like Alice. "Look how sad he looks," she whispered, motioning toward Frank. "He must be our age."

"I don't like how they are all so close-shaven," said her dark-haired companion. "No man is handsome unless he has whiskers." They left for the tailor shop, their voices drifting away.

In the tailor shop, Arthur Hewitt watched the visitors' blithe ignorance—the girls' pouty insouciance, the boys' empty posturing. It had been a long time since he'd had a woman, much less stood so close to one, and he wondered how schoolgirls compared in the sack to others he had known. When a couple passed his bench, he closed his eyes and breathed deeply. Rosewater . . . they smelled like rosewater, one of the many things he remembered about the first girl he'd had in bed. He opened his eyes and saw a schoolgirl standing close, studying his face. His lip curled up in a lazy, lascivious grin. The girl went white and Hewitt quickly dropped his eyes. A guard stepped forward and told her, "You'll want to step away, ma'am, he's a bad one," and Hewitt breathed in her fear as palpably as any perfume. He wondered if these visitors could read his thoughts as easily as he could theirs. If they could, they'd know that in a few days he'd be out of this place or dead. He bent back to sewing a metal button on a jacket. This vision of the outside world had been unexpected and exciting. Maybe he'd go to Lawrence and visit that little dark-haired tart in her college dormitory. How would she like that? She certainly wouldn't forget it. He smiled to himself and the button. Maybe it was a sign.

ARTHUR HEWITT KNEW he was not as smart as his friend Tom Kating, but he'd learned the patient art of watching and waiting, an art that creates the most deliberate of men. He'd learned that patience in the Hole. Except for Clark and Kating, he'd probably spent more time in the Hole than any other inmate in Leavenworth. He knew the way the cell and his body communicated, exchanging temperatures at night and in the morning, absorbing the gritty smell and feel of the floor and walls. Like most men in isolation, he lived in a separate space, knowing that memory was the one thing the guards could never take away.

An imprisoned professor of languages whose name is unknown

today, once said in Hewitt's hearing, *Being is memory*. At first, Hewitt wanted to shut his mouth for him for talking so highfalutin and thinking he was better than the rest of them. But then, in the Hole, Hewitt realized the truth of what the professor said. Being *was* memory, at least for a prisoner, and when he got out he thanked the professor one day. His words had made sense of what he'd experienced all these months and years in the Hole. "They did?" the professor asked, studying the man's face, a dull face actually, slow and heavy and coarse, yet suddenly he felt humbled, realizing there were depths to these men he hadn't understood.

Hewitt had learned this: A man could spend his time in the Hole remembering every slight or rising ounce of anger and burn himself up, or he could examine his past mistakes and chart a way to survive. Most men in the Hole became consumed by their rage. This was what the bulls wanted, so they could throw you in again. This was what happened to Bob Clark, and why he came out nearly insane. It was unjust to punish the poor man in a world so corrupt, but that was the way it was. Look at robber barons like Rockefeller, how society treated them like heroes for stealing millions while all Hewitt had done was steal a horse, and for that he got tossed in this hell. Look how the rich men's mines and trains and factories killed and maimed thousands, while his 1901 escape killed one damn guard.

The anger ate him up when he thought about it, so he thought of other things. A man's actions defined him, and in the Hole he practiced those actions over and over in an infinite train of thought, replaying them in his memory. Evidence suggests that Hewitt was in the Hole at the same time as a man who'd stabbed a fellow prisoner to death with a homemade shiv. Such killings were still unusual, but even so they sometimes happened. The victim had stolen his tobacco, so the man had assumed the role of judge and jury, slipping the knife between the second and third button of his victim's oversized jacket, pumping it up to the hilt in the middle of his chest. He felt the thief's life trembling through the knife, a feeling so gentle and intimate it was more like an act of love. The man told Hewitt he'd looked in his victim's eyes as he'd killed him. They worked in the laundry together; his victim was a trusty, yet no one else was around. He went to the floor to finish him, cradling him like a baby. The knife cut through the skin like butter, no resistance whatever. His victim whispered "Please," just once, and then there was silence.

As Hewitt listened to the account of murder, he imagined himself as executioner and Lemon as the man he cradled. The image frightened and calmed him, for he knew he could do it easily. But they'd kill him afterward, hang him in the yard before all the other prisoners, and he couldn't let that happen because they'd been trying to kill him ever since Waldrupe's death, and he couldn't let them win. He could live for escape or he could live for revenge, and to choose the latter meant death or madness. Escape was the only sane way out. He went over every inch of the "world's best prison," looking for the chink in the armor, the crack in the wall.

The train was the only way. He'd been working on another plan, half convincing a prisoner whose term was about to expire to throw some revolvers over the wall near the brick kiln. A man in the tailor shop said he could get a blade to saw out his cell window. Yet Hewitt knew that plan was doomed. It was too much like the 1901 mutiny, plus it wasn't like the early days, when Charles Ennis could stroll into the unguarded worksite and hide the guns. Throwing two pistols over a thirty-five-foot wall flanked by manned gun towers and spotlights was a lot different from creeping into a dark palisade. Hewitt wondered how close the man would have gotten before his courage gave out and he ran the other way.

The only practical way out was through the West Gate—not that this was very practical. The steel gates formed the openings of the forty-foot stone enclosure prisoners sometimes called the railroad chute; it was open from above, and anyone caught inside would be like a duck in a shooting gallery for the armed guard manning the tower immediately overhead. The fields beyond were flat and open, where pursuers could ride them down in minutes. The only solution was to hijack the engine. Kating, with his experience as an engineer, could drive the train, but how would they grab it without weapons?

Hewitt wasn't the only one to see the possibilities. Several prisoners had made such plans. One group actually set a day, but at the last minute their courage failed them. Several times Deputy Lemon called men to his office to accuse them of planning such a breakout. It was perhaps the best-known secret in Leavenworth, and half a dozen guards had gone to Lemon and McLaughry to warn them of the danger. They begged McLaughry to install a switch outside the prison that could derail all engines. McLaughry agreed that something was needed but said his hands were tied until Congress appropriated the money.

On March 31, 1910, a miracle occurred in Hewitt's life—at least it seemed that way to him. On that Thursday, he was double-bunked with Theodore Murdock, and everyone knew Teddy Murdock had a genius for making things. The idea came in such a flash that he discarded his other plan. Sometime that weekend, when neither man had duty and spent most of the hours in their cell, Hewitt raised the subject, keeping his voice low so no one in a neighboring cell could hear. He asked Murdock if it was true that he could make most anything, like people said.

"You heard that, huh?" Murdock grinned. "I don't know. I made coins, cabinets, paper money, and chairs. I even made a fiddle once, and it looked nice if it didn't sound so good."

"You think you could make a gun?"

Murdock laughed. A man would need a foundry for that, he said. Hewitt shook his head and said no, a fake gun, carved out of wood and painted to look real. Could he make three or four and carve 'em so real they'd fool the guards?

When Murdock yelped in surprise, Hewitt told him to keep it down. "What would you do with 'em?" Murdock asked, appalled. "It's not like you could shoot your way out with toy guns."

Hewitt smiled. No, but a good bluff was something else. Why not wait till the Thursday train was past the inner gate and well in the yard? By then the tender would be uncoupled and the locomotive would have its steam up, ready to go. They'd make a rush, him and Kating from the tailor shop, Murdock and Bob Clark from carpentry, each holding a dummy gun. They'd board the engine and force the engineer to run it out at gunpoint.

"What if the gate's closed already?" Murdock asked.

"I guess we'll see which is tougher, a steel gate or a few tons of train."

Teddy Murdock studied his new cellmate, his initial horror turning to intrigue. The plan was so audacious it just might work; it all depended on how skillfully he could carve those guns. His pride was at stake. Murdock had all the vanity of the frustrated artist. Getting the blocks of wood for the barrel, cylinder, and stock would be no problem; loose wood lay all over the carpenter shop, and snapping up a carving knife would be a cinch too. The shop was so loud and loosely guarded he could probably build a Trojan horse and the guards wouldn't see. The problem would be in keeping it secret from other inmates, since he'd be carving the guns every free minute he had. He'd also need paint and shoe blacking, but Hewitt said he could get those from the tailor shop, no worry there.

They started their preparations on Monday, April 4. Hewitt worked at getting a message to Kating, in the Hole since February 21. He told his friend to admit defeat to Lemon; it was the only way he'd be released and sent back to work. Passing a message to Bob Clark was easier. Murdock served as the carrier, slipping a note to him in line. "You think it'll work?" Murdock asked after Clark read and swallowed it. "Depends," Clark answered.

"Depends on what?"

"On how good you make them guns."

Almost from the beginning, Frank knew something was up—as did John Gideon, who sat on the other side of Murdock in the shop. Few inmates rushed through their work, since that always meant extra duties from the foreman, yet they watched as Murdock rushed through his jobs like he was getting paid by the piece. Once finished, he reached beneath his table for a large block of wood, watching the guards with one eye while trying to keep the other on whatever it was he carved. John Gideon was the first to approach him; Murdock tried to brush him off, but Gideon wasn't dumb. Once while Murdock was away from his bench, Gideon found a carving knife, sandpaper, a small can of shoe blacking, and something hidden under a rag. He lifted the corner and saw the block carved into a rude right angle, bulging in the middle and tapered near the ends. Almost like a gun.

Gideon lifted the rag to show Frank, then placed it back carefully before Murdock returned. They waited a second as he settled in his place; then Gideon slid his stool over and said, "Okay, Teddy, what's with the block of wood?"

That night, Murdock told his cellmate that Gideon and Grigware knew. He worked right between them and couldn't keep it secret any longer; it might even be an advantage to have them acting as lookouts while he worked, he said. He'd sure get more done if he didn't always have to keep his eyes peeled for the bulls. Hewitt had to think about this new development. Tom Kating was usually the one who dreamed up plans; Hewitt's strength was that everybody liked him, so he was able to rope people in to their schemes. Though he was unaccustomed to sudden changes, he tried his best to think this through. The more people involved, the more chances for a leak, yet Gideon and Grigware already knew. Gideon was no problem: anyone who held up a mail train alone had ice in his veins. But he knew nothing about Grigware. He seemed likable enough and had been jailed for train robbing, but he always insisted he wasn't part of the gang. He peeked over the edge of his bunk at Murdock. "Will the kid fold when shooting starts?" he asked. "Does he understand we stand a good chance to get killed?"

"He said he'd rather die than stay here any longer," said Murdock.

"You believe him?"

"He's a lifer, ain't he?"

Hewitt was forced to eat his words. "Okay," Hewitt decided. "Just make sure he understands he's on his own when the shooting starts."

"I think he understands."

Frank understood, all right. He'd learned that lesson well. He'd learned it in the Omaha court with its dark wood paneling like Dr. Byrne's office. He'd learned it in the Hole. A man was on his own in any of this country's temples of justice. He was far from justice within the place of justice, especially if he was poor. He'd vowed he'd be damned before he spent his entire life in this place, and now he had a chance to make good on that vow. It might be the only chance he had. No judge was going to free him from Leavenworth. He had to do it himself, be it on the westbound train or in a coffin sent to Peckerwood Hill.

On the surface, the next three weeks at Leavenworth passed normally. On Tuesday, April 12, the same day as the coeds' visit, Warden McLaughry left for Joliet, Illinois, to attend the wedding of his youngest son. Like his father and older brother, William McLaughry had cast his lot with prisons, working in Joliet thanks to his father, hoping someday to follow his family to Leavenworth. A young man with connections could build a future in corrections, especially as the crime rate rocketed. Leavenworth was just the first step in a prison-building boom.

On Friday, April 15, Tom Kating sent a note to Deputy Lemon. His health had improved, he wrote, and he promised to return to work in the tailor shop and obey the prison rules. Lemon wondered what caused this change of heart. He checked with his stoolies but found no rumored mutinies. Maybe Kating had just grown tired of the Hole. On Saturday, April 16, after sixty-four days in Isolation, Kating returned to the cellblocks. He went back to work the following Monday.

The day after that, on Tuesday, April 19, Warden McLaughry returned from his son's wedding, feeling the glow of an accomplished old age. He was proud of his sons, proud of his prison, proud of all he had done. Leavenworth might seem hard duty, but he'd built it from the ground up through his own force of will. Now his sons would follow in his footsteps, and someday it would be written that he'd founded a prison dynasty. McLaughry listened as his deputy reported that everything had run smoothly in his absence. He remembered the rumors concerning Lemon—that he was brutal, that he was involved in a kickback scheme. McLaughry accepted that Lemon was harsh, lacking the polish that catapulted men to higher positions. He would never be a warden, at least not in the federal system. With that Stetson hat, he was too much of an anachronism. Yet hard men were needed in hard places, men willing to do whatever it took to keep recalcitrants in line. "You did a good job," he told his deputy, meaning every word. Lemon smiled.

The next afternoon, on Wednesday, April 20, Theodore Murdock turned to Frank and John Gideon and said that he'd finished the guns.

Frank looked at Murdock's handiwork and was astounded. There were three fake pistols, each a thing of beauty, each impossible to distinguish from the real article unless you held it in your hand. "Amazing," Frank said. Teddy Murdock had carved exact imitations of Colt revolvers, each detail pulled from memory. He'd taken them to his cell at night for touch-up or sanding, the guns tucked away in the loose folds of his oversized uniform. The barrels were painted a dull steel color, the stocks a rich walnut. Even the brass cartridge butts and round heads of the slugs had been carved into the cylinders, then each painted so accurately that no guard would dare argue back. Murdock looked proud.

Frank stared again at the guns and remembered something. "Tomorrow's Thursday."

"Less time to worry," Gideon said.

That night in his cell, Arthur Hewitt was overjoyed. The results of Murdock's handiwork were better than he ever could have dreamed. As Murdock pulled the guns from a hiding place, Hewitt turned them in his hands. He took one for himself, took another for Kating and left the third for Murdock. "I don't want it," Teddy said unexpectedly. Hewitt was surprised by his cellmate, then had a rare flash of insight. He'd had the nerve to carve the fakes for three straight weeks, knowing full well what would happen if he'd been discovered. All that time, he was completely on his own. It was funny the forms that courage took. He'd had the nerve for that, but didn't trust his nerve to face down a guard.

Hewitt told him to hand the gun to Clark or Gideon; since Murdock didn't like Clark, he said he'd slip it to Gideon in line. Hewitt wrote a quick note to Bob Clark: "We have been waiting a long time for the guns. We will go in the morning. We will take the big engine." He handed the note to Murdock to pass over in the morning.

That night, before sleep, Frank had an attack of nerves. He wondered what it felt like to die. He'd heard that when a bullet hit there was no pain at first, just a blow and, if fatal, a rapid weakening as if life spiraled down a drain. He'd heard that for survivors the pain came later, especially with infection. Yet survival was rare. The repeating rifles of the tower guards had high muzzle velocities; the bullet produced a shock wave that stacked up tissue as it traveled through the body. The exit wound was always bigger than where the bullet entered, and a head shot was even worse. A high-velocity bullet entering the skull could burst the brain like a bubble. Sometimes the head exploded. He wondered what it was like to die so gruesomely. Did it hurt? Was there a strange lightness as one's brains flew over the ground?

Maybe it was healthier to contemplate other things. Frank tried to make future plans. If he did get out, where would he run? He had no idea. He couldn't go to Alice. That was the first place the law would look. Spokane was out: after a man's girl, the law checked his family. He couldn't visit Denver, Kansas City, Omaha, Wallace, or any of the places he'd stopped for the last four years. Anything he'd done in the past was now off-limits. To those he'd known and loved, Frank Grigware would have to be dead.

He lay in bed and tried to sleep but found sleep impossible. If he lived through tomorrow's escape, he'd have to run to the ends of the earth. He'd always wanted adventure and, boy, he'd gotten his wish. He laughed at the thought, then bit his hand to stop the nervous giggles. He was a bundle of nerves and feared he would go crazy.

The next cell over, a man started snoring. A guard's slow footsteps rang on an upper tier.

He finally dropped asleep, exhausted, and slept like the dead.

THURSDAY, APRIL 21, 1910, started pleasantly enough, the kind of weather old-timers called a "balmy spring day." Frank rose as always with the sun, washed his hands and face, stood at attention outside his cell when the tier doors slid open, did a smart right-face, and marched in close order to the dining hall. He watched from the corner of his eye as Murdock nudged Bob Clark in line and passed the note; in shop, he saw him slide close to Gideon and pass him the gun. The guards didn't notice; Frank thought the warden might as well put out blind men. All in all, it seemed like just another normal day.

Life seemed peaceful everywhere. Theodore Roosevelt reached Paris at seven-thirty that morning, one of many stops in a global tour begun after leaving the Oval Office the previous year. Later that day he told an audience at the Sorbonne that a nation's success depended upon "the way in which the average man, the average woman, does his or her duty," both in the ordinary affairs of life as well as "in those great occasional crises which call for the heroic virtues." That day, Roosevelt's account of hunting hippos in Africa appeared in *Scribner's* magazine. When the hippos charged his boat, Roosevelt wrote, he "poured lead into them from a rifle at Gatling-gun speed."

The sad news that day was the death of Mark Twain. He died in his home at Redding, Connecticut, of "angina pectoris" at 6:30 P.M. The man whose writings humanized the frontier once planned to extend the saga of Huck Finn, Tom Sawyer, and Becky Thatcher into the West but abandoned the plan after concluding that an honest portrayal would be too brutal. Notes later found showed one scene in which their wagon train was raided by Indians, who raped and killed Becky. Twain's white house was on a hillside with a green slope beneath it; he could see a trout stream flowing through a long meadow. The previous fall, Twain's daughter drowned when seized by epilepsy in the bath. The stabbing pains in his chest began soon afterward. "Mark Twain died, as truly as it can be said of any man, of a broken heart," one newspaper eulogized.

That day in Kansas City, six dogs and a frog were poisoned with strychnine to demonstrate its effects in the murder trial of Dr. B. C.

Hyde, charged with poisoning an entire family. That morning in a field near Leavenworth, a thirty-three-year-old farmer was cutting and burning cornstalks when his fence caught fire. When he tried to save the fence, his clothes ignited. He was burned beyond recognition by the time neighbors, hearing screams, ran to his aid.

Leavenworth would be the big news that day, at least for those who lived on the old frontier. At 8 A.M., the Union Pacific mogul backed slowly through the gates, whistling once from outside as always. Frank looked up from his workbench. The larger mogul was better for their plans than the Porter engine, its extra weight perfect as a battering ram. He watched for signs of wariness among the guards, but nothing caught his eye. He watched as the flatcar stacked with lumber backed through the inner gate; as Captain Zerbst and Guard Reed jumped on the ladder and took their free rides back to the scales. It dawned on him that they probably enjoyed the weekly routine. The engine hissed to a stop, and he saw that the inner gate stayed open while the outer gate had closed. As always, the engine stopped about four car lengths from the inner gate. Would that be enough track for it to build up speed? None of them knew. He watched as Zerbst and Reed dropped off the ladder and Zerbst sauntered to the scales. As always, Harry Reed stood guard by the tender, club in hand. Reed seemed to be humming to himself, enjoying the fine weather. There was a hiss and a clank as the flat cars uncoupled from the tender. Frank looked at the others. It was the signal to run.

The four of them rose. There was a ringing in Frank's ears, his heartbeat pounding, but it sounded more like a stamp press drowning out all other sounds. Gideon swung around fast as the guard started forward and pointed the gun at his chest, ordering him down on the ground. The guard took one look at the gun and dropped to his knees with his hands in the air. Frank grabbed a hatchet and Murdock a thick piece of wood. Clark opened the door and all four of them piled through it, Guard Reed simply gaping as they sprinted ten to twenty yards in the open, toward him. Gideon took the lead, pointing the gun at Reed's head. Reed dropped the club as he threw up his hands; Gideon forced him forward at gunpoint into the locomotive cab.

In the tailor shop, Tom Kating and Arthur Hewitt encountered more resistance. They too rose at once, each with a gun in his hand. Prisoners near them froze in disbelief, as did all but one of the guards. Tom Brummett was new to the shop, an inexperience that may have inured him to the general paralysis. He was standing by Kating when he saw the Colt in his fist. "Put up your hands!" Kating cried. Something in Brummett's mind kicked into automatic, for he grabbed the pistol and it cracked in his fist, the barrel snapping in his hands. Kating threw up his own hands to protect himself but was not fast enough: Brummett swung with his nightstick and caught him across the skull, knocking Kating down. Hewitt ran up before Brummett could turn and threw him across the room; Brummett, crash-landing in a pile of machinery and inmates, was stunned by the impact and out for the rest of the show. "Get up, hurry!" cried Hewitt, picking Kating off the floor. The tailor shop was farther back from the tracks than the carpenter shop; Hewitt half dragged Kating as they ran the twenty to thirty yards to the engine.

A surreal sense of astonishment seemed to freeze the entire yard. The break for freedom occurred within full view of Captain Zerbst, the armed guard in the West Gate tower, and the guards and inmates in the other shops, yet no one intervened. It somehow seemed staged: One moment they all ran across an endless open space; the next, they crowded into the locomotive and John Gideon placed his gun to the head of Charles Curtin, the engineer.

"Run her out!" yelled Gideon. "Pull the throttle wide open!"

Curtin said it couldn't be done. He pointed down the engine to the forty-foot chute: at the end was the massive iron barrier. "The gate's still closed."

"Do as I tell you!" Gideon answered, poking Curtin in the ribs with the fake revolver, no hint in his voice that the threat was less than real.

"They'll shoot us from the tower!" cried the fireman, Miller Heeter.

"Don't bet on it," Clark replied. "I was in the 1901 mutiny, and they won't fire as long as another guard's in here with us. They won't chance killing one of their own."

Curtin opened the throttle as told. Frank glanced back as the engine lurched forward, wondering about Hewitt and Kating, then saw them limp from the tailor shop and jump onto the rear of the tender. Kating's scalp bled freely where he'd been struck; he acted woozy and had to be supported by Hewitt as they climbed over the tender and took their places with the others. They passed the inner gate. Frank stared at the gate at the end of the chute, built to withstand assaults from outside. We'll never make it, he thought, but was somehow too excited to be scared. He almost felt invulnerable, every sense sharpened, living more intensely than ever before. Engineer Curtin moved instinctively to stop the engine as they rushed toward the gate, but Gideon nudged him in the back with the revolver. "Keep your hand off that throttle," Gideon warned the trainman. "Hit it hard!"

The engine slammed into the outer gate with the greatest ringing crash Frank had ever heard. A shudder passed down the entire length of the engine. Frank watched as if from a great distance; time seemed to freeze as the convicts and guards watched the era's most irresistible force crash head on into what was assumed to be an unmovable object. Then the gate ripped free. It folded like cardboard, warping along its length as the mogul pushed it aside. The engine, neither derailed nor badly damaged, rushed on.

The guards in the yard and surrounding towers watched helplessly as the Leavenworth train gained speed. The guard in the West Gate tower aimed his rifle but couldn't tell the inmates from Reed or the trainmen and held his fire. "Stop them!" cried Zerbst, running forward from the power plant, but there wasn't a lot anyone could do. Someone hit the emergency siren as the engine cleared the outer buildings. Frank heard himself cheer—the others around him, too. Ahead was freedom!

The passage through the gate seemed to waken Kating from his stupor, and he told the engineer, "Give her all she'll stand." He told the fireman to shovel coal as he'd never shoveled before. As they sped west on the prison spur toward the main line, Kating yelled to Hewitt if he recalled working on this stretch of track during the winter of 1901. "I do remember that," cried Hewitt. "God, it was cold." Kating agreed, and added, "I'm glad we did it, now."

Curtin tried to slip the throttle back a notch, but Gideon nudged him in the ribs with his pistol, and Kating reminded him to keep it shoved forward as far as it would go. Hewitt kept his gun on Harry Reed. Frank glanced at his own hand and was surprised to see the hatchet. He didn't remember anything but jumping from his bench. Where did that come from?

Their train headed north for less than a minute, climbing from the valley of the prison and curving quickly northwest on a steep gradient bounded to the south by Mount Hope and to the north by Government and Sentinel hills. Past the hills the track curved again to the southwest, the grade dropping sharply from 940 to 800 feet above sea level as the train descended into Salt Creek Valley. Frank leaned from the cab and felt the wind snapping at his clothes and tugging at his hair. The valley ran roughly northeast to southwest, cross-hatched with farms and fences, plowed fields, and those filled with stubble. It was ripped down the middle by the meandering Salt Creek, a deep cut in the landscape heavily grown with cattails, cut-grass, cottonwood, and pine. Hund's Station and Hund's Schoolhouse lay in the center of the valley just across Salt Creek, at the junction of a road west to Easton and a road north to Kickapoo. Two tracks crossed here also: theirs, the old Leavenworth Northern & Southern Railroad tracks, which followed the path of the Oregon Trail north into Nebraska, and the Kansas Central & Union Pacific Railroad tracks, which ran six miles west to Easton and then straight as a zipper into the Kansas prairie. Either way was a good route to freedom; past the creek lay miles of open country where they could fire up the engine to 60 mph or more. Frank took his first deep breath of fresh air in months and smelled traces of the smoke from farmers burning stubble from their fields. There was the green hint of growing things. He'd forgotten what fields smelled like. He would have given his life for this moment. Now he had it, and he'd give his life to never go back.

The train had reached a speed of about 25 mph when it began the straight slope into the valley from up in the hills. Kating told the engineer to put on more steam when the unbelievable occurred: Curtin yelled over the wind that the Shanghai bridge over Salt Creek was under repair. New pilings were being driven into the mud and rock; the bridge was jacked up for repairs. If the train passed over, the bridge would collapse and kill them all. "It's a trick!" yelled Gideon, but the engineer persisted in his warnings, even when poked in the ribs with the gun. "If we hit that bridge in its weakened state," Curtin yelled back, "it means death for us all."

Kating stared at the wooded creek ahead of them and after a second told Curtin to slow down. They had arrived at a point about two and a half miles west of the prison, where heavy timber grew on both sides of the track. They could see the pile driver with their own eyes and realized Curtin wasn't lying; if they hit the bridge at speed, bridge and engine both would topple into Salt Creek. Kating nodded to the engineer and Curtin eased up on the throttle, stopping the train at the edge of the water.

Frank stared at the bridge in disbelief, then glanced back over his shoulder toward the prison. His disbelief rivaled the night he was arrested for train robbery, the afternoon the judge ordered him sent for life to Leavenworth. It seemed like one of those impossible plot twists that only occur in moving pictures. How was it possible that one moment he'd been within reach of freedom, only to be in jeopardy again? Was there really no such thing as justice, just endlessly cruel reversals that pumped up one's hopes only to dash them again? Maybe his life was someone else's movie, just like that poor elephant whose execution was relived nightly, a loop of life and death played for the entertainment of paying customers who relished the knowledge they'd never endure such pain. As the engine settled into silence, he heard the prison siren yowling in the distance, and the sound brought him back to earth. From here on, every man was on his own.

Gideon, an old railroader like Kating, now took charge. He told Curtin to wet down the coals of the fire so the engine would be dead and he wouldn't be able to return to the prison immediately, bringing searchers on their trail. Since their prison uniforms would act like beacons, he forced Curtin to give up his cap and coat. That set off a frenzy of demanding and donning clothes. Kating, Clark, and Hewitt took the engineer's three new pairs of gloves; when Curtin protested, saying he'd only just bought them, Gideon called it the fortunes of war. Hewitt and Clark looked at the fireman and told him to take off everything. The idea of the fireman riding back to prison in his long johns struck Kating as funny, and he sounded a voice of reason. "Boys, he won't be able to get back into town if we take *all* his clothes. You don't want that, do you?" After all, he *had* shoveled coal as fast as humanly possible into the furnace; that must be worth something. The others reluctantly agreed and let Heeter keep his pants and shoes. Someone ordered Guard Reed to disrobe, too, but the siren's distant wailing made them too nervous to wait any longer. "Leave him be," snapped Hewitt. "Let's go."

It was obvious to Frank during all the divvying up that he'd be left out of the spoils. As the others divided the coats and shirts, Frank grabbed the engineer's dinner pail. He backed away, expecting some kind of challenge, but Hewitt, Kating, Gideon, and Clark jumped off the fireman's side of the cab and ran south into the dense brush and woods. Frank leapt off the engineer's platform and ran north and west through a stand of trees. He crossed a stubble field and sprinted toward thick woods. Murdock took off after him, but the kid ran across that field faster than seemed possible. Where did that boy learn how to run? All Frank could think about was putting as much distance as possible between him and the train. He didn't know which direction he was headed; he just moved his feet the instant they touched the ground. His mother always laughed at how fast he ran; well, he'd never run so fast as now. He left the edge of the stubble field and saw a dense stand of brush back among the trees. He crashed through the bushes, their branches stinging his hands and face. Before him was some kind of hole. He rolled into it, still clutching the dinner pail to his chest; he reached up and pulled leaves and fallen branches over him. He lay still and caught his breath, listening as his heart pounded back to normal. It seemed the prison siren would never stop. Someone crashed through the brush nearby and he thought it was probably Murdock, but he didn't take a chance and reveal himself. He lay still as the dirt around him. He didn't peek from his hideout. He'd gone to ground like the animals he'd hunted in the forest. If he could see no one, maybe no one could see him.

FRANK WASN'T THE only one thrown into panic when the siren announced the escape. Farmers in a ten-mile circle around the penitentiary left their teams in the fields and armed themselves with guns of every make and model, some little more effective than the escapees' wooden colts. Women locked their horses in their barns to keep them from being stolen, then locked themselves and their children inside their houses. Those living outside the siren's ten-mile radius were reached by phone, the party-line operators spreading the net. Memories were still too fresh of the 1901 mutiny.

As soon as they were able to get the engine's steam back up, Curtin and Heeter ran the train back to the prison and Reed told his fellows what had happened. By then, armed guards had been thrown around the prison gates in case any other inmates attempted to break free. McLaughry and Zerbst phoned the night guards from their sleep and ordered them to the prison to join the chase. Although some of the day guards were added to their numbers, few could be spared from their normal duties. Within thirty minutes of the breakout,

McLaughry had formed a fifty-guard posse; within the next hour, Engineer Curtin shuttled three loads of guards out to the place where the escapees had fled. The guards formed into lines and dove into the brush after them.

John Gideon was the first inmate to be spotted, possibly as early as 9 to 9:30 A.M. He was discovered by Frank Murray, a guard who lived close to the prison and was among the first of the night shift to reach Leavenworth. Murray had returned to the Shanghai bridge with the first trainload of searchers and was checking the area south of Hund's Station when he saw someone creeping through the undergrowth. Murray ordered him to halt and the man whipped around, pointing a revolver. "Let me pass," he said.

It was John Gideon, still carrying one of the fake pistols. He pointed the gun at Murray's head and demanded right of passage. But Murray, acting remarkably calm given the circumstances, stood pat, staking his shotgun against the revolver. The two men stood like that another moment, until Gideon knew his bluff had failed. He lowered the pistol and surrendered. Murray marched him back to prison, and McLaughry threw Gideon in the Hole.

The next contact with the escapees occurred thirty minutes later, about 10 A.M. By now the countryside was saturated with farmers, and Fred Frey, a retired guard who now farmed a plot in the Salt Creek Valley, patrolled a dirt road with his seventeen-year-old son, Claude. They were about a mile southeast of Hund's Station when they saw three men up ahead. Frey yelled for them to halt, but the only man to obey was the one in the rear. It was Bob Clark. He'd fallen behind Hewitt and Kating in the tangled brush and had been struggling to catch up; he looked back and saw the old man's shotgun pointed at his back and automatically stopped, throwing up his hands. Hewitt and Kating looked back and then rushed to the woods bordering the road. Clark watched as Frey and his son approached, pulling revolvers from their pockets. It was strange, but they only seemed relieved when they had him covered with the smaller-caliber guns.

He was right. There was a certain irony to Clark's capture; he was stopped with an unloaded gun. When Frey first heard the alarm and grabbed his 12-gauge, he mistakenly scooped up 10-gauge cartridges and did not discover the mistake until he was well into the woods. Before he was able to go home and correct the mistake, he spotted the three fugitives. Hewitt and Kating were out of range before he could drag his pistol from his pocket, so he trained the shotgun on Clark. Like the prisoners with their jailers, Frey bluffed Clark with a useless gun.

That left four inmates free, though by this time there was some confusion concerning how many prisoners had actually hopped on the hijacked train. Some guards thought five had escaped, while others insisted there were six. Somehow Murdock was not noticed among the missing until a roll call revealed his absence. This also confirmed Frank's escape, which instantly started a rumor that he'd fled with the other Mud Cut defendants. A quick check confirmed that Fritz Torgensen, Dan Downer, Bill Matthews, and Jack Golden were in their cells or shops where they were supposed to be.

To add to the confusion, false sightings of the fugitives were constantly being phoned in to the prison. All sounded urgent, but the one given most credence came about 11 A.M. A woman told Frank Lemon she'd seen three prisoners run into a cave at Hund's Vineyard, about eight miles west of the prison. As Lemon and a small force of guards rushed to the scene and surrounded the cave, they phoned for reinforcements, and sheriff's deputies armed with repeating rifles soon joined the others outside. Confident of their overwhelming force, they rushed the entrance, expecting shots, but were greeted instead by silence. The cave was empty. Lemon was enraged. They'd lost two hours on the empty cave; the prisoners were probably miles away!

In truth, the Salt Creek Valley around Hund's Station was so packed with searchers that the fugitives made little headway. After Hewitt and Kating escaped from Fred Frey, they hid in the treeline, watching the farmer and his son march poor Bob Clark away. They knew the treatment he'd get; right now, the Hole was the least of his worries. Lemon and McLaughry would probably kill them all. They waited for another hour before spying an approaching wagonload of guards sent there by Frey and his son. There wasn't much cover in the trees, so they headed south and west, a route also anticipated by their pursuers.

Guard J. F. Maxey and three others passed the place where Frey had seen the men run off and slowly worked their way up a wooded ravine. They heard some movement ahead and cried out for whoever was there to stop. The order was not obeyed. Maxey came to a spot where the ravine narrowed and deepened; it was choked with brush and treefalls before opening into a field. It was the perfect place to hide, he thought—unless, of course, someone already guessed you were there. Maxey placed two of his men at the field end of the cut, shotguns ready, and entered the ravine with his other man from the forest end. It was like beating high grass for rabbits. By 2:30 P.M., Hewitt and Kating popped out of the woods ahead of the beaters and into the hands of the waiting guards.

That only left the two fugitives who'd run to the north, Murdock and Grigware. McLaughry made it known that he wanted them back. It didn't matter in what condition; it didn't even matter if they came back alive. He wanted them back. No one broke free of his prison so audaciously and got away scot-free.

WITH NIGHTFALL came a change in the weather, a wind from the west that brought widespread destruction over the next few days. Anyone caught in the open during that storm, which brought rain and snow through wide swaths of the nation during April 21–24, 1910, would wish he'd died and gone to hell. At least it would be warmer there. On April 22, a 40-mph wind blew a wildfire through the prairie town of Salem, Nebraska, instantly turning it to cinders. That night, snow and freezing rain hit the upper Mississippi Valley, destroying millions of dollars in fruit crops. The waves along the Great Lakes reached record heights, beaching the Goodrich steamer *Iowa* halfway between Kenosha and Racine on the Wisconsin shore.

The first night of the storm, that Thursday evening, saw the front move in a line all over the Missouri Valley. In the woods above Salt Creek, Teddy Murdock weighed his options. He knew he was in a trap and thought his best chance of escape was to play a waiting game. Like Frank, he'd headed northwest from the engine, passing the younger man in his woodland hole. The northern stretches of Salt Creek Valley were more wooded than in the south. Murdock decided that Hewitt, Kating, and Clark had fled south out of instinct, choosing the route they'd taken during the 1901 mutiny. John Gideon followed the men he considered the most experienced; logical enough, though it proved his undoing. The northern woods lay in a cul-de-sac bordered to the north and east by the Missouri River, while to the south lay open country sprinkled with several farming villages. Like Frank, Murdock hid in a clump of bushes, where he stayed in a fever of anxiety as armed farmers and guards passed and repassed his hiding spot on a nearby road. They passed so often that by evening he'd concluded that as long as he lay still in the forest he was safe. Yet the route to freedom lay west, over roads, railroad tracks, and open fields where he'd easily be seen.

His hunters knew that too. By Thursday evening, the search was consolidated under Lemon's command. He wanted the fugitives back as badly as McLaughry; no one made an ass of him. He'd take his time with his old friends Hewitt, Clark, and Kating once he got back to the prison; right now he had to prove that no one could escape on his watch, at least not do so and live. Earlier in the day he'd rushed fifty guards west to Easton to block the line of escape. That night, he extended these guards in a line and worked them east toward the prison at the same time that McLaughry started a line moving west from Leavenworth. They hoped to squeeze the fugitives between them and force them into the open. Lemon thought Murdock and Grigware would lie in hiding until nightfall, then enter a farmhouse, trade their uniforms for civilian clothes, and maybe steal some horses for a cross-country run. The crossroads near Hund's Station was guarded, and Salt Creek Valley was "fairly alive with searchers," claimed the *Leavenworth Times*. Hope ran high among the searchers that they'd bag their prey by Thursday night or, at the latest, Friday morning. "With the almost certain fact that the prisoners . . . are between here and Easton, their escape seems impossible," the local paper assured its worried readers.

Yet Thursday night brought a shift in fortune as well as in the wind. Early in the night, clouds obscured the moon, throwing the Salt Creek Valley into complete darkness. By midnight, a heavy rain set in. The wind picked up to 28 mph, while in the early morning hours the mercury dropped to 46 degrees. Many of the searchers were driven indoors. They could only hope that the fugitives did the same or died from exposure in the storm.

Once it grew dark, Murdock moved from his hidey-hole and back-tracked slightly, moving northeast around the wooded edge of Sentinel Hill and away from Salt Creek and the crossroads. He crossed a stream where he could get all the water he wanted but still couldn't find any food. From the heights he could see lights from lanterns and motorcars down in the valley, the only visible signs of life for miles. He dug into the leaves and brush for warmth, trying to get some sleep, realizing he faced a real problem. If he sought protection from the storm in a barn or farmhouse, he would surely be discovered and sent back to prison. But he'd had nothing to eat since breakfast, and this was not even the season for apples or green corn. His stomach knotted and growled as he thought of food. Surely the sounds would give away his hiding place. At least he could hope that with the dawn he would finally get warm.

The searchers also prayed that something would soon save them from this miserable storm. Their hopes leapt up at 1 A.M. that night when two men were seen walking along a byroad three miles southeast of Easton. The two were probably hoboes, who seemed to drift frequently through the wide area between the major rail junctions of Kansas City and Omaha, and had been spotted by a boy accompanying one of the many posses. The two strangers dove into the woods the moment they knew they'd been spotted; the boy spread the alarm and the woods were surrounded by guards and volunteers. When the news was phoned to the prison, Lemon hurried ten more guards to the scene. By 2 A.M., the woods had been searched without result. There were no other sightings that night and no rumors of missing food, horses, or clothes.

By Friday morning, as forty guards continued to scour the area between Leavenworth and Easton, the rest were pulled off the hunt to fill their regular prison duties. The searchers were tired and hungry and had been told there would be no relief until later in the day. Some respite came from the weather; the mercury rose from 50 degrees Fahrenheit at 7 A.M. to 62 degrees by noon. Unfortunately, the rain continued, deepening the malaise despite the warming.

By Friday morning, the state and local press indulged in a paroxysm of speculation, having little else to report besides false leads. "Confederates on the outside had succeeded in smuggling at least two revolvers," wrote the *Kansas City Star*, raising the specter of an army of armed ex-convicts roaming the countryside. Newspapers said the escape's split timing proved the plans had been in the works for "months, or perhaps years. The making of the wooden revolvers alone must have occupied months as they could not have been made only in minutes when the guards were not watching." Others reported that Murdock and Grigware were traveling together and carried one gun between them, taken from a guard. Opinion was divided over whether that gun was loaded.

By Friday morning, McLaughry knew he must shift to damage control if he hoped to survive the crisis. He was no longer worried about armed squads of confederates; he had the fake guns in his possession and believed he knew what had occurred. It was an embarrassment that fakes of such detail could be produced in his prison under the noses of his guards; even more embarrassing was the fact that he'd been warned by his own guards about the means of escape by rail, not once but several times. If that got out, it could be his undoing.

As soon as the first four fugitives were returned to the prison on Thursday, McLaughry sent them straight to the Hole. Gideon and Bob Clark proved tough nuts to crack, so McLaughry turned his spite on his old friends Kating and Hewitt. At first the two men said they didn't know who made the revolvers, but their resolve slipped quickly as Thursday afternoon turned to evening, suggesting they received more than a gentle persuasion from the guards. By night they said they'd been given the guns by another inmate, whom they still refused to identify. As midnight neared they softened further, blaming Murdock, who was still free.

By 8 A.M. Friday, McLaughry faced a horde of newsmen in his office. He despised them for their prying questions but knew their good or bad opinions could make or break him, so he had little choice but to play along. The fugitives had "seized the very opportune moment when the engine was ready to move out," he said. "The fact is that the engine ought not to be permitted to deliver cars inside the prison yard, and we wanted long ago to build a switch outside for cars, and they could be brought in at our convenience, but Congress did not give us an appropriation to enable us to do it. I can't say that the guards were negligent, but circumstances gave these fellows a chance they were looking for, and they took advantage of it and broke through the gate before anyone could stop them. We have 124 life men, and have to work them in all parts of the yard. . . . The prison is still under construction, and we have to take chances." He passed out fliers with descriptions and photos of Frank Grigware and Theodore Murdock and said he was adding an extra $200 apiece for their capture, this in addition to the standard $50 reward always offered for escapees. McLaughry pointed out that he had tacked a warning at the bottom of the printed fliers: TAKE NO CHANCES WITH THEM. GET THE DROP ON THEM FIRST. THEY ARE BOTH BAD MEN.

The $500 reward brought armed farmers and their sons out in droves. Teddy Murdock quickly discovered that he could make no headway in his flight—everywhere he turned were barking dogs and armed farmers. Over and over he was tempted by cold and hunger to return to the prison, he resisted the temptation only by focusing on the fact that if he did go back he'd get thrown in the Hole, a place he'd never been. The worst thing was his hunger, which drove him into a frenzy. If he begged at a farmhouse, the alarm would go out and pursuers would arrive in minutes. He stayed in the woods, eluding the manhunt, chewing leaves and grass to allay the hunger pangs.

It rained all day. By 5 P.M. on Friday, April 22, Lemon's searchers were ready to give up when news arrived that once again brought hope. A seventeen-year-old boy had spotted a man answering Murdock's description sleeping in the brush. He'd been walking in the woods about four miles southeast of Easton when he saw the man stretched out in a thicket. It was approximately the same area where the two hoboes had been seen the night before. The boy hurried home and grabbed a gun, but by the time he returned the man was gone. J. F. Maxey—the same guard who'd captured Hewitt and Kating— took five local farmers to the spot and searched without luck. At about the same time, a rumor began circulating that Grigware was seen three miles northeast of Easton, in the opposite direction. By then it was evident to Lemon and McLaughry that false sightings and rumors would keep arriving until they all dropped from exhaustion. Yet to be on the safe side they kept twenty-five guards in the Salt Creek Valley and sent the others home.

Those who remained on the search were too tired to do any good. They'd been patrolling now for two days and nights without relief. They were wet and cold, contenting themselves with patrolling the roads leading from the valley, watching for skulking figures who might try to creep from the hills to break through their lines. They alternately hated the fugitives for causing their misery and McLaughry and Lemon for keeping them out here. Sometimes they felt sorry for the poor escaping bastards, who didn't even have the benefit of occasional shelter and a hot meal. On Friday night a break came in the storm; the moon shone through rents in the clouds, outlining the trees and farms in a harsh, cold light. Only the deeper hollows remained in shadow. It was Lemon's opinion that at least one of the prisoners was still in the valley, and he thought it would be Murdock. One more night and they'd have him, Lemon said. McLaughry agreed, but also believed that if the two did succeed in getting through the guards, they would follow the Missouri River north to more familiar territory. After all, Grigware had been arrested in Omaha, and Murdock had a wife in Chicago. The U.S. marshal in Omaha was forewarned of Grigware's possible route, while the Chicago police contacted Emma Murdock. When they told her of her husband's escape, she laughed and said she'd turn him in the minute he showed his face. No love lost there, Chicago detectives agreed.

That Friday night in Easton, farmers stopped two hoboes walking through a field about four miles north of town. They phoned the prison and McLaughry sent out three guards in a fast Model T; to avoid mistakes, they took the fugitives' photos and measurements and hurried down the dark dirt roads, careful not to run over any searchers. It was a long drive. When they arrived, they saw immediately that the two tramps in no way resembled Murdock or Grigware. It was becoming obvious that, if this kept up, any number of innocent people might be shot, never mind the fugitives. The farmers, thinking they'd just earned $500 in reward money, held double-barreled shotguns to the hoboes' heads. The two captives were "on the verge of nervous prostration" when released, but had enough energy and presence of mind to leave an area inhabited by so many dangerous and disappointed farmers.

That Friday night, a rumor began circulating that Frank and Murdock had held up two farmers earlier in the day. According to this tale, they'd taken the men's clothing and were now dressed as civilians. They'd also broken into a farmhouse and grabbed something to eat before running back to the woods. A fear settled on the farms around Easton that Frank and Murdock were the most dangerous of the ones who'd escaped. They became bigger than life, capable of laying waste to the countryside. That night, McLaughry sent out 3,000 copies of the wanted posters, almost certain that the two had slipped his net and gotten away.

On Saturday morning, the search for Grigware and Murdock was finally called off. The exhausted guards went home. It had been two full days since the breakout, and despite all rumors the fugitives had never once shown themselves. No one believed they could combat hunger this long. McLaughry admitted to the papers that they were probably miles away.

*   *   *

BY SATURDAY MORNING, Theodore Murdock had only been able to work his way two miles west of where he'd jumped from the engine. Every time he tried to punch out of the Salt Creek cul-de-sac, some damn farmer or guard appeared in the distance, silhouetted against the sky with a rifle or shotgun. He'd learned through snatches of overheard conversation that all his fellow inmates except Grigware had been recaptured. Where was Frank? he wondered. He hadn't seen the boy since he sped across the stubble field. He was the least likely of all of them to get out of the trap: even though he'd been sent up for life, he'd seemed like a complete innocent in the rough world of cops and crime. If anyone had laid odds on which of the six escapees would be the first to be caught, smart money would have bet on Frank Grigware. More likely, Frank had succumbed in some gully to the wind and the cold. Months later, a farm boy plowing the fields would find rotted pieces of his uniform, some scattered bones, and tufts of hair.

Murdock decided that if he didn't do something quick, the same would happen to him. It had rained off and on through Friday night, and by Saturday morning the cold front had arrived to stay. By 7 A.M., the mercury read 35 degrees. By 11:20 A.M., there were 40 mph winds with 45-degree temperatures. By afternoon, snow flurries accompanied the northerly winds. He was soaked to his bones, and if he didn't die soon from hunger, he certainly would from cold.

By that evening, Murdock huddled at the edge of the dripping woods. His hunger had grown beyond endurance; he shivered so violently he was convinced he'd caught pneumonia. It was hard to think straight anymore. He crawled to the edge of a nearby thicket and spotted a haystack a short distance away. *Warmth*, he thought. Maybe he could hide in the hay, go to sleep, and at least get warm. He made a run for it, but when he reached the lee side of the haystack he almost stumbled into young Johnnie Forgery, who was driving cattle from pasture back to his home. The boy spied the number on his coat collar and started screaming, while Murdock did an abrupt about-face and darted back to the woods. Johnnie Forgery ran home screaming, leaving his confused cows behind. He told his mother, Mary, who phoned the prison.

By then Lemon was disgusted with false sightings, as were all the searchers. Yet Mary Forgery sounded so convincing he couldn't afford to ignore her words. He set off for her farm in an automobile, a wagon filled with armed guards chasing behind him. But Mary Forgery wasn't waiting for help to arrive all the way from Leavenworth. She put out a general alarm through the operator, and within minutes neighbors arrived. Among the first were Rollin Flynt, a driver at the prison; John Moore, a farmer; and Peter Mertes, a soldier. Johnnie Forgery took them back to the haystack where he'd spotted the prisoner, and all three entered the thicket after the man. It wasn't long before they saw him staggering through the woods up ahead. They called for him to halt, and Murdock sat down. He almost seemed happy to be caught, his bravado so reduced by exhaustion and hunger that he did not seem capable of flight. He limped slowly from the woods at gunpoint, leading the small procession.

They'd barely left the treeline when Lemon and his troops arrived. Murdock greeted the deputy almost happily. "For God's sake, take me back to prison where I can get something to eat," he pleaded. "I'm nearly dying from cold and want of food." They put him in the guard wagon and headed back. As they drew in sight of Leavenworth, he told the guards around him that the prison "looked like heaven."

In his cravings for food and warmth, Murdock had forgotten what awaited his return. He was given a bath and a meal, dressed in stripes, and chained to the "baby." Like the others, he was thrown in the Hole.

All that night, all of Sunday, and into Monday, McLaughry and Lemon gave Murdock the third degree. Who made the guns? Murdock quickly confessed; he figured the others had already been broken, so what did he have to lose? How did he do it? Without trying to boast, which might have been fatal, Murdock described the care with which he'd carved and painted the guns. Were there other confederates? Just the men with whom he'd escaped, Murdock replied, adding that he felt badly disappointed that he'd worked so hard yet still not gotten free.

The last question was asked most persistently. Where was Frank Grigware? Murdock didn't know, even after the third degree. Where was he headed and what were his intentions? Teddy Murdock knew nothing of his plans. Frank had mentioned long ago that he might head north into the Iron Hills of Minnesota if he ever escaped, but that was all that Murdock knew. In his opinion, Frank Grigware had not survived the weather. McLaughry hoped he was right, but over the next three days he mailed another 10,000 wanted posters from coast to coast, including several to the Bureau of Criminal Identification, the brainchild of William Pinkerton.

Take no chances, warned the posters. Francis John Grigware, 6768, was a desperate and dangerous man.

CHAPTER NINE

A Face in the Crowd

WHERE WAS FRANK Grigware?

It was a question asked with increased regularity in grange halls, general stores, and other gathering places throughout the country-side. Theodore Murdock's capture on Saturday, April 23, gave fresh hope to Salt Creek Valley farmers that Frank and the $250 reward for his capture had not slipped away. A man could furnish a house for $250 from Sears, Roebuck and still have money left for a week in Kansas City.

In the prison, a rumor started among the inmates that Frank had drowned while trying to swim the Missouri River north of the military reservation, but McLaughry believed the young fugitive was still alive. "It is almost a certainty that sooner or later Grigware will be recaptured," chimed in the *Leavenworth Times* on Sunday, April 24. "Usually an escapee falls into his old ways, and the first time he is arrested and Bertilloned and his fingerprints taken, his detection will surely follow." It was a season for escapes, not one of them success-ful. On Monday, April 25, five inmates attempted an escape from the state prison in Cannon City, Colorado, by dynamiting the walls. Two prisoners were shot dead, three others wounded, and no one got away. The forces of law and order always prevailed.

That same day, a tramp passing through nearby Doniphan, twenty-five miles north of Leavenworth, got a sampling of that law. He stopped in a general store and bought a nickel's worth of ginger snaps, then asked the way to Atchison. The clerk watched him saunter down the road, then phoned the Atchison sheriff to be on the watch for a suspicious man heading his way. The man looked like Grigware, the clerk said. The wanderer was arrested as he entered town. Although he turned out to be a man who was simply "escaping from work," not prison, he was jailed overnight and released the next day with a warning.

The captured escapees did not fare so well. The four fugitives caught on the same day they broke out were chained to the "baby" and thrown in the Hole until Monday, April 25; Murdock, taken on Saturday, received comparable punishment. Since Murdock was the only fugitive not sentenced to life, McLaughry told him he would be tried for conspiracy and his prison term lengthened once his ten-year counterfeiting sentence was served. After all five were released from isolation, they were clothed in stripes, shaved bald, deprived of reading and writing privileges, and assigned to solitary cells from which they were not released for any reason save work and meals. They exchanged the "baby" for an Oregon boot, a thick steel doughnut that clamped around the ankle and was held up by a foot brace hooked to the boot. According to McLaughry's special order of April 25, the five "returned to shops in which they worked" and were fitted with the Oregon boot "for continuous wear." The boots came off eight months later, on December 24, 1910, an early Christmas present, records showed.

The Oregon boot had a unique history. It was actually the generic name for a heavy iron manacle correctly called the Gardner Shackle, named for its inventor, Warden J. C. Gardner of the Oregon State Prison. Gardner patented his invention in 1866, had it manufactured at his prison by convict labor, and required every inmate to wear one for the entire length of his stay. After 1878, it was barred from use for anything but punishment, but wardens throughout the West loved it as an alternative to the ball and chain. A man wearing a boot just could not run. As unlikely as it seemed, a prisoner could run while wearing the ball and chain; he could carry the cannonball in his arms, if he was strong enough, or cut the chain with a sharp ax or other edged tool. With the boot, this was impossible. The shackle, which came in different weights of six to fifteen pounds, was bolted around the ankle and could not be cut away. Gardner's invention was so popular that three other manufacturers produced imitations. One of them, the Leininger Patent Shackle, advertised that it was "Entirely Humanitarian in its Application," as did competitors. The main selling point, however, was laid out in Gardner's application to the U.S. Patent Office: "This improved shackle has been repeatedly tried by me upon inmates . . . and found to be the only kind of shackle to prevent the escape of desperate characters."

The disadvantage for the prisoner was that it tore up his calf and ankle; if worn long enough, it also damaged his knees, hips, and spine. "Inside of three days" of being shackled, wrote Kating in his letter to President Wilson, "the Oregon boot had begun to cut into our legs." In his own defense, McLaughry said the boot was "lightweight" and was placed around Kating's ankles to prevent "his traveling at as rapid a gait as he did on the day that he escaped." The boot "does not hurt him so long as he walks as he should do and behaves himself," McLaughry claimed. But Kating demurred, citing first-hand knowledge. "An Oregon boot, if worn long enough, has a tendency to deform a man," he said. "We were made to keep up in line . . . and going up and down stairways, and as a result Hewitt almost jerked his hip joint out of place and could hardly sit down, but he did prevail on the Deputy to put the boot on the other leg." One result was that their legs were "raw and sore about half the time," he said. "Murdock's leg got in such an awful fix that the Doctor sent him to the hospital and wanted the Boot taken off, but the Deputy went to the hospital and said, 'God damn him, he can get well or die with that boot on,' and took Murdock to isolation, where he soon went insane, became stark raving mad."

Murdock's madness, if it did occur, was only temporary, but there is strong evidence that after eight months of the boot, his health was permanently damaged. He'd been fit when he came to Leavenworth in July 1909 and up to the day of the escape, but after he wore the boot his health steadily deteriorated, year after year. In 1910 "he began to complain of vague symptoms involving in particular his legs which could not at the time be corroborated by physical examination," Dr. Yohe would write in 1913 to McLaughry's successor, Thomas Morgan. By July 1911, Yohe prescribed a truss for Murdock "on account of the man's hernia," recorded as "of no particular consequence" during his 1909 admittance but which by 1911 "had increased greatly in size." By 1913, Murdock's health had diminished further, the complaints again centering on his legs. He complained of pain frequently, and Yohe administered "electric massage" for temporary relief; this was apparently a reference to early massage therapy, which had gained greater acceptance in America by the 1890s when Swedish massage was routinely being offered in YMCAs, YWCAs, and private sanatoriums. Murdock was admitted to the prison hospital for most of February 1913, then placed there permanently on April 12 of that year. "The diagnosis in Murdock's case is now unquestionable," Yohe wrote. "The man has Locomotor Ataxia," a general incoordination of movement. Murdock "is growing progressively worse and the end is inevitable," he said.

Hewitt and Kating escaped this fate by once again teaming up to survive. Soon after returning to the tailor shop, they cut strips of cloth and wrapped them beneath the shackle and down along the braces. Guard Tom Brummett, still smarting from his treatment on the day of the escape, "reported this to the Deputy, who gave him orders not to allow us to do this, but as the guard did not try hard to enforce this order, we kept padding them." The longer the boots stayed on, the more their legs scarred up and refused to heal. Finally the two obtained a measure of relief when they used McLaughry's concern for his public image against him. "Almost every day at noon there were visitors in the dining room," Kating wrote. "Our boots would rattle against the brace as we walked, and it seems visitors enquired of the Warden what were we wearing on our legs. [An] officer of the prison, probably sympathizing with us, said one day that the Warden was awful sore about the boots rattling when visitors were around, that we should wrap a strip of cloth around the brace . . . keep our pants legs pulled down over them, and step easy at such times, because if we didn't the Warden might never take the boots off."

FRANK NEVER LEARNED of these punishments, but he could imagine such retribution as he lay in his forest hole. As the days following the escape stretched out, his will battled his cold and hunger; unlike Murdock, he'd grabbed the engineer's dinner pail, one of the wisest things he could do. While Murdock starved, Frank divided up Curtin's food, always staying hungry but never approaching his friend's extremes.

Frank stayed in his hole for several days. His place of concealment was not far from the prison, but he was exhausted and didn't know what else to do. Though he heard the shouts of the searchers, he never actually saw anyone while hiding there. He heard them in the woods around him but did not know how close they came to his hiding place. Though he later thought he hid there for three or four days, he wasn't sure, since he lost all track of time.

What did he think as the temperature dropped from 62 degrees on noon of Friday, April 22, to a few degrees above freezing on Saturday and Sunday? As it rained without end? No doubt he thought of his family, especially his mother, and how they would take the news of his escape. Would it be the last nail in the coffin, proving to them that he was guilty after all? He thought of Alice and how he'd never see her again. He thought of that bittersweet night in Denver, how warm it had been curled against her. He wondered about the future and where he could go. The United States was huge, but not so huge that he could forever evade the law. Maybe he'd be safe in another country, but where? If anything, it was hard to plan. The shouts of his searchers distracted him, driving out all other thoughts; the nearby crack of forest animals against the fallen branches or the patter of rain on the leaves sounded like manhunters stealthily closing in.

More than anything else, he thought about food. He remembered with nostalgia the seemingly endless supply of onions they'd eaten lately in the dining hall. During the last two weeks before the break-out, both the federal prison and the state prison at Lansing reeked of green onions, since both prisons' farms yielded bumper crops that year. On doctor's orders, they'd stewed, boiled, poached, and roasted onions into every main dish to drive off scurvy. When the guards complained of the smell, they were supplied with all the onions they could take home.

Frank stayed in his hollow until Saturday evening, only venturing out to get water. When he could no longer stand the hunger, he left his hole for good. He still had no plans and had not selected a course of action. When he saw the factory smoke from the penitentiary, he walked in the other direction.

He waited for darkness before leaving the forest, then headed northwest, his timing fortuitous. By then Murdock had been captured, so farmers' hopes were up, yet because the guards had been recalled, whatever search remained was far from organized. Frank wisely stayed away from the roads and followed the railroad tracks, keeping in cover as he paralleled the grade. He made a second wise choice before reaching Hund's Station, at a point where the two railroad lines crossed at an angle of about 45 degrees. Frank stayed on his train's original heading, north by northwest and roughly following the old Oregon Trail, a choice that took him into the less densely populated country north of Easton. He moved slowly in the darkness, making little noise. It seemed to him that he moved in a dream.

By morning, he was walking by the tracks when he spotted a farmhouse. Although separated from each other by considerable distances, prairie farms by then were not completely isolated. Rural Free Delivery, or RFD, had started in 1896; telephone lines ran across the landscape, making seclusion more bearable. Party lines had become the new town center. Every farm around Leavenworth, Atchison, and Easton knew of the breakout, as shown by the reactions of Mary Forgery and others. Farmers plowed their fields with handguns in their pockets; farm wives kept a loaded shotgun by the door. Frank later estimated that the farmhouse was a half mile from his hiding place, but by then he'd walked throughout the night and a better guess would be that it was situated four to six miles north of Easton, maybe less, considering his weakened condition. He watched for signs of life but didn't see a soul. He crossed the field to the back door and knocked. A woman answered, and he asked for something to eat.

There was a meaningful pause as the woman sized up her visitor. He still wore the prison denims, did not have a hat, did not have a penny to his name. If the woman suspected him of being the last fugitive, she did not show it. "Perhaps she did not think an escaping convict would stop so close to the prison to ask for food," he later said. "She fed me and gave me an old hat. I don't recall just how and where I got rid of my prison shoes and other things I wore from there."

Who was this woman? Like Alice Evans, she was one of the more poignant characters in Frank's saga, and like Alice Evans, one of the least known. She enters and leaves the stage unidentified, a nameless face in the crowd. A few details can be gleaned, some by omission. Given the saturation of newspapers and wanted posters, as well as the heightened state of the countryside, she must have suspected that Frank was the remaining escapee. Since the fliers carried Frank's description, as well as information about his prison uniform, her identification of him almost seems certain. If nothing else, the big metal buttons on his coat, each stamped U.S. PENITENTIARY, were a dead giveaway. It was not unusual for a woman to be alone on the homestead during the day; by daybreak her husband would have been in the fields, especially in the growing season. Her shotgun was in easy reach, but she made no move to grab it. Instead, she studied him. A young man would notice and remember if she were young and pretty or, conversely, old and crusty; since there was no mention of her looks, we see her inhabiting an anonymous middle age. If she had phoned in his arrival, as had the clerk in Doniphan after the hobo bought ginger snaps, there would have been excitement, a search, and a story in the *Leavenworth Times*. Instead she did not to betray him and chose to help him flee.

For insight into Frank's silent savior, we can go to a contemporary. In 1909, Elinore Pruitt, a railroader's widow with a two-year-old daughter, left her job as a Denver "washlady" to keep house for a Wyoming rancher. It was a common position: Urban women with no hopes or future placed classifieds in local newspapers, hoping to start over on the plains. Elinore's rancher, Clyde Stewart, proposed marriage after six weeks, a result of such employment that was also not unusual. Her letters describing homestead life to a friend in Denver were first published in the *Atlantic Monthly* and eventually compiled in 1914 as *Letters of a Woman Homesteader*, a book that gave voice to women, like Frank's savior, who silently settled the plains.

It was not an easy life. In addition to cooking, cleaning, and caring for her daughter, husband, and a cackling flock of Plymouth Rocks, Elinore Pruitt Stewart was also a partner in planning the farm's success or failure. She experimented with new crops provided by the U.S. Department of Agriculture. Bulletins from the state experimental station outlined problems in each new strain of seed. She drove the hay-mowing machine, hitching the horses at first light; she milked seven cows every morning and did most of her cooking at night. She did her own canning and preserving, putting up thirty pints of jelly and an equal amount of jam in one season, using wild fruits—gooseberries, raspberries, and cherries—that she picked on her own.

Balanced against the unending work were memories of the poverty she'd fled. She wasn't poor out here. She worked hard for what she had, and she was proud. "To me, homesteading is the solution of all poverty's problems, but I realize that temperament has much to do with success," Elinore Stewart said. "[P]ersons afraid of coyotes and work and loneliness had better let ranching alone. At the same time, any woman who can stand her own company, can see the beauty of the sunset, loves growing things, and is willing to put in as much time at careful labor as she does over the washtub, will certainly succeed; will have independence, plenty to eat all the time, and a home of her own in the end."

One particular point of pride was her home. Homestead walls were often hung with a heavy gray building paper, good for insulation; over that was pasted wallpaper with a bold rose pattern, a style that sold in red, pink, or yellow. Oval family portraits, in ancient tintype or more modern silver emulsion, hung on the walls. The woodwork was stained a walnut brown with an oil finish, the floors the same. Since Frank knocked at the back door, he'd be looking into the kitchen and could see in the middle of the room a square table made of pine. Some throw rugs lay on the floor beneath it, often braided in white and blue.

Frank looked into the neatly kept kitchen and thought of his mom and how he'd probably never see her again. He grew sad at the thought, and it showed on his face, which the woman noticed. She didn't ask what he was thinking, since that was considered forward, but she did ask if he had a mother or sweetheart somewhere. The kitchen reminded him of his mother, he said. Her name was Jennifer, but everybody called her Jennie. She liked pretty things, like what was in this kitchen, he explained.

The homestead woman looked more closely now at Frank than she had earlier. He said in later interviews that she was alone. That suggests there were no children peeking around her skirts or roaming around the yard. This is telling, if not unusual. For all the disappointments and hardships of homestead life—the foreclosures and crop failures, the slow strangulation from the railroad rates and instant apocalypse of natural disasters, the creeping madness and suicide— for all of these, the hardest thing to bear was the death of a child. On the plains, childhood ended quickly; child mortality was high. Elinore Stewart lost her own newborn son by her rancher husband to erysipelas, a disease caused by a streptococcal infection that brought fever and large red welts on the face and legs. She held him in her arms until the last agony was over and then dressed the little body for the grave. Her husband was a carpenter; he made the coffin himself. They selected a chapter from John, and some neighbors came over for the funeral. In time the sorrow was not so keen, but a loneliness set in that matched the loneliness of the setting. Maybe this woman looked at Frank and thought of such a child.

Perhaps he'd been a boy. Perhaps he would have grown up like this, with an open face and quiet manners, with something about him that seemed decent even though she knew he was a wanted man. The world was full of trouble, yet that trouble wasn't always a person's fault. Sometimes it was his fault, but only by the slimmest margin. Who was to say that the law always protected the innocent? Sometimes it seemed as if the innocent suffered most, through no fault of their own.

So she warmed to the young stranger and asked him inside. There was no need to feel threatened, and she put the gun away. She fed him—better, perhaps, than at any time since 1906, when he told his family he was leaving to see the world. She dug through old clothes for a jacket, a shirt, denim pants, and shoes. A slouch hat would cover his face . . . from the sun, she said. She never mentioned Leavenworth, for it was more convenient for both to say he was a hobo, but she drew on some paper the layout of the roads. The old Oregon Road went north past the Cumberland Presbyterian Church and into the Kickapoo Reserve. A few miles later it met the tracks again. There was a station there, and a water tower for the engines, and near that a "jungle" where hoboes hung out till boarding a train. "There ain't no quicker way across the prairie than on a fast train." Frank looked at her in surprise, then smiled, for she was telling him how to escape. Frank never detailed how long he stayed at the house, but it may have been a couple of hours. He left before her husband returned for the midday meal.

Much later, when she was alone again, she burned the prison uniform until no trace remained but the metal buttons, then buried them deep in her garden. She smiled as she stirred the ashes and raked the disturbed soil. Helping that boy escape was illegal, but did that make it wrong? No matter. It was her secret. No one but her and her God would know that a fugitive had passed by.

THAT AFTERNOON FRANK followed the old Oregon Road. As he walked along the highway, he met many people going and coming, but they paid no attention to him. "I soon found they were apparently unconcerned as to who I was or where I was going," he later said.

That seems amazing today, given the manhunt, but perhaps no one could imagine a prison fugitive passing boldly among them. Like Frank, the travelers were entranced by the beauty of the prairie spring. The meadowlarks sang in the fields as if they were glad to see him; the dandelions spread over the hills like a yellow brick road. The blue spikes of larkspur grew as high as his waist; along creeks the cottonwood seeds floated like snow. To the Indians, the prairie was a tame place, not wild like the first settlers saw it. Even as he walked, he saw traces of that vanished West: a cow skull on a fence post, the round circles of buffalo wallows where the grass grew greener and thicker thanks to a hundred years of buffalo urine, which changed the chemical composition of the soil, aiding growth long after the buffalo were gone. Evening turned to night, and he reached the tracks as the woman said. He came to the water tank, and the jungle was busy tonight. He pulled his hat low and walked toward the fire.

Hoboes, like so much else in the West, were a legacy of the Civil War. When it ended and many veterans had no homes left, they wandered the countryside looking for work. Many sought jobs as migrant farm workers and carried with them their own work tools, especially hoes. It was thought that they were originally called "hoe-boys," a term later shortened to hobo. Others failed to see their beginnings in such a pastoral light. William Pinkerton, who saw crime even in unemployment, often sent undercover operatives into the hobojungles to find wanted men. Pinkerton likened hoboes to more organized bands of Gypsy thieves and dated the origination of their name to the 1880s. "As late as twenty years ago, one tramp meeting another and wishing to be sure of his identity as a professional tramp would address him as 'Ho-Beau,' " footloose slang for *Hello, buddy*, said Pinkerton, in a series of speeches delivered before businessmen and police officials from 1900 to 1907. "This expression subsequently developed into the word 'hobo,' " he claimed.

Whatever the derivation, hoboes were a fact of life by 1910. Their numbers grew from 60,000 in the 1890s to possibly 900,000 by the turn of the century. Various hobo organizations flourished, and from 1906 to 1923 men riding the freights in the West were wise to carry the Little Red Card showing membership in the radical union, the Industrial Workers of the World, or Wobblies. The red card was seen as the badge of an honest migratory worker, and trainmen tended to be easy on these "bindle stiffs," even letting them ride free. "Privates," or private citizens, called all such migrants hoboes, but the hoboes themselves distinguished their ranks into three types: hoboes, who worked and wandered; tramps, who dreamed and wandered; and bums, who drank and wandered. Whatever the cause of their wanderlust, their numbers only grew. By 1934, the U.S. Bureau of Transient Affairs would estimate that 1.5 million Americans rode the rails.

Jungles like this were their crossroads, a place to eat, sleep, and catch a train. They were also the site of a "mulligan," the famous hobo stew. Mulligans consisted of "hoppins," any and all vegetables that could be begged, borrowed, or stolen, and some meat, usually "gumps," or chicken, acquired the same way. The law of compensation, endemic to every camp, required that a 'bo could not take from the mulligan unless he put something in.

Frank had something left over from the farmhouse, so he put something in. As he sat around the fire, he soaked up the latest news. Some talked about the prison break, and he worried that his thrown-together wardrobe would give him away. A little observation proved otherwise. His clothes meant nothing to them, since they all had on about as many different kinds of clothes as could be imagined. Given his circumstances, a hobo jungle was the safest place Frank could stay. There was a fraternity among the tramps, and one of the bylaws was "no questions." If he was recognized that night, no one gave him away.

Another advantage to the jungles was that they were the main repository of hobo news. Water tanks, like the one above them now, also served as tramp directories. Hoboes carved or scrawled on the sides of the tank their "monicas" (later known as "monikers"), date of arrival in the jungle, and direction of travel. Hoboes studied the tanks like newspapers, hoping to find news of old pals. The writer Jack London, one of the more famous turn-of-the-century hoboes, saw one water tank in San Marcial, New Mexico, that conveyed the following: Begging on the town's main street was a fair way to make some cash; police there did not bother hoboes; the local roundhouse was okay for "kipping," or sleeping; and residents were not generous in San Marcial.

Frank lay back but the night was too beautiful to sleep, the moon hanging over the prairie like a prison spotlight. He listened as the 'boes discussed the local railroad bulls. Their job was to keep tramps off trains and away from the train yards by any means possible, which meant instilling in them the fear of God. Railroad bulls were known for throwing tramps off moving trains, for shooting them, or for beating them with fists and saps. The most feared hobo stalker in the nation at that time was Jeff Carr of Cheyenne, Wyoming. He was a big guy straight from the dime novels, with a slouched mustache, cowboy hat, and pair of revolvers strapped low on his hips. He had a habit of galloping up to a train on his white horse, catching the ginks still hanging from the steps, and throwing them off. It was a man's bad luck if he fell under the wheels. Such accidents were sufficiently common that the hoboes had special names for those mutilated by the wheels. "Sticks" was a 'bo who lost a leg; "Wingy," one who lost one or both arms; "Halfy," a man who lost both legs above the knee. In time, Carr was laid out by stiffs waiting in ambush with a coupling pin, yet after his death he was still said to hunt hoboes. Even his white horse came to be possessed of demonic powers.

A third advantage of the water tanks was that in 1910 steam locomotives still made frequent stops to take on water. Freight trains then were dominated by boxcars, their doors left open or ajar when they were empty. This afforded a natural and protected ride, which was exactly what Frank and his companions wanted. "When a train stopped that night, with others I scrambled into a boxcar," he later said. "I did not know where it was going. I didn't care, for even yet I had no plan—just a desire to stay at liberty." He rode north, skirting the backsides of cities and towns. Wind blew through his "boxcar Pullman": the previous load was powdery, probably flour, and he traveled part of the distance in a white cloud. They rode through the night and into the day. Sometimes a deer or calf lay beside the track, back snapped, body broken. The dumb things never knew what hit them when a train barreling along in the bleakness ran them down.

Sometime later, he heard his fellow tramps say they were approaching Minneapolis. They began to jump off, and Frank jumped too.

He floated in a kind of dream. He didn't fear to walk down streets where he knew he would be seen by policemen. He was uneasy at first, but when they paid no attention to him, he paid no attention to them. Instead, he concentrated on day-to-day survival. He begged for food, becoming a "moocher," but such a life grated on his pride. He wanted a job, and there was plenty of work around.

One day he steeled his nerve enough to ask for a job with a contractor named Hoggins. The foreman asked his experience and Frank said he was a carpenter. They needed carpenters, so the foreman asked his name. At this point, Frank finally snapped out of his dream. He'd never thought about this moment, yet realized how stupid he'd been for not seeing it and recognized his need for a new identity. On impulse he answered, "Fahey," his mother's maiden name. The foreman glanced up at his hesitation and added, "Jim?" to help him out. Lots of guys were on the skids these days, and the foreman was old enough to know that a thin line existed for everyone between employment and beating the pavement in search of that ever-elusive job. If these men wanted to start over as someone else and they did an honest day's work, who was he to judge?

"That's right, my name's Jim Fahey," Frank answered, liking the sound.

❧ PART III ❧

Flight

Hell hath no limits nor is circumscribed
In one self-place; for where we are is Hell,
And where Hell is, there we must ever be.

—Christopher Marlowe, *The Jew of Malta*

❦ CHAPTER TEN ❦

A Wanted Man

AS THE SEARCH for Frank broadened, he was pursued with that special doggedness reserved only for those who successfully evade the law. The United States had a long-standing vow to keep after mail robbers until they were captured or dead, and proof of that death was final; federal penitentiaries also vowed to keep after fugitives. At regular intervals, the Post Office Department sent out "case cards" on Frank, which included his name, description, picture, fingerprints, and Bertillon measurements, plus the offer of a $50 reward for information leading to his capture. The Department of Justice received its own case card on April 29, 1910, and placed it in the active file. At similar intervals over the next two and a half decades, Leavenworth authorities sent out circulars offering a reward that eventually increased to $200. The cards and circulars were sent all over the United States and into Canada and Europe. Though the intensity of the search waxed and waned with time, interest, politics, funding, and evolving styles of law enforcement and the media, it never went away. The search for Frank would be a constant in a rapidly changing world, clinging like an unassuming barnacle to the consciousness of federal, state, and local lawmen, outlasting years of labor violence, the sinking of the *Titanic*, the Great War, the flu pandemic, the Red Scare, the Black Sox baseball scandal, the rise and fall of Prohibition, the Roaring Twenties, Black Tuesday, and the worst years of the Dust Bowl and the Great Depression. Frank's photo hung in post offices, courthouses, and precinct rooms for so long it seemed part of the wallpaper. He gazed at the new world in youthful bewilderment, bowler set on his head with quaint precision, tie pulled askew.

If there was a constancy to this search, it was a gambler's hope of winning the lottery. Frank was seen everywhere, nowhere, and all places in between. He seemed most often spotted in small-town America, recognized in the unsuspecting faces of barbers, railroad brakemen, miners, former lawmen, and sons-in-law. It was Omaha redux, friends calling the law on their friends, minus the frenzy sparked by a reward worth a fortune. Frank became the grail of the wanted posters, a mystery to be solved. Not only had he pulled off one of the nation's most spectacular prison breakouts, he'd succeeded in doing what most fugitives only dream about—vanishing without a trace and staying free.

The first big push to find him began the summer after he fled Salt Creek Valley. Though aided by Pinkerton agents, post office inspectors, big-city police chiefs, and small-town sheriffs, the power behind the search would always be the U.S. Justice Department's Bureau of Investigation, direct forerunner of the FBI. In 1910, the Bureau was in its infancy, with about four hundred agents nationwide. It was still headed by its original chief, A. Bruce Bielaski, a Maryland native who'd attended Columbia University in New York City. Congress had qualms about creating a national police agency, fearing it could be used for political oppression, especially if its power was concentrated in the hands of one man. Given time, these fears would be realized. In the beginning, however, Bielaski seemed attuned to such concerns, urging caution in the use of the Bureau's wide powers. Seven years later, for example, in 1917, when America entered the Great War and an anti-German, anti-Socialist, anti-alien hysteria gripped the entire nation, Bielaski would urge restraint concerning the prosecution of targeted political groups. "The meetings engineered by the Socialists are now covered throughout the United States without any specific instructions," he wrote to his boss, U.S. Attorney General Thomas W. Gregory. "I think there is a need rather for more caution than more vigorous efforts," meaning that although his agents watched the Socialists, he saw no need to drag them into court just for their unpopular beliefs, advice that would be ignored by Gregory and President Woodrow Wilson.

Indeed, the bureau created in 1908 had the soundest of intentions, to fill the national law enforcement gap unofficially covered by the Pinkertons. Its original mandate was to handle crimes that involved the crossing of state lines, as well as banking and antitrust offenses and violations of the Mann Act, the law passed to fight "white slavery." On August 8, 1910, the Bureau opened Case No. 1088, the pursuit of escaped federal prisoner Frank Grigware. There had already been some activity, though uncoordinated. McLaughry had sent out reward circulars, and on July 4, 1910, post office inspectors from San Francisco and St. Louis attended the Jeffries-Johnson heavyweight boxing-title bout in Reno on a tip that Frank would attend. On that day, he was hammering nails in Milwaukee. Two months later, a Bureau agent left the Kansas City office to pursue a more methodical trail. Although the agent's name was blacked out in FBI documents, his style was similar to that of his Pinkerton predecessors. The Bureau's investigative technique came straight from the Pinkerton play book, especially in its reliance on undercover work, extensive use of criminal files, and, later, scientific detection. Although no documentation seems to exist, it is reasonable to believe that not a few Pinkerton veterans—fed up, like Charley Siringo, by their agency's growing imperiousness and taint of corruption—left for the higher pay and status of a government job.

The agent's first stop was Leavenworth, securing from McLaughry "all available data," then returning to the Kansas City office to file his report. From August 10 to 21, he trekked through the Oklahoma State Territory [*written: State 1907*], still the most lawless place in the nation; there was a good chance it was Grigware's hiding place, since it wasn't far from the prison. The agent followed leads through Muskogee, Tulsa, Sapulpa, and Kiefer, where he learned finally that the man he had been trailing was not Grigware after all but an itinerant Irish gambler. In disgust, he entrained for Omaha. From August 22 to 26, he talked to Omaha police, postal inspectors, Union Pacific detectives, former U.S. Attorney Charles Goss, Pinkerton men, and others involved in Frank's arrest and trial. The Pinkertons seemed most helpful. In their opinion, Frank would only be found in the Pacific Northwest; they used as support their files on members of the Mud Cut Gang. All but one,

Bob Splain, had been jailed with Frank, and he'd been suspected in the failed breakout attempt during the Omaha trial. Frank's family also lived in the region, and there was a good chance he might attempt to contact them. On August 26, the agent caught a fast train to Spokane, where he stayed until August 31, when he headed home.

The Bureau's month-long search set the pattern for the next twenty-four years. It collaborated with the prison to handle periodic mailings of wanted posters; it followed provocative leads, often into the back country of Texas, Oklahoma, and the Old Southwest. It formed a picture of Frank as one of the last unredeemed outlaws, based more on his elusiveness and the résumés of his Mud Cut co-defendants and those participating with him in the escape than on his own history. In time, a search ensued for all of them—for Jack Golden, Bill Matthews, Dan Downer, Fred Torgensen, and Bob Splain, as well as for Tom Kating, Arthur Hewitt, John Gideon, Bob Clark, and Ted Murdock—on the assumption that Frank's criminal nature would win out and he'd hook up again to resume his evil ways. Sometimes, there were glimmers of insight among the false leads. "If he is still alive and in the United States, most likely he would be very careful to lead a quiet, law-abiding life in order to avoid any possibility of being arrested and later identified," a harried agent wrote in 1928, after eighteen years of dead ends.

More than anything else, that first month of investigation laid the groundwork for the surveillance of Frank's family that continued in various forms for the next fifty years. On Saturday, August 27, 1910, that surveillance began. After talking with Charles Riddiford, the Spokane postal inspector who identified Jack Golden, the agent "was engaged in shadowing the Grigware house," he wrote, always in a distant third-person voice, as if he'd truly turned to shadow.

Frank's conviction and escape had devastated the Grigwares, a blow from which few of them ever completely recovered. Jennie took it worst of all. At first she hoped for some sign of innocence; later she prayed that Congress would pass a parole bill and save him from that federal hell. When it did in 1910, it was too late for Frank, who'd already fled. "No one could figure out why this happened since [Frank] had always been an exceptionally hard worker and of good reputation," Jennie's daughter-in-law said years later. "We could only think he fell in with bad company." After the escape, they expected some word, but as time passed they began checking reports in various parts of the country of deaths of unidentified men whose descriptions sounded vaguely like Frank's. They would be relieved when the deceased was not Frank and then would slip into a deeper sadness, as they wondered if they'd ever learn what happened to him.

The family splintered after Frank's arrest; after his escape, the disintegration hastened. The first to go was Edward, returning from his son's trial wrapped in a gloom that soon turned to anger. Not long after that he moved out, blaming Jennie and the Fahey clan for filling Frank's head full of fantasies about the vanishing West. If the boy had stayed home and worked, none of this would have happened, he said. Edward eventually left Washington with another woman, appearing again in Long Beach, California, where he worked as a fisherman and carpenter, as if he could regain the life he had had in Michigan before succumbing to the lies of the West and moving to Spokane.

Jennie was left to care for the children alone. In addition to her dressmaking, Jim and Joe brought in money, but they were young men and she knew they would soon start their own families and move away. Jim married in 1911. His first child came in 1913, followed by one every year until 1916. He moved from the house on South Grant Street into a place of his own. Her oldest son, Joe, left because he was dying. In 1914, he moved to Arizona to combat tuberculosis, but returned a year later and died on March 17, 1917, in the Kearney Sanatorium in Spokane. Eddie moved in 1915 to Chicago to attend art school, after a few seasons with the Spokane baseball team. Sometimes his team traveled north into the Canadian provinces of British Columbia and Alberta, where he often wondered if Frank watched him from the crowd. Sometimes he felt *something*, he didn't know what, some presence or closeness he couldn't pin down. He quit the game when he began to watch the crowd more than the ball. By 1917, the year of Joe's death, both of Jennie's girls had married and moved to Seattle with their husbands. Jennie sold the house on South Grant and moved to a small apartment not far away. Jim and his sisters watched as she grew quieter and more fragile; in 1923 she left Spokane forever, moving to Seattle to live with one of her daughters.

As the years rolled past, it dawned on the Grigwares that they were all being watched, though the surveillance centered on Jennie and Jim. Jennie took the interviews with Bureau agents in stride, coming to expect their visits during holidays and near the anniversaries of

Frank's arrest and escape. The agents might change, but they always asked the same questions. Have you received any word from your son? None, she replied truthfully. If she had, she wouldn't tell them. It was men like this who'd thrown Frank away in Leavenworth, ignoring his pleas of innocence. She served them something warm to drink and maybe a snack, these men in gray suits and white shirts, plain straw hats and dark conservative ties. They seemed surprised by her hospitality, and with that advantage she turned the question back to them. Had *they* received any word of her son? They said they knew as little as she. A curious sympathy for Jennie developed in the agents' reports, as if they felt guilty for bringing this woman nothing but pain. Jennie grew sadder with each visit. She grew more convinced that Frank was really dead.

It was different with Jim. He'd known, ever since his third degree following Jack's panicked telegram from Denver, that the Pinkertons, Spokane police, Post Office department or Bureau of Investigation could at a whim destroy his life and that of his family. They followed him to lonely Napoleon, Washington, where he opened a meat-packing business on the Colville Indian Reservation; they later followed him to Tonasket, where he owned a butcher's shop, grocery store, and cold storage plant. "He has been quite successful there and is well thought of," one report said. When Jim's first son was born, they came to visit. The boy's name was James Dean Grigware, born on April 21, 1915, the fifth anniversary of Frank's deliverance.

Jim knew his mail was being watched, as did Jennie, thanks to friends in the post office who warned them to be wary. The post office traced all mail going out and coming in. Prior to J. Edgar Hoover's ascendance to director in 1924, the Bureau relied primarily on mail tracings for long-distance surveillance, a laborious process in which the handwriting on an envelope was traced on opaque paper for comparison to a handwriting sample. The comparisons were notoriously inaccurate and sent agents on numerous wild goose chases. Frank's sample, taken from his file at Leavenworth, was watched for certain "markers." As one expert wrote, the Bureau watched all incoming letters for "the small e being finished just below the line, the following letter being begun independently; the *wa* as joined in both; the peculiar angle and careless finish of the final *a*; the end of the letter *k*; the *a* and *n* and the little additional slant given the small *l*."

Jim worried because he knew some secrets but wouldn't tell them to the agents until years had passed and even he thought that Frank was dead. He didn't tell his mother, either, for fear that through her words or actions she might alert the agents. Shortly after the escape, a package of Frank's belongings had been sent from prison to the Spokane post office, but before he could pick it up someone had forwarded the package to Vancouver, British Columbia. He asked Eddie and Joe if they'd done it, but both swore ignorance. At first it was a mystery, but later he suspected Bob Splain, based on a rumor he heard. Word drifted to Jim that, in 1913 or 1914, Splain had seen Frank at a construction site in Edmonton or Calgary in Alberta, Canada.

Starting now, a picture of Jim Grigware develops in the records that has a surface deception. Pinkerton and Bureau notes of 1909 through 1915 portray him almost as a rube, easily intimidated by police, folding quickly under the mildest interrogation. Later records show, however, that Jim knew far more than he ever let on. He was immensely protective of his mother and felt himself a steward of the secrets of his closest brother, Frank. If one word could sum up Jim Grigware, it would be "responsible." He took responsibility for everything. He inherited his father's faltering meat-packing business when Edward abandoned the family; he relocated the business twice, turning his holdings into a small fortune. Family stories painted him as tight with a buck, but more than anything else, Jim Grigware got things done. In 1914, records later indicate, he decided without telling his wife or mother to locate his brother. At the time, the only way to do so seemed to be by contacting Bob Splain.

So Jim let it be known through the Spokane grapevine that he wanted to meet Dan Downer's old compadre. The particulars of this meeting are speculation but can be pieced together through later Pinkerton and Bureau notes, as well as other known details of Spokane's criminal underground. They met sometime in 1914. Splain was a stocky man in his mid-thirties, standing 5 feet 10 inches and weighing 175 pounds. He was well built and good-looking, with a dark complexion and brown eyes, but a missing tooth made him look like a punch-drunk middleweight who'd seen better days. The best place to meet was at an Italian place on Spokane's Front Street, near the Coeur d'Alene Hotel. Jim arrived first and watched as Splain was greeted by characters who looked equally rough. According to Bureau files, this was a yeggmen's hangout, a safe house for safecrackers and sneak thieves. All throughout 1913 and 1914, police believed, yeggs had drifted here before skipping out to Buenos Aires to escape the law. According to a paid informant, Splain was the "mastermind of this crowd." A Northern Pacific Railroad detective said he had "no doubt that Splain and Grigware are corresponding" and that Splain had knowledge of Frank's whereabouts. The Bureau, Pinkertons, Secret Service, and Spokane police all wished to pick Splain's brain but feared it was "necessary to work through an informant, as it is not believed that Splain will divulge information . . . to an official." To that end, the Bureau's Spokane office was authorized to pay a snitch the "lowest practical compensation" to get close to Splain.

Did Splain know of the government's interest? Apparently so. During this time he was always on the run, moving between Kansas City, San Antonio, Portland, and Spokane as fast as trains would take him. He was rarely in one place for more than two weeks at a time. The Bureau was convinced Splain was key to finding Frank, and one of the major efforts of this phase of the search was to locate Bob Splain. There is a suggestion that Splain may have even known the identity of the snitch and fed the man a pack of lies. According to a memo dated March 19, 1913, and penned by an unidentified agent in the Bureau's Chicago office:

> My information is that shortly after Grigware was taken to the penitentiary at Leavenworth to serve his life term, Splain told some of his friends that he was going to visit Grigware and slip him the articles necessary to enable him to make his escape; and in order to frustrate such plans the Warden was warned and furnished with a picture of Splain so the gateman could identify Splain should he try (to) pass the gate. Splain did make an attempt to get a visit with Grigware but was refused admittance by the gateman. He then went to Topeka, Kansas, and worked there as a common laborer on some sewer extension work and is said to have disappeared the same day Grigware made his escape; and the belief is that Splain did in some way aid him in his successful effort, and it is also said that the two men have been in constant communication ever since.

The information was provocative, and possibly even believable, but from whom did it come? McLaughry never mentioned such a warning, and there was no notation of Splain's visit in Frank's prison file. In addition, the tales of Murdock, Kating, and the others belied any part played in the escape by Splain. It is hard to believe that Splain would name himself as an accomplice in the most spectacular American prison breakout to that point, knowing he'd be inviting vengeance from the law. The clincher came in the memo's next paragraph:

> My informant is of the belief that Grigware is now in Panama and working for the Isthmian Canal Commission at Colon, and says that if we get a line on Splain through the Portland police and keep a cover on his mail, we will be able to locate Grigware without much trouble because they correspond regularly.

Everything in the memo was wrong, though Bureau agents couldn't know it then. Frank's Latin American route was a theory favored by agents, as was their suspicion about Splain's role. If anything, the Chicago snitch was skillfully manipulating his masters, maintaining his steady government income while telling the agents exactly what they wanted to hear.

On this day, however, Bob Splain was not lying. Jim Grigware didn't have patience for small talk, especially with a thief, and asked Splain immediately whether he'd seen Frank in Edmonton or Calgary as the rumors said. Splain looked startled and told Jim to keep his voice down. "I heard the rumor too," he said. "But it wasn't me who saw him."

"Who was it, then?"

"You sure you want to know? The more you know, the more you're in it, and once they find that out they're always after you."

But Jim insisted and Splain shrugged, telling what he knew. The man's name was Herbert Fife, a contractor in Spokane. Frank had worked for him on some framing jobs before leaving for the Coeur d'Alenes. In fall 1913, Fife was in Edmonton when he saw Frank in a hotel lobby. He was surprised and called out, but Frank got a frightened look and bolted into the crowd. The following Sunday Fife spotted Frank again, this time among worshipers leaving Catholic Mass. It seemed like Fife was looking for him, knowing his religion, though he never said. This time he approached Frank without announcing his presence, but Frank was on the lookout and spotted him. He hurried in the opposite direction, losing Fife again. Though Fife looked all over Edmonton and asked for Frank by name, he never saw him again.

"So now you know," Splain said. The federals were after him because they thought he knew Frank's hideout; if they ever heard Fife's story, or got wind that Jim knew it, they'd come after him too. If Jim contacted Fife himself, it would eventually get out, Splain said.

Fife was one of those people who couldn't keep a secret. When Bureau agents finally did reach him themselves, the contractor gave full details of his sighting Frank in Edmonton but said nothing about contacting or being contacted by his family. Every year or so, when the agents came on holidays, Jim would have to read their minds, Splain said. Did they know or not? Splain spelled it out for him: "I been in the sweatbox, I know their tricks. I can't say the same for you." Would they act like they knew something when they didn't, trying to draw him out? Would they pretend ignorance, knowing that he'd heard? Jim would have to keep the secret if he wanted to spare his brother, knowing full well that the Bureau could ruin his life if they thought he played games with them.

All Jim Grigware had ever wanted was to work hard and be a success. Now, like his brother, he too would be pursued. Like Frank, Splain, and anyone remotely touched by the Leavenworth escape, he'd have to stay one step ahead of the law.

THERE WERE HUNTS within the hunt, for friends, distant relatives, former associates, and associates of associates—for anyone who might have the slightest clue to where Frank had vanished. The search for Alice Evans was the saddest of them all.

She was called a "prostitute" by the Pinkertons, Frank's "sweetheart" and "fiancée" by the Bureau during the early search, a "dalliance" by Frank's father, "a woman in a house of prostitution" by frustrated Bureau agents as the search dragged on. This much is true: By August 1910, four months after Frank's escape, she'd returned to Spokane and knocked on the door of his family. They accepted her and she took an apartment nearby. On August 29, 1910, the third day that the Bureau agent shadowed Jennie's house, he observed "a girl who answered the description of Alice Evans . . . come out and mail a letter." The post office opened the letter and discovered that it was nothing more than payment to a bill collector in Portland,

Oregon. The agent followed Alice back to her apartment at 422½ Sherman Street, not far from where Jennie later moved. He traced all mail to and from the address but found nothing of interest.

He lost her soon afterward, and only then seemed to realize what he'd lost. Who else would a lonely young fugitive be more likely to write than his girlfriend? But by then she'd left Sherman Street in Spokane. On October 8, 1910, the agent left Kansas City again to check out a tip in San Antonio; on October 23 he headed east across the rough Texas landscape to Waco. He talked to a mounted police officer who said Alice had once told him that Frank "had a rich uncle in the lumber business," but the policeman forgot "where Miss Evans said that uncle lived." The agent found the young man engaged to marry Alice before she fell for Frank; not surprisingly, the young fellow still held a grudge. He assured the agent that "he would render him all possible assistance in locating and apprehending Grigware."

But where had Alice gone? She'd disappeared like Frank, and the suspicion crossed the minds of Bureau agents that she'd hooked up with her fiancé and both had gone underground. Agents kept a watch on her Spokane address and put a nationwide trace on her mail. They heard she was in Portland but could not find her; interceptions of her mail in December 1910 came up with two possible clues. A letter was addressed to Alice from Tempe, Arizona, with handwriting that resembled Frank's, and a second letter sent shortly before Christmas was signed *Frank* and mailed from Waco. But they only proved to be false leads.

San Antonio, Waco, and points south seemed to mock the Bureau's efforts with a string of false leads. On September 1, 1911, a man who called himself Grigware's former friend told a Chicago agent that Frank traveled under the name of Holoway and had left Chicago that summer for Juarez, Mexico. From there he transferred to Mexico City, where he worked for the National Railway of Mexico. Four days later, on September 5, 1911, a Joe Wright of San Antonio said that Grigware hung out in saloons and gambling houses in that Texas town. Frank supposedly worked for a yegg gang. "When a man is robbed by the gang," said Wright, "Grigware would follow him and see if he made connection with the officers."

On September 6, 1911, the ubiquitous and talkative Chicago informant made a claim that would change Frank's life forever and stalk him through the years. That day, he told his handlers that

"Grigware has said a number of times he will never be taken alive; he will be killed before he goes back to the penitentiary." The Chicago agents believed the warning, filing away his unsubstantiated claim for posterity.

On October 7, 1911, Frank was said to be in Mexico City, waiting for a bunch of pals from Chicago to board a train and meet him on October 17. They'd hook up in the American Bar in Mexico City, "a resort for a number of criminals." One begins to suspect that organized crime was playing with the Bureau, sending agents scampering all over the map, wearing thin their ranks and thus ensuring less heat at home. The Bureau seemed willing to believe anything. On April 4, 1913, a railroad switchman in Waco was sure he'd spotted Frank and wanted the reward money immediately. He said Frank worked with him as a switchman on the Missouri-Kansas-Texas Railroad; the wanted man, whose knees twisted "slightly to the right," could be found somewhere on the line between Waco and Denison. The Bureau gave special credence to the sighting: "The statement . . . appears perfectly straight," the memo claimed. The switchman was

> a man of about 55 years of age, having been in the railroad service of the roughest character almost all his life, and has the face of a confirmed criminal, although his statement is very straightforward, and Agents believe that there is likely to be something to the facts given by him. It will be borne in mind that at the time this Department was trying to locate Grigware, two or three years ago, he was supposed to have a woman in a house of prostitution at Waco.

The Bureau was desperate to find Alice, now firmly convinced she was not Frank's fiancée, but his whore. It is a documentary pattern seen repeatedly in the paper trail: A rumor reported in an early memo becomes a fact, given sufficient time and frustration. The fact that agents cannot find someone translates into their certainty that he or she is guilty. In February 1915, the order was given again to track down Alice Evans. Agents found a Mrs. Alice Evans on Spokane's Augusta Street, but she was too old, as well as a Miss Alice Evans who was "rated as a laundry worker," but the agent "doubted this one also, as the original was a clerk in one of the big stores." On February 2 of that same month, the Bureau renewed its order with the post office department to cover Alice's mail, but none was forthcoming. On February 5, 1915, the final memo concerning Alice was posted by the Bureau: "About three and a half years ago, she married. . . . [S]he died about a year after the marriage."

After a five-year hunt for Alice Evans, it boiled down to this: She wed in August 1911, about a year after traveling to see Jennie Grigware, the woman who would have been her mother-in-law. She died a year later, probably in childbirth, as Bureau agents called her a whore.

TIME PASSED, AND America changed in ways no one ever conceived. Where Frank was hiding, the changes appeared to have little bearing on his life. His hideout seemed so distant from the America he'd known that it could be on another planet. He was wrong.

The year 1913 would loom large in Frank's fortunes, though no one could know at the time. In March 1913, Captain John Edgar Hoover of the Cadet Corps, Central High School, Washington, D.C., led his teenage troops down Pennsylvania Avenue for President Woodrow Wilson's inaugural day parade. Sixteen years of Republican government were coming to an end with Wilson's election, and the United States was headed toward a period of unprecedented upheaval. In Russia and Europe, people were overwhelmed by war and revolution, while in the United States, labor unrest had become the major concern. Nearly half the labor force toiled excessive hours in dangerous and nightmarish conditions and then went home at night to slums. In all the years of strikes and violence that started with young James McParland's defeat of the Molly Maguires in 1876, nothing would compare to what loomed on the horizon. America was about to experience a wave of strikes like nothing it had imagined, and a million U.S. socialists would demand the overthrow of capitalism. Soon company guards gunned down workers in Ohio. A seven-month strike in Ludlow, Colorado, ended with a machine-gun battle between Colorado National Guardsmen and armed miners; when the charred and twisted bodies of eleven children and two women were pulled from the wreckage, the press reported the "Ludlow Massacre" to the world. Soon members of the Wobblies were lynched, many others jailed, their right to protest squelched by vigilantes who claimed that only they were "100 percent American." The rule of force supplanted that of law.

The intolerance and violence would just grow worse as America entered World War I. "War is the health of the State," wrote outspoken pacifist Randolph Bourne in 1917. "It automatically sets in motion throughout society those irresistible forces for uniformity, for passionate cooperation with the Government in coercing into obedience the minority." Yet by 1913, even before he wrote this, Americans already warred against themselves. For young men of ambition, it was a good time to be policemen. Where order was craved above all else, policemen could be heroes, including, with time, the young and stern cadet who marched in the van of his teenage troops that inaugural day.

In Leavenworth that year, President Wilson swept out the old regime. Robert McLaughry saw it coming, his dreams of founding a prison dynasty swept away. Like James French before him, the breakout killed his career. Two months after Frank's escape, on June 26, 1910, he announced that all sightseeing tours were barred from the prison; a week later, a derailing switch was finally installed on the tracks 150 yards west of the prison, making another escape like Frank's impossible since the engine would quickly be derailed. Neither measure saved him. In the increased scrutiny of the months that followed, the allegations of prisoners like Tom Kating and former guards about corruption and cruelty reached more receptive ears, resulting in the firing of Deputy Frank Lemon and his closest cronies. The new administration paid more attention to the charges than to McLaughry's achievements through the years. The warden felt old. He no longer wanted to fight. In June 1913, three months after Wilson's inauguration, McLaughry handed in his letter of resignation. The old Scotsman was succeeded by Thomas W. Morgan, editor of a newspaper in Ottawa, Kansas. A prison history called him "a new broom."

On August 12, 1913, three years after Frank's escape, an investigation of the Mud Cut Robbery trial by postal investigators was handed to President Wilson. The investigators noted in their report the highly circumstantial evidence used for conviction, the confusion of witnesses when distinguishing between Frank and Jack Golden, the prejudice or proven perjury of some witnesses, as well as the likelihood of even more perjury given the public reaction to the unprecedented reward, the distribution of which had still not been settled in the courts. Without comment, Wilson pardoned Jack Golden and set him free. Despite the testimony of lawmen that Jack had a long criminal history prior to his Omaha arrest, the Bureau now noted that his only prior conviction was a liquor charge in 1905 or 1906, which had earned him ninety days in jail. Jack's incipient tuberculosis also contributed to Wilson's leniency. Given the fact that the slim evidence against Frank was the same as that against Jack, given U.S. Attorney Frank Howell's strong doubts about the case, it is almost certain that Frank would also have been pardoned—if he'd still been there.

In October 1913, the huge reward by the Union Pacific was finally handed out in the Mud Cut Robbery. Judge Munger awarded $2,700 each to the six boys who filed suit, and $5,400 each to the Denver policemen who arrested Golden and to an Idaho marshal who arrested Matthews. Five of the six boys, now no longer boys, planned to use the money to buy or rent farms or homes in South Omaha. The other boy, still in school, wanted to buy a shotgun and, as he told one detective, "buy a tub full of ice cream."

That same year, Wilson commuted the murder charges of Tom Kating, Arthur Hewitt, and Bob Clark, all charged with Waldrupe's killing in 1901. He signed the papers, again without comment, on July 21, 1913, one month after McLaughry retired. The three were made trusties after their commutation, never once written up for violations. On July 21, 1914, exactly one year later, they were given $10 each to start a new life and a one-way rail ticket taking them wherever they wanted. They left the Big House forever on the early train.

In 1913, the sentences of Dan Downer, Fred Torgensen, Bill Matthews, and John Gideon, all convicted of mail robbery, were reduced from life to ten years. A change in the federal law in 1909 had altered the sentence for mail robbery from life in prison to 10 to 25 years with "good time" deductions, yet courts throughout the nation haphazardly applied the new law. Judge Munger had never mentioned the change during the Mud Cut Robbery trial, and the defense lawyers did not even seem aware of it. Once in Leavenworth, of course, the prisoners' access to appellate lawyers had been tied up by Deputy Lemon's kickback scheme. Once again, McLaughry's replacement, Warden Morgan, passed their cases up the line to Wilson; once again, the president signed. Only Ted Murdock was unaffected by the change in law or administration, since he, of all the prisoners involved in Frank's fate, had been charged with counterfeiting, not train robbery or murder. Yet two years later, in March 1915, he too would have his sentence commuted by President Wilson for health reasons brought on by his punishment at the hands of Lemon and Mc-Laughry. Thin to begin with, he looked like a skeleton and limped out on crutches when released on March 30, 1916. Teddy Murdock, like the others, stuck his $10 in his pocket and took an early train.

Throughout these years and later, others were mistaken for Frank and arrested, despite their protests of innocence. They stayed in jail until a new circular arrived from Leavenworth or, in the most promising cases, an official from the prison or the Bureau. Their freedom often came about only after officials looked for webbing between their toes, but even then release was not guaranteed. It was thought that Grigware could have had the webbing removed surgically in the intervening years. By now, the Pinkerton style of justice had apparently taken wider root in law enforcement: If a man was suspected, he was jailed. Once jailed, he was guilty.

Throughout the 1910s and 1920s, Frank's description, photo, and Bertillon measurements were still the primary means for identification, not his fingerprints, though they too were included on the reward fliers and case cards. Despite Matthew McLaughry's well-publicized experiences at Leavenworth, the old, comfortable, and faulty system of identifying suspects was used everywhere by state and local lawmen. So it was that in Sterling, Kansas, a barber named Frank Waters who looked vaguely like Frank's wanted picture spent a few nights in jail; in Pueblo, Colorado, a man named Arthur Burleson whose handwriting resembled Frank's suffered the same fate. A deputy sheriff in Tacoma, Washington, recognized Frank in the face of a recently arrested short-change artist named R. R. Boyer: "I shall expect to receive the reward of $200 offered for his delivery," the triumphant lawman said. A deputy sheriff in Flat River, Missouri, arrested an itinerant diamond miner named Frank Gregoire, then reluctantly let him go. Two months later, a deputy U.S. marshal made the same mistake and arrested him in Joplin. Only after removing all of his clothes, including his shoes and socks, did Frank Gregoire persuade the marshal that he wasn't, in reality, Frank Grigware.

From 1912 to 1927, requests would come to Leavenworth from all over the nation seeking detailed information about the wanted mystery man. In addition to general mailings of thousands of circulars, special requests came from Salt Lake City, Utah; Crawfordsville,

Georgia; Enid, Oklahoma; Waverly, Alabama; Richmond, Virginia; and Clovis, New Mexico. Frank was seen "headed west" in Aberdeen, South Dakota, in October 1920, and hundreds of wanted posters papered public buildings in cities and small towns throughout North Dakota, South Dakota, Montana, and Washington. During this sighting, he was thought to be a salesman for the C. D. Kenny Coffee Company in New York City, traveling west one last time to see his family before filling a new post in Rio de Janeiro. During this time, the Pinkertons offered to get reinvolved. An October 26, 1920, letter from R. E. Mason, superintendent of Pinkerton's Spokane office, to Leavenworth's then-warden, A. V. Anderson, stated that since Frank's mother and sister Mary lived in the area, it was "barely possible Grigware may show up here, if he has not already done so." Mason made his pitch: "Should you desire our agency to make any investigations for you, please communicate with our office at Kansas City, as you understand we do not work for rewards and would only charge for time put in and any necessary expenses incurred." There is no evidence that Warden Anderson acted on the offer.

The rumors of Frank's whereabouts often took strange, bizarre, or conspiratorial turns. He was said to be part of a gang of safe blowers headed by a yeggman named "Toronto Jimmy" and suspected of murdering a Chicago diamond dealer. The Illinois state attorney general was certain Frank sat in the state penitentiary, convicted of murder under a different name. A man caught wandering through the basement of the post office in Norfolk, Virginia, claimed he was a detective who'd tracked Frank to North Carolina; he promised to lead authorities to him, but only if first paid the $200 reward. Further investigation showed he'd recently been released from a mental institution and had received his detective's "certificate" from a correspondence school; he was declared insane again. On July 20, 1922, the Bureau received an urgent message from the Spokane Police Department that an Officer Germaine had learned that "Grigware was seen in Spokane within the last month in the robes of a Catholic priest." That lead fell apart when Germaine was killed the next day in a motorcycle accident. Two years later, Special Agent Thomas F. Rooney of the Union Pacific Railroad believed Frank was involved in the robbery of a Southern Pacific train in the Siskiyou Mountains in southern Oregon.

No one was safe from suspicion, neither relatives nor former lawmen. On March 5, 1915, a telegram reached the Bureau that Frank had been arrested in Parkman, Maine, a small village in the center of the state. One day earlier, Constable E. L. Smart had arrested his son-in-law, who, until recently, he'd believed to be a decent enough fellow named Hibbard R. Steeves. "With the arrest was revealed a tragedy such as this section of Maine has seldom, if ever, seen," a dramatically inclined reporter said.

The arrest followed a mailing of the circulars. Many such arrests seemed to take place that way; a bored official who happened on Frank's photo was reminded of a friend or acquaintance, and imagination did the rest. Smart was sitting in his town hall office, sifting through the mail a piece at a time. Posters of fugitives from all over the nation seemed to arrive daily. Criminals were scarce in Parkman, especially escaped criminals, and he cast aside each poster until reaching the bottom of the pile. One suddenly caught his eye. He looked at it again, a sick feeling growing within him. "Then something in my brain snapped," he said.

He'd recognized his son-in-law, with whom his twenty-year-old daughter Lucy had eloped shortly before Christmas of the previous year. The marriage of his only child surprised him, a case of love at first sight while away at a nearby women's college, she told her doting dad. Smart got over his shock and even blessed the union, and the young couple had lived in his house for the three months since the wedding. One wonders how much anger was suppressed in the name of being a calm and loving patriarch, how much resentment the doting father harbored against Steeves for deflowering his little girl. Then he saw the WANTED poster.

For three days the constable wrestled with his conscience. He could not sleep, at least not well. He stayed late at work for one excuse or another. What should he do? Should he burn the circular and wipe it from his life, or do his duty to the law? He couldn't decide. When he slumped home at night he'd see his daughter, so happy with her new husband, and decide to burn it. But when he returned to the office in the morning, he could not throw it in the fire. He remembered his oath of office, yet to whom was his duty greater, his family or the law? Finally he called a friend, Dr. A. H. Stanhope of Dover, twelve miles away. Stanhope would know what to do. His old friend advised him to stay put, then sped to Smart's office with a Dover deputy sheriff in tow. They drove to Smart's house, a rambling New

England farmhouse, and walked inside. Lucy and her husband were cuddled together on the loveseat in the sitting room. Without a word, unable to glance at his daughter, Smart and the others stopped in front of the scoundrel he'd naively believed to be Hibbard R. Steeves. "You're under arrest as Frank Grigware, an escaped convict of Leavenworth," the Dover deputy said.

There was silence. Before Steeves could raise his voice in denial, Lucy fainted. A servant carried her upstairs. Smart ordered his son-in-law to submit to a physical examination by Dr. Stanhope; Steeves looked at the three men staring hard at him and knew he had no choice. In every detail, the doctor said Steeves matched the wanted man: height, weight, hair, eyes, scars. Smart pointed to a chair. Steeves sat back in disbelief, the wind knocked from him at the unreality of what was happening, as the doctor untied the laces, lifted off his shoes, then stared at three toes grown together on his right foot. "It is the man," Stanhope said.

No longer "he," but "it." Already demonized. Of course, it was not the man at all. The physical defect was not the same. Steeves's accusers had remembered that *something* was wrong with the wanted man's feet but forgot in their excitement the fact that the second and third toes of *each* foot had grown together in the real Grigware. Any imperfection was proof. Steeves was thrown in jail until a prison official arrived by train to say they'd arrested the wrong man.

Hibbard Steeves was released. No follow up articles mentioned whether the young couple continued to stay with Constable Smart, but the answer is not hard to imagine.

Six years later, it was a lawman who found himself faced with a quick trip to Leavenworth. On Sunday, May 22, 1921, Pennsylvania State Police arrested Frank J. O'Boyle in his home in Carbondale, a small coal mining town northeast of Scranton on the Lackawanna River. O'Boyle had been Carbondale's chief of police from 1914 to 1919, after which he retired. "He had a reputation of being a remarkably competent police official, and while in power reorganized the police department," said the *Philadelphia Public Ledger*. Not surprisingly, "his arrest has caused a sensation in Carbondale."

O'Boyle was actually identified twice, both times by zealous lawmen. The first tip arrived by letter in January 1918, while O'Boyle was still police chief; a Lackawanna County sheriff's deputy (who also happened to be the sheriff's son) made the identification, yet no action came of it. Two years later, police officers themselves were flipping through the newly mailed reward circulars when they came to Grigware's photo and were stunned by "the remarkable resemblance" to O'Boyle. The police wired Leavenworth, which immediately wired back: USE EVERY PRECAUTION POSSIBLE IN MAKING ARREST. VERY ANXIOUS TO HAVE HIM RETURNED. KEEP MATTER ENTIRELY TO YOURSELF, AS HE WILL SKIP OUT IMMEDIATELY IF INFORMATION LEAKS OUT.

O'Boyle was arrested at his home and taken to his old police department. One wonders about the reaction there. His Bertillon measurements were taken, and officers affirmed that the scars on his body seemed to match those described for Grigware. Yet when O'Boyle's shoes were removed, the telltale toes were not joined.

In a perfect world, that would have been the end of the matter and O'Boyle would have been freed. But the former police chief had been apprehended, making him guilty. Worse, he did not seem to have a friend in his successor, Police Chief Harry Kegler. WE ARE FRANK TO SAY THAT WE BELIEVE THIS TO BE YOUR MAN, Kegler cabled Leavenworth's warden. True, the arrested man's nose was "somewhat different, but O'Boyle admits that he has had his nose broken." There was no webbing between O'Boyle's toes, "but there is a possibility that the web could have been removed and still leave no trace," Kegler said. Finally, there was the problem that O'Boyle's fingerprints and measurements did not match, but Kegler had an explanation for that:

> With all due respects to your office, I would advise you, knowing the man as I do, to investigate your records regarding "Grigware" very closely. We are inclined to believe something has been fixed somewhere. O'Boyle is capable of pulling it.

Politics were one explanation for poor O'Boyle's woes. The former chief lost his job when the "political complexion of the Carbondale government changed," said the *Philadelphia Public Ledger,* and since then had made his living driving a laundry wagon. There were also gaps in his alibi, his jailers claimed. O'Boyle had been born in Carbondale but moved west with his parents while still a boy. He returned to his birthplace in 1913. During his years out west, he'd been employed as a railroad brakeman and served in the army from 1909 to 1910 during the border trouble with Mexican revolutionaries, he said. No one ever had reason to doubt his word, but now, when he was asked to produce his discharge papers, they couldn't be found.

There is real irony in this, for O'Boyle's department and even O'Boyle himself would have arrested others with similar holes in their stories. How does one prove the truth of a life? By the word of neighbors and family? By a lifetime of service? Or by a stack of documents neatly filed and instantly accessible? Few people file and order their lives on the assumption that someday they will have to prove themselves to authorities, yet as the century progressed police interrogations increasingly hinged on that presumption. The Gaze grew wider, demanding documentary proof of a life lived by the rules. Without such proof, guilt was presumed.

Suddenly O'Boyle found himself cast as the lead in a Kafkaesque role that became a common theme in the century's popular culture: that of the "wrong man," a victim of mistaken identity. It was the ultimate paranoid nightmare, a flight for survival from a state that had grown increasingly omnipotent and omnipresent, yet lacked a complementary omniscience since its Gaze could not penetrate beneath the surface to see the truth. A flawed God, built and maintained by man. The movies especially loved the story, and of all film directors we immediately think of Alfred Hitchcock: his films of flight included *The 39 Steps, The Secret Agent, North by Northwest,* and *The Wrong Man.* But the theme was not confined to celluloid dreams. The nightmare was canonized by the end of the century when the U.S. Supreme Court ruled that it was not illegal to execute the wrong man. In the controversial 1993 case of Texas Death Row inmate Leonel Herrera, who challenged his impending execution based on the discovery of new evidence of his innocence, Chief Justice William Rehnquist wrote in the majority opinion that it was not unconstitutional to execute an innocent man if all procedural rules had been upheld. In his dissent, Justice Harry Blackmun responded. "The execution of a person who can show that he is innocent comes perilously close to murder."

When O'Boyle was unable to produce his discharge papers, his old colleagues threw him in jail, suddenly demonized like Hibbard Steeves. He stayed in jail for two nights, until the evening of May 24, when a Leavenworth official arrived. The federal man took one look at the prisoner and told the Carbondale authorities they'd jailed the wrong fellow.

Frank O'Boyle was released. No connection was ever made by the police or press—or even O'Boyle himself—that Frank Grigware had also claimed to be a victim of false identification.

THERE WAS A brief hiatus in the search, a three-year gap in which there were no sightings, no mailings, and no unlucky innocents facing entombment for the sin of vaguely resembling Frank Grigware. These were the years 1917 through the beginning of 1920, when too much else was going on in the world to bother with one fugitive. On April 6, 1917, the United States finally entered the Great War in Europe; conscription began a month later, swelling the U.S. Army to more than 4 million. By Armistice Day on the eleventh hour of November 11, 1918, 21 million people had been wounded, a rate of about ten for every minute of the war, and 8½ million had died. America left more than 115,000 dead in Europe, about half of them succumbing to disease.

The disease came home with the troops during the flu pandemic of 1918. By the time it subsided, between 550,000 and 675,000 people had died in the United States and between 20 to 40 million worldwide. The figures were imprecise because people died so fast—sick at dawn, dead by dusk. Doctors had never seen anything like it; a single sneeze could spew 85 million disease-causing germs into the air. The killer was a particularly virulent strain of influenza, misnamed the "Spanish flu" because Spain was devastated early on. In Philadelphia, the dead were left at streetside and stacked in caskets, waiting for burial owing to a nationwide shortage of gravediggers. The death toll toppled actuary tables, bankrupting insurance companies.

By spring 1919, the disease disappeared as abruptly as it began. But after the one-two punch of the Great War and the flu pandemic, nothing would be the same. Where before it was the frontier that was dangerous and unpredictable, now nowhere seemed safe. Death came quickly and quietly, without the romance of the West, without reason or dignity. If only life would return to normal. If only things could again seem ordered and reasoned.

It wasn't to be, at least not in 1919. During the "long hot summer" of that year, racial violence swept the country, resulting in at least twenty serious disturbances that included major riots in Chicago, Knoxville, Omaha, and Washington, D.C. The worst was in Chicago, where, as in other major cities, wartime prosperity had accelerated the great migration of blacks from the rural South to the urban North. Blacks and whites competed for jobs and housing, with blacks gradually replacing European immigrants in the urban ghettos. In Chicago, the riot erupted on a Lake Michigan beach when a black youth crossed the unofficial color line dividing whites and blacks; whites threw rocks and killed the youth, leading to a melee that ballooned into a riot engulfing the whole city. The violence followed a pattern that was repeated across America—white aggression and black retaliation—and police took a role that fanned the flames. Discriminatory law enforcement, once directed at European immigrants, helped create the tensions. During the riot itself, police often ignored white violence, convincing blacks that retaliation was their only defense. The police arrested blacks in disproportionate numbers. Finally, police officers often became rioters themselves. Lawlessness prevailed for more than a week; when the Chicago riot was over, 23 black and 15 white victims had died, 500 people were injured, and arson left more than a thousand black Chicagoans homeless.

That same spring and summer of 1919, as Vladimir Lenin in Russia called for world revolution, the American middle class was shocked by a new wave of labor strikes—3,000 that year alone. This was followed by a bombing campaign, including a midnight attack on the house of the new U.S. Attorney General, Mitchell "Fighting Quaker" Palmer. Many remembered the similar attack on former Idaho governor Frank Steunenberg more than fourteen years earlier. The Senate called for the probe of an alleged plot to overthrow the government; Congress funded an investigation of radicals. The great Red Scare began.

In the Justice Department, the boy who led the teenage cadets down Pennsylvania Avenue during the inaugural parade six years earlier, now an obscure government bureaucrat, was made special assistant to Attorney General Palmer and head of a new section designed to gather evidence on radicals. John Edgar Hoover compiled a massive card index on "left-wingers" and communist sympathizers that included 500,000 names and 60,000 biographical notes. In the days before instantaneous data retrieval by computer, Hoover's index proved astoundingly efficient, capable of locating names and cross-references within minutes. It was, up to that point, a milestone of political and social control.

Now began a season of oppression that was "the sorriest episode in the history of our country," wrote Judge Lawrence Brooks of Massachusetts, who witnessed much of what followed. It was a season in which the Roman poet Juvenal's classic warning—"Who will police the police?"—was forgotten in a climate of hysteria and fear. On November 7, 1919, the second anniversary of the Russian revolution, Bureau agents and local police raided the offices of the Union of Russian Workers in a dozen cities. Using names pulled from Hoover's file system, hundreds of suspected revolutionaries were arrested and many beaten. In more ways than just Steunenberg's death, the Red Scare echoed the "Big Troubles" in Idaho. Although a law had been passed making membership in a radical group a deportable offense, most of those arrested were released for lack of evidence or violations of their rights. On January 2, 1920, the "Palmer raids" began, in which police and Bureau agents arrested 10,000 people in twenty-three cities, again with brutality and the suppression of civil rights. And again, most of those arrested proved innocent of any offense and were released, but not before experiencing a taste of the third degree.

"There is a Doctor Jekyll and Mr. Hyde in nations as in individuals," Theodore Roosevelt once wrote, and the years 1917–1920 nurtured and strengthened America's Hyde. The Sedition Act of 1918, born in the midst of war hysteria, legalized oppression in the name of security. The Act, signed into law by President Wilson on May 16, 1918, seemed to promise for many the return to a golden age when things were kinder and gentler, before the forces of chaos arrived. Now anyone could be jailed for twenty years and fined $10,000 for sins ranging from inciting insubordination, discouraging army recruitment, and obstructing the sale of Liberty Bonds to uttering, writing, or publishing "any disloyal, profane, scurrilous, or abusive language" about the Constitution, the flag, the armed forces, their uniforms, or the form of government of the United States. Under its aegis, perennial Socialist candidate and veteran labor leader Eugene V. Debs was charged with sedition and sentenced to federal prison, first in Moundsville, West Virginia, then in the Atlanta penitentiary. His crime: making a speech in which he denounced the Wall Street Junkers who robbed the poor and "the gentry who are today wrapped up in the American flag." Under its aegis also, federal prisons filled up with people charged under the Sedition Act; with its blessing, federal agents raided Socialist headquarters across the nation, periodicals were banned from the mails, uniformed soldiers attacked civilians and disrupted meetings they considered unpatriotic. By 1920, the Bureau's greater purpose had shifted from chasing white slavers to arresting the outspoken, and the number of agents had tripled from 400 to 1,200.

An evil had been let out of the box that many observers felt might never be put back in. "Emotion had replaced all reason," Herbert Hoover wrote in his memoirs. "I wouldn't have believed the American people could so completely lose their sense of balance," remembered Montana Senator Burton K. Wheeler. "A screaming hurricane of hate swept America," recalled Alvin Johnson, founder of the New School for Social Research. "Democracy in America has been trampled underfoot, submerged, forgotten," said Wisconsin Senator Robert F. LaFollette.

On December 22, 1924, the man who now signed himself *J. Edgar Hoover*—in imitation, some said, of A. Bruce Bielaski—was appointed the new director of the Bureau of Investigation. Like Allan Pinkerton before him, who signed himself *Founder*, Hoover answered official correspondence as *Director*. The paths of power were not dissimilar. The Bureau that Congress had hesitated to create in 1908 for fear it would become an instrument of oppression had already proved those worries true. Under Hoover's direction, it would also become the most powerful police organization the United States had ever known.

In Seattle, Jennie Grigware finally accepted that her fugitive son was dead, a victim of the deadly, more ruthless world. During the war, she believed he'd served in an army—American or Canadian, she wasn't sure which—and had died in the trenches. Her intuition told her so. Otherwise, he would have sent word to her somehow that he was still alive.

The Bureau thought otherwise. In 1928, they reopened the case, silently and secretly watching Jennie in Seattle, Jim Grigware on the Indian reservation, and far-flung Grigwares back in Michigan. Agents talked to their acquaintances, monitored their mail. "This investigation having been dormant for several years, it is believed that care should be exercised to avoid giving subject or his relatives and friends any inkling of the present activity," said a Bureau report penned in Seattle and forwarded to Washington.

The Director agreed. "Please be advised that the Bureau does not believe that this investigation should be permitted to become inactive nor should further investigation be conducted by correspondence only," he wrote in a letter to some doubting Thomases in the Detroit office on October 6, 1928. "To the contrary, the investigation should receive the most vigorous personal attention."

By then, Frank had been a fugitive for eighteen years. He was the longest-standing fugitive from any federal lockup. His escape was among the most spectacular of all time, reported across the nation, humiliating the Justice Department, destroying careers. Catching him now, after so many years, seemed almost impossible. Yet bringing him back to Leavenworth would show the world that no one could outrun the new Bureau of Investigation. It would be a publicity coup.

An urgency arose in official correspondence concerning Frank's pursuit that had never appeared before. "He is believed to be a dangerous man and would kill or be killed rather than be captured," warned a memo dated July 21, 1928, a subtle yet important change from the tale of the Chicago snitch in 1911, who without ever talking to the wanted man told his masters that Frank "will never be taken alive, and he will be killed before he goes back to the penitentiary."

For Frank, it was a deadly embellishment.

For his pursuers, it was a license to kill.

CHAPTER ELEVEN

A Man of Substance

FRANK WAS NEITHER hiding in Buenos Aires nor helping to build the Panama Canal. He did not buy and sell coffee beneath the massive statue of Christ the Redeemer in Rio de Janeiro nor sip tequila with fellow yeggmen in Mexico City's American Bar. He never rode desperately at midnight across the high plains of North or South Dakota, nor parade openly as a fast-talking cousin in Midland, Michigan. He was not, as various lawmen suspected, living with surgical alterations and under a different name in Windsor, Vermont; Walla Walla, Washington; Des Moines, Iowa; Boston, Massachusetts; Lansing, Michigan; Oklahoma City, Oklahoma; Jefferson City, Missouri; Jacksonville, Florida; Sacramento or San Francisco, California; Salt Lake City, Utah; Columbus, Ohio; Lincoln, Nebraska; Newark and Jersey City, New Jersey; or Albany and New York City, New York. He had not visited any of these places. Frank Grigware was dead.

James Lawrence Fahey lived. What traces remained of the scared boy running from Leavenworth were buried deep, deeper than the metal buttons of his prison jacket, and only struggled to the surface at night in his dreams. Lately those dreams had gotten bad. He stood on a gray plain with no life in sight, and behind him the grayer bulk of Leavenworth thrust from the soil. A pounding came from within, like the pistons of a great machine. Wherever he ran, no matter what the distance, he'd glance back and the prison would still be there.

No one knew that dream. The nightmare doppelgänger was his burden and his alone. To all the world, he was Jim Fahey from the States, builder, former mayor, naturalized Canadian, with a lovely wife and three lively children. He'd found what he'd been seeking when he left home in 1906. He'd staked a claim on the American ethos that any man could jettison the past and be whomever he wanted. He'd done so in Canada.

FRANK STAYED IN Minneapolis until the end of summer 1910, working for Hoggins construction company and breaking in his new identity. He always felt jumpy, expecting the hand of a city policeman or Pinkerton detective to drop on his shoulder at any time. He knew they were looking for him, knew the posters with his Omaha or Leavenworth mug shot hung in every courthouse and post office, though he didn't exactly go looking for them. Staying free would take adhering to two strict rules. The first—never commit a crime, no matter how small—was not a problem—he wasn't tempted in that direction, no matter how others portrayed him. The second was harder. He had to cast off all ties to the past, completely and thoroughly. He could never contact a friend or relative; he could not write Alice or his brother Jim. He couldn't write his mother. He wondered if she still kept the locket he'd given her before his leave-taking, or whether she'd thrown it away. He wondered if she thought he was dead. He could never go back to Washington or Idaho, never again visit Waco or Denver, Kansas City or Omaha. He wasn't one for bars or pool halls, but he'd loved baseball and the prizefights, and detectives would look for him there. He'd have to remake himself entirely. What had been could no longer be.

It was with a sense of relief that Frank started out for Canada with Hoggins's brother Ingval, whom everyone called "Shorty," where a boom was going on. First they hit Duluth and worked on an ore dock; then by spring 1911 they moved to Winnipeg, Manitoba, getting a job with Pollock's Siding doing tin work on grain elevators. They worked west, building elevators in Winnipeg; in Rainbow, Saskatchewan, and in the southern plains of Alberta around Lethbridge. It reminded him of the American Plains, though the conditions were harsher. He wondered how these farmers survived. Hailstones, insects, wheat rot, wind, and interest rates could wipe them out in hours, even minutes. During summer, the sun beat down on the wheat fields of Manitoba and Saskatchewan and on the rolling rangeland of Alberta, the mercury spiking in the hundreds. He felt he was roasting, perched upon a ledge of tin. In winter, the winds whipped the dry snow across the prairie and into the little towns, their only spots of warmth the light seeping through cracks in windows nailed shut with building paper or blankets to keep out the cold. Standing beside the tracks in every town was at least one mammoth elevator, looming from the snow like a tin cathedral. One or two empty boxcars sat alone beside it on a railroad spur.

Frank marked his and the railroads' progress west by the tin cathedrals. As in America, the railroad was the historic fact tying the country together, a political reality threaded with steel. These prairie provinces were the great middle of the nation, backwaters cut off from the bustling maritime centers, which was fine for someone hiding from police but a detriment for everyone else. The early 1900s was a period of expansion across Canada's prairies, and two railroads—the Grand Trunk Pacific and the Canadian Northern—were building on parallel lines. In 1903, the Grand Trunk began building west from Winnipeg to the Sheena River in British Columbia, while three years later the Canadian Northern started building to Vancouver. In time the overlap and operating inefficiencies would cause both companies to go bankrupt, their rolling stock absorbed in 1923 into the government-owned and operated Canadian National Railway. But Frank's trek across the Canadian West occurred during the boomtime, when thousands of jobs opened up for engineers, surveyors, packers, freighters, carpenters, and other laborers. The railroads set up temporary camps as they were building, and these became instant towns.

Canada's southern prairies were the northern reaches of the "Great American Desert," and like the American lines in their own prairie expansion, Canadian railways laid track in return for large cash payments and huge grants of land. Like their American cousins, the Canadian lines colonized the prairie, since the way to profit lay in selling this land to settlers. In some basic ways, the similarities ended there. Frank noticed as he worked from depot to depot that these farm towns seemed laid in a plan. They were lonely, but not *as* lonely as on the American plains. As early as 1877, Canadian surveyors warned that "the present opportunity would never occur again" for railroads to develop a well-regulated society that also catered to the railroads' needs. Towns were created at regular intervals along the main lines, imposing a discipline on expansion that the Americans had ignored. It was social engineering with an eye on profit, yet the companies themselves went bankrupt while many of the little towns survived. As originally envisioned, these towns existed to provide services to, and gather harvests from, the surrounding farm districts; since horse and wagon were still the principal means of transportation, the towns were built six to eight miles apart, a distance geared to the wagons' limitations and speed. Divisional railroad points—home to train yards, engine sheds, and machine and repair shops—were planned as major population centers and were spaced at 100- to 150-mile intervals, with a 125-mile distance considered ideal, since this was the distance a locomotive could comfortably steam without refueling. It was a marvel of planning and organization, and Frank, as a builder, was impressed and amazed.

Despite local idiosyncracies, the prairie towns basically looked the same. The railroad track ran in a straight line through their middle. The station was the town center, the focus of news, supplies, and people, as compared to American towns, where the station was pushed to the far edge. The loading platform, branch bank, post office, general store, and other shops clustered around the depot. Two to five grain elevators jutted from this center, each actively grading and cleaning the grain. Just as the depot was the communications center, the elevator was an economic nucleus, funneling the grain harvest from surrounding districts to the grain companies and cooperatives and then straight into the bellies of the railroad cars. Wheat production had shot up with the introduction of Red Fife wheat, which matured faster during the shorter Canadian growing season, tempting more settlers to start up farms. It was the kind of boom Frank had seen in the fields around Spokane. He'd arrived in Canada in the middle of a wheat boom that just kept getting better; as grain production mounted, the railroads added larger engines and more cars, increasing their debt to handle demand. By 1914, the Transcona yard in Winnipeg could accommodate 7,500 grain cars. By 1928, the year of Canada's greatest wheat crop, the prairies produced more than 500 million bushels of grain.

Like everyone else, Frank decided to cash in on the prosperity. By spring 1912, as the Bureau agents searched for Alice and watched his family, Frank and Shorty Hoggins signed with the Canadian Northern Railway in Edmonton, the provincial capital of Alberta. They were hired as bridge men for more than they'd ever made in their lives and sent 85 miles south to Blackfalds to work for foreman Charlie O'Connor on the Blind Man Bridge.

Trestle work paid good wages, but it was also an easy way to get killed. More grain cars meant the development of heavier locomotives, which called for steel bridges instead of the old wooden kind. In 1909, hundreds of workers built a steel viaduct across the deep valley of the Belly River, later called the Oldman; at one mile long, 314 feet high, and supported by thirty-three towers, it was Canada's longest and highest railroad bridge. Three men died during its construction, while others fell off bridges undergoing similar upgrades far up the Fraser River. In the mountains, men died in rock slides and avalanches, sixty dying in 1910 alone in slides in the Rogers Pass. A man could be dead in an instant, just another number on the statistical tables.

Notwithstanding this, Frank liked the life from the start. The bridge gang at Blackfalds was about two hundred strong. They lived in crowded two-story boarding cars called "hotels on wheels," working dawn to dusk over the ravine. The towers were built in sections from the ground up, then the long steel platform laid from end to end. Sometimes when the wind kicked up he could feel the platform sway. The track was laid with a gantry, a long wooden structure shaped like a guillotine and built onto a flatcar; a locomotive pushed it forward as it placed the rails with a series of cables and pulleys. The gang was a rough-talking bunch of Canadians, métis, Russians, Ukrainians, and Americans, but Frank got along with almost everyone. To them, he was Jim Fahey from the States: the Canadians pronounced the last name "Fay." These Canadians took some getting used to. "The meat of the buffalo tastes the same on both sides of the border," said Sitting Bull while camped in Canada after annihilating Custer, but Frank could see real differences. While growing up in Spokane, he knew that the Canucks lived "up there" in the Great White North, yet that and an awareness of the Mounties was the extent of his knowledge about Canada. If Americans seemed benevolently ignorant of Canada, Canadians seemed touchy about the States, keeping themselves almost malevolently well-informed. A major part of the Canadian identity was that they were *not* Americans, while Americans rarely thought twice about their northern neighbors—an attitude that only increased Canadian ire. There were Dumb Yank stories aplenty, the most famous not coming until the 1920s when Al Capone purportedly said, "I don't even know what street Canada is on." What Americans saw as clout, Canadians saw as bullying; what Americans saw as straightforwardness, Canadians saw as loutishness, indicating a general lack of sophistication. This was not a problem for Frank, since he was quiet and soft-spoken to begin with, but it caused conflict with the other Americans in the bridge crew, including Shorty, who could get mouthy at times.

One of the oddest things to Frank was the language. A whiner was a "suck," a bootlicker was a "keener," and every question seemed to end in "eh?" They celebrated July 1, Dominion Day, instead of the Fourth of July. They ate their "brown bread" with "back bacon," then washed it down with Caribou, a mix of wine and grain alcohol, which was separately called "alcool." Since the railroads outlawed drinking to keep the peace in camp, the men downed their liquor on the sly. Whatever name they gave it, these Canadians were expert moonshiners, and both Caribou and alcool could give a man an awful kick in the head. Frank laid off the stuff, and though that occasioned some ribbing from his fellows, he figured it was better than what might happen if the booze loosened his tongue and they learned his real name.

Individually, the Canadians were open, friendly, and maybe less dogmatic than Americans, but something seemed self-defeating in their make-up that took him awhile to understand. He came to see it was tied to their relationship with the wilderness: Where the conquest of the frontier had taught Americans that anything was possible, Canada's unconquerable Northwest Territories taught skepticism. Everything had a limit, even man. Like the American West, the North was a challenge and a barrier, but here it had proved impossible to overcome the cold. The country itself was a huge lopsided rectangle of almost four million square miles, the world's second-largest nation, nearly half of which was the North. Stretching across a quarter of the world's time zones, the North was a place where wolves and bears raided towns and carried off pets, where waterfalls froze in mid-plummet and mountains reared up over two miles high. Canada itself was a place where a million lakes, streams, and rivers made up a third of the world's fresh-water supply, where some bays and lakes were bigger than entire states, and one single forest was six times bigger than France. The cold was so intense that shifting ice, killer blizzards, and battering winds put a stop to nearly everything. Canadians were humbled by their country, while Americans rarely had the good sense to be humbled by anything. Though Canadians seemed to take the North for granted, it was always there—huge, unknown, and looming above them, relatively unexplored. The Inuit (whom Americans called Eskimos) had a word in Inuktitut for that helplessness: Ionamut, "It can't be helped," an attitude adopted by many Canadians. They were able to accept the climatic barriers with a shrug. Where Americans could barely conceive of losing, Canadians saw little reason to expect quick victory. Where Americans were all win or lose, Canadians hung in there, just wanting to do well.

The aggressive American sense of entitlement worried Canadians, a concern with roots in history. The two countries had been enemies in the French and Indian War, Revolutionary War, and War of 1812: the rest of the nineteenth century was one of peace, though at times uneasy. By 1846, the great flood of settlers into the Oregon Territory forced Britain to surrender that region; by 1849, the advance of Americans into the upper Mississippi River threatened the Canadians' two-century trade dominance there. The Americans seemed everywhere, like ants, and like ants they never stopped spreading. Anglo-American antagonisms flared during the Civil War, worrying Canadians again. As the Union Pacific and Central Pacific railroads approached completion of North America's first transcontinental railroad, Canadians were not comforted when on February 3, 1869, the *Daily Alta California* of San Francisco proclaimed:

> That the U.S. are bound finally to absorb all the world and the rest of mankind, every well-regulated American mind is prepared to admit. When the fever is on, our people do not seem to know when and where to stop, but keep on swallowing, so long as there is anything in reach. To use a popular Californianism, we "go for everything that is in sight."

The Canadian rush to build a railroad from coast to coast was as much an attempt to ensure that it kept a firm grip on territory that might otherwise be taken by its upstart southern neighbor as it was to link the country. A *Washington Post* editorial on the eve of the Spanish-American War in 1898 predicted:

> A new consciousness seems to have come upon us—the consciousness of strength—and with it a new appetite, the yearning to show our strength. . . . Ambition, interest, land hunger, pride, the mere joy of fighting, whatever it may be, we are animated by a new sensation. . . . The taste of Empire is in the mouth of the people even as the taste of blood in the jungle.

After winning that conflict, the United States indulged in a frenzy of expansion, annexing Puerto Rico, the Philippines, Guam, Wake Island, and Hawaii. These days, Canadians weren't as worried about territorial annexation as they were about an American economic and cultural takeover. Americans apparently thought they owned a right to everything.

Complicating matters was the fact that American settlers were solicited for the Canadian plains. Since there were many Americans in Canada, Frank was not really an oddity. Since British-controlled Canada had banned slavery in 1841, fugitive southern slaves fled across the border on the Underground Railroad. In the late 1890s, the Canadian government and the railroads began a campaign to lure American homesteaders north with the promise of the "last best West." Even as American railroads helped lure Frank's parents west, Canadian railroads created a vision of their own land of plenty. Agencies established in the Midwest encouraged farmers to relocate north of the border; promotional literature had titles like *Prosperity Follows Settlement* and *Canada, Land of Opportunity*. In 1914, a Minneapolis, Saint Paul & Sault Saint Marie Railroad special filled with settlers from Colorado rolled north to central Alberta, where thousands of miles of irrigation canals had been cut by the railroads; nailed to one car was a banner reading SOLID TRAIN LOAD OF SETTLERS FOR ALBERTA. By then, about one million Americans had settled ahead of them.

For Frank, it meant he was not alone, but he also stood a better chance of being recognized by old friends or acquaintances. He kept his eyes open and his head down, better reason to stay quiet and not draw attention to himself. At first he worried about the Mounties, the national police force, but they were more concerned with keeping order in the camps and preventing bootleggers from selling whiskey to the workers, and soon those worries passed. By midsummer he'd gained a reputation as a steady worker and excellent carpenter and was asked to follow the bridge gang north to Entwhistle, set in a straight line west from Edmonton toward the Rockies. He said good-bye to Shorty, who'd grown tired of the job and went his own way.

Entwhistle lay on the Pembina River, deep within the foothills of the Rockies. It lay 140 miles east of the Yellowhead Pass, at 3,729 feet the lowest point through the mountains to British Columbia. Both railroads were building lines toward the pass, part of that duplicated effort that would eventually bankrupt both companies. The Grand Trunk Pacific got there first in 1911, and a small town grew around the railroad. Frank's employer, the Canadian Northern, did not arrive until 1913. Though he would not see the small town for another twelve years, he heard idyllic descriptions of a self-sufficient community built at the junction of the Athabasca and Miette rivers, surrounded on all sides by snow-capped mountains towering ten to eleven thousand feet above sea level. There were geese, silver fox, cougar, and mountain goat in the high country; bears and caribou, plentiful even in the foothills, would stand off and watch from a distance as men laid track or worked on a trestle. It seemed a pristine place cut off from the rest of civilization, a place that lay far from the reach of the American law. Maybe he'd come back some day and check the place out. When he finally did, the small town was named Jasper.

Right now, however, he was too busy for sightseeing. They were more isolated here than south on the plains, and if possible the work was more taxing. This was the end of the track, what railroaders called the end-of-steel. It was an amazing sight, a narrow thread advancing through muskeg swamp and forest choked with grading crews, track-laying crews, bridge crews, plus a gradually shifting supply train piled with rails, fish plates, ties, spikes, gravel, timber, and other supplies. A second train with additional supplies waited on a siding a short distance back. The end of steel was a town in itself, a beehive of blacksmiths, track layers, teamsters, carpenters, surveyors, cooks, medical staff, supervisors, and the occasional visiting railroad executive. All had their billets on the trains, whether it was the large boarding cars for the workmen or the smaller cars for supervisors and executives. The cooks, many of them Chinese, got little rest: an

Anglican minister reported that the men "work like horses, eat like hogs, and sleep like logs"; one laborer reported sick to the doctor after eating twenty-seven breakfast sausages. The makeshift town pushed ahead as the track advanced; at the end of a day's work, it might be three or four miles from where it had started that morning.

The Mounties spent their days outfoxing bootleggers. Whiskey was smuggled into camp in pigs' carcasses, stitched tight at the belly so the bottles wouldn't show. Two female bootleggers carried whiskey in hot water bottles strapped to their chests; tubes for the liquid ran to spigots tied to their legs. A quick flip of the skirt sold the stuff, and a Mountie only caught them after noticing that their chests, apparently buxom when first entering camp, seemed to deflate with time. There were other threats to order, too: a pair of prostitutes, dressed in nuns' habits they'd rented in Edmonton, reportedly collected several thousand dollars. The deception was discovered belatedly, when genuine nuns entered camp the day after they departed.

There was a different attitude here toward Mounties than that held by Americans toward their own lawmen, Frank observed. The British Canadians, at least, seemed to take a more reverential posture to authority; where Americans adopted a skeptical stance to their national police forces, Canadians trusted the Royal Canadian Mounted Police. They also played a different role from their southern counterparts, especially on the local level. The Mountie was the chief agent of law enforcement, but in provinces like Alberta, where the RCMP also contracted as the provincial and local police, he could serve as unofficial judge, father confessor, and family counselor. In feuds he was consulted as a disinterested party rather than as a threat who might toss everyone in jail. The Plains Indians of Canada suffered dark and desperate days during the nation's westward expansion, but in some very important ways the Mounties served as their advocates, thus preventing the kind of extermination and near-extermination of whole tribes that occurred south of the border. During the Yukon gold strike, Mounties served as unofficial immigration officers, sitting in tents atop mountain passes and turning back prospectors who didn't have the funds, supplies, or character to survive a full year's stay. Their reputation of saving lives was honestly earned, especially during the harsh winters when they plunged into the forests with their packs of sled dogs. Not that they were universally loved: the French Québecois viewed them, like the Irish did the British, as unwelcome interlopers. On the whole, however, Mounties kept a tighter hold over western settlements than did American lawmen, and with far less violence. The six-shooter never became a symbol of freedom or civilization in Canada.

In late summer 1912, Frank nearly died while working on the Entwhistle bridge. He was standing on a forty-foot tower, setting an overhead cable for bridge work, when he felt the structure sway. At first he thought it was the wind, then someone on the ground screamed, "Watch out, it's coming down!" Even as he heard this, he felt the sickening lurch as the wooden scaffold crumbled.

He glanced to his left and saw the guy rope used for guiding the cable; he didn't even think as he leapt for it, knowing if he missed he'd plummet to the rocky ground. He caught it and held on, only then realizing that he'd reacted in the same instantaneous fashion as when John Gideon pulled the wooden gun from his pocket and yelled, "That's the signal! Let's go!" A man's life could compress into a single instant, and nothing else existed but the loud beating of his heart and the object upon which his instinct for survival, or freedom, became focused. Frank wrapped the rope around his calf as he understood how close he'd come to death. He started to tremble.

As the crane lowered the guy rope to the riverbank, the entire population of the end of steel seemed to drop their tools and run up beneath him, their voices merging into one wild cheer. Hands grabbed him under the shoulders and held him up before he touched the ground. Charlie O'Connor, his foreman, ran up, and, between claims that Frank's leap was the goddamnedest thing he'd ever witnessed in his life, finally asked if Frank was all right. "My legs feel a little shaky, Charlie," Frank admitted. "You mind if I sit down?"

O'Connor let him sit out the rest of the day. Everywhere he went, he waded through a barrage of thumps on the back and congratulations on his good fortune. Finally, to get some peace, he walked up to the outfitter overlooking the river, the Pembina Coal Company store. Even there, his exploit had preceded him. The manager, G. D. MacRae, told him to put away his money, he didn't need it, and opened a bottle of beer. Frank usually didn't touch the stuff, but after what he'd been through he figured he deserved one. MacRae was a cheerful fellow but tough, the kind of man who knew that although wildernesses were opened by adventurers, they were civilized by builders and storekeepers. They went outside to sit on the store's front stoop, the wall behind them hung with pelts and steel-tooth traps, the spaces around the bench cluttered with casks of nails, minnow nets, bamboo casting rods. In one corner, overlooking the river, a long spyglass on a tripod was pointed at the trestle work. Even without the telescope, Frank could see the pile of sticks that had been his tower. "Bravest thing I ever saw, leaping for that rope," MacRae commented.

"I didn't have time to think about it," Frank admitted. "It's not like I'm a hero." MacRae pulled on his beer and commented that sometimes heroes were made simply by staying alive. They talked awhile that day and several more times that summer, becoming the best of friends.

By fall the bridge was finished, as well as a water tank for engines outside MacRae's store. The crew shipped eighty miles west to Macleod River Crossing, where Frank helped build twenty-seven company houses in the winter of 1913. It was bitter cold, in the minus digits, but that hard winter at the Blue Jay had helped prepare him for such conditions. Still, the cold and boredom were hard on everyone. The Canadian railways' first murder occurred that winter when two men got into a dispute and one pulled a pistol and started shooting, ending the argument in the time-honored American way. Even the toughest men could die from the cold. A Russian worker came down with double pneumonia, his skin turning yellow; the man coughed and fought for breath until one night he bolted straight up in his cot, then sank back with a horrible gurgle and died. Frank decided he'd prefer a quick death like a drop from the tower to such a lingering agony. Somehow, it reminded him of Leavenworth. There was little enough mercy on this earth. At least you could hope for mercy when you died.

That spring of 1913, Frank and some friends quit the railroad, built a raft, and floated down the Athabasca River to Athabasca Landing, an end of steel 85 miles north of Edmonton. The landing was the jumping-off point for settlers heading to the Peace River region, the province's northernmost point of civilization except for Fort Mc-Murray, an old fur trading post near Saskatchewan. The homesteaders in Peace River were true pioneers. From Athabasca Landing they struck out nearly 200 miles across rivers, lakes, deep forest, and muskeg swamp along a trail that was little better than a mud stream. Tiny settlements were springing up around the main town of Peace

River Landing, and the idea of traveling that far started Frank's wanderlust again. He thought about the frontier as he made his float trip, a 150-mile journey that proved plenty hard. The river was in full flood and rougher than they'd anticipated, and a couple of times he thought they'd crack up on the rocks; instead, they'd whip around bends in the river and get stranded on sandbars. Once they rounded a bend and ran into a bear. They'd neglected to bring rifles, but the bear was just as scared and both parties quickly went their unharmed and separate ways. That summer—as President Wilson pardoned Jack Golden, now a diseased shell of his former self—Frank and a real estate speculator opened an Athabasca fox farm. Though silver fox stoles were the rage, Frank's heart was never in it. He looked at the poor beasts in their cages and again thought of Leavenworth. It was as if anything could call back those old memories. By fall 1913 he sold his shares to his partner and returned to Edmonton, now at a crossroads in his life, biding his time by selling Athabasca real estate to investors.

That was probably when he saw Herbert Fife—or, more accurately, when Fife spotted him. When Frank had first come to Alberta and seen the number of Americans running loose, he'd expected discovery at any moment and stayed away from crowds. But three years had passed since his escape and he still hadn't been recognized. He grew careless. One day he went to the lobby of a hotel where a possible buyer stayed when someone across the room cried out, "Frank! Frank Grigware!!" He whipped around and there was Herbert Fife, a contractor for whom he'd worked in Spokane. He looked around, expecting stares of horror at the fugitive unmasked, but no one seemed to pay the least attention. Frank saw an exit down a hall and escaped before Fife could reach him. The discovery threw him into a panic of uncertainty. Fife would surely talk and the law would hear. He felt again as if the prison walls were closing in. He tried not to go out for the rest of the week, hoping Fife's business had ended and he'd returned to Spokane. He laid low until Sunday, then as always attended mass. As he was leaving services, he saw the man again. This time Fife seemed actively on the hunt, planted near the steps of the city cathedral and watching as people left the sanctuary. He must have remembered that Frank was Catholic. His eyes locked on Frank's face and he headed straight for him, but Frank scooted in the opposite direction and soon lost Fife in the crowd.

How long now? He wondered how long it would take before Fife started talking, before the law heard and followed, before he was shackled back aboard the Leavenworth train. He realized now that his safety had been an illusion; he was and always would be a fugitive, forever on the run. His dream of a normal life was only that—a dream. It struck him that the only reason he'd remained unseen until Fife's wake-up call was that he'd stayed away from cities, working in places no one from his past life would have reason to visit. If he valued his freedom, he'd have to become a ghost on the edge of society.

Through his real estate connections he heard that his old storekeeper friend, G. D. MacRae, was planning to open stores with his brothers in the Peace River country, the very kind of wilderness he required. When MacRae came to town for supplies and Christmas shopping, Frank said he wanted to go too.

They left not long after Christmas, in the winter of 1914. The wait seemed to take forever, every day of waiting another in which his pursuers could pick up his trail. Like most settlers to the north country, Frank and the MacRae brothers went by train to Athabasca Landing, then drove up the iced-over river by horse until reaching the town of Smith. They continued by the Little Slave River to Lesser Slave Lake, where they crossed the ice to the Catholic mission at Grouard. Though the Grouard Trail to Peace River usually took eight days in spring or summer, it took nearly twenty in the snow. When they finally struck Peace River Crossing, it was 62 below.

They built the store in time for the arrival of the spring's first homesteaders; theirs was the first independent operation outside those run by the large trading companies. The Grouard Trail was murder, even after the thaw. It wound through muskeg, bush, and nearly unfordable rivers. When the settlers emerged from the trees at Peace River, even the hardiest among them groaned that it had been no picnic trail. Many came in wagons hauling their possessions, but sometimes it was easier to walk than ride. In one instance, a woman was riding in a wagon and carrying her baby when the wagon hit some rocks and the child bumped clean out of her arms. It dropped into a mud hole and sank from sight but was plucked out before it drowned. As the new arrivals camped at the edge of town, they staggered to Frank's store and those of his competitors, where they applied for homesteads. They signed their names in a census book: if they worked hard for two years and "proved up," the parcel was legally theirs. Frank sold them supplies and watched as they trudged off for more backbreaking work, invariably building log houses with sod roofs. The owners said it rained three days inside these houses for every one outside.

All during that year of 1914—as Frank James died in the States at age seventy-two; as on June 28, Archduke Franz Ferdinand was assassinated in Sarajevo, Bosnia, plunging the world into war—the homesteaders kept arriving. It was as rough and isolated a country as Frank had ever seen. Wolves raided the livestock, and in some of the farthest-flung towns the residents got isolation pay. When government officials came through to take the census, they drove pack mules before them, killing their own food as they went or stopping in isolated cabins along the way. The only preachers at first were circuit riders; then, slowly, churches began to send missionaries. Yet even with this, Frank was surprised by the number of Americans. The census takers found American after American in the isolated homesteads, all of them responding to Alberta's offer to snap up free land. Frank wondered which American newcomer would be the one to know him and turn him in. As Canada entered the war and shipped troops to Europe, he wondered if he shouldn't join the army too and disappear. In the end, he decided that he stood less chance of discovery at the edge of the wilderness than he did amid the regiment halls and the reams of military records.

And to tell the truth, he was happy here. Every day did not begin with the possibility of arrest; more and more evenings ended with a feeling of freedom. As 1914 became 1915, Frank was made a partner with MacRae and his brothers; though the larger company stores undercut their business in the main town of Peace River, MacRae opened a new store in West Peace River and Frank opened a confectionery. They opened two stores seventy miles southwest in the town of Spirit River, with a population of 200 souls. He built all the stores himself, as well as a home for his old friend MacRae. He built a Presbyterian church for the Reverend J. M. Pritchard in Spirit River and served as chairman of the church building committee. He was the fastest shingler in the region, nailing up five rows at once on the church while the wind kicked up a little hurricane. He was a conservative builder, drawn to plain substantial structures, opposed to unnecessary frills. He moved permanently to Spirit River, managed the store himself, took up the sport of curling on the frozen lakes, and learned to deliver the heavy stones down the ice like a pro. In 1916, he was chosen chairman of the school board. Soon afterward, his friends asked him to be mayor. He hesitated briefly, but figured the exposure would be no worse than as manager of the town's largest store. Up here, people accepted a man for what he was, not caring overly what he had been. It was the way of the frontier—the way the American frontier had been billed. He was building a country in western Canada, something he'd only dreamed about in Spokane. He worked hard and made good, daring to dream of the future and hope he could succeed. In the modest terms of a pioneer community, he was a man of substance. He had no enemies in the Peace River country. He had the respect and trust of his friends.

THEN HE FELL in love.

It happened one day in spring 1915, when the town organized a picnic and everyone played baseball. Frank noticed in the outfield a petite dark-headed woman whom he'd never seen before. He thought maybe she was a schoolteacher and liked the way she walked, with a very short stride. The other girls kidded her that she'd never make it to first base with those tiny steps, but in truth it was hard for all the women to play ball in the tight skirts they wore. She was running bases when she tripped and fell on a mound beside a badger hole; she knocked the wind out of herself and was a little shaky getting up, but she brushed herself off and kept playing.

"Who is that?" Frank asked Bertha Baby, a friend who ran the town's hotel. Frank had talked with Bertha about opening a confectionery in the lobby like he'd done in Peace River, and Bertha thought enough of Frank's business sense to consider investing.

"That's Ruth Broderick," Bertha answered, quizzically appraising her friend. "Jim Fahey, I think you're interested." Bertha was plainspoken, as were many of these north country girls. "Here all the girls had given up on you as a monk. Shall I make the introductions?"

Ruth Gwendolyn Broderick had moved with her father, older brother, and sisters to Spirit River in 1914, the previous year. She was eleven years Frank's junior, and somehow the story started wherever she went that she was a schoolteacher, perhaps because petite features and quiet charm were associated with young teachers. If anything, she was as tough as any homesteader, and possibly more well traveled. Her parents had left Cornwall, England, years earlier and sailed to Hawaii with the idea of starting a pineapple farm. Instead they grew coffee, and Ruth was born during that period, on June 2, 1897. Life would seem idyllic in a tropical paradise, but the reality was otherwise. Hawaii was isolated, the farm was in trouble, and Ruth was eight years old when her mother died of tuberculosis. Her brother steamed back to England to enlist at the outbreak of hostilities with the Kaiser; he'd barely reached the front before he was wounded and discharged. In a way he was lucky. Nineteen fourteen was one year before the Germans used gas at the Second Battle of Ypres, two years before the British lost 19,000 men and had another 38,470 wounded in one unimaginable day in the Battle of the Somme. During his recuperation, he heard of free land in Canada being offered to veterans for homesteading, and saw a way for his family to solve their financial woes. Soon the Brodericks headed for the north country.

Spirit River was good to them. Their homestead was a success, and the work helped Ruth's father and brother overcome their losses. One sister, Nora, married the town pharmacist. Ruth married the mayor, Jim Fahey.

Neither really knew what hit them after that introduction on the baseball field. Years later, when Frank's children asked how they met, Frank said he liked the way their mother walked, and would then mince around the kitchen in imitation as the children giggled. Ruth thought Jim Fahey was a gentle man for such a hard country, not coarse at all. There was a quietness to him she couldn't exactly fathom, but in the year they were engaged she found him to be dependable and decent and came to trust that he would never let her down.

Once during these early years she asked about his family. He never talked about them. He was Jim Fahey from the States, and that was all that anyone knew. He was quiet to begin with, but the question made him quieter still. He said his family was lost to him. His voice was sad, like they were truly lost, like something horrible had happened that he couldn't bring himself to divulge. It was a given that many men came north to escape their pasts and start over; they ran from heartbreak, from a failed business venture, or debt and poverty. Sometimes they ran from the law. He hadn't hurt . . . or killed . . . someone, had he? she asked, and felt relief when he laughed and said he hadn't, no. Then she asked a tougher question: "Have you broken the law?" Again he said no. Though she would wonder about his silence afterward, she never asked again.

Frank thought many times about his answer. As he stood alone in his store or worked steadily on a house, her question echoed in his mind. It was true, he hadn't broken the law, though he had been convicted. Was it against the law to escape from prison if you weren't guilty to begin with? The game made him disgusted with himself. Who was he fooling by splitting hairs? Should he tell her everything? He knew what an honorable man would do. Yet in so doing, he risked losing everything. Before Ruth, there'd been no reason to reveal himself to anyone in the north; before Ruth, he'd never thought he'd have a normal life again. There'd been no other woman in his life since Alice: he could never think of her without watching as she cried on the witness stand. In the end, all he brought to her was pain. Back in the States, everything he'd touched seemed doomed, but here he was respected, here he was a builder of the nation, here the impossible had happened and this surprising woman took one look and decided Jim Fahey was worth her love. On a good day he could see himself becoming the man she seemed to see in him. *Correction: that she saw in Jim Fahey, not Frank Grigware.* If he told her the truth, he'd be calling back the old doomed ghosts; if he told her the truth and she rejected him, the reason would get out. In a little place like Spirit River it *would* get out, and there'd be no place for him to hide. He'd have to run again and take yet another name. He didn't know if he could give up his entire second life. If he told the truth of Leavenworth, he'd lose Ruth, just as he lost Alice and his mother. It would be easier to die.

Once or twice he tried to tell her, but each time he lost his nerve. Why was he such a coward? he berated himself, and yet everyone thought so highly of him. If only they knew. At such times she'd see the sadness in his face and touch her fingers lightly to the back of his neck or hand. Ruth was a woman of small gestures, but Frank felt at peace within those gestures and in the quietness of her eyes. She believed in him. How could anyone believe in him? He couldn't bear to lose that, not again. Sometimes he'd see her wrapped in a heavy coat, eyes on the ground, lost in her thoughts. Friends would see him gaze at her searchingly, lost in her.

They married on December 20, 1916, with the Reverend Pritchard officiating. The whole town turned out, as well as much of Peace River. She was High Anglican, he was Catholic, and Pritchard was a Presbyterian. People made jokes, but it didn't matter. Frank looked around proudly. He was getting married in the church he built, which stood in the middle of the town he'd put together. He thought of his mother, knowing she would be proud.

Every year after that he thought he'd tell her the truth, but every year something happened. In early 1917, Frank and Ruth applied for a homestead on Spirit River, and on August 14 of that year he became a naturalized Canadian citizen under the name James Lawrence Fahey. Was the marriage legal since his name was false? Who would ever know? With his naturalization, Frank had completed the last step in his legal reinvention; in the years before the 1935 Social Security Act and the establishment of the nine-digit numbers that tracked adults throughout their entire working lives, it was still easy for a man or woman to assume a new name and identity free from a growing paper trail. True, many criminals were discovered, thanks in part to their Bertillon and fingerprint records, thanks in part to a tendency to backslide, but on the whole, identity was still as malleable as it had been during the Wild West days. Every year seemed to take him one step further from Frank Grigware. By 1917, the United States had entered the war in Europe; by August 1917, his brother Joe had died five months earlier in a Spokane sanitorium, while Alice was already five years in her grave. That year, on November 16, ~~1917~~ 1907, the last vestiges of the Old West died out as well, apparently taking all memories of the Mud Cut Robbery with them. Oklahoma—once called the Indian Territory, haven for Tom Kating, Arthur Hewitt, and other escapees—was granted statehood, the last of the Great Plains states to be admitted to the Union. In 1918, he and Ruth proved up on their homestead and filed a title of certificate. He'd built homes for other people. Now he built and owned his own.

The next year, on April 19, 1919, their first child was born. Jack Edward Fahey was hearty and healthy, and only Frank knew he had the same first name as his childhood friend. A new family sparked Frank's ambition, and in 1921 he sold the Spirit River homestead for $3,200 and went into the cattle business, buying 160 Black Bell Angus beef cattle at $120 a head. Cattle ranching seemed a good bet in those days. Ranching had developed in Alberta since the 1880s in anticipation of the coming of the railroad, and since then the two industries had gone hand in hand. Yet the cattle business was more vulnerable than the railroads liked to admit, the export of beef subject to price fluctuations, changing import regulations, and the price exacted by shipping cattle long distances. In 1921, Frank's first daughter, Louise Irene, was born at the ranch. Two years later, in 1923, a catastrophic slump in prices drove the cost of cattle down to $8 a head. Frank was nearly ruined and sold out while he could still get anything.

It was at that low point that he remembered the pretty little town in the mountains that he'd heard so much about while building the bridge at Entwhistle. Maybe there, he suggested to Ruth, we can pick up and start again.

FRANK SAW IMMEDIATELY that Jasper in 1924 was a growing town. The previous year, the Canadian National Railway had risen from the ruins of the Canadian Northern and Grand Trunk Pacific; in the wake of that realignment, Jasper became the CNR's junction through the mountains. Railroad employees from the old divisional point in Lucerne, British Columbia, were transferred to Jasper almost daily. Approximately six hundred workers and their families lived in Jasper, and 225 children filled the wood-frame schools. More important, the railroad planned to turn Jasper into a tourist town. Just as the trains had promoted prospecting and prairie farming, now they tapped tourism as a pot of gold. Encroachment on some of Alberta's wildest and most beautiful places was just beginning, but for the people who already lived there, it suddenly meant money and jobs. The 1920s were a Busby Berkeley spectacular of growth and glitter throughout North America, the prolonged boom before the Depression-era bust, and the Canadian Rockies got its share. For years the railroads had dreamed of opening "chateau"-style hotels up and down the Rockies; the largest for years was the Banff Springs Hotel, which opened in 1888 and accommodated 280 well-heeled guests. Banff was Canada's first national park, just as Yellowstone was America's, and upper-crust tourists from all over rode the rails to the wood-frame turreted structure that enclosed the waters of the local hot springs. The success of Banff was replicated elsewhere. In 1907, the area surrounding Jasper was set aside for parklands, and in 1927 this was extended south to Bow Pass, approaching Banff.

The railroads imported mountaineering guides from Europe to lead climbing groups into the Rockies and the Selkirks; a Challenge of the Mountains promotional campaign showed a shapely young female climber dressed in a red wool sweater, jodhpurs, and calf-length climbing boots pointing invitingly at Banff's mountains. By Frank's arrival in 1924, the Jasper Park Lodge, another Banff-style chateau, was in its early construction stages; it too would be a turreted redoubt with magnificent views of the mountains, world-class chefs in the kitchen, climbing excursions for all skill levels, and the best shooting and fishing around.

Frank, Ruth, and their two children came to Jasper on June 16, 1924. They stayed that summer in temporary dwellings on the site of the Jasper Lodge. That first summer he worked as caretaker of a local school and then, during the winter, got a job as storekeeper for William S. Jeffrey, a genial man he'd met through his old friend MacRae.

Frank and Ruth fell in love with Jasper. Something about the place seemed sublime. It was a town of rustic architecture, cobblestones, and timber that lay in the heart of the Athabasca River valley; from town they could look out and see the surrounding mountains—the Whistlers, Signal Mountain, Mount Kerr, Old Man, and even Mount Edith Cavell, twenty-two miles away. It was a town where deer roamed the lawns and had to be skirted on sidewalks; where bears grubbed through the garbage and a man could be fined for throwing a rock at one. The town physician, Dr. O'Hagen, made house calls with his cane and his little dog Pepper, his vest pockets stuffed with nickels for the children. Late at night, they could stand outside and hear the hounds of hunters baying on the track of a cougar or bear.

A year after their arrival, their third child, Marie Leona, was born, on October 25, 1925. That same year, the provincial election approached and Colonel James V. Cornwall, a pioneer legislator, was asked to create a slate of candidates from Canada's remote regions. Cornwall had known Frank as Jim Fahey for a long time and asked if he would run. Frank said he'd only lived in Jasper for a year so far and declined the honor, though his true reasons were more cautious ones. Cornwall pressed his friend, almost certain he would win: Fahey was a strong promoter of amateur sports, a churchman of influence, a builder and contractor, a one-time journeyman carpenter who'd helped build up the remote lands of Canada. Frank was touched: Did people really feel that strongly about him? Was he really so well liked? What would become of that regard if they found out the truth? He declined again, reluctantly, and the matter rested there.

By 1925, Frank had returned to the construction business, going into partnership with a new pal, Jack McCaw. He built his own house on 719 Maligne Street. Since this was Dominion land, he could not actually buy the property but easily acquired it on a 49-year lease from the government. Every winter he and McCaw worked on the Jasper Lodge, which always seemed to be expanding; the two of them framed and finished nearly half the town's municipal buildings, including St. Martha's Hospital. Folks liked his house so much they asked him to build similar homes for them. By 1929, the year the Great Depression hit in Jasper as it did in Canada, America, and the rest of the world, Frank could honestly say that just as he'd done in Spirit River and Peace River, he'd helped build this corner of the world.

By then, Frank sometimes took long walks in the woods surrounding Jasper, just to be alone. Newcomers had to be careful up here: the altitude seemed to do something to their senses and they'd wander off in confusion. One summer a soldier recently discharged from the Philippines war stepped off the train and disappeared. The Mounties did not find his body in the forest until weeks later, by which time his bones were picked clean by wolves. By now, though, Frank knew his way around. There was still snow in the small hills and valleys of the back country, even in June. The water was crystal clear and cold. The ground was spongy with alpine furze and moss; lodgepole pine towered overhead. He rounded a corner in the trail and spotted a caribou on the other end of the meadow guarding her newborn calf; the cows could be as threatening as bears in the calving season, and he raised his walking stick overhead to make himself look bigger. With a snort, the mother and calf walked off; he waited another couple of minutes to give them time. Everything was quiet out here, and he was the intruder. The only living things that did not seem cautious were the sparrows, which hopped from branch to branch and watched his every move.

It was easy to believe during these walks that Frank Grigware had never existed, that he'd always been Jim Fahey and Leavenworth was just a product of bad digestion and unwanted dreams. His life in prison seemed too long ago to be real. His son Jack was becoming a young outdoorsman and liked to fish with his father. His eyes were brown, not blue, like Frank's, but they had the same straight look; his hands were long and lean, with Frank's long fingers; he had the same silences. Louise played the piano, and was shy and reserved. Marie was the lively one, and no one was a stranger to her. When anyone came in the house, she grabbed a book and climbed on their knee, demanding that they read to her. By now, Frank was captain of the curling club, and people called him a sportsman. These forests were like the Coeur d'Alenes to him, silent and magnificent. He laughed at that thought. It was such a long time since his dream of quick riches in the Coeur d'Alenes.

By now he'd hiked into the deeper woods, where his progress was slower, and at times it was harder to pass through. There were fallen trees on the slopes and he had to avoid their branches, but that was difficult because the light grew dusky in the gloom beneath the trees. Still, he was not afraid. Occasionally there'd be an opening in the canopy through which he could see the snowy peaks. Amid such grandeur he better felt his tininess—how small he seemed, how silly all his fears, unless somehow they were part of a bigger purpose or design. At such times, his thoughts turned to the subject of God. Ruth believed in God with a simple, direct belief that seemed to admit no questions, but in his youth, during the trial, during his time in prison, while he hid in the culvert outside Leavenworth and knew that at any second the dogs could find him—during all that, he'd known there was no such thing as God. God was a story parents told their children to make sure they obeyed the rules. If he ever thought of the Almighty it was in negative terms. He remembered the Reverend Pritchard's sermon one Sunday on poor Job: *Behold, I cry out of wrong, but I am not heard: I cry aloud, but there is no judgment.* Why, like Job, were men and women built up in their hopes only to watch them knocked to the ground like sticks? Why did honest people seem the playthings of the corrupt and powerful? Maybe the answer was beyond understanding, Pritchard lamented, or maybe the answer could be found in Job's cries. *Behold, the fear of the Lord, that is wisdom; and to depart from evil is understanding.* Frank thought he'd lived in fear so long, he probably had wisdom to burn.

But these days were different. Maybe he'd been wrong. He seemed a lucky man after all. Maybe all men and women suffered through some period of their life, and the suffering made them better. Maybe his own suffering had taught him the value of patience. Maybe God was not a grand design. Maybe God was part of the details.

But sometimes events arrived from the outside world to remind him whom he had been and what could still be. In 1929, he read about the capture of an escaped American lifer in Edmonton. James Manning broke into summer houses in the woods south of Edmonton, then was caught trying to fence the stolen goods. It was a classic case of what happened if a fugitive succumbed to temptation and returned to his former ways. When he was arrested, a routine check of fingerprints revealed that James Manning was actually Roy James, a fugitive from the Iowa State Penitentiary, who'd broken out with two others on September 17, 1926. Roy James had been convicted of murder during a train robbery and sentenced on January 7, 1915, to life behind bars. Manning's wife, like Ruth, did not know about her husband's history. Frank recalled the inked whorls and loops of his fingerprints, which he'd disparaged that first day in Leavenworth; he read the story again but only found the briefest mention that Manning's fingerprints were checked in Ottawa against prints sent there by the U.S. Bureau of Investigation. Manning was sent back to Iowa to serve his life term. I am not a thief, Frank tried to assure himself. The same can't happen to me.

In 1931, Frank's partner, Jack McCaw, was suddenly killed. He was rounding a curve at Lake Beauvoir when he lost control of his car. Frank found it hard to take, for he and Jack had been friends and they worked together well. Yet the Depression gave few choices for starting over, and you did well to hang on to what you had. Sometimes these days he needed extra help, and he'd wander past the hobo jungle at the edge of town. He'd ask the 'bos if any were carpenters and wanted some work. He remembered how he'd been like them and wondered if any were running from the law.

The movies were the great escape from daily life, and every Saturday Frank took his family to the Chaba Theatre downtown. In Jasper, downtown was just a few blocks' walk away. The Chaba was a large theatre for the town, fronting the rail station, with art deco fittings and uniformed ushers. The chairs had wooden backs with a green upholstery of which Ruth approved. Before each weekend feature there'd be a raffle, and winners took home china dinner plates or sets of what was later called Depression glass. Frank often brought some prize home from these drawings. His family saw him as the lucky type, always winning something that way.

One night they walked to the Chaba as usual and Frank failed, as usual, to notice the name of the feature. He settled back as the Pathé newsreel showed the plight of the Bonus Marchers in Washington, D.C. On the screen slogged men who were ragged, apathetic, and weary, whose faces showed no hope: a crowd of twenty to eighty thousand war veterans who'd arrived by freight train to the capital from all over the country. They demanded relief in the form of their war bonus, a $500 certificate of compensation not due until 1945. They wanted passage of a bill that allowed immediate payment and felt that if Congress could give millions to bail out large industrialists, it should pay those who'd risked their lives serving their country. *Washington Star* editorialist Thomas R. Henry called their pleas a "flight from reality," for, he cynically reminded America, only the rich could lobby Congress for passage of such bills. As expected, the Senate ignored the marchers. Frank watched as the army, in which the veterans had served, swept down on them with tear gas, bayonets, and tanks, burning their tent cities and driving them away.

The film started: *I Am a Fugitive from a Chain Gang*, with Paul Muni. Frank watched as the movie charted the downward course of a man from war hero, to hobo, to unjustly railroaded criminal and fugitive. It was a bitter and uncompromising film, an enraged condemnation of a society in which the nation's best became the hunted and the chain gang stood for all America. Frank sat in the dark and blinked in surprise as Muni stepped off the train from the war and told his mother over supper, "I want to get out—build, construct, create, do things." Frank's heart sank as Muni's film mother answered, "Follow your heart. You've got to be happy, got to find yourself," and Muni took off across America on construction jobs. It was as if Frank were watching his own life, as if the writers stole their story straight from his experiences. He glanced to the side, and Ruth and the children were munching their snacks, oblivious to him. Frank watched as Muni was unjustly charged with a robbery, as he was sent to a chain gang where another convict said, "There's just two ways to get out of here. Walk out or die out." Frank stared as Muni escaped and fled north; as the WANTED posters circulated throughout the country; as Muni changed his name and became a builder, specializing in bridges. He said to a girl that he liked: "Roads, bridges, for people to use when they want to get away from things. But they can't get away." The girl, who was small and petite like Ruth, looked at him and smiled. "You're a strange, moody person," she told him. "You need someone to pull you out of your doldrums."

Frank was sweating now, for he knew exactly where the movie was headed. He wanted to yell warnings to Muni but knew that would be madness. He wanted to leap from his seat and escape, but to do so would give himself away. He gripped the armrests as, at the height of his success, Muni was discovered by the law. Two detectives came with their cuffs; the northern city where he lived fought the extradition order; the local newspapers emphasized the story of a man who, regardless of his innocence or guilt, had made good. *Are we not a merciful people?* his defenders asked. *Haven't we progressed beyond simple vengeance to a higher order of justice?* The publicity grew so hot that the prison authorities relented. They said they were willing to make a deal. If Muni returned to the chain gang voluntarily and paid all expenses, he'd be paroled in ninety days.

"Can you trust them?" Ruth—no, the girlfriend—asked.

"I don't see why not. Besides, I want to get it all cleared up," Muni answered. "I'll be free, always, and we'll be together, always."

A train took Muni south back to prison; Frank felt a twinge of panic as on the screen it headed straight at him. It looked like the Leavenworth train. Once Muni arrived, the prison officials went back on their word, just as Frank knew they would. "Crime must be punished," snapped one official. "Hard men must be punished. The purpose of prison is to crush and discourage crime." Frank watched silently as Muni was told he would stay in the chain gang indefinitely. He remembered what it felt like as his on-screen doppelgänger seemed to go crazy. He knew that the only thing left, besides death, was to escape again.

Which he did. Another year passed. Muni hid outside his girlfriend's house and called to her when she came home. He was a bearded hobo, dressed in gray tattered clothes. She reached for him, but he backed off, not wanting to pass his infection to her. "I haven't escaped," he told her. Frank knew the words by heart. "They're still after me. They'll always be after me. Keep running, that's all that's left for me."

"How will you live?" Ruth asked. Footsteps approached and

Frank's face faded into the shadows. He answered from the darkness, "I'll steal!"

That night, as they all walked home and the children skipped ahead, Ruth grabbed his hand and asked why he was so silent. Did his old nation trouble him? It seemed such a violent and unforgiving place. Frank just shook his head and answered, "The movie made me sad."

That night, as the others slept, he remembered being seen by Herb Fife in Edmonton and knew that somehow, somewhere, a net was tightening around him.

That night, as his family dreamed, Frank's nightmares began.

❧ CHAPTER TWELVE ❧

The Net

ALTHOUGH A NET *had* tightened around him, the hand guiding its progress was still unsure. Frank's pursuers worked on instinct, sensing rather than knowing that they were on the right track, believing that in all likelihood he had escaped to Canada yet unsure where he had gone to ground. They hoped that, like James Manning, Frank would make a mistake that gave away his presence. But Frank Grigware was smart, and after more than two decades of freedom, the Leavenworth fugitive was either exceptionally canny, unusually lucky, or dead. And so they cast a wide net and waited, hoping that the day-to-day challenges of surviving the Great Depression would make Frank slip up, if only for a second yet long enough to give himself away.

The Depression brought desperation into nearly everyone's lives. When the New York Stock Exchange lost $30 billion during those black weeks in autumn 1929, the Western world's economies crashed with it—and none so hard as Canada's. Heavily dependent on the export of grain and raw materials, the Dominion of Canada suddenly saw this lifeline pulled back as former customers retreated into economic nationalism. Nearly a quarter of all Canadian wage earners were thrown out of work; tens of thousands of young men drifted from town to town by road and rail. In Alberta the prairie regions suffered worst, the wheat farmers hit three ways at once—by drought, a plague of locusts, and the plummeting grain market. Thousands of farm families verged on starvation, barely kept going by government relief that did not meet its own prescribed survival levels; in 1934 a family of five received $32.36 a month or $388 annually, barely half the $700 set by the government as the minimum poverty level.

Frank tried to avoid that route. He figured he'd weathered worse, and at first he hoped to weather this as well. Relief recipients received vouchers instead of cash, which branded them as indigents. Whether they knew it by the old name or not, Americans and Canadians both still bowed to the Gospel of Wealth, especially during the prosperous 1920s. Success went to the deserving—until, in one ruinous swath, the middle class watched their jobs and savings vanish and their banks foreclose on their mortgages. If wealth came by merit, unemployment meant personal failure. What happened to the continental dance of prosperity that seduced Americans and Canadians alike? Had it all been a lie?

Frank had ridden this wheel before. He'd gone from young dreamer and suitor to criminal, from convict to fugitive, from wanted man to man of substance in successive rapid spins. As everyone else enjoyed the 1920s prosperity, the cattle market plummeted and he'd dropped to the bottom. He'd worked his way up before and knew comebacks were possible, but this time the options were limited. Even if one held a job, a dollar could be a day's wages, or the wages for two or three days. And that low-paying job could suddenly vanish without warning. Money, once a necessity, now became an obsession, the subject mushrooming in popular culture. The board game Monopoly was born, the fantasy of amassing millions in fake money being better than the reality of having next to none. Hollywood churned out more comedies about the rich than dramas about the poor. Politicians in Canada and America alike rose to power by promising hard cash to voters. From every RCA Victor, Capehart, Philco, and Spartan radio streamed songs of money in various keys. Some songs were wistful, like "We're In the Money," others cynical, like "Life Is Just a Bowl of Cherries." Some were as bleak as the Depression itself, like "Brother, Can You Spare a Dime?"

Frank thought about money: a lot. Most folks in Jasper did. The mountain town depended on the railroad for jobs and tourists, and, though not as devastated as the prairie regions, it too was hit hard.

Railroaders were laid off, many forced to take relief. The tourist trade fell flat, closing inns, stores, and restaurants that depended on their business or trimming their hours to subsistence levels. There was a smell to poverty, a musty smell that ate at the frayed edges of trust and hope until finally they gave way to bitterness and morbidity. It was the last that caused people to fall "accidentally" from twelve-story windows. The newspapers always seemed surprised by Depression-era suicides or family murder; variations on the theme "Nothing wrong with his accounts; happily married" were common. In Canada, the papers were filled with stories that writer Pierre Berton would later call "death by Depression." A migrant worker in Cabri, Saskatchewan, could not bear the shame of poverty when arrested for vagrancy and killed himself with a .22 rifle on his release from jail. A man in Ste. Perpétue, Quebec, beat his four sleeping children to death with a hammer in his despair over the loss of his farm. The stories never focused on the dwindling bank balance, the determination that loved ones would live an accustomed style of life, the stiff upper lip taught by the stern grandmother from the old country.

Having been through it before, Frank was more sensitive to the signs in others. He wondered at what stage one's poverty became apparent to strangers. Was it the wearing of the same suit, so obsessively brushed and pressed that it finally became shiny in the knees and elbows? Was it a sudden droop in the shoulders that hadn't been there yesterday? A look in the eyes that changed overnight from hope to furtiveness?

The nights were bad for everyone, Frank included, when all a man could see was darkness ahead. He went over in his mind everything he'd done to avert the inevitable. He went over his life insurance policies and realized with a start that he was worth more dead to his family than alive. He went over the dwindling bank balance like counting sheep: "three hundred and forty dollars," "two hundred and ninety," "two hundred and forty-five." When dawn broke, he was still awake. The birds outside were singing, happy in their ignorance of such things as salary. He'd heard of men who stopped every clock in the house, as if that could stop the dollars' trickle. People got leaner and more close-mouthed with each passing day.

Frank had thought his past experiences might toughen him to the hardships, but by January 1934 he too was being worn down. He was almost forty-six and Ruth was not yet forty; they had been in

Jasper for ten years, a long time. He'd already been president of the curling club; she, a member of good standing in the Ladies' Auxiliary. The Depression had settled so firmly in their lives and those of their neighbors that sometimes it was hard to recall prosperity. In small towns like this there was a safety net; everyone was in the same boat, and together they'd sink or swim. No one actually starved, but the big problem was lack of money. In spring, Frank had debts to pay. The mortgage and other bills were coming due. The Depression brought construction work to a standstill, and the Jasper Lodge, that old standby, had not bid on jobs since tourism slacked off in 1931 or 1932. Over the summer he was able to find small repairs, but with winter this too tightened up until there was no work at all. People he knew, railroad men, owed him for work, but they were out of work themselves. He could have pressed for payment, even threatened to take them to court, but he remembered too well what it was like to have his back up, and he hated it when someone put themselves out to pay.

"You're too easy, Jim Fahey," Ruth chided. "They have debts but we have debts, too." She made him promise to ask for payment, but she knew there was no heart in his words. She'd fallen in love with him for his decency toward others; now that decency could be their downfall. His friends called him generous, but the truth was he couldn't bear to bring pain to others. He'd done it in the past to the ones who'd trusted him most. He couldn't do it again.

Sometimes, late at night, he lay awake as Ruth slept beside him, searching for a way free that he might have missed. There was a natural cycle of feast and famine for carpenters, made a hundred times worse by the Depression. Even in the best of times there was little carpentry work during the winter and the debts piled up; the saving grace had been that people immediately needed work done with the spring. This spring the debts would be the worst they'd ever faced, yet this time there was no guaranteed relief from contracts coming in.

What could he do? Sometimes he thought about hopping a freight to a southern state, where there might be work the entire year. He'd live frugally in a flophouse, hoarding his pay and sending it back to Ruth to head off debt this spring. Surely no one was looking for him now. He looked nothing like his old mug shots taken in 1909. He'd aged by a quarter century. True, the blue eyes and dark hair were the same, but his cheeks had sunken, all boyish fat in his face and body long gone. The United States had enough problems without worrying about the ramblings of one lone fugitive.

Yet his fate was still tied to his birthplace, just as—for better or worse—the fates of the two nations were tied. When the American stock markets crashed, Canada was the first country to follow; in the financial and social chaos that followed, both nations' economies spiraled downward together. The United States was already invested in Canada's resources: as America's banking system collapsed, taking with it nearly $3 billion of depositors' savings, Canadian banks and businesses also started to fold. By 1932, a quarter of America's work force was unemployed, the same percentage as in Canada. The U.S. money supply dwindled by 33 percent; unemployment in major cities like Chicago, New York, and Toledo ranged from 50 to 80 percent; the drought and hardship that hit the Great Plains of America spread to the High Plains of Canada, forcing up to a third of all farmers in both nations off their lands. In 1930, three years before Franklin Delano Roosevelt swept Herbert Hoover from office with his vow of a New Deal, Canada's Conservative Party leader Richard B. Bennett knocked Liberal perennial Mackenzie King from the premiership with similar promises. "Mackenzie King promises you conferences," Bennett thundered, "I promise you action. He promises consideration of the problem of unemployment, I promise to end unemployment. Which plan do you like best?" In America, Hoover's name became synonymous with blight: there were "Hoover blankets" (newspapers used to ward off cold), "Hoovervilles" (the shanty towns of the homeless), and "Hoover flags" (pockets that were empty of money and turned inside out). When Bennett's promises turned out to be worthless, his name was similarly disparaged: "Bennett buggies" were cars pulled by horses or oxen because the owners could no longer afford gasoline. The thousands standing in breadlines and soup kitchens in America looked exactly like the thousands queued up in Canada. Hunger and poverty did not stop at the forty-ninth parallel.

If one thing separated the two nations, it was the violence in America. Its continuing crime, murder, and corruption apparently resisted all efforts at control or comprehension. To Canadians and Americans alike, the violence was a self-made monster that had been unleashed at some uncertain point in the past and now ran out of control. Though each decade found a new expression, the basic violence remained. The 1890s had seen the last gasp of the Old West; the early 1900s, labor violence; the 1920s, Prohibition and the Roaring Twenties; the 1930s, gun battles between cops and criminals, both sides armed with tommy guns, the new weapon of choice in the peacetime war. In the 1920s, Canadians read lurid accounts of rumrunning, bootlegging, Al Capone, "Legs" Diamond, "Bugs" Moran, gangsters and rackets, the St. Valentine's Day Massacre, murder as a trade. In the 1930s, the headlines screamed of the kidnapping of Charles Lindbergh's baby, John Dillinger, Machine Gun Kelly, Pretty Boy Floyd, the Barker-Karpis gang, and Bonnie and Clyde. Sometimes the violence jumped the border, as in the snatching of Ottawa brewery king John Labatt one week after the Lindbergh kidnapping, but such instances were rare. In many ways the experiences of Canadians and Americans seemed interchangeable, yet the violence set them apart. What caused America's Frankenstein?

Friends often asked Frank this question. A Canadian like them, he was still "Jim Fahey from the States," thus acknowledging that in some crucial sense he inhabited both worlds. If they only knew the half of it, Frank thought, taking care to keep such musings to himself. Was the American man innately homicidal, walking around with a gun in his pocket in the same manner that a carpenter hung a hammer from his belt? What explained the American veneration for firearms? Fathers gave sons a rifle as a rite of passage; respectable ladies could buy a .22-caliber Young America Ladies' Revolver from the Sears, Roebuck catalog. Frank was of two minds when his Canadian friends asked such questions, though he didn't let on. He'd never felt particularly murderous, yet he too had carried a gun, the .38 Colt purchased in Spokane as protection from cougars, the same gun used as evidence against him in his trial. He'd never pointed it at anyone during his trip across the interior West, yet its presence made him feel safe just by being there. The fact that he was seen carrying it did nothing but damn him to the jury, yet the same western jurors probably felt owning a firearm was every American's right. If pressed, they would have said there were times a man wasn't complete without his gun.

Frank never thought twice about it back in the States, but now, in another country, America's ties to guns and violence seemed as virulent to him as any germ or virus, worse than the flu that killed millions or the tuberculosis that plagued Jack and Fritz Torgensen, and cut short the lives of the prisoners in Leavenworth and his brother Joe. It passed down the generations, repeating through the years. The new "social bandits" like Bonnie and Clyde and John Dillinger were glorified and romanticized in the same way that the James boys and Butch Cassidy had been. Each brand of outlaw rode across the same landscape, whether on the backs of fast horses or behind the wheels of fast cars; they struck at the same banks and big businesses that were still seen as preying on the working man. An inevitable doom followed in their tracks, whether in the form of Pinkertons hunting Jesse James, the Bureau chasing Dillinger, or the lawmen of Texas pursuing Bonnie and Clyde. The press started each morning with headlines of the latest sightings or victims, feeding off the doom. Lawmen made their careers from the hunt, gaining power and status as the chase grew to mythic proportions, an epic struggle between good and evil, aided in the telling by the bandits, the lawmen, the media. Everyone danced Death's crazy reel.

From Frank's aerie in the mountains it was as if he could take a longer view and watch the contagion spread. The social violence that began in 1866 with the James-Younger gang stretched in a long crooked trail of personal connections and tradition to John Dillinger and Charles "Pretty Boy" Floyd. It formed a bloodline, like a red-stained family tree. Even after the James-Younger gang broke up, following their last disastrous bank raid in Northfield, Minnesota, their style of armed gang robbery was carried through the 1880s by Belle Starr, Cole Younger's common-law wife, and in the 1890s by the Dalton gang. The Daltons, kindred of the Youngers, were wiped out in 1892 when trying to rob two banks at once in Coffeyville, Kansas. A host of imitators followed, from legends like the Wild Bunch to flash-in-the-pans like the Mud Cut Gang. One of the most serious perpetrators of the tradition was Belle Starr's nephew, Henry Starr, who robbed his first bank by horse and his last bank, during which he was killed in 1916 by a shotgun blast to the face, by car.

The violence begat a meanness that seemed to resist all efforts at control. A large part of the failure could be blamed on the forces of "good." Frank had seen the failure from the inside, one of the truths about himself he never told his Canadian friends. He'd seen the brutality of his keepers in Leavenworth, the sheer love of power practiced daily by Deputy Lemon and his cronies, far worse than anything he'd seen among the inmates. He'd seen the way the Pinkertons and the prosecutors twisted the facts of the Mud Cut Robbery to ensure convictions and make examples of them all. The men he'd known in Leavenworth had come to prison down a hundred different routes, yet the treatment they received from those in power seemed a blueprint for bitterness, sure to keep them on the criminal road. The very ones to sabotage the Leavenworth experiment had been the ones entrusted with its care; the foxes ran the henhouse. As long as it wasn't too obvious, no one seemed to mind. As the guards grew more corrupt, the inmates grew more brutal. A good man who came in as a guard either quit or became brutal to survive. When a man was finally released, his days flowed in a haze of anger, and his nights were punctuated by dreams of revenge. *That* was the legacy of Leavenworth and the other prisons inspired by its example. *That* was the dance lasting through the generations.

Supreme Court Justice Louis Brandeis voiced this fear during the 1928 wiretapping case *Olmstead v. United States*, but his cautionary note of dissension placed him on the losing side. He wrote:

> Decency, security, and liberty alike demand that government officials shall be subjected to the same rules of conduct that are commands to the citizen. In a government of laws, existence of the government will be imperiled if it fails to observe the law scrupulously. Our government is the potent, the omnipresent teacher. For good or for ill, it teaches the whole people by its example. Crime is contagious. If the government becomes a lawbreaker, it breeds contempt for law; it invites every man to become a law unto himself; it invites anarchy. To declare that in the administration of the criminal law the end justifies the means—to declare that the government may commit crimes in order to secure the conviction of a private criminal—would bring terrible retribution.

Sometimes Frank wondered if the nightmare he'd lived in Leavenworth hadn't leaked through the high walls into all of America. Surely there were communities in America like Jasper, where people banded together for the common good and made a tough life at least bearable. Where friends took care of friends, and daily decency was honored with a nod of thanks and a silent smile. Yet these days a meanness seemed pervasive, a coarsening of feeling that invaded all men. "We are now engaged in a war that threatens our country," U.S. Attorney General Homer Cummings said in 1933, in calling for a national war on crime. The true war was waged on an unseen level between agents of the law and anyone who was poorer or different. Sometimes Frank still wandered to the hobo jungle to see if he could recruit the occasional worker. They were young like he had been when he'd ridden the rods. Some had come from the States and had a haunted look in their eyes. He dropped enough hints for them to know he'd been in their shoes too. With those who were willing to talk, he asked what it was like in Depression-era America.

It was murder, they said. Perhaps they'd lived stories like those Frank saw in the magazines. One boy said there was a war on between police and blacks; he'd heard a policeman in Charleston, South Carolina, say that his ambition was to kill a Negro. "I almost did it once," he'd bragged. "I arrested a nigger and he put up some show of resistance, so I threw my club on the ground and said, 'Pick it up, you goddamn son of a bitch!' and he reached to get it, had it in his hand, but dropped it like it was a coal of fire. In another minute I'da shot his brains out. And there was my defense: nigger resists arrest, grabs club, starts to attack officer of the law."

The war wasn't limited to race. Differences in circumstance seemed enough to call forth some atavistic impulse, a bloodthirstiness that seemed ready to spring forth at any time. Another boy told of leaving Atlanta by rail with three other "wild boys."

> We were rounded up in the railroad yards by five detectives carrying pistols and shotguns. They caught eighteen or twenty of us after beating the bushes about the yards. They herded us to a bank beside the railroad, all of us young, none over twenty-five except a middle-aged man looking for a place by some river to jungle-up for the winter. They examined us for scars from shackles, threatened us with three months in the chain gang. I saw one of the cops go a short distance away, take all the cartridges from his pistol, then return and sit down close to a tough-looking young man. The cop's pistol butt was in easy reach of the boy's hand. Another cop was watching. Had the boy grabbed the empty pistol from the cop's holster he would have been shot to give the other tramps a lesson, to keep them out of Atlanta.

Frank heard these tales and abandoned all thoughts of tramping through the southern states. Something had happened to his old home that was terrifying. If he went south and the law caught him, he'd never return to Jasper alive. But that still didn't solve the problem of money. He asked Ruth if she had any ideas. Calm as always, she answered that something always turned up in the spring.

IF ANY ONE group benefited from the Great Depression, it was the body soon to be known as the Federal Bureau of Investigation. That appellation would not be given until 1935, but in 1933–34 J. Edgar Hoover's "G-men" were already national heroes for their highly publicized wars against the mobile midwestern criminals. The Lindbergh kidnapping in 1932, followed quickly by the exploits of Dillinger, Bonnie and Clyde, and others, convinced the public it was gripped by a "crime wave" at the very moment when the crime rate actually declined. The end of Prohibition and the Depression saw the first time in the twentieth century when America witnessed a *decrease* in the numbers of crimes. The homicide rate dropped by 50 percent between 1933 and the early 1940s; the rate of other serious crimes—rape, robbery, burglary, and assault—dropped by a third. But falling crime rates were not in the best interests of the Bureau's tenacious and ambitious director. Instead, by exaggerating the threat of crime and posing as the last bulwark of law and order at a time when economic collapse heightened public fears of chaos, Hoover was able to expand the size and scope of his agency. He became a master of public relations, cultivating his image for political advantage and, in the process, becoming a major force in creating the crime hysteria of the 1930s.

In some very important ways, director Hoover was a new breed of government functionary. He was among the first to understand the role of the mass media in shaping public attitudes. Disturbed by Hollywood's glamorization of criminals, he committed himself to the creation of an alternate image—the cop as hero. He skillfully manipulated the media by transforming a group of otherwise ordinary criminals into "public enemies," and standing fearless against them was the almost superhuman Bureau agent; stalwart, professional, and relentlessly efficient. The top agent, of course, was Hoover himself.

Something strange began to develop in the press and popular culture of the 1930s, an almost Manichaean struggle between the forces of light and dark, an epic and unending war between cops and criminals for America's very soul, a theme that continues today. Hoover understood instinctively that great heroes need to do battle with great villains, and so the lone Dillingers of the Midwest suddenly saw their reputations inflated to the vanguards of the advancing legions of crime. It was the same technique used by the Bureau's predecessors, the Pinkertons, first with the train robbers and then with the "underground" of yeggmen and anarchists, when the Founder and his sons pitched their agency as the last defense of their corporate clientele. John Dillinger himself became the most famous criminal in the Bureau's history. In late 1933 and early 1934, Dillinger was robbing banks and businesses in Indiana and Ohio when he was caught and thrown in jail in Crown Point County, Indiana. It was there he pulled the brazen trick that made headlines around the world and put him on the Bureau's hit list. On March 3, 1934, he talked his way out of jail by waving a fake wooden gun, locked a succession of guards in prisoners' cells, stole the sheriff's car, and drove to Chicago. By driving a stolen car across state lines, he put himself within the Bureau's jurisdiction. Across the West and Midwest, his escape revived memories of the similar Leavenworth escape, and a few newspapers carried stories of the 1910 breakout, mistakenly identifying Frank as "Fred."

By then, Hoover's reformed agency had been quietly looking for Frank for years. During this time, Hoover had transformed the Bureau of Investigation in well-nigh miraculous ways. Soon after his appointment as director in 1924, Hoover fired the deadwood, cutting the number of agents to 339 and closing twenty offices across the nation. He closed the Buzzard's Roost, a room where agents had swapped dirty stories while polishing off a bottle. He realized that to change the image of his organization he must change the image of his men, and he did this with a fervor that approached religiosity. New agents had to be between twenty-five and thirty-five years old, with a background in law or accounting; they were paid $2,700 a year, plus travel allowances, and were expected to go anywhere in the United States at any time. They arrived at work dressed in a pressed suit, white shirt, conservative tie, and plain straw hat. They signed an oath of office, in the early days a terse statement promising to defend the Constitution "against all enemies, foreign and domestic," which changed in time to a catechism:

> Humbly recognizing the responsibilities entrusted to me, I do vow that I shall always consider the high calling of law enforcement to be an honorable profession, the duties of which are recognized as both an art and a science . . . in the performance of my duties I shall, as a minister, seek to supply comfort, advice, and aid . . . as a soldier, I shall wage vigorous warfare against the enemies of my country . . . as a physician, I shall seek to eliminate the criminal parasite which preys on our body politic . . . as an artist, I shall seek to use my skill for the purpose of making each assignment a masterpiece.

Hoover thought of his agency in superlatives, and his belief that everything in the Bureau was "the best" filtered down to newcomers. One agent remembered how the instructors explained that the FBI motto "We never close a case" was better than the mounties' "We always get our man." The agent added, "It was difficult to understand why, since never closing a case meant never solving it, but no one wanted to contradict our serious and hard-working instructors."

Of even more importance for the Bureau's growth was its emphasis on scientific crime detection, adopting and expanding the national theme started by Allan Pinkerton. The aura of modern science became a major dimension of the Bureau's image during these hard years. In 1930, Hoover won the responsibility for administrating the landmark Uniform Crime Reports (UCR) system, the nation's first national crime-record system, in effect becoming America's clearing house for reports of "crimes known to the police." In 1932, the Bureau opened its crime laboratory for the examination of hair and blood specimens, firearms, and other evidence from crime scenes. Yet nothing would reflect the Bureau's power and centrality to police work more than its huge index of fingerprint files.

Hoover seemed to have a genuine mania for prints; he loved his collection as a lepidopterist loves his tagged butterflies. When he moved into his office in 1924, he brought with him several boxes containing 10,000 dog-eared fingerprint cards from William Pinkerton's brainchild, the National Bureau of Criminal Identification. Hoover also took over Leavenworth's file of 800,000 fingerprint cards, accumulating ever since Matthew McLaughry started his single-handed experiment in identification in 1904. The cards would be the key to Hoover's growing empire, changing a small agency with limited jurisdiction to a facility upon which all state and local police departments came to depend. During the 1920s and 1930s, the fingerprint bureau grew from a small file room to a huge L-shaped clearinghouse situated high in the Department of Justice. Hoover accomplished such exponential growth by persuading the nation's police chiefs that a centralized fingerprint system was essential in an increasingly mobile country. The media blitz emphasizing the mobility of Dillinger, Ma Barker, and the others enhanced this strategy. When local forces started sending copies of their print files to Washington, numbering in the thousands daily, the increase in arrests proved Hoover right.

The decade of the 1930s saw the consolidation of the Director's empire. On March 1, 1932, the international exchange of fingerprints was initiated between the Bureau's Identification Division and other nations. The exchange had already been going on with Canada on an informal basis, but now it became official. On February 15, 1933, a Latent Fingerprint Section was established, and on November 10, 1933, the U.S. Civil Service Commission turned the prints of 140,000 government employees and applicants over to the Bureau. Because of this, the Civil Identification Section was established. It would soon dwarf the criminal files. By 1939, the number of sets of prints controlled by the FBI totaled slightly less than 10.8 million.

By 1933, J. Edgar Hoover had amassed one of the greatest tools for social control ever seen in America, greater than the Pinkertons' criminal files, greater even than Hoover's own card index that he'd used with such success during the 1919 Red Scare. Yet Hoover had greater plans. As the success of his fingerprint files became obvious, he envisioned a "Universal Fingerprinting" system in which the prints of every citizen, innocent or guilty of crimes, would be held on file. With August Vollmer, head of the Berkeley, California, police force from 1905 to 1932 and principal author of the 1931 Wickersham Commission's *Report on Police*, as well as other prominent politicians and law enforcement officials, Hoover began advocating taking the prints of every American citizen. By 1935–36, a national campaign had started to voluntarily secure every citizen's prints. Such prominent Americans as Walt Disney, John D. Rockefeller, Jr., and even

President Roosevelt submitted their prints to Hoover's Civil Identification Division. Local officials embarked on similar campaigns in several cities: in Berkeley, for example, Vollmer's influence convinced half the population to voluntarily submit their fingerprints. Within two years the campaign died out, yet Hoover's organization continued its relentless collection. By 1946, it would collect its hundred millionth fingerprint card, making it the largest repository of fingerprint files in the world.

It was a fantastically swift accretion of power—more power than had ever been wielded by any single public or private lawman in the entire history of the United States. The rise truly accelerated with the 1934 "Public Enemy" campaign against Dillinger and his ilk, and by 1936 would put Hoover beyond criticism when his universal fingerprinting campaign fizzled. Even then there were warnings that Hoover was being allowed—by the President and Congress, by the nation's police chiefs, and by the enamored American public—far too much state-sanctioned control. When warnings did leak to the press, they were buried on inside pages, kept brief, or ignored. One such moment came in early March 1934, when U.S. Attorney General Cummings and the Bureau embarked on their campaign of "Shoot to kill, then count ten" against Dillinger. At that point, though state warrants had been issued against him for escape, murder, and robbery, Dillinger had committed no federal offense other than driving a stolen car across state lines. It was an offense for which "the offender is seldom shot on the spot," noted Turner Catledge, Washington correspondent for the *New York Times*.

During this time the search for Frank Grigware pushed forward slowly, involving untold man-hours by field agents in Chicago, Kansas City, Omaha, Seattle, Spokane, Portland, and Butte, Montana. Hoover was always in the background, directing the bureau chiefs (known as special-agents-in-charge, or SACs) to retrace old leads, goading them into swifter action when he considered an agent's or office's performance "rather superficial." Considering his other projects and obsessions of this period—consolidation of all fingerprint records and crime statistics, campaigns against kidnappers and the midwestern bandits, the spread of the Bureau's power in Washington and its growing influence over state and local jurisdictions—Hoover's micromanagement of affairs in the far-flung offices was phenomenal. He was already legendary among his agents as a hard taskmaster, more so than the Pinkertons' crusty James McParland had ever been. Minor transgressions by agents resulted in a letter of censure (every agent earned a stack of these); graver sins meant almost immediate transfer. The ultimate sanction, dismissal "with prejudice," meant a man could never again hope for federal employment or a expect a Bureau recommendation for another job. Nonetheless, the agents formed a close bunch, developing an esprit de corps that was the envy of other agencies and receiving better pay and fringe benefits than similar federal employees. Hoover expected each agent to be, like him, a Bureau man twenty-four hours a day, willing to pick up and follow every lead, willingly subject to the risk and draconian discipline that were considered natural parts of the job.

Why was Hoover given such free rein in the Bureau's early critical days? People tend to forget today the respect and admiration then given worldwide to public figures who moved swiftly and decisively, even when they turned authoritarian. Mussolini was admired for the efficiency he brought to the Italian train schedules; Hitler, because he "was doing something" about Germany's Depression. One of Hitler's greatest American admirers was Henry Ford, who'd made millions through efficiency and who now developed his own home-grown brand of fascist anti-Semitism. Huey Long, the near-dictator of Louisiana, was spoken of as a future President; Father Coughlin, a Canadian expatriate, who advocated by radio his own brand of authoritarian rule, had an immense following. Canadian Prime Minister R. B. Bennett was applauded for raging that revolutionaries be crushed under "the iron heel of ruthlessness."

Although the harried Bureau agents prospered or failed at Hoover's whim, and they acknowledged the fact by their private name for him, "Kid Napoleon," they seemed to love him and loathe him in equal measure. The twenties and thirties were hungry years, and the Bureau was an institutional home, a shelter from the chaotic world outside. In many ways, the agents who hunted Frank saw the Bureau in the same light as Frank saw Jasper—as a safe haven from the dangerous world outside. Instructors told new recruits that the Bureau was "the greatest organization ever devised by the human mind." They quoted Emerson's dictum, that an institution was "the lengthened shadow of one man," in this case Hoover's. The Bureau became their extended family, with Hoover, the patriarch, doling out punishment and praise.

THE BUREAU JUMP-STARTED its new effort to locate Frank by revisiting his family. In 1928, a distant cousin named J. H. Fahey, who worked as a post office inspector, was located in Los Angeles; though Fahey said he was "willing and even anxious to get information that might aid" in his cousin's arrest, he really knew nothing. Although Fahey's name itself was a tip-off for new investigative avenues, there were no indications that the Bureau got the hint. In 1929, agents reinterviewed Frank's mother, his brothers Jim and Eddie, and a sister in Seattle. All believed Frank had died in the Great War. Bureau agents interviewed his extended family in Michigan, who almost unanimously considered Frank a "family disgrace." They would gladly turn Frank over to the agents if they knew anything, they said.

In important ways, 1929 was a pivotal year in the search for Frank. That year saw the beginning of a wild goose chase that lasted through 1933. Paul Deford, married to Frank's first cousin Mary, part of the Michigan Grigwares, told an agent that he'd talked to a soldier, "name unknown, who was near [Frank] at the time of his death in France" during World War I. The Bureau immediately investigated the rumor. They checked the fingerprint records of the U.S. Army, Navy, Marine Corps, and Coast Guard: the army was the first to require fingerprints of new recruits in 1905, followed in 1907 by the navy, and quickly after that by the remaining services. Though the move showed an increasing reliance on fingerprint records, the agents only proved that Frank had not enlisted in the United States' armed services. By August 2, 1929, "a search of the records of the Department of Militia and Defense, Daly Building, Ottawa, Canada, fails to disclose that subject was ever in the Canadian Army." It was noted that "in the Canadian Army, the fingerprints are not taken of soldiers."

In 1931, Deford was contacted again and added more details. He said he was visiting Bay City, Michigan, and was sitting in a soft drink parlor when a wounded veteran dressed in uniform asked if he was the Paul Deford related to Frank Grigware. Deford said he was shocked: when he admitted to the veteran that he was indeed Frank's relation by marriage, the man said that Frank had fought in France under an assumed name, and "the same shell that had wounded him had killed" Frank Grigware. Unfortunately, Deford still could not remember the veteran's name. In May 1932, Deford remembered a little more: The veteran said Frank had enlisted in Detroit and now said his cause of death was from a bullet wound rather than shrapnel. Deford also said he had seen Frank in a Detroit saloon in 1917. On March 30, 1933, Deford's son finally decided to end this line of inquiry. Paul Deford was a drinking man, his son admitted, and "heard the rumor at the same time he had taken too much strong drink, and therefore, it was to be greatly discounted that he had been told anything of the kind."

The year 1929 saw the beginning of a push by Hoover to locate Frank's former criminal associates. By then, most had died or disappeared. Among the Mud Cut robbers, Bill Matthews was dead or dying in Portland, while Fritz Torgensen was known to have caught a freight train south from Spokane and was never seen again; he passed into oblivion, the most unstable and volatile of the Mud Cut crew, in all likelihood another hobo fatality whose body was plunked into a handy river or dropped into a shallow grave. Among those who broke out of prison with Frank, Bob Clark and John Gideon had similarly disappeared. Arthur Hewitt died in 1916, two years after his release from Leavenworth, and Teddy Murdock died in 1929 in Tacoma, Washington. Of the escapees, only Tom Kating was left, working peacefully as a tailor in downtown Tulsa, Oklahoma, his identity protected by members of his family.

That left Dan Downer and Jack Golden. Downer was reticent and reclusive. He had returned to his old ranch outside Spokane after his release from Leavenworth in June 1919, but the ranch went belly-up and he was not made welcome by police when he returned to Spokane. By 1929, he'd moved on. In 1931, agents tracked him to Helena, Montana, where it was rumored he'd been a bootlegger and highjacker during the Prohibition years. He'd been recently arrested for running a still and then released on bond. Agents found him on July 18, 1931, through his lawyer. Downer said he had not heard of Frank directly or indirectly since his escape in 1910. He said he'd actually watched the escape when it took place and had been floored when he saw Frank run for the train. Downer didn't believe the later rumor that Frank drowned while swimming the Missouri River. Grigware was smarter than that, he said.

Downer's words were useless, which left Jack Golden. Leavenworth had ruined Jack's life. These days he was a vagrant, tolerated only if he stayed away from the places he once called home. His pardon from Leavenworth had not come quickly enough, for he was a "lunger," racked by tuberculosis to the end of his days. Soon after Frank's escape he wrote to Frank's mother. Jennie Grigware never revealed the contents of that letter, yet after that she seemed to experience a change of heart toward Frank's old friend. Within a year of his 1913 release, he was running his father's ranch five miles northwest of Spokane. By 1914, his mother was dead and one of his brothers in Everett owned a hotel and other property while renting cribs to prostitutes. Jack's course after his release seemed continually downhill. In September 1917, he was charged in Missoula, Montana, with petty larceny. On July 14, 1921, he was charged in Spokane with disorderly conduct under the name John Gordon (a variation of Frank's alias in South Omaha); the charge was suspended on the condition that he leave town. He was arrested again in Spokane on July 24, 1927, for selling a stolen diamond; though acquitted, he was told again to leave. Things got worse. On March 28, 1928, he was charged in Spokane with driving while drunk; three months later he was again charged with vagrancy. In April 1930, he was charged with vagrancy in Portland. By then the Bureau was looking for him in earnest, convinced he had knowledge of Frank's hideaway. But Jack, thought to be a liquor runner going by the name of Tommy Burns, remained elusive. He was middle-aged like Frank, still running from his demons across the West, still hiding from the law. If he ever thought of his old friend, it was in the belief, shared with so many others, that he had died long ago. In Jack's case, he probably considered Frank the lucky one.

Yet for all these false starts, 1929 was also the year that the Bureau first learned of Herbert Fife's sighting of Frank in Edmonton in 1913 or 1914. Whether the clue first came through Jim Grigware or Fife himself is uncertain, but by October 15, 1929, the Seattle office gave details of Fife's close encounter in a letter to Hoover. On January 10, 1930, J. R. Burger, the SAC of the Bureau's Kansas City office, "respectfully" suggested to Hoover that the Bureau contact Catholic priests in Edmonton with a copy of Frank's photo, as well as contact the police and local lodges of the Knights of Columbus. "It is to be remarked that since the investigation has been instituted, Herbert Fife has been the only person located . . . who has seen Subject," Burger wrote. Shortly afterward, Hoover gave his imprimatur.

So it finally happened that twenty years after Frank's escape, in the first year of the decade that would forever be associated with the

Great Depression and the rise of Hoover's FBI, all eyes were trained to lonely Edmonton in Alberta, still a backwater at the time; Frank was two hundred miles due west, living high in the mountains. The Bureau started its campaign on a subdued, politic note. "If it is not too much trouble," wrote D. H. Dickason, SAC of the Butte, Montana, office, to RCMP colleagues based in the provincial headquarters in Calgary, "would you have this given such attention as you think it merits and have it ascertained, if possible, whether this man is still around Edmonton or is even there?" Frank's photo, Bertillon measurements, and fingerprints were sent to the RCMP's Criminal Investigation Branch in Edmonton, to the headquarters of the Alberta Provincial Police in Calgary, and to the RCMP's International Branch in Ottawa. By March 8, 1930, Alberta officials said they'd found no trace of Frank Grigware in the province, but added they had leads on a man named E. Hollingshead employed by the national railway at Macleod, where Frank helped build company houses during the winter of 1913. Ten days later, they wrote again. They'd found the man and checked both his prints and his feet. E. Hollingshead and Frank Grigware were not one and the same.

The search continued, looking for Frank's associates in prison, interviewing his family. Agents tried to find Alice and failed. In January 1933, "exhaustive inquiries" made in Alberta again turned up nothing, and by now it was evident that all the heart was out of the search for Leavenworth's most successful fugitive. True, if he was located it would prove beyond a shadow of a doubt Hoover's claims about the importance of the fingerprint system, and it would show the nation and the world the sheer doggedness of Hoover's G-men, already thought of as incorruptible, untouchable, and famous for their war against kidnappers and gunmen. Catching Frank would be more, much more, helping to transform the Bureau into the eye of the state, the omnipotent and far-reaching Gaze. Yet even the most zealous agents were being worn down by a chase that seemed neverending. Other investigations beckoned, and there were far more dangerous criminals. In all probability, they believed, Frank Grigware died long ago.

On March 31, 1933, the Chicago office—at the time one of the Bureau's most important field offices—gave the first hint in a letter to Hoover that the Grigware search was believed a lost cause: "Since it has been twenty-three years since the subject escaped from the

United States Penitentiary at Leavenworth, Kansas, it is being left to the sound discretion of the office of origin . . . whether his apprehension is still desired." There was no immediate answer. Two months later, on May 29, 1933, the Portland office tried. An unsigned memo to Hoover suggested that "apparently the only possible means whereby the subject will ever be located will be through fingerprints or possibly handwriting, there being little likelihood of his being identified from [his] photograph at this time." The memo added that the last picture taken of Grigware was taken when he was twenty-three. He would now be forty-seven, "if alive."

Again, there was no answer from Washington. We can only wonder what went through Hoover's mind. By now, Bureau instructors were teaching new recruits that "we never close a case"; by now, the Bureau tackled straightforward targets that offered easy prestige, and nothing was more straightforward than bringing to justice one of the most spectacular and brazen fugitives in American history. By now, Hoover was in the first stages of his campaign to establish universal fingerprinting, and finding Frank Grigware would only glorify that effort. If anything, Hoover played for time.

Finally, on December 5, 1933, C. C. Spears, SAC of the Portland office, took a chance. In a letter to the Director, he said what others had only hinted: "It is respectfully requested that permission be granted to close the file."

Hoover took sixteen days to decide. On December 21, 1933, in a letter to Spears, he answered:

> Dear Sir:
>   The Division has given consideration to your letter dated December 5, 1933, and concurs in the suggestion made by you that active investigation in this case be discontinued.
>   The Division, however, will not cancel the Identification Order in this case and will maintain the Wanted Notice now on file in the Identification Unit.
>
> Very truly yours,
> Director

By Christmas 1933, the active hunt for Frank was over. But the plain and tented arches, whorls, and loops of his inked fingerprints stayed on file.

*   *   *

THE NEWS WOULD have been welcomed by Frank, for God knows there was little enough good news that year. By late January 1934, no jobs were in the offing, and his mortgage was coming due. When a friend in similar straits suggested that they do some trapping in the park lands to make ends meet, Frank hesitated, then thought of his debts. True, it was poaching, a violation of park regulations, but few people in this part of the country saw much wrong with shooting the occasional deer or taking the odd fur. How often had his own workers done as much? his friend asked. What could happen? There were times when your family's welfare was a bit more important than game regulations, he told Frank, a direct if unintentional parallel with the motives of Jean Valjean, who stole bread to feed his family in Victor Hugo's *Les Miserables*. Frank let himself be talked into it, just as he'd let Jack Golden lull him into complacency when he suspected the boys from Spokane. In late February, as snow the size of Liberty dollars fell on Jasper, he entered the forest again.

He knew these woods well. There were two places near Jasper known for their winter trapping, the Snaring River to the north and Trapper's Creek to the east on Lake Maligne. Trapper's Creek was less accessible from town in winter, which meant game should be more plentiful; the only way to get there was to take his friend's dogs. In this weather it was a trip of at least three days. They tied their tent, traps, sleeping bags, and other supplies to the sled; the big sullen clouds overhead promised a heavy snowfall soon. They set up camp near nightfall, cutting a bed of sweet-smelling balsam before staking the tent, collecting wood for the fire, and slicing meat into the sizzling pan. The trees around their site seemed immense, their tops rocking and groaning in the wind in the strangest way. Frank always had the feeling that he was being watched, whether by lawmen or the eyes of God. The scents of their campsite put him more at peace: the attar of balsam, the pungent smell of burning wood, the fragrance of cooking meat, the sharp whiff of gas from the carbide lamp. After he crawled into bed the tent became a cave around him, strange and primitive, his figure throwing grotesque shadows on the blue wall.

When he woke, he hardly remembered where he was. He could almost hear the silence—not a branch seemed to stir, not a tree moved. He stuck his head out the flap and saw that new snow had fallen, pressing the tree branches low to the ground. Every now and then a tree would drop a load of snow with a *whumpf!* and he knew better than to linger close if he didn't want to be buried. It reminded him again of his winter in Idaho and how he'd survived that terrible blizzard. His whole life seemed composed of circles, of scenes endlessly repeating themselves, an odd collection of déjà vu.

Trapper's Creek was named because it was one of the few sources of running water during the winter, which meant fur-bearing prey came down from the highlands to drink, followed by predators. Frank and his companion were after stone marten, with their white throat and thick brown fur. He remembered how he'd trapped pine marten that winter in the Coeur d'Alenes. Pine marten had a yellow throat, that was the main difference, but both were long and graceful animals with short legs and toes armed with sharp claws. They lived in the hollows of trees when not out hunting the rodents and birds that made up their food; the fresh-fallen snow made their tracks easy to spot, and Frank spent the day setting his traps along the game trails. They left the traps overnight, and next morning, when the cold seeped through the sleeping bags to wake them, they found two marten apiece, each pelt worth $100 or more. They gutted the animals and headed back. Once home, Frank nailed the raw pelts to the barn door, flesh side out to dry.

Once again, as with Jack Golden, he'd listened to advice and assurances that were not in his best interest. Once again, as in Edmonton, he'd grown careless. The consequence arrived in the form of a friend. On the morning of Saturday, March 10, 1934, Game Warden Franklyn Bryant dropped by for a chat and a strong cup of tea. Frank had known Bryant almost since his arrival in Jasper; his son Joe attended school with Frank's younger daughter, Marie. Game wardens were considered outsiders, since locals figured game laws were made for tourists and tenderfeet but not for them. As an outsider himself, Frank could sympathize. By the mid-1930s, in fact, a game warden's job had grown sufficiently dangerous that Bryant now strapped a Colt .38 to his hip when he entered the park. Park Warden P. H. Goodair had been killed by a grizzly near the Tonquin Valley in 1929, but more dangerous than griz were the poachers drawn by the extraordinarily high prices paid for the long-haired furs of lynx, fisher, and marten. The combination of high prices and hard times led to an increase in poaching. Bryant started wearing his Colt after getting shot at once by a poacher; the pistol and Bryant's khaki uniform, so like the ones worn by Fort Leavenworth's soldiers drilling in sight of the prison, reminded Frank of his days in the West. He opened the door at Bryant's knock and welcomed him in. But as the two men mounted the back steps, Bryant glanced across the yard. "Jim," he said, his face clouding, "why did I have to come this morning? Look what you have been up to." He pointed at the marten pelts, caught out of season. Bryant's duty was clear.

Frank patted him on the back and told him he could "do his duty later," after drinking his tea. It was just one of those things. They walked to the courthouse together and Bryant served a warrant for poaching on his old friend. On Monday, March 12, he pleaded guilty before Judge A. B. Campbell, Jasper's veteran stipendiary magistrate, who gave him a choice: pay the $200 fine for poaching or spend two months in jail.

Frank chose the former, though he knew he'd have to get a loan for part of the amount, probably from Dr. O'Hagen and William S. Jeffrey, both old friends. The fine was another burden, but they knew he would pay them back, and he had to endure the good-natured kidding of friends for being caught and punished for something of which almost every man in Jasper had at one time or another been guilty. In fact, the only real shock of the whole episode came early that Saturday, when Bryant walked him to the RCMP barracks and Detective Corporal S. C. Coggles said he'd have to take his fingerprints.

Frank looked at Coggles and his face went white. "What are these for?" he asked, trying to keep the quiver from his voice. Coggles looked up, his sixth sense as a policeman telling him something was amiss, though he had no idea what it could be.

Coggles was an easygoing man, with sad eyes and the broken nose of a prizefighter. Like everyone else in Jasper, it seemed, he too was counted among Jim Fahey's friends. In the winter he was regularly seen stumping around town in his peakless fur cap with the fold-down earflaps, since the famous flat-brimmed hat, though better looking, was uncomfortable and cumbersome. Though Coggles was no prize to look at, the RCMP placed a lot of faith in him. Jasper was regarded as an important post, because officers came in contact with visitors from all over the world, many of them famous, who must be given cordial and intelligent attention. Out of Jasper went special expeditions into the backcountry, places that could not be reached except by plane or hard overland trails. Coggles had done his share of lifesaving, had seen his share of danger, and was a good judge of men. Jim Fahey was a good man, but something, he knew, was wrong. He'd not seen his friend so rattled since his partner Jack McCaw died.

In fact, Coggles didn't usually get involved in poaching cases, leaving that to game wardens like Bryant. If it were not for the blasted fingerprints, the RCMP would not get involved at all. He told his friend that prints were required these days. If he'd been charged two years earlier, taking prints for something as minor as a violation of park regulations would not have been considered. It was not the same as breaking the law. But since 1932, practically everyone had gone through the process, even vagrants. With the Depression-era labor strikes, Ottawa had visions of revolution lurking around the corner. The government sought to ferret out and docket all potentially dangerous characters.

"You're not a dangerous character, are you, Jim?" Coggles asked, making a joke and trying to put his friend at ease. "The bureaucrats won't be happy until they bury us all under paperwork." Bryant laughed, though he too had noticed the sudden change in his friend.

"I'm just surprised, that's all," Frank finally said.

What could he do? If he refused to give his prints, he'd only raise suspicions worse than he already had. He pressed his fingers to the ink pad and rolled them on the heavy card. He remembered the record clerk at Leavenworth saying they'd only started printing prisoners a couple of years before his arrival. Here, he was two years too late. He could only hope the prints went no farther than the Jasper barracks. Surely, with all the problems in the world, no one paid attention to the prints of a small-time poacher.

He was wrong. That same day, copies of Frank's prints were sent to the Investigative Branch in Edmonton, then on the International Branch in Ottawa. From there they were sent to criminal identification bureaus in London, Paris, Berlin, and Washington, D.C. On Friday, March 16, or Saturday, March 17, 1934, an unidentified records clerk in Ottawa, following existing routine, was about to drop James Lawrence Fahey's fingerprint card into its classification slot, based on the arrangement of its Galton Details. He stopped short, surprised. Another card was already there, also filed by the Galton system of loops and whirls, but this one had been sent long ago from the U.S.

Bureau of Investigation under the name Frank Grigware. The clerk lifted it from the slot. In every detail, the prints on the old card matched those of James Fahey of Jasper, Alberta, Canada, taken a week earlier.

Ottawa wired the U.S. Department of Justice's Division of Investigation in Washington to check their files. Visitors to the division's facilities on Constitution Avenue were told how many chances there were in a trillion that the lines and whorls of a finger pad on one human digit would be duplicated by another. Visitors were shown how, by a system of punched cards and whirring machinery—the same punch-card-based Hollerith machines even then being used in Germany to tabulate a census that would categorize Jews, homosexuals, and Gypsies—experts could classify a new fingerprint in a matter of seconds. A clerk then dropped it into its proper classification, adding the card to the millions of records, each representing a single person, already stored in Bureau files. When a Bureau clerk checked Ottawa's findings, he pulled the original card. It was yellowed and dusty and had been entered on April 29, 1910.

Twenty-four years after his spectacular and famous escape, less than three months after the search for him was suspended, one week after he was caught for trapping out of season, telegrams were fired to every Bureau office that ever participated in the search. The message was identical:

FINGERPRINTS OF JAMES LAWRENCE FAHEY PROVE HIM IDENTICAL WITH FUGITIVE FRANK GRIGWARE. STOP. PLEASE RUSH IN-STRUCTIONS.

The wheels of justice turned. By Monday, March 19, the Bureau wired Ottawa to please arrest Frank at once before his position dawned on him and he slipped the net again. He would be held to await extradition back to Leavenworth, where he would serve out his life term. At first it was thought he was already in custody, but news that he was simply under observation caused a flurry of telegrams between Ottawa and Edmonton, Butte, Montana, and Washington, D.C. On March 25, the U.S. legation in Ottawa notified H. M. Collins, the U.S. consul to Edmonton, to have Grigware arrested, but the RCMP in Edmonton did not act hastily. They checked again with Ottawa and Washington. ARE YOU SURE THIS IS GRIGWARE?, they asked. COULD THERE BE A MISTAKE? PLEASE ADVISE. The prints were double-checked in both capital cities. From Washington came word: SEE IF HIS TOES ARE WEBBED.

It was up to Corporal Coggles to do the dirty work. He was aware of what Americans thought of Mounties: tall, principled, and slow to anger—an aura that Hollywood would soon attach to Nelson Eddy in the 1936 film *Rose-Marie* and to Gary Cooper in the 1940 *North West Mounted Police*—lonely and vulnerable in a strong sort of way. Coggles was the farthest thing from a movie star, but he certainly felt heartsick and alone. It was his responsibility to arrest the man known in America as Frank Grigware, but here in Canada the same man, Jim Fahey, was his friend.

He donned his uniform, as he always did for funerals, and placed the flat-brimmed hat he so roundly hated square on his head. At 7 A.M. on Monday, March 26, he caught the train from Edmonton, where he had gone to receive his orders in secret, and arrived in Jasper at 1:50 P.M. He walked down the street as the curious Jasperites noted the peculiar sight of Corporal Coggles wearing his dress uniform; he knocked on Fahey's door. Ruth Fahey answered, small and wide-eyed at the familiar man standing uncomfortably on their porch wearing the buttoned red blazer. He asked if Jim was home and Ruth said he was downtown at the site of a possible job. He would be home soon, she added. Would Corporal Coggles like a cup of tea as he waited? Could she ask what he wanted Jim for? Coggles looked down at the woman he had known for nearly ten years and felt sick, like a traitor, like the lowest form of life that lived in these woods. "Just a matter of the fine, ma'am," he answered. "It really won't take long." Perhaps relieved, Ruth told him where he could find Jim.

Coggles found James Fahey exactly where his wife said he would be. He said there was some trouble with the moneys due on the fine, and the wanted man, straightforward as always, offered to pay it right there. "Nothing that drastic," Coggles answered. "You'll have to come to the barracks and sign a release." He watched again as Jim's face grew bloodless and realized that he must already know. He'd known since he'd been forced to give his fingerprints; that was why he'd acted shaken then. What would he do, he wondered, if the man tried to break away? But nothing of the sort occurred. Jim Fahey walked with him to the barracks. They strolled casually down the street as they had done so often before. Old friends nodded greetings, eyeing Coggles' uniform with surprise, wondering what was going on. As they entered the barracks, a second Mountie, a Corporal Baynes, was waiting. He handed an official looking document to Coggles. Dejectedly, Coggles handed the paper to Frank. "Sorry, old man," Coggles said.

The time was 3 P.M. Once again, all motion and sound seemed to stop except for the slight twitch of the paper and the sound of Frank's heartbeat in his ears. "Open it, Jim," the corporal said softly.

Frank nodded as if hypnotized. "Yes, I guess I had better," he said. He unfolded the document and saw an extradition warrant from H. M. Collins, U.S. Consul in Edmonton, calling for the arrest of one Frank Grigware, escaped lifer from Leavenworth, alias James Gordon, alias E. E. Hollingshead, alias James Lawrence Fahey. Frank slumped down upon the bench, still holding the document, his heartbeat roaring in his ears. Coggles feared he'd been knocked out by the blow and grabbed him by the shoulder, shaking him back to life. "This . . . this is not right," Frank mumbled. "I am not that man."

"I was told you might say that and have been commanded to have you take off your shoes to look for webbing between your toes," Coggles answered, knowing by now it wasn't necessary. "The second and third toes of each foot, to be exact."

Frank looked up at Coggles and his face had grown ashen. Coggles had seen such eyes before in unsuccessful rescue missions. His old friend smiled, and the smile was so ghastly the hardened corporal had look to away. This was the look of the dead.

"That's not necessary," Frank said. "The warrant is right. I escaped from the prison, though I had nothing to do with the robbery that put me there." He looked up at the ceiling as if in that second the entire weight of the world would press down on the three numbed men in the lonely barracks. He released his breath. "I guess you should go and get Ruth," he said. He paused. "I guess I'll finally tell her."

Oh, my God, Coggles thought, having glimpsed an abyss he could never have imagined. He never told her. *She doesn't know.*

CHAPTER THIRTEEN

The Ends of Justice

RUTH FAHEY *DIDN'T* know, though by nightfall of March 26, 1934, she, and Jasper, knew. There were so many accounts of Ruth's initial reaction that it is impossible for us to know today exactly what happened. If anything, the confusion mirrored the uproar in the town. According to the *Toronto Daily Star*, Ruth collapsed when she came to the RCMP barracks and Frank told her the news. According to the *Edmonton Journal*, Frank was at home in a rocking chair and Ruth in the same room, sewing, when Coggles arrived with the warrant. According to a later account in *True Detective Mysteries*, Ruth took one look at the warrant, screamed, "It can't be so! Say it isn't true, Jim!" and then fainted. According to Spokane's the *Spokesman-Review*:

> When they had restored Mrs. Fahey to consciousness and she had got upon her knees before him and begged him to tell the truth, he admitted that it was all true. He was Grigware, the escaped felon, and he would have to go back to Edmonton with the officer and later back to Leavenworth to resume serving his life term in the carpenter shop where he had left it 24 years ago.

For all the overwrought staging, the scenes portray a very real fear. This was of extradition, the surrender by one sovereign power to another of a fugitive from justice. Ever since conventions signed between the United States and Great Britain in 1842, 1889, and 1900, American fugitives fleeing into Canada, and vice versa, had been seamlessly escorted across the forty-ninth parallel. James Manning's arrest in Edmonton was typical of the two nations' no-frills practice of extradition. More famous was the 1917 flight and extradition of homicidal millionaire Harry K. Thaw, sent to New York's Matewan Hospital for the Criminally Insane after pleading not guilty by reason of insanity to the 1906 murder of Stanford White, famous architect and lover of Thaw's celebrated showgirl wife, Evelyn Nesbit. The Canadians handed Thaw back to U.S. officials almost immediately. No one could remember a recent case in which an extradition request between the two nations was not honored.

In Frank's case, there was at least one legal complication. It is an almost universally held rule that a state will not surrender its own citizens to a foreign power. Frank had become a naturalized Canadian citizen in 1917 and, as such, a subject in the greater British Commonwealth. Yet the fact that he'd done so under a false name, as a felon, could easily void his citizenship.

On the night of his arrest, Frank was placed in the RCMP lockup while Ruth made arrangements with neighbors to keep the children. At 12:15 P.M. the next day, March 27, Frank, Ruth, and Coggles took the train to Edmonton, where Frank was signed over for another night in jail. Barrister W. H. Howson was retained to represent him, a good choice since Howson, as leader of Alberta's Liberal Party, had political pull. While Ruth stayed with friends, Howson prepared for the arraignment before a magistrate, the first stage of Frank's legal ordeal.

On March 29, 1934, Canadians and Americans alike woke to a world that moved fast, seemed incomprehensible, and switched rapidly from the astonishing, bewildering, and mysterious to the routine and mundane. That day, Albert Einstein, with thirty-six other prominent Germans, was deprived of his citizenship for conduct that "violated his obligation of fidelity to the Reich and its people," i.e., being a Jew. Jean Harlow announced she had written a novel. Robert L. Ripley, the Believe-It-or-Not Man, announced he was leaving to visit an isolated island in northern Japan to search for a tribe of "little people with tails." On that day, Kansas City Sheriff Thomas B. Bash declared war on gunmen after four people were shot to death during recent city elections. Will Rogers's folksy aphorisms appeared in papers in both nations. The mysterious "Tutankhamen's curse" claimed its twentieth victim, Canadian architect Arthur E. Weigell, who had been present at the tomb's opening. G-men chased John Dillinger across Indiana. Lawmen in Fort Scott, Kansas, searched for Bonnie and Clyde. The worst month of the Dust Bowl was beginning, bringing winds howling from the north. And, President Franklin Roosevelt took to sea aboard the white yacht of millionaire friend Vincent Astor for a short vacation. For Frank, that holiday would prove bad timing.

On March 29, 1934, Canadians woke to breaking news of Frank's arrest and the tale of his twenty-four-year flight from justice. Although brief mentions ran in American papers, fuller accounts did not appear until Friday, March 30, or later that weekend. A marked difference between the coverage in the two nations could immediately be seen. In America, Frank's arrest was described as yet another tale of evil unmasked, of crime and its inevitable punishment. There was almost always a presumption of guilt, an unswerving belief in the moral weight of authority. Typical of the coverage was the *Leavenworth Times* headline, A JAIL CELL FOR "JEKYLL AND HYDE" PRISON FUGITIVE, or the *Kansas City Star*'s RELENTLESS ARM OF JUSTICE CLOSES ON A CRIMINAL WHO HAS "GONE STRAIGHT" FOR YEARS. Evil was always discovered, whether through the law's relentless pursuit or due to its own unconcealable needs. Order was restored. An unspoken poke at Canadian naïveté also crept in. Some stories drew a comparison between Frank's escape and Dillinger's more recent breakout from Crown Point, Indiana, focusing on the bluff with the wooden gun. Some reporters speculated that Dillinger might have gotten his idea from the Leavenworth break. The message was implicit: All criminals are the same.

In Canada, from the beginning, the theme was the opposite of that in America. There was a presumption of innocence for Frank; if not that, at least one of mercy. Frank's guilt was the folly of youth; because of his actions in building Canada's wilderness, he had shown himself redeemed. There was a good deal of melodrama to both approaches. The American angle was the dark dream of vengeance, repeated endlessly in the best-selling mystery pulps. The Canadian angle was that of the radio soap opera, coming at a time when soaps were the theater of the masses. This was not unusual: Canadian papers of the 1930s and 1940s tended to shape their lead stories in the soap formula of ordinary people facing and surviving almost impossible odds. The soaps' titles said it all: *Brave Tomorrow, Bright Horizon, Against the Storm*. Their stories were of family disruption and threat, often taking place in a pastoral setting, usually a small town like Jasper. Happy endings were de rigueur. Though the end of Frank's personal soap seemed anything but happy, his family's sudden turmoil grabbed Canadian readers by the throat and refused to let them go.

The *Toronto Daily Star*, Canada's largest and most aggressive newspaper, took the lead, eventually working in apparent partnership with the more localized *Edmonton Journal*. The *Star*'s headline for its first interview with Frank proclaimed MAN OF TWO NAMES "JAMES FAHEY" NOW FEELS HE HAS ATONED FOR CRIME CHARGED AGAINST HIM, yet after that the coverage switched to the plight of Ruth and her children. UNSUSPECTING WIFE COLLAPSES AS HUSBAND'S IDENTITY REVEALED, read the paper's subhead for its March 29 story. This was followed by LAW'S LIGHTNING BOLT FLICKERS OVER HEADS OF HAPLESS CHILDREN, and FEAR-FILLED EYES SHOW MRS. FAHEY'S TORMENT, HER WORLD SHATTERED.

Something bigger was at work in the Canadian newsrooms and living rooms, something touching an almost mythic chord. Here was an American, James Fahey, who'd fled to Canada to be free. He'd wanted a second chance and found it only in the Dominion of Canada. He'd spent his adult life building the Canadian North, and now he was being dragged from his family by the American colossus.

By 1916, Canadian papers had already defined themselves by what they were *not*—and that was American. They were never as consistently "yellow" as the famous U.S. dailies; a comparison to William Randolph Hearst in news circles was a term of contempt. Toronto, the heart of Canada's news business, demanded reputability and respectability, but though that dour face had changed by the 1930s, the old nationalistic bias still remained. Harry Hindmarsh, the *Star*'s managing editor, covered major stories by throwing entire squads of reporters at them, and the paper's opening salvo in Frank's story promised an unfolding drama of social justice, immediately comparing Frank's plight to "some of the most imaginative writings of Dickens or Victor Hugo." The theme was not an isolated anomaly but was always ready to spring forth with its own vengeance, as seen in an unrelated story two months later when, on May 28, 1934, the

Dionne quintuplets were born in Ontario's backcountry, beginning a saga that dominated headlines in Canada and America for a dozen years. When American promoters attempted to "tour" the quints, the Canadian press pounced, deriding "cheap American publicity."

"The lives of children are a bigger concern in Canada than profits," declared Arthur Roebuck, Canada's Attorney General, on July 27, 1934, drawing a virtual line in the sand against "exploiters from American cities." It was us versus them, Canadian values versus American madness, the Canadian home versus an American monster that threatened to break through the door.

Whether the style was Canadian soap or hard-boiled American hype, no reader or writer could resist Frank's situation. As new angles arose daily, reporters, regardless of nationality, attacked their typewriter keys. "Who can even imagine the mental anguish of those twenty-four years when he was living two lives?" cried the *Kansas City Star* on April 8, 1934:

> To the world about him, to his wife and children, his life was honest and upright, open and above board. But, as he says, every moment of that twenty-four years he was living another life. Always within the shadow stood that specter of the mailed fist of the law, the haunting fear that sometime the fist might strike.

The *Spokesman-Review* investigated Frank's roots, taking a certain pride that he delivered their paper as a boy. If one thing caught the imagination, it was that horrible moment when Frank's hidden past was revealed. Every newspaper story, magazine piece, and book section devoted to Frank's tale in the days and years that followed almost invariably quoted the same two lines from Oscar Wilde's "Ballad of Reading Gaol":

> For he that lives more lives than one,
> More deaths than one must die.

Every account gave some portrait of Frank's revelation to Ruth, leading thirty years later to a bizarre rendition where "Weeping and holding her husband's dazed hand, she sobbed [the biblical] Ruth's words, 'Entreat me not to leave thee, or to return from following after thee, for whither thou goest, I will go.' "

More than anything else, Ruth's actions in those moments determined everything that followed. If she had denounced Frank as a liar
and abandoned their marriage, all of Canada would have abandoned
him. She held his life in her hands. As Frank watched her struggles,
did he remember Alice or the unnamed Kansas farm wife, both of
whom were thrust into similar situations, both of whom had done
their best to show him mercy? He usually hid his emotions from the
press, the habit of concealment still paramount even when no longer
needed, yet sometimes his feelings peeked through the reserve. Once,
when a reporter asked Ruth about her plans, she said, "We're going
to make the best of this, aren't we, Jim?" Frank turned his eyes on
her and smiled. "I don't know what I'd do without you," he answered. "You've been a tower of strength to me." Another time he
said, "You've been brave to stand by me," to which she answered
quietly, "No, it hasn't taken bravery."

Exactly what happened in front of Coggles was blurred by the
conflicting accounts, but Ruth's subsequent actions shine clear. She
accompanied Frank to Edmonton, where she was mobbed by reporters. Ruth was described that first day in Edmonton by the *Edmonton
Journal* as quiet and "wide-eyed with anxiety over the imminence of
a tragedy which threatens to darken completely the lives of her husband, herself, and her three children." She was "desperately confused" by both the fate confronting her and her mobbing by the
media. But there was no confusion about her ultimate intent. Asked
about her plans, she answered, "I don't know what I'm going to do
yet, but I do know that I will never lose faith in my husband." Asked
about that faith, which had certainly been tested, she acknowledged
her shock: "I never knew anything about this trouble. The first I knew
about it was Monday, when they came to take my husband away."
But when asked what would happen if Frank returned to Leavenworth, the woman in the oversized coat who never quite got used to
the harsh Canadian winters stared straight at the flash cameras and
stated simply: "Nothing will ever break up our home."

Nothing will ever break up our home. Those words came early in
the ordeal, on March 29, a single statement that seemed to make up
Canada's mind for it more than all the writers ever could. In that one
brief instant, Frank's flight and discovery became more than another
two-nation tale of crime and punishment. It became something every
man and woman felt at a deep level in those hard Depression years.

The home would survive. When little else remained, at least a man or woman had dignity.

At 10 A.M. on Thursday, March 29, Frank appeared in the District Court of Edmonton before His Honor Judge G. L. Crawford, where he was formally remanded into custody. Collins, the U.S. consul, told the court that according to the formal terms of the application for extradition, the president of the United States would ask the governor general of Canada to deliver Frank to a U.S. marshal for return to prison. Frank's lawyer responded that he would seek executive clemency or a pardon from Roosevelt, although there was some debate whether it would be better for him to waive extradition entirely, go back to Leavenworth as a sign of good faith, and then seek clemency. That was a lawyers' debate, for there was no doubt in Frank's mind what he wanted. He remembered Paul Muni's fate in the chain-gang movie he'd seen two years earlier; he recalled what happened when Muni made the same good-faith deal. Sure it was a movie, but like most viewers he knew it was based on a true story published in 1931's *True Detectives Mysteries*. He sat on a back bench with Ruth, their hands tightly clasped, as the lawyers argued law. To the reporters sitting in the courtroom, they seemed so puny compared to the immensity of the proceedings around them and to the nations gathered here. Yet when the debate was over, the two of them and their children would be the ones to pay. "The 'Faheys' have won the fullest sympathy of all who have come in contact with them," asserted the *Edmonton Journal*. "Their appearance is all in their favor. Fahey is a man of small stature with hands hardened by many years of honest toil. . . . His wife is a cultured, attractive woman of pleasing personality." As Frank listened, the judge asked his lawyers whether they would seek to have their client released on bond. This was unprecedented. It was generally held between nations that extraditable fugitives were high "flight risks" and so were not granted bond. Understandably surprised, the U.S. consul objected. To grant bond was not in keeping with Canada's treaty obligations, he said. But the judge was unfazed. "I do not promise to grant it," he said, "I only promise to consider it." The judge quizzed the consul how long it would take before the United States could formally request extradition in court; the answer was that it might take two weeks or longer. The judge set the next hearing for 10 A.M. on Friday, April 13, and Frank was led back to his cell.

Following news of the arraignment, something extraordinary occurred. The people Frank had helped or simply befriended during his
years in Canada began coming to his aid. The groundswell started
spontaneously in several parts of Alberta. Petitions were circulated in
Jasper, Edmonton, Peace River, Grande Prairie, Spirit River, and
throughout the province calling for Frank's release and freedom. The
petitions, to be sent to the White House and to Canadian Premier
Richard B. Bennett, pointed out Frank's "exemplary life" since coming to Alberta; they were signed by people from all walks and stations
of society: mayors, police chiefs, magistrates, school principals, lawyers, farmers, railroaders, ministers, housewives, and laborers. In Jasper, Franklyn Bryant, the game warden, circulated a petition,
saddened by his part in Frank's unmasking; it was said that Corporal
Coggles did also, though this never was confirmed. Friends and acquaintances from the past began trickling into newspaper offices to
relate their small pieces in the puzzle of Frank's fugitive years: C. F.
"Charlie" O'Connor, his old boss at the Blackfalds railroad bridge;
Roy Anger, a railroad worker who'd watched him jump for his life
to grab the dangling guy rope; the Reverend J. M. Pritchard, who
married Frank and Ruth in Spirit River. The trickle of signatures,
stories, and memories became an avalanche as Frank awaited return
to the penitentiary on the plains.

If one thing acted as the trigger, perhaps it was a wire sent by the
Jasper Chamber of Commerce to President Roosevelt at 8:50 P.M. on
March 29. Bypassing diplomatic channels was considered a breach of
etiquette by British subjects, and the writers begged forgiveness for
their presumption. The next day, at 8:52 P.M., the Jasper's Women's
Institute, a homemakers' group to which Ruth belonged, wired its
own plea to Eleanor Roosevelt, begging the First Lady to use her
influence to "help a suffering family." Both Roosevelts still cruised
off the Florida coast in Vincent Astor's yacht, so it is uncertain how
quickly the wires reached them. The telegram to FDR, the most
widely reproduced, began without preamble, as if it too were a cry
of desperation:

A GREAT TRAGEDY HAS HAPPENED HERE IN THIS BEAUTIFUL SUM-
MER RESORT. ONE OF OUR PROMINENT CITIZENS, JAMES FAHEY,
WHO HAS LIVED IN CANADA FOR TWENTY TWO [SIC] YEARS AND

JASPER FOR THE LAST NINE YEARS OF THIS TIME HAS BEEN PROS-
ECUTED FOR TRAPPING IN THE PARK. HIS FINGERPRINTS SHOW
THAT HE ESCAPED FROM LEAVENWORTH PENITENTIARY IN 1910,
BEING 18 WHEN CONVICTED. SINCE COMING TO CANADA HE MAR-
RIED A SCHOOL TEACHER, THEY HAVE THREE CHILDREN. BUT WIFE
DID NOT KNOW OF HIS RECORD UNTIL FAHEY WAS ARRESTED A
FEW DAYS AGO. WE, THE CITIZENS OF JASPER, ARE APPEALING TO
YOU, MR. PRESIDENT, TO SAVE THIS MAN FROM BEING RETURNED
TO PRISON; HIS RECORD IN CANADA HAS BEEN THAT OF A GOOD,
LAW ABIDING CITIZEN. WE ARE ALSO APPEALING IN BEHALF OF HIS
WIFE AND THREE CHILDREN TO SAVE HIM FROM ANY FURTHER
PUNISHMENT. SURELY TWENTY FOUR YEARS OF ANGUISH HAS PAID
IN FULL. GIVE THE BROKENHEARTED WIFE AND CHILDREN A HUS-
BAND AND A FATHER. KINDLY IF POSSIBLE GIVE THIS MATTER IM-
MEDIATE ATTENTION. IMPERATIVE MEASURES BE TAKEN AT ONCE,
MAN LIABLE TO IMMEDIATE EXTRADITION. WE KNOW WE ARE PRE-
SUMPTUOUS IN WIRING YOU BUT HOPE YOU WILL FORGIVE US UN-
DER THE CIRCUMSTANCES.

Saturday, March 31, brought good news. That morning, Judge
Crawford ruled that Fahey could be released on bail bonds totaling
$10,000. He would not be released, however, until after a hearing on
April 2. That evening, the lawyers told Frank that Premier Bennett
said he "would be disposed to exercise whatever influence he could
properly bring to bear" to secure leniency from the United States.
Things were looking up, said Frank's lawyer, W. H. Howson. Yet
there was still no word from Washington.

Frank stayed in jail during the Easter weekend, visited by friends
who promised to help, visited by Ruth, who hurried to and from the
barracks in an attempt to escape the mob of reporters and curiosity
seekers posted outside. He could tell this was hard on her, maybe
harder than on him. She worried about the future, about the children,
about why there had been no word from Roosevelt. During this time
he told her the details of his former life so there would be no more
surprises. His attorneys visited and assured him that thousands of
people across Canada were working or praying for his release. They'd
never seen anything like it, they said. But when everyone had gone,
it was quiet and cold in the jail cell, no matter how many blankets

he was given, and he remembered the days in Leavenworth when he'd looked about him at the walls and other prisoners, knowing that a life sentence would either kill him early or drive him insane.

He wondered what would happen if he did return. He wondered how he could possibly survive another day in that place. He remembered the scene in the movie when the prison authorities had Paul Muni in their grasp and reneged on their promise of leniency. Examples had to be made to show no one escaped the law, they explained. That was what the American papers said now; an example must be made, though mercy could be shown when he arrived. He'd experienced justice first-hand in Leavenworth: he may not have said it publicly, but he had few illusions about the quality of mercy there. On Easter Sunday, April 1, the Christian celebration of rebirth, he recalled being thrown in the Hole twenty-four years earlier, remembering with every bone in his body what it felt like to be buried alive.

For years he'd skimmed the papers for news of his old prison, and if anything Leavenworth seemed worse now than when he'd been there. The penitentiary had turned into a charnel house, a machine for processing prisoners. By 1919 the last of the cellblocks had been completed; by 1926 the dome was finally erected, and in 1927 all work on the prison was said to be done. Yet all the improvements could not hide what had grown inside. In 1924, W. I. Biddle, Leavenworth's fifth warden, officially ended the prison's idealistic beginnings when he announced that Warden French's ideas had been abandoned. What started as a reformatory for 1,200 to 1,400 young men from the West was now a maximum security prison for 2,700 hardened criminals from across America. Prohibition brought gangsters to the cellblocks, although drug offenders accounted for the majority of admissions. By mid-1925, the prison count jumped to 3,345; by 1934, there were nearly 4,000 inmates there. "This is the most modern, both in housing and equipment, of any prison in the world," Biddle claimed, echoing French's boast of twenty-seven years earlier.

By 1934, the very worst prisoners in the federal system were shipped by prison train to "the Rock" at Alcatraz. The prospect that he would not meet "Doc" Barker, Alvin "Creepy" Karpis, "Machine Gun" Kelly, or other so-called public enemies was perhaps a relief, but it did little to allay Frank's impending sense of doom. Death was still a common cellmate in Leavenworth, visited in some form on everyone. The inmate death rate was as bad as during his tenure:

seventeen died in fiscal year 1933, nine in 1934. Four more guards had been killed in the line of duty since Waldrupe's death in 1901. The first was Andrew Turner, knifed to death in 1912 before 1,200 inmates in the dining hall by Robert F. Stroud, eventually called the Bird Man of Alcatraz. Stroud killed Turner with his homemade *shiv*; a prison knifing in 1912 was still unusual, but shivs were common now . . . almost standard equipment among prisoners. Guards Edgar Barr and Andrew Leonard died next, in 1917 and 1922. On June 20, 1929, laundry foreman W. G. Warkne was beaten to death with a lead pipe by Carl Panzran, who boasted of having killed twenty-two men. Panzran was executed a year later, the first legal execution in Kansas since 1888 when a federal prisoner was hanged in Wichita. "I wish all mankind had one neck so I could choke it," Panzran said before his hanging, on September 5, 1930. At 6 A.M. that morning, he was marched from his cell to the gallows erected behind the isolation building, old haunt of Deputy Lemon. He spat at the guards. The hangman placed the rope around Panzran's neck and adjusted the knot behind his left ear. At 6:02 A.M., he pulled the iron lever and Panzran shot through the trap, head flopping to one side when the vertebrae broke. His body spun slowly. No one spoke or moved. Panzran exemplified every prisoner's hatred for his keepers, but killing him didn't kill the rage.

By 1934, Frank's escape was legend in the Big Top's folklore, yet there had been other escapes, in 1911, 1920, 1927, and 1928. In 1929 a riot that began in the mess hall spread across the institution. Burning mattresses were thrown against the windows, causing the glass to explode. Brass railings torn from the galleries rained down like missiles. The guards regrouped and charged back in a battle reminiscent of 1901's mutiny.

On February 28, 1930, two mail robbers named Holden and Keating walked out through the front gate with a forged pass. Eight months later, their buddy, train robber Frank Nash, walked away from the deputy warden's residence where he'd been assigned as a trusty and was allegedly picked up on Metropolitan Avenue in a car driven by Keating. They drove to Kansas City and formed the nucleus of a midwest robbery gang. Nearly three years later, Nash was arrested and was being taken back to Leavenworth when "Pretty Boy" Floyd, a fellow gang member, tried to spring him at the Kansas City train station with a machine gun. Four lawmen were killed, including

Bureau man Raymond Caffrey; Nash also died. Congress passed a bill authorizing Hoover's G-men to carry weapons.

On December 11, 1931, seven convicts armed with revolvers escaped out the front gate using Thomas White, the sixth warden, as a shield. The guns had entered the prison wrapped in cut-up inner tubes and sunk into a barrel of dye delivered to the shoe factory. The seven stormed the front gate and ordered it opened, but the guard refused, saying he was an old man and if they wanted to shoot him just go ahead. Instead, they stormed the warden's office; and knowing they'd kill the warden if he refused again, the feisty guard finally let them out. A passing car was hijacked and the fugitives sped southwest, Hewitt and Kating's old route, stopping at a schoolhouse to terrorize teacher and students before speeding on. Pursuing guards cut them off and they swerved down a farm lane. One prisoner, enraged by the turn of events, shot Warden White in the arm and left him for dead. The farmhouse was on a rise and the inmates fought it out like the mutineers of 1901; when the battle was over, three of them lay dead, three surrendered, and one slipped away in the chaos only to be captured three days later. The warden recovered, but retired within two months.

Fred Zerbst was appointed in his place as Leavenworth's seventh warden. This was the same Fred Zerbst who was guard captain during Frank's escape. He had achieved what his old bosses Robert McLaughry and Frank Lemon had only dreamed about, making federal prisons his lifelong home. He'd been posted to several federal institutions, served as deputy warden in both Leavenworth and Atlanta, and ended his career back where he started. If anything, he'd learned the prison lesson: To prosper, one must survive. He'd survived the 1910 breakout and its repercussions, survived power struggles in the Atlanta federal penitentiary that reportedly drove one assistant warden to suicide, and survived a murder attempt after Carl Panzran killed laundry foreman Warkne. Survival excused everything; with time, survival proved one right. Zerbst never had the vision of James French or the public adulation of Robert McLaughry, but he had the respect of his prison colleagues for being a survivor who had seen it all. He even survived a corruption scandal during his second year as warden, when in August 1933 a counterfeiting ring was discovered inside the prison walls. Drums of the different-colored inks used in making bogus bills were found in the print shop; although there were never any charges, it was thought some prison officials had to be involved. The old corruptions remained, just more elaborate and sophisticated than Frank Lemon's alleged kickback scheme. There would be a symmetry if Frank returned during Zerbst's reign. *Glad to see you back, number 6768,* Zerbst might say in his quirky, ironic voice. *It's been a long time.* Zerbst was not a bad man, not compared to others Frank had seen on both sides of the bars. Even Frank might smile, if only a little.

By the time Zerbst took over, Leavenworth had helped develop, at least in part and simply by its continued survival, a system of controlling and changing people that was born in the asylum but transferred more efficiently to the modern industrial prison. These were innovations in discipline that by the end of the century would transfer to the school, hospital, factory, military unit, and office cubicle. They were first stated in different terms in Jeremy Bentham's *Panopticon*, the idealized institutional circle of being that inspired Benjamin Henry Latrobe and, through him, Leavenworth's designer, William Eames. Bentham's prison utopia isolated every inmate in a small lighted cell where he could be watched at all times by an observer in a central tower. The results, Bentham claimed in his preface, were many: "Morals reformed—health preserved—industry invigorated—instruction diffused!" It didn't work that way. But his principles—there were five, each smoothly incorporated into the Leavenworth machine—would be recognized by office workers and students everywhere.

The first principle was *spatialization*: There was a place for everyone, and everyone had a place. Where a man was located indicated his identity and importance, from the trusty in the office down to the lowliest third-class prisoner in the Hole. It wasn't much different in school, where the best student moved to the head of the class and the dunce was sent to the corner.

The second principle was *the minute control of activity*: Every minute at Leavenworth was controlled and scheduled until the timetable was canonized. Otherwise, idle minutes could permit the devil's handiwork.

The third principle was that of *repetitive exercises*: Tasks were endlessly repeated, in the prison shop as on the factory assembly line, the military parade ground, and in the school. Sufficient repetition made reaction second nature, without thought, achieving a mindless state of mechanical perfection, a modern state of grace.

Next was the establishment of *detailed hierarchies*, that complex chain of command and training where each level of the hierarchy kept watch over the lower one. Just like the guards and staff, the prisoners formed their hierarchies, jealously guarding privileges.

Finally, there was a self-regulating system of *normalizing judgments*, a continual analysis of whether one was sufficiently disciplined. It was a subtle form of power, working on the transgressor from within: the pure Gaze taken finally to its logical conclusion, Pinkerton's "unblinking eye" accepted by and in every man.

If the prison succeeded in its task, it created a docile worker who did as told without question, "guarding" his own behavior and re-forming himself along entirely new lines. The process started with constant observation and the imposition of penalties for the smallest infraction. The structured schedule and constant repetitive work installed the proper work ethic. As the inmate's behavior became more "normal," he was granted greater privileges, culminating for some in parole. The man who did not reform and conform was channeled into safe alternatives, becoming the eternal recidivist, the permanent criminal safely enclosed for the rest of his life out of sight of society. In some important ways, Warden French's prison vision succeeded after all.

IN THE MIDDLE of these cell-bound thoughts, Frank had an Easter visitor. Frederick Griffin was a reporter for the *Toronto Daily Star* sent 2,166 miles from Toronto to Edmonton to ferret out Frank's tale. He arrived early on Sunday morning and learned immediately that although reams had been written about Frank's arrest and the support rising for him across Alberta, no newsman had actually gotten into jail to interview the prisoner. He decided to be the first, scooping the rest of North America, and spent the remainder of the morning wresting the needed permission from various lawyers and police officials.

It is fashionable to romanticize mid-century newsmen, but Griffin seems absolutely tireless in this day and age. In many ways he was a product of his culture, that adrenaline-soaked urgency that seemed to rule the *Star*. The paper's expense account was princely, its feature writers resourceful, and stunts like the time a *Star* man stole an airplane from a rival were quietly smiled upon. Griffin wasn't even a star at the *Star*: that mid-1930s honor went to Gordon Sinclair, who traveled all over the world and was once asked in Tibet about the health of the Dionne quintuplets. Indeed, by Griffin's own account, he got the Edmonton assignment because he was the nearest warm body when the story broke, plus he'd shown a willingness to go anywhere at short notice and had the ability to crank out long columns of type in a day. He loved the reporter's life, basking in "the experience, the quickened living, the freshness of interest" that journalism brought to him. A 1934 picture shows Griffin perched on a log beside a grizzled gold prospector. The newsman's looks were of the type that today would make him a broadcast celebrity: an aristocratic face with a high forehead and prominent cheekbones, a dimpled chin, hands seemingly too clumsy for tiny typewriter keys. In 1912, he'd arrived in Canada by steamer to escape Ireland's poverty, and for him this was truly a New World. Before his landing, he'd never used a telephone or flicked on an electric light, never ridden in an auto or seen a typewriter. In many ways he was as lost as Jennie Grigware's parents. Yet he suddenly found himself assigned to write about the modern age. He'd reported on the Florida real estate bubble, in which so many Canadians lost money, traveled the goldfields of the North, and would shadow events in the Soviet Union like the more famous American expatriate reporter John Reed. As with many reporters, he'd one day be forgotten by his own paper, but it was a fate he fully seemed to accept. The only permanence was the endless flow of time and news, a passage newsmen liked to call "the Big Parade." This was the man whose stories on Frank would run coast to coast and who did as much, if not more, than anyone or anything else in shaping public opinion concerning his tenuous future.

On Easter Sunday afternoon, Griffin watched as James Lawrence Fahey was led slowly into the Edmonton guardroom, a taciturn man of small stature, reluctant to talk of the past. It took two hours to eke out the story, yet in the end it was worth it, Griffin thought. He scribbled notes on a steno pad as Fahey claimed innocence of the Omaha train robbery; he spoke in slow, defensive sentences about how he had knocked around the West, trying to find an America that no longer existed and maybe never had. He told how he became entangled in the robbery arrests, how he hopped on the train as it crashed through the Leavenworth gates, of his flight into Canada and freedom. As Frank talked of his adventures, the astounded Griffin discovered that he liked the man. More important, he also believed Frank's tale.

"Here is a man of two names, two lives, two identities, whose past, which he thought dead, has arisen with the threat of sending him back to complete a life sentence interrupted by twenty-four years of honorable freedom," read Griffin's lead. His story ran the next day in the *Toronto Daily Star*, was picked up quickly in other papers in Canada and the United States, and a week or two later made the global jump into papers throughout the British Empire. "He is John Francis Grigware [sic], American born citizen, alias James Fahey, British subject. Fiction holds no stranger story than that of the spectre which arose, after 24 years, to tear him from his family, his friends, his home, to expiate a crime of his youth, of which, he declares vehemently, he was not guilty."

On Monday, April 2, Griffin caught a train to Jasper to interview Frank's friends and children; on Tuesday, April 3, he hurried back to Edmonton to interview Ruth. By then the *Star*'s editorials claimed that Frank should be pardoned. In line with that stance, the paper on April 4 sent Griffin 2,000 miles south by rail to Omaha to determine whether Frank was innocent or guilty of the charge that sent him to Leavenworth, and whether he'd received a fair trial.

That Tuesday night, Frank was released as expected from jail on two $5,000 surety bonds paid by Jasper friends. One bond was paid by Frederick A. Jackman, a longtime resident and reported curling enthusiast; the other was paid by William S. Jeffrey, the store owner who'd been Frank's first employer when he arrived in town. Although Frank's release was opposed again by the U.S. consul, it moved easily through the courts; the conditions for the bond were that Frank stay in Edmonton until the April 13 extradition hearing and report every morning at 10 A.M. to the RCMP. Judge Crawford ordered it done, the attorney general's office approved the paperwork, and Police Magistrate George B. McLeod (a friend from Frank's days at McLeod River Crossing) stamped the order and set him free.

Everyone was hopeful about the way events were proceeding. News stories speculated that Frank would get a pardon, as if by wishing hard enough it would finally come true. But the only person who could call off Frank's return to Leavenworth was President Roosevelt himself. And on April 2, a White House spokesman told the press that Roosevelt was extending his vacation to go fishing in the Bahamas. Nothing would be decided until he returned.

WITH HIS RELEASE on Tuesday night, and Roosevelt's continued sabbatical, Frank entered a limbo of waiting. Unlike most extradition matters, this one would not be settled quickly. While most Canadians seemed to want some resolution, no one in Washington seemed willing to act until Roosevelt returned. The first extradition hearing, scheduled for April 13, was delayed until April 19, ostensibly because the extradition papers were not yet in order. Actually, the situation was informed by the fact that the president had still not returned. He came home the next day, on April 14. But when April 19 arrived and the United States was still not ready, the hearing was delayed to May 14.

The wait took many forms. It may have been hardest on the Fahey children. Frank's neighbors in Jasper tried to shield Louise, Jack, and Marie from the news that their father might go to prison, but by Saturday, March 31, with the story in the papers, on the radio, and on every lip, it proved impossible to keep secret. In her letter of that Saturday, reproduced on the front page of the *Edmonton Journal*, Louise wrote: "Dear Daddy, We have heard the news and know everything, but I love you just the same as ever—if not more." She told how the local priest was saying a special mass on Easter Sunday and "everyone is so kind." It just heightened the melodrama, and readers couldn't get enough. On Sunday or Monday, their mother wrote the children that "we must be brave for a little while yet."

For Frank, there were bittersweet reunions. On Easter Sunday, he received a wire from his brother Jim, even as he was talking to Fred Griffin in the RCMP guardroom. Jim was a merchant in Tonasket, Washington; Eddie was a noted artist in Chicago; Mary and Genevieve were married and living in Seattle; and Mother was doing well. But Joe had died soon after Frank's escape, and the telegram did not mention Father. Jim ended the wire by adding that he'd do whatever it took to help him.

"I never knew where he was," Jim told a phoning Edmonton reporter on Thursday, April 5. "In all the time I didn't know if he was alive or dead. I never heard from him. When I heard about Frank's identity being disclosed in Jasper I wrote to him. Hearing that he was alive was like receiving a message from the dead."

Eddie was reached by phone too. He told about Frank's early life, the arrest and conviction, and the fact that Jack Golden had been pardoned from prison. If Frank had not escaped, he would have been pardoned too. Eddie remembered how proud and envious he was of his older brother, as he took off across the mythical West and as he stuck out one of the coldest winters on record while mining for silver. He remembered the day Frank "proudly stated to his dad and mother and we, his sisters and brothers, that he was going out to see the world." Eddie had always believed in his brother and missed him. "My faith and belief in Frank's innocence has never wavered," he said.

As hard as it was to wait for resolution, it quickly became obvious that each day's delay seemed to work in Frank's favor. On Easter Sunday, prayers were offered up in churches in Jasper and throughout Alberta for a happy ending. By Monday morning, five thousand Canadians had signed petitions calling for a presidential pardon, and more were signing daily. That night, the Hon. John Brownlee, premier of Alberta, said he favored leniency. That same night, the Alberta provincial legislature unanimously adopted a resolution calling for a pardon or clemency, the only time in Canadian history that a legislative body voted an official certificate of character on a man with a price on his head. Every major paper in the nation called for Frank's release. Prime Minister Bennett forwarded Alberta's resolution to Canada's minister in Washington, urging him to lobby personally Roosevelt for a pardon—once, the president came home. The White House, the U.S. State Department, the U.S. Department of Justice— all were flooded with calls, wires, and letters demanding "Fahey's" freedom. U.S. officials had never seen anything like it. These Canadians were usually so reserved, even docile. Now it was like the whole damn country had gone nuts. What had gotten into them?

Things got especially testy around the Bureau, which, with Frank's discovery and arrest, thought they'd scored a major coup for modern crime detection only to watch that victory come apart at the seams. Memorandums to Hoover and Assistant Director Clyde Tolson, the Bureau's number-two man, showed a series of calls from *Star* reporters, first asking questions about the hunt for Frank and then demanding access to his criminal file. The queries, in each case stonewalled, grew increasingly confrontational. On April 18, a reporter talked for twenty minutes about the injustice done to Frank until the press liaison refused to say more and hung up. When the reporter called again on May 1, "I stated that unfortunately I was too busy to spend any more time concerning this matter" and hung up again, the spokesman wrote. *Right!* scribbled Hoover at the bottom of the page.

The wait continued, flushing old names from Frank's past like rabbits from the brush. On April 3, Dan Downer came out of hiding after being tracked down by reporters in Spokane. Prison records showed that while still in Leavenworth he'd given a statement attesting to Jack Golden's innocence, not Frank's, but the statement was loaded with contrived and inaccurate details, and officials finally believed that he felt guilty for his part in Jack's incarceration, which in turn had led to his worsening tuberculosis. Dan had lied in hopes of winning Jack a pardon, and in that way at least partially atone. Even now, Downer refused to discuss the Mud Cut Robbery. He gave a statement to the papers that really said nothing at all: "Grigware, being a young man, might have been easily influenced, and not realizing what he was doing, got into bad company and trouble." One week later, on April 10, Jack finally came out of hiding too. He said Frank was innocent of the train robbery, but only used as evidence the factors that led to his own pardon from President Wilson—the perjured testimony, the circumstantial evidence, the hysteria over the reward. If the witnesses in their trial "did not commit willful perjury, [they] did unconsciously exaggerate the stories they told in the hope of gaining part of the reward," he deposed. When asked if he remembered Jack, Frank answered, "Yes, I remember him." That was all he said. Nothing more, ever again, at least not publicly. He did not mention that he remembered that day in court when Jack came within a hair of saving him but lost his nerve. He did not mention the betrayal. Twenty-four years after the fact, his old friend, like him, was caught by the recurring patterns of his life. Once again, Jack was trying to help—and once again, Jack Golden suffered a failure of will.

Of more help were Fred Griffin's stories filed from Omaha. The peripatetic journalist had made the long rail trip to Nebraska and analyzed in long news reports the circumstantial nature of Frank's trial and conviction. He pointed out how witnesses said they could not see the robbers' features, how they confused Frank and Jack in their identifications. Roy Prawl, the fireman on the Overland Limited, told Griffin he was certain that Frank was not one of the Mud Cut

Robbers. Frank Howell, the U.S. attorney who fought Frank's appeal but privately thought that he would have never found him guilty, for the first time expressed his doubts publicly. "I was never convinced, never, that Grigware or Golden [were] guilty," he said. "The poor devil was convicted because he was caught in bad company." Even Charles Goss, the federal prosecutor whose arguments sent Frank to prison, moderated his view. The case against Frank was entirely circumstantial, he said, though he felt that was all that was needed. He said he felt Frank should be returned to Leavenworth as an example of the law's unerring reach but then almost immediately be pardoned or given clemency. He smiled when recalling Frank's escape. "To be frank, I rather admired his daring when he got away."

Then Goss leaned back in his leather chair and dropped a bomb. By now he was the white-haired chief justice of the state supreme court. His chambers were paneled in dark wood and set within the Nebraska capitol building, its dome rising 400 feet from its base. That made it bigger than Leavenworth's, supposedly the biggest dome at the time between Chicago and San Francisco. In the century's early decades, a domes race had gripped state capitols out west, and few, if any, took the three decades needed to raise Leavenworth's. The Nebraska capitol building sat on Omaha's highest prominence and Goss looked out his window at the crowded, sprawling, industrial city.

"I have known for twenty years that Grigware was in Canada," Goss said.

"But how?" blurted Griffin, absolutely startled. We begin to sense that poor Fred Griffin waged a constant war to keep his emotions in check; he fought and lost, and so they often controlled him. "Why was he not caught? He told me himself that in his twenty-four years of freedom he was never once in danger."

Goss smiled benignly at the baffled reporter. It was good to shake up members of the press from time to time; it kept them humble. "I was told," he said, "by a post office inspector that, within a year or two of his escape from Leavenworth, word was received that he was seen in Vancouver or Victoria. I thought at the time he was making his way into the wild country of the North to hide out."

"Why was he not then caught if his presence was known?" Griffin asked.

"The inspector reported it, but there was some jealousy of him." Goss looked at the reporter and shrugged. "No action was taken."

It was a mystery that would never be explained. By all accounts, Frank never made it as far west as Victoria and Vancouver in British Columbia during his flight, yet there remained the strange matter of Frank's belongings sent after his escape from Leavenworth to the Spokane post office, which were then mysteriously forwarded to Vancouver. It is possible that Frank was briefly stationed in Vancouver while working for the railroad. Perhaps Herbert Fife's sighting of Frank reached the unidentified postal inspector in an altered form, and he reported it to Goss. In any case Goss, given mistaken information, reached the right conclusion. As a former federal prosecutor, he could have pressed for action. Instead he sat tight, perhaps as a way to pay forward his own doubts about Frank's conviction.

An odd assemblage of American supporters began speaking in Frank's favor. Henry Dunn was a South Omaha police captain in 1909 when Nels Turnquist brought Downer, Torgensen, and Grigware in for questioning; he would become police chief and eventually police commissioner. "This man should not be brought back, or, if he is, he should be the nation's guest and promptly given his liberty," Dunn said. "He has rehabilitated himself. That's all a prison can do at its best for men." John W. Leedy, the governor of Kansas from 1896 to 1898, when Leavenworth was first announced, sent a telegram to Roosevelt on April 3. BELIEVING IT TO BE IN THE INTEREST OF THE PUBLIC WELFARE THAT MEN SHOULD BE ENCOURAGED TO ABANDON EVIL ASSOCIATES AND WAYS, AND AS THIS MAN JAMES FAHEY HAS SET AN EXAMPLE THAT SHOULD ENCOURAGE OTHERS TO FOLLOW, I WOULD HEARTILY RECOMMEND EXECUTIVE CLEMENCY," the eighty-five-year-old Leedy wired. Even a sitting congressman pitched in. "Canada, stand by your guns," urged Representative Francis Henry Shoemaker of Minnesota. "Don't allow for one minute this man Fahey's Canadian home to be broken up by a travesty of justice."

Shoemaker was an odd choice for an ally. The junior congressman himself served time in Leavenworth for sending libelous matter through the U.S. mail; his sentence began on December 29, 1930, and ended on November 4, 1931. The alleged victim in this case was one of Shoemaker's many political enemies; the trial and conviction stank so badly of politics that Roosevelt pardoned Shoemaker after the fact in 1932. Shoemaker had already been elected at-large that year as a populist Farmer-Labor candidate to the Seventy-third Congress; the presidential pardon allowed him to serve legally for one term before he was voted out again. During his tenure, he made news by calling his foes "jellyfish," "alley cats," and "ravenous fiends," and made headlines for getting into fistfights with workmen using an acetylene torch outside his hotel room and with a Washington, D.C., cabdriver, whom he punched in the face at a traffic stop. Francis Henry Shoemaker was not a run-of-the-mill congressman.

In line with his volatile temperament, Shoemaker made no secret of his feelings about Leavenworth. "Plenty of men," he said, "have been railroaded to Leavenworth on the flimsiest of evidence, third-degreed over, and over so the officer of the law, many times the black-sheep relative of some politician, can get something on him. . . . The system would not be tolerated in any other country in the world."

Yet not everybody was on Frank's side. Thomas Munger, the trial judge in the Mud Cut case, believed that when a jury returned a verdict and the court handed down a sentence, the accused must serve the sentence in its entirety. He did not believe in appeals, pardons, or paroles. In 1934, as in 1909, he was a sitting federal judge; as the original trial judge, he could have terrific impact on moves to pardon Frank or extend any kind of clemency. He *did not* like the hoopla surrounding Frank's return. When Fred Griffin stepped into his chambers, Munger greeted him with a tirade about "newspapers creating false sympathy for a potential murderer by pandering to the lowest tastes of moron readers!"

To the newsman, these were fighting words. "You call Grigware a potential murderer?" he shot back, the Irish in him rising, his emotions winning out once again.

"He robbed with a gun in his hand!" Munger fumed.

"You don't think he deserves a pardon?"

"Certainly not."

"Do you not think he has shown redemption?" By then they were arguing, never mind pretensions of a civil interview. The judge launched into a broadside accusing newspapers of encouraging criminals to think that all they had to do was escape and hide in Canada for a number of years to deserve a pardon. "Can there be no mercy?" Griffin cried.

"There is no question of mercy," Munger shot back. "This man had a gun in his hands."

By now the two men were shouting so loudly that Munger's bailiff, waiting in the outer office, heard their voices through the closed door. He turned the knob and stepped inside. If any one moment showed that Frank's case had moved beyond reasoned debate, this was it. To Griffin and his readers, Munger represented all the American stereotypes: vengeful, autocratic, unwilling to admit error, convinced irrevocably of the rightness and absolute morality of his view. To Munger, Griffin was the embodiment of every muddle-headed Canadian who favored coddling criminals and was ample evidence of why America was becoming the greatest nation on earth while Canada lagged so far behind.

Even Griffin later conceded that he'd lost his professional cool. An interview is lost once the knives are drawn. "I had had about as much as I could stand, even from a United States judge," he wrote in his news story. All his outrage over the handling of Frank's case seemed to break forth in a tirade as great as Munger's. "I said, 'You have attacked newspapers, I could attack the judiciary. I could talk about shyster lawyers and venal and corrupt judges, but that would gain little. You have a right to whatever opinion you like about Grigware, but I cannot see that you have any right to attack me, my newspaper, or our motives, about which you know nothing. Thank you very much, judge. Good day.' " He had picked up his notebook and slammed the door behind him. Only later would it dawn on him how easily he could have been thrown in jail too.

If anything, the incident and others like it illustrated the depths of anger called up by Frank's case. Two styles of justice—redemptive and retributive—were at war over his fate; in such a charged atmosphere, there might be no compromise. Frank tried to act calm and strong for Ruth, his children, and all those who'd come to his defense, but within himself he shuddered to think what would happen if he returned to Leavenworth. If Munger became involved in his fate— which, as original trial judge, was a distinct possibility—he wouldn't have a prayer. His best chance lay with Roosevelt, yet a *New York Sun* editorial, widely quoted in Canadian papers, pointed out FDR's difficulties. While a president's powers were absolute in extradition matters, his feelings as an individual must be weighed against his duty as the nation's chief executive. "The president's first concern is what course to adopt to safeguard the United States," the *Sun* argued. "After that he can take thought of the individual, his years of responsibility, and his family."

Frank had another surprise on Wednesday, April 11. That morning, Fraser Duncan, one of his lawyers, handed him an envelope mailed from Seattle. Inside was a crisply folded letter from his mother, who lived with his sister Genevieve. It was in his mother's handwriting, which he recognized immediately. He read it through, then handed the letter back to Duncan, covering his face with his hands. His shoulders started to heave. Duncan discreetly left the office and faced the reporters outside.

"It is the most beautiful letter I have ever read," Duncan said, trying to keep his own voice in control. "Poor Fahey feels very much upset."

Frank would never reveal the contents of the letter to the public; the next day, he talked to his mother and brother Jim over the phone. Like many of the moments in Frank's very public ordeal, this too remained private. On April 13, the day before his first scheduled extradition hearing, he sat down and wrote a letter to his mother and brother. Only part of that letter survives.

> My Dear Mother and Brother:
>
>   To hear your dear voices again in person is very much like a dream. After all these long years, I can't actually believe this hearing to be true.
>
>   Nevertheless, it is an act of God and I am beginning to think that perhaps I am very fortunate that things are coming to a head before it's too late. I am sure happy you are alive, dear Mother, and my big desire is to see you as soon as possible.

The next day, the first extradition hearing was held; the case was delayed five days. On April 19, Frank returned to court again and the case was reset for May 14. Everyone was frustrated by the postponements, including the judge. He ruled that Frank could return home and keep vigil in Jasper, provided he reported twice a day to the RCMP barracks where he had been arrested. Since the barracks was within walking distance, Frank could do this easily.

They came home to Jasper on Friday, April 20. At first the town had planned a big celebration, but Frank and Ruth asked that their arrival be kept simple and quiet, attended only by their children and the friends who had cared for them. The train pulled up to the station in the morning and Ruth alighted first. The children ran up and, one by one, threw themselves into her arms. Frank stepped off next, carrying two suitcases.

A white-haired woman stepped slowly from the small group of adults waiting for them. Frank looked up from his children and stared. There was a silence. It was his mother, Jennie, now seventy-one. No one had told him that she would be here. She'd started out by car from Seattle with his brother Jim, but the road had been blocked by a rockslide in Vernon, British Columbia. Jim had turned back and planned to come later, but not before he wired ahead and put his mother on the Jasper train.

"Frank," she said. She wore a dark blue high-necked dress, and around her throat hung the little silver locket he'd given her twenty-eight years earlier when he said he was going off to see the world. She touched it, perhaps unconsciously, as she tried to speak. "They told me you were dead, but I didn't want to believe them."

Frank dropped the suitcases and held his mother to his chest. "Forgive me, Mother," he answered. "I wasn't dead."

IF ONE GROUP disliked the sudden turn of events it was the Bureau of Investigation, and no one more than J. Edgar Hoover. On the surface, he played it cool. When asked about the case by reporters with both American and Canadian papers, he said that his Bureau had worked "hand in hand" with the Mounties yet he refused to give details. "A case is never dropped until the fugitive is found or his demise is definitely established," he added, neglecting to mention that the Bureau *had* dropped the case three months before Frank's discovery, which would not have even occurred if he hadn't been charged by his friend, the game warden. In fact, it turned out that Frank's identification occurred only by a narrow thread of luck and the Mounties' love of fingerprinting. It was generally *not* the law at the time in Canada that a person arrested for an unindictable offense, like breaking park regulations, had to give his fingerprints. When Frank was asked to do so in early March, he had no legal compulsion to submit. Had he voiced an objection, Corporal Coggles would have been surprised and wondered why his friend was being obstinate, but he could not have forced him to press his fingers to the ink pads.

Soon after the arrest, Frank's discovery was billed as a great victory for the Bureau. "The identification of this fugitive after the lapse of nearly twenty-four years through comparison of his fingerprints is but another illustration of the efficacy of the fingerprint identification system," claimed a May 1, 1934, press release called the "Fugitives" that was regularly sent to press and police throughout the United States, the two groups that Hoover tried most to sway. Frank's arrest would be hailed as a victory for the rest of the century. Yet even as early as April 9, before the first scheduled extradition hearing, Hoover was being left out of the loop in talks about Frank between Hoover's boss, U.S. Attorney General Homer Cummings, and U.S. Secretary of State Cordell Hull. And even before that, members of the Bureau were growing worried that their prize might slip away.

On April 3, D. H. Dickason, SAC of the Butte, Montana, office, wrote in a "Personal and Confidential" letter to Hoover that the "Grigware matter" was progressing well. But two days later, in a letter dated April 5, Dickason noted with alarm that the Alberta legislature had drafted a resolution seeking Frank's freedom. In the same letter, he disputed Dan Downer's affidavit of support. "You will note that this statement does not say that Grigware was not guilty," Dickason wrote. "I cannot see how he can claim that he was innocent when the time to advance the plea was at the time of his trial in Omaha, Nebraska"—a plea Frank actually made in 1909.

By April 16, two days after Roosevelt's return to the White House, Dickason's worries about losing Frank had intensified. The winds in Washington were definitely shifting. In a letter to Hoover, Dickason complained about the Canadian defense of Grigware:

> I cannot see why this propaganda of a good citizen prevails when the records show that he was convicted of [poaching] and sentenced therefor in Canada. He was fingerprinted at this time and this was his downfall.

Dickason then went on to state what would become the Bureau's position on Grigware:

I would respectfully suggest that it will not be beneficial to our work in Canada if this man is not brought back to the United States. The officers there are like the Division—silent as to their feelings in the matter, but it would be a decided set-back for our work if he is released there. So far as any action after he reaches the penitentiary is concerned, if it is shown that leniency should be granted, that is all right, but for the good of our work and the capture of other criminals in Canada, I would, from my knowledge of this case, which extends over a number of years, respectfully suggest that the man, if possible, be brought back. He could then go through the regular course of investigation for a pardon or parole and any action taken would be very satisfactory to everybody.

Finally, Dickason attempted to cast doubt on the petition drive. "A list of the signers of the petition for Grigware's release at Jasper show a number of them sign as 'Mrs.————' and 'Mr.————,' which would indicate that the petition was prepared by someone, as these persons, if signing themselves, would sign their given names instead of Mr. or Mrs." Whether Dickason was simply suggesting that the petition was not entirely spontaneous, as reported in the press, or whether he also suggested that the petitioners be investigated is subject to interpretation.

By April 27, a week after Frank's return to Jasper, there was no record of any call to Hoover from Homer Cummings for comment on the case. So the Director took it upon himself. However, he proceeded carefully. In a memo to the Attorney General on that date, he sent Dickason's letter in its entirety without comment. His only addition was a brief preamble: "In order that you may be advised of the status of the case . . . I desire to call your attention to the following letter." Cummings did not acknowledge receipt of the letter; neither did he give Hoover any indication of which way his or Roosevelt's thoughts were headed.

Hoover had reason to tread lightly where Cummings was concerned. In 1933, when Roosevelt entered the Oval Office and Hoover was up for reappointment, Cummings seriously considered another man, former Department of Justice official Wallace Foster, for Hoover's job. But then Foster died unexpectedly. In the end, Cummings and Roosevelt decided to keep Hoover in his post, and on July 29, 1933, his reappointment was announced. Yet Hoover in April 1934 was not yet the national hero he would be a few months later, when John Dillinger was finally cornered and riddled with bullets outside Chicago's Biograph Theater on the night of July 21. He was not yet the J. Edgar Hoover who in 1935 and 1936 could lobby passionately for something as potentially abusive as the Universal Fingerprinting System. He still covered his bases, letting others speak for him when he sensed potentially damaging opposition. Like Frank Grigware and Fred Zerbst, he'd developed a sixth sense for survival, with good reason. Cummings was beginning to regret his advice to Roosevelt to reappoint Hoover. He would later call it "one of the biggest mistakes I ever made." The Director was "difficult to handle, could not be controlled, and had the faculty of attracting too much attention to himself."

This time, however, the Director did not get his way. On Saturday, May 12, 1934, two days before Frank's scheduled extradition hearing on May 14—on a beautiful spring day when two garden parties were scheduled at the White House and the Weather Bureau finally promised rain for the drought-stricken Midwest, when Secretary of State Cordell Hull told public officials and newspapermen that they "should analyze carefully the fundamentals behind the surface of events"—Attorney General Homer Cummings drafted a short letter to Hull:

> My dear Mr. Secretary,
>
> In reply to your letter . . . relative to the proceeding for the extradition of Frank Grigware from Canada, I desire to say that after careful consideration of all the facts bearing on this matter I have reached the conclusion that the ends of justice would best be served by not insisting that Grigware be extradited.
>
> I shall, therefore, be glad if you would be good enough to withdraw the request for his extradition.

To the press, there was no mention of justice. Cummings's statement to reporters was even shorter—"No good purpose could be served by bringing about the return of Fahey"—as if, in Cummings's mind at least, Frank Grigware no longer existed. After all those years of flight, only James Fahey remained.

To Hoover, there wasn't even the courtesy of that brief note. Cummings sent no official notice to the Director, no personal memo. On June 1, after hearing the news from every avenue but the official ones, Hoover shot a memo to the Justice Department. "Kindly advise the Division whether the arrangements for the extradition of Grigware have been withdrawn or whether he will be returned to a penal institution within the United States."

Four days later, Cummings's assistant, Joseph B. Keenan, answered: "I beg to advise you that the application for Grigware's extradition was withdrawn."

Forty-six days later, when he heard that John Dillinger was shot to death, Hoover said the words that seemed to express his feelings for all fugitives who eluded justice far too long. "I am glad Dillinger was taken dead," he snapped, then echoed the old Indian fighter Philip Sheridan: "The only good criminal is a dead criminal."

FRANK WAS DOING repairs in McLean's store in Jasper when the news from the States arrived. He'd been offered a number of jobs since his return from Edmonton, including a substantial repair contract at the Astoria Hotel, but even the extra work could not diminish the growing tension. For the past week rumors had come from his lawyers that some final decision would probably be made before the May 14 hearing. Fred Griffin had heard the rumors, too. By then he'd returned from Omaha and planted himself in the Canadian National telegraph office in Jasper to be first with the news.

It was late morning when Griffin rushed into the general store and read the message. Frank took the news stoically, the whitening of his face and tightening of his lips the only betrayal of emotion. "I hope it's true," he said. "I hope to hear from my lawyers soon now." He stared outside the store into the street, where people were smiling and looking at him through the big glass windows. It dawned on him that he would always be looked on in that fashion, as an oddity, and for a moment he seemed confused. "I'm going to have to tell the people now," he said. Carefully laying aside his carpenter's apron, he walked through the pines to the home he had built for his family. Griffin followed him but stayed back a discreet distance as Frank walked inside. He knew Frank's elderly mother still remained in Jasper for the decision from the courts; all the worry and excitement had weakened her, and she'd been laid up in bed for the past several days.

Tomorrow was Mother's Day, Sunday, May 13: maybe this would cheer her up, Griffin thought. He could imagine the look on Ruth's face when Frank told her the nightmare was over, the three children running up for a hug.

It was probably the happiest ending to a story that Griffin would ever write, yet even so the news from Washington was not perfect. The United States government had only dropped the extradition proceedings. No pardon had been granted. Should Frank ever cross the border into the United States, he could still be subject to arrest as a fugitive from justice. Officially, he could still be sent back to Leavenworth to serve out his time.

Right then it didn't seem to matter. Everyone floated in a sea of relief. Later that evening, near sunset, Griffin visited Frank for a last interview. At first Ruth stayed with them. They stood on the back porch and talked about all that had passed. Griffin told the story about his shouting match with Judge Munger, and all three of them laughed. Micky, the family's water spaniel, glanced up from his nap and then dropped his head back on his paws. They watched some deer stroll from the trees across the back of their property; one small deer with oversized ears poked an inquisitive nose through the porch railing. "They are all pets here," Frank said of the deer. "They come around almost every day in the winter to be fed."

It was getting late, and Griffin had to file his story. He turned to Ruth and asked if she had any last things she wanted to say. She looked at the reporter with her luminous eyes. "You have been very good to me, but please don't say anything more about us," she told Griffin. "Jim is working now, and all we want is to be left alone." She squeezed his hand gently, smiled once more into his face, and went back inside.

Frank and the fiery reporter stood outside in silence watching the sun go down. Frank breathed deeply as if in relief and smiled. "It's a lovely spot, don't you think?" he said. They watched as the sun finally vanished behind the mountains; the snow on the higher peaks was faintly luminous in the gloaming. Frank thought about his life and all that had happened. He still found it hard to comprehend all the fuss that had been made about his capture and all the support he'd gotten from strangers and friends. They saw in him something he couldn't see, for he never felt that special. He was not a hero, like some said. He'd run to save himself, and if that was an achievement, he felt it was a most ordinary one. He was not the only man ever to seek his future far from home, and he certainly wasn't the first. He was not the only man to flee the bitter ends of justice. Plenty of other young men had been swept up in the romance of the life ahead and told their families, "I'm going to see the world." He thought of what the Spokane prospector-turned-businessman Jacob Goetz had told him as Frank prepared for his own journey: how he'd known many young stampeders like Frank and himself, men full of spit and vinegar with the same high hopes and the same lack of sense, all looking for some bright promise. Frank realized now that Goetz was right. Better men than he had not made it out alive.

Frank looked at the dark sky above him. There were times when he remembered all he'd been through and felt bewildered by each mile he'd traveled, each nail he'd pounded, each person he'd befriended, each horror he'd observed. He thought of the friends who'd gone into Leavenworth with him in 1909 and of the ones who'd escaped with him that spring morning five months later, all staking their slim hopes on a train. Not a one had been as lucky. He remembered Alice Evans, remembered the lonely woman in the farmhouse, the hoboes in the jungle who'd shown him how to nail a drag. They'd all seen something in him, maybe a bit of themselves. They all were ordinary people, living the myth together. Trying to catch the train before it left them behind.

He looked at the stars in the darkness and thought how clear they were in the mountains. All of it seemed so far beyond his imagination; more than ever he felt so small. He wanted to cry out, but there were no words for such longing. The stars went on forever. Please God, let me cry out, he thought. But he could only catch his breath, amazed.

"He Should Therefore Be Considered Dangerous"

AT FIRST IT seemed that Ruth would get her wish. Her little family was "left alone,"and life returned to what it had been before the international headlines. The spirits of Frank's mother also soared with the news from the United States. On the day following U.S. Attorney General Cummings's statement, Jennie Grigware thanked her president, the federal government, and "all in Washington who were instrumental in the dropping of the extradition proceedings." She added a wish: "I hope the president will see fit to grant a full pardon to my son." The *Edmonton Journal* seconded that hope in an editorial headlined NOT THE "PERFECT ENDING" YET: "Until that pardon is issued, Fahey will still be a fugitive from justice and will not be able to visit in that country where he has relatives. No doubt Mr. Roosevelt will extend this clemency in his own good time."

That same day, on May 14, justice officials declared that no pardon would be issued, at least not for now. The department preferred to hold the case in the status it had occupied for the last twenty-four years, a spokesman said. It was disappointing for Frank, but his lawyers told him to be patient. The United States had to save *some* face, and their decision might quietly change with time.

Nonetheless, the summer was a happy one for Frank and his family. Jennie extended her stay, and the girls were overjoyed to learn that their new grandmother was an expert seamstress. "I had more clothes when she came up than any other time," Marie remembered many years later. "Any little scrap she would put together as a dress." Frank's brother Jim finally arrived, bringing his wife, Lucille, and those of their seven children who still lived at home. They worked on Frank's second house, on Tonquin Street at the edge of town. It was a wooden two-story house with a cross-gable roof and wood shingles that he'd started in 1929, to which he kept adding until 1938. That summer Eddie came up also, teaching painting to the children and their friends in the kitchen on Tonquin Street. Frank watched his brother and realized how much he'd missed; when he'd left in 1906, Eddie was still a kid whose greatest dream was to play baseball. Later that summer, Jennie went back to the States with Eddie. Despite all their hopes otherwise, she would never return to Canada.

Except perhaps for Frank, Eddie would be the most noted of Jennie's children. In 1934 he was a commercial artist in Chicago, but by 1936 he'd moved to Cody, Wyoming, the town east of Yellowstone that Buffalo Bill helped found in 1895. Eddie's house overlooked a canyon of the Shoshone River as it wound toward a cleft in the mountains. In World War II, he would be a War Record painter for the U.S. Navy: one of his best-known pieces during this time was of an anthropomorphic "globe" listening in on a woman's phone conversation. The legend said KEEP MUM: THE WORLD HAS EARS, a subject all the Grigwares knew about. After the war, he returned to Cody, where he made a name painting realistic murals of the Old West. The best known were a mural of western expansion in Cody and a history of the Mormon Church painted in its Los Angeles temple. Some of the cowboys in his paintings were dark-haired and blue-eyed like the brother he'd admired.

In October 1934, Frank legally changed his name to James Lawrence Fahey. On March 29, 1935, one year after his arrest, the *Edmonton Journal* did a short follow-up, noting that Frank still hoped for a pardon. On March 25, 1936, he still waited. That winter he traveled to Vancouver with the Jasper curling team to take part in a regional competition. Jim came up to see him, but their mother was too sick to travel, he said.

Frank told reporters that life was quiet, yet the idyll had begun to end. In 1935, he heard that his father had died in Sedro-Woolley, Washington, at the age of seventy-five. Edward Grigware had never gotten back with Jennie and died shunned by his family. Frank briefly considered going to the funeral, but with the unresolved status of his pardon, he decided not to test America's generosity. He'd been lucky once. If he got stopped while crossing the border, he might not be lucky again.

Frank lived quietly in Jasper for the rest of the thirties, yet by decade's end something began to change. Maybe Jasper itself was changing, no longer as isolated, now that hardtop roads connected it to Banff and Edmonton. Maybe the change was in him. His spring of notoriety had passed, yet he could never be plain "Jim Fahey" again. He would always be the man who escaped from Leavenworth. He would always feel the eyes of the curious following as he passed. Even with his closest friends, something basic had changed.

In the rest of Canada, his story was pushed aside by the greater madness over the birth of the Dionne quintuplets on May 28, 1934, sixteen days after Frank's extradition was canceled. In an era when childhood innocence was seen as balm for a troubled world, the quints were Canada's answer to Shirley Temple—and there were *five* of them. Every aspect of their birth and childhood was carried in the press: their premature delivery, their feeding schedule, the squads of doctors and nurses guarding them from disease and infection, their developing personalities. One detail that caught Frank's attention was the fact that the second and third toes of each girl's feet were webbed together, said to occur in only one out of every 1,000 children. No one made a fuss about it. He hoped the defect did not cause the girls as much trouble as it had caused him.

When Hitler's Germany overran Poland on September 1, 1939, an era that made stars of innocents gave way to one where evil seemed everywhere, like a bad seed. By then, Frank showed signs of moving on. In 1938, he sold the house on Tonquin Street to William Jeffrey, the friend and store owner who'd bailed him out; Jeffrey gave the house to his son and daughter-in-law. The trigger to move came in 1940. That year, a "baby Fahey," listed in provincial records as a stillborn birth, was buried in plot 058 of the Jasper cemetery, an unmarked grave atop a green hill north of town. Even today, the graveyard prizes anonymity, and according to the regulations posted at the gate, gravestones are optional.

By 1941, Frank had briefly moved to Edmonton to run a concession during the war. Though Jack and Louise were in their twenties,

Marie was a teenager and still living at home. She turned nineteen in 1944, a young woman ready to tell her own parents she wanted to see the world. That same year, news arrived from Seattle that Jennie Grigware was dying. She was eighty-one and had never gotten better after her first and last trip to Jasper; she wished desperately to see Frank one more time. The Grigwares made discreet inquiries to some unidentified friends in the government but got the impression that there would never be a pardon. Frank's brothers warned him that the house and hospital might be watched. Jennie died that year and was buried in Seattle. Frank never saw her grave.

He thought of her often now, just as he'd thought about her during his fugitive years. After Jennie's death, Marie began to sense a "great sadness" in her father that never completely disappeared. A bitter resentment began to grow in his children toward the United States. "It's as though law enforcement there could not ever admit they made a mistake," Marie later remembered. "As though authorities could never admit they were wrong." Stories drifted north that distant members of the Grigware clan painted Frank as a black sheep. A photo kept by the Grigwares in Michigan mentioned a Francis "Train Robber" Grigware. Kay Werner, one of Jim's granddaughters, now living in Washington State, later said, "It was always drilled into us that you don't bring shame to the family." She believed the dictum started when Frank was a fugitive.

Not everyone in the States considered Frank guilty. Some saw him as a symbol of deepening faults in American justice, an unpopular opinion after the war and during the rest of the century. On November 1, 1946, a letter to Leavenworth penitentiary from Baltimore attorney Samuel Rubin asked about the lessons of Frank's case. "The innocence of Grigware was established," Rubin wrote. He requested more information about Frank's case because, he said, he was trying to develop a study on the need for better publicly funded counsel for indigent defendants. This would include a staff of investigators hired to work with public defenders, detectives whose efforts would counterbalance the police evidence used by prosecutors, thus evening the scales of justice and making the process more fair. The imbalance is one of the great weaknesses of the American criminal system, one that remains today. There was no reply to Rubin's letter from the prison, and no record that the Baltimore lawyer ever wrote again.

After World War II, Frank's case may have been forgotten in

Canada, but not in the institutional memory of the FBI. The Grigware case was stamped closed on June 12, 1934, and at first it seemed destined to stay that way. When Jack Golden was arrested in Seattle for grand larceny on October 31, 1941, the local sheriff wrote to the FBI about a federal notice for Jack's detention. Hoover wrote back that the notice "may be removed inasmuch as Grigware is no longer wanted." Then, in early 1957, there were questions as to whether Frank could come back home.

They were initiated that year by his brother Jim. In 1956, Jim's wife Lucille died in Spokane at the age of sixty-six, and once again Frank did not attend the funeral. Ironically, there was no evidence that the family was watched from the end of the war to the mid-1950s, so it may have been a window when he could have slipped in and authorities would not have known or even cared. Yet the temper of the country had once again changed. In 1957, the year Jim started to feel more lonely, Senator Joseph McCarthy died of cirrhosis of the liver. Yet damage had already been done by his political exploitation of America's second Red Scare. The Cold War was a fact, "brink-manship" and "massive retaliation" were public policy, and Sputnik circled the globe. Opponents of the first civil rights march in Washington, D.C., and school desegregation in Little Rock, Arkansas, labeled them the results of communist agitation. Enemies were seen everywhere, inside the border and out. The turn-of-the-century fear of anarchism had been updated to the even more apocalyptic Nuclear Age. Nineteen fifty-seven was the year that *Masters of Deceit*, billed as a manual on "Communism in America and How to Fight It," was being ghostwritten by five or six Bureau scribes; Hoover would be credited as author, and its publication in 1958 would see it sell 250,000 copies in hardcover and two million in paperback. Jim Grigware could not have made inquiries at a less fortuitous time.

By then, Frank's brother Jim was sixty-nine. The trips to Canada were getting harder. Frank had often said he'd like to share the travel expenses and visit Jim in Washington and Eddie in Wyoming. One of Jim's daughters or granddaughters, who remains unidentified in FBI records and whose husband had some connection to the government, made initial and innocent inquiries into whether Frank could finally visit his childhood home.

The inquiry mushroomed unexpectedly. On March 5, 1957, a memo passed the desk of Clyde Tolson, still the FBI's Assistant Director, asking whether Frank would be arrested if he entered the United States. A handwritten note at the bottom of the memo said, *It certainly seems to me he should be apprehended if he comes to U.S.* On March 8, Hoover sent a memo to Assistant Attorney General Warren Olney III of the Criminal Division, asking for an opinion. Hoover's note was deceptively light on details. Regarding the reason for the 1934 cancellation of Frank's extradition proceedings, he only wrote, "We do not know why request for subject's extradition was canceled." Olney responded on March 26 that, since Frank was still classified as a fugitive, "There is no reason why this subject should not be apprehended to serve the sentence imposed against him since such sentence has neither been served nor commuted."

On March 29, 1957, Hoover sent memos to FBI offices in Kansas City, Denver, Seattle, and another unidentified Washington field office, as well as to the FBI's Foreign Liaison Unit and to the legal attaché in Ottawa "to establish appropriate coverage" of Frank's relatives to monitor the chances of his return. Twenty-three years after it ended, the surveillance of the Grigwares began again. By April 18, 1957, memos were sent to FBI offices throughout the West and in Detroit identifying Frank's kin in Washington, Michigan, Colorado, and Wyoming. As agents found more relatives, more memos flew.

Starting on that same date, April 18, 1957, Frank's status as a threat dramatically changed. Underlined and printed in capital letters across the bottom of the memo was the warning: IT HAS BEEN REPORTED THAT GRIGWARE WOULD KILL OR BE KILLED RATHER THAN BE RECAPTURED AND HE SHOULD THERE-FORE BE CONSIDERED DANGEROUS. It was the same unsubstantiated rumor first reported by the old Bureau's Chicago office in 1911, made by a paid informant who never talked to Frank yet told his willing paymasters that Grigware drank tequila in Mexico City's American Bar while awaiting a visit from his yegg pals. As during the original hunt, Frank was labeled dangerous, yet this time the message was hammered home with each new memo. Once again, it was a license to kill. By then, Frank was seventy-one.

From that day forward, every memo issued about Frank Grigware prominently displayed the warning that he WOULD KILL OR BE KILLED RATHER THAN BE RECAPTURED. His brothers and sisters, nieces and nephews, third, fourth, and fifth cousins were tracked by FBI agents to Los Angeles, Manhattan Beach, and Bakersfield, California; to

Caseville, Lake, Saginaw, Bay City, Marlette, Dearborn, and Grand Rapids, Michigan; to Seattle, Kettle Falls, Evans, Tacoma, and Whidbey Island, Washington. By early August 1957, Jim Grigware had apparently gotten word that his innocent question had backfired. He warned Frank to stay out of the country.

There seems little doubt that Frank would have gone back to Leavenworth this time if he'd crossed the border. The FBI meant business and had more power than in 1934. On August 28, 1957, when the Kansas City office accidentally left the warning of Frank's perceived dangerousness off two reports, an advisement went out from Washington "to make proper insertions." The warnings continued throughout 1958 and 1959. On January 9, 1960, Eddie died in Cody; as in the past, Frank dared not attend the funeral. It was a wise decision, since by then he was being watched. The FBI had tracked Frank and Ruth to Moberly Lake, British Columbia, about 250 miles northwest of Jasper and 115 miles due west of Spirit River in the northern Peace River country. He owned a summer resort, built and sold houses, and was a partner in a Hudson's Bay Store. He'd sometimes vanish into the woods to trap fur. He'd made a big circle in his life, helping build yet another town in the forest, returning to that region where he'd earned his first acceptance and perhaps his greatest peace. If there was a direction to his life, it was always toward the winter forest: the isolated outposts in Moberly Lake, Spirit River, and Jasper; the near-fatal winter at the Blue Jay mine when he found what he'd been looking for, though he would not realize it till later. His boyhood in the woods outside Caseville started the pattern, when his father taught him how to set traps for fur. Perhaps he was an anachronism and should have been born a hundred years earlier; in his own silent way, he would have prospered. The continental Gaze had not yet developed. There were no trains to Leavenworth then. He would have been free.

By 1961, the FBI heard rumors that Frank might leave Moberly Lake, and they wanted to know if the reports were accurate. On March 13, 1961, Hoover wrote that contacts in Canada should poke around to learn more. On April 23, a month later, an agent knocked on Jim Grigware's door in Kettle Falls, Washington. Jim was seventy-three by now, growing sick and five years away from death; he was the last of the family to go up and see his brother, a fact known to the FBI. The agent quizzed him about Frank, and the old man bragged that his older brother had built a new house, just the newest of several. Moberly Lake was a tiny place in the woods, he said, with a few homes, a store, and a post office. It suited Frank very well. Jim said Frank's children lived in British Columbia; in his report, the agent tracked down their locations. The agent also added that Frank was "reportedly very spry for his age." Three months later, on July 20, an FBI agent or a Canadian informant made the trip to Moberly Lake and asked around. "It is common knowledge among the population that [Frank] is a fugitive from the United States," the report said. Friends in the area no doubt told him about the stranger asking questions. The man they knew as James Fahey nodded, easily guessing for whom the stranger worked. He was seventy-five years old, still building houses at the edges of civilization, and the FBI continued to call him a dangerous man.

Perhaps the FBI's Canadian contacts saw this as objectionable. In any case, on December 5, 1962, Canada's legal attaché in Ottawa wrote Hoover that there were no indications that Frank ever considered visiting the United States and informed the Director that they were closing the file on Grigware "due to his advanced age." The attaché also believed that FBI requests to check on Frank to verify his presence at Moberly Lake "shall perhaps be a little less frequent." It was a polite and proper Canadian brush-off, and Hoover seems to have gotten the message. There is no record that the Canadians were asked to check on Frank again.

By 1965, the FBI's Kansas City office, which once again inherited the case since it had been the "originating office" decades before, had apparently come to the conclusion that continuing surveillance of a man who would soon be eighty was a waste of resources and time. On February 1 of that year, the Kansas City SAC asked Washington for permission to close the Grigware file. Ten days later, on February 11, 1965, he got his answer. "The case may be closed by your office; however, all stops should remain effective," Hoover wrote. As in 1933, Frank's case was closed, but not completely. Another alarm would go off in the Identification Division if Frank's fingerprints ever again passed through their system. By now the FBI fingerprint files were a huge and twisting labyrinth, the cards still classified and stored by Sir Francis Galton's Details, the twelve basic minutiae that arched, whorled, looped, and spiraled, that could trap men and women forever in an endless inky maze. They ran like rats; they ran forever; and at the end, they found their own personal Minotaur. By the 1960s, the numbers of cards representing American citizens, the quick and the dead, the innocent and guilty, had long since sped past the hundred million mark; the total would reach two hundred million in 1971, the FBI later said. By 1965, the year Frank's case file was once again closed, FBI literature regularly boasted that its fingerprint cards, if stacked one atop the other, would reach 113 times higher than the Empire State Building.

By 1965, Frank was seventy-nine years old. He'd been pursued, processed, indexed, cataloged, discovered, debated, forgotten, and reinvestigated by the FBI and its predecessor for fifty-five years, more than two-thirds of his life. His file was closed three times—in 1933, 1934, and 1965—but always with a final stop order that never really closed it entirely. There were nearly 660 pages of documents in his file: not a record by FBI standards, which kept reams of documents on public figures ranging from congressmen to communists, from Dr. Benjamin Spock to Walt Disney, as well as the fingerprints of millions of private individuals. Still, it is safe to say that it was among the longest-lived cases in FBI files.

When his brother Jim died in 1966, Frank chose once again not to attend the funeral. He was eighty by then, the last of the four brothers, a walking if largely anonymous witness to history. He wanted it that way. He thought often about America as he and Ruth grew old. In the years before Jim's death, his brother would tell him about changes in the United States, especially in the West. The towns there now, like the ones he'd ridden through in his youth, were still forlorn and proud. Instead of being linked by steel tracks, they were connected by concrete and asphalt—endless miles of road. The road would flow out of the western emptiness past a fringe of service stations, bars, and motels, cut through a couple of blocks where the town widened to storefronts, ranch houses, and green lawns, and then pass out the far side through a skein of gas pumps and junkyards, vanishing once more into the distance.

Frank would have liked to have seen the changes. He'd never forgotten the savage beauty he'd witnessed down there. He remembered the cyclone in the distance, its thin finger reaching from the clouds to lay waste to the earth; the black electric storm clouds that boiled up as fast as soup; the mountains that rose straight above him, dwarfing everything by comparison, as beautiful and ominous as gods. He remembered the sparkling vein of silver he'd found and lost; that deadly winter when the cougars came down from the mountains. He remembered the day the Leavenworth train broke through the gate with a mighty metal crash, and he turned his face west toward the Salt Creek Valley and smelled the ash where farmers burned stubble from their fields.

By the 1960s and early 1970s, others had run, like him, across the border. He watched on TV as Canada became home to American draft dodgers, fleeing what they considered an unjust war. Slaves, draft dodgers, Frank Grigware, others like them—they were linked through the centuries. All fled a vengeful justice, when questions of guilt and innocence took a backseat to the rhetoric of power, the expediency of politics, the prejudice of rage. America liked to see herself as the land that made men's futures. She never saw herself as the spirit of vengeance, hunting men till they died. It didn't start that way, yet by century's end there was little doubt that public policy had grown more punitive. By the year 2000, nearly two million Americans were behind bars and roughly fourteen million feared the likelihood of imprisonment at some point in their lives. America's rate of imprisonment was the highest on the planet, and many of those imprisoned were black, Latino, or some other minority, just like the first official prisoners in the nation's first federal penitentiaries. There were thousands of prisons in America—local, state, and federal; publicly and privately operated—and by the year 2000, the business of building and running prisons was the greatest area of growth in the public sector.

Through it all, Leavenworth survived. Though billed as the nation's oldest federal prison, it is no longer the most expensive to run or the most visionary. On January 19, 2001, it housed 1,645 inmates in the walled prison and another 456 in the prison camp outside the walls. It is still one of America's toughest prisons and, according to government sources, the largest maximum security prison in the nation. The West Gate and the railroad chute have been demolished, the red-brick wall plugged with concrete. The railroad tracks have been torn up, the bridge over Salt Creek at Shanghai Crossing nothing more than blackened posts rotting in the mud.

All things pass, even prisons, and in the town of Leavenworth there are occasional rumors that the Big House has grown too antiquated and will be closed, demolished, or turned into a museum like Alcatraz.

So far, the rumors have never proved true. Such a move would be disastrous for the first city in Kansas, where seven prisons comprise its employment base and banners strung across the street declare Leavenworth PRISON CITY, USA. Yet even if it passes, what matters is its legacy. It started the nation's fingerprint revolution, molded the modern prison, perfected the art of control. Today, Leavenworth is the most famous prison in the prison nation. Like Louis Brandeis said, importance lies in influence. By the start of the new millennium, Leavenworth had led the way.

By then, Frank was dead. In the late 1960s or early 1970s he and Ruth moved to Lacombe, Alberta, halfway between Calgary and Edmonton, to be near Marie and Louise. They lived in a senior center not far from the site of Frank's first railway job on the Blackfalds bridge. He was hearty until the year before his death, when he had a fall and his health deteriorated steadily. He died on April 12, 1977, at the age of ninety-one, of what his children called a general shutdown. On the day of his death and afterward, there were no obituaries in the papers in Toronto, Calgary, Edmonton, Jasper, or even Red Deer, the closest city to Lacombe. He achieved in death the anonymity he'd sought in life, his passing unnoticed publicly.

He is buried today in Lacombe's Fairview Cemetery, a crowded if peaceful place where the oldest graves are in the back and people of every creed and nationality lie side by side. The names are Irish, English, Asian, Russian, Eastern European, Middle Eastern, or of indeterminate mix, all running from something at sometime in their lives. I visited there in the summer of 1999, one more pursuer following Frank's trail. The graveyard is flanked by tall pines and cedars that sigh and rustle in the breezes but moan and creak in stiffer winds, an early warning system for the summer storms that roar off the western mountains, bringing with them hail the size of marbles and a biting cold. The storms end as quickly as they start, leaving oblong pools that shine like the deadly mercury forming amalgams with gold. Seen from another angle, they simply reflect the sky. After the storm, black-and white magpies drop from the branches. They strut among the gravestones, looking for something shiny that blew in from the west or worked up from the soil. When something glitters, they clutch it in their beaks and quickly fly back home.

People do remember Frank in Jasper, though by the name Jim Fahey. They say that Trapper's Creek got its name from him. The records say otherwise, yet legends change constantly, like original intentions and identities. The Jasperites remember the tale of Frank's unmasking, the vengeance that crashed down on him after all those peaceful years. The town is much as it would have been then. Deer and bear no longer wander the streets, but the architecture is still similar, the tree-lined streets, the mountains that glow in the sunset, the Chaba Theatre where Frank got a glimpse of his future. The house on Tonquin Street still stands. In the summer of 1999, Phyllis Jeffrey, daughter-in-law of the man who helped spring Frank from the RCMP lockup, still lived inside. She welcomed me while giving painting lessons at the kitchen table to her granddaughter, a world-class snowboarder. It was the same kitchen where she took painting lessons from Frank's brother Eddie in 1934. She was proud of her house and its solid construction. "They don't make them like this anymore," she told me.

Ruth lived for more than a decade after Frank, until her death in the early 1990s. Today she is buried by the side of the man she would always call Jim. She never liked to talk about "the dark days of 1934," her younger daughter remembered, and the children—Louise, Jack, and Marie—respected her wishes. It was only in 1998 or 1999 that Marie, by then living with her daughter and her family in Grande Prairie, part of the Peace River country, finally told them the tale of her father's journey and of those dark days.

Not that she was ashamed. She'd simply assumed her father's mantle of self-sufficiency. Whose business was it, anyway? she wondered, when I called her on the phone. What reason did she have to trust me, one more American Nimrod, chasing her father after all these years? It seemed there were too many prying eyes in the modern world. Still, Marie admitted, her father was a handsome fellow. Quiet and always lean, built like a sprinter. "Once I tried to beat him in a foot race," she recalled, "and he put me in my place." As he pulled ahead, they both started laughing. As he sped away, she never felt more proud.

There are times in life when children see their parents as they are to others and, more important, get a fugitive glimpse beneath the skin. This was one of those moments for Marie. She saw now that he ran for the joy of it, nothing more. As Jennie Grigware had promised in another century, no one would ever catch him, no matter how hard they tried. If Marie's father was not a hero, at least he was a messenger. If we never do find justice, perhaps we can find peace, he seemed to say, and for a time the world had listened. That was heroic enough for Marie. She laughed quietly at the memory of those long legs tearing up the ground beneath him and then said, almost to herself, "My father could run like a deer."

Notes

Preface

ix "as a pretty a spot as you can find on God's green earth." James W. French, quoted in *Proceedings of the Annual Congress of the National Prison Association of the United States, 1895*, p. 184.

xi "a 3,100-bed jail in Harris County . . . and dozens more." Cited by Eric Schlosser, "The Prison-Industrial Complex," *Atlantic Monthly*, December 1998, p. 77.

xi "given up to the dreams of fancy, and . . . innovators." Alexis de Tocqueville, *Democracy in America*, ed. by Richard D. Heffner (New York: Penguin Books, 1956), p. 44.

Prologue: The Stuff of Dreams

Details of the "big mutiny" of 1901 were primarily taken from the *Leavenworth Times*, November 9, 1901, and thereafter. The conditions under which the prisoners labored were found in many general sources, but most specifically in the letter of prisoner Thomas Kating to President Woodrow Wilson.

1 "the Hot House, after its lack of ventilation." For a better description of this heated milieu, see Pete Earley, *The Hot House*, pp. 25–26.

1 "whispered group jealousies . . . filled every minute with peril." Charles S. Wharton, *The House of Whispering Hate*. Wharton, a former Illinois congressman and one-time attorney of Harry K. Thaw, the millionaire murderer of architect Stanford White, was convicted in 1929 of conspiracy to rob the U.S. mail and served time in Leavenworth until 1931.

1 "a giant mausoleum adrift in a great sea of nothingness." Quoted in Earley, *The Hot House*, p. 30.

3 "This prison when completed . . . leave the prison a reformed and useful citizen." *Leavenworth Times*, March 21, 1897.

6 "Old prisoners claimed that stragglers were whipped." Thomas E. Gaddis and James O. Long, *Killer: A Journal of Murder*, p. 176 and footnote p. 363. Gaddis heard the tale from Robert Stroud, the Bird Man of Alcatraz; it was related to him by J. S. "Heck" Wallace, an alleged march survivor and fellow prisoner. Carl Panzran, the subject of Gaddis's book, also worked at the Leavenworth construction site and heard the tales.

7 "The typical midday meal was beans flavored with . . . floating hairs." Letter of Thomas Kating to President Woodrow Wilson, April 20, 1913. Kating was one

of the ringleaders in the 1901 escape and gives a prisoner's view of life in Leavenworth from 1900 to 1913. The charges in his twenty-page, densely handwritten letter have credibility for no other reason than what happened after President Wilson read it: Kating's life sentence was commuted and as Leavenworth's warden was replaced after fourteen years at the helm.

8 the new warden saved the Justice Department $50,000 in wages. Ibid. p.

9 "I have a bucketful of notes . . . even if I have to come out and do it myself." Ibid., p.

9 "dog poisoning fiend." *Leavenworth Times*, November 8, 1901.

9 The captain of the watch . . . not to worry about plans made by any "Territory bums." Letter of Thomas Kating to Woodrow Wilson, p.

12 "A penitentiary never sheltered a more desperate character than 2064 . . . brought into subjection." *Leavenworth Times*, November 8, 1901.

11–12 The near-fatal meeting of Frank Thompson and Andrew Leonard is described in the *Leavenworth Times*, November 8, 1901.

14 "the base of the forehead, halfway straight back through the head." *Leavenworth Times, November 8, 1901.*

14 "several ounces of fluid from the brain oozed down." *Leavenworth Times*, November 16, 1901.

15 "At night, he was chained to a metal staple in the floor of his solitary cell." Letter of Thomas Kating to Woodrow Wilson,

16 "Leavenworth is hell, and I guess I'm the chief devil." Quoted in Gaddis and Long, *Killer*, p. 177.

Chapter 1: The Grand Tour

Details on Frank's journey across the vanishing West are contained in the files of the Pinkerton National Detective Agency, *True Detective Magazine, Edmonton Journal,* and *Toronto Daily Star.*

25 "The railroads had even shaped time . . . did not officially adopt standard time until 1918." John F. Stover, *American Railroads*, p. 157–158.

29 "all honorable work is noble and confers honor upon the one doing it." Quoted in Stella Luke, *100 Years of Mining*, self-published in conjunction with the Mining Museum of Wallace, Idaho, p. 35.

38 "Of late years . . . the act of the dead man." *Spokesman-Review*, June 5, 1909.

38 "The lure and lust for gold was unrelenting. . . . Those who worked for mining companies probably fared worse in death that lone prospectors because of the hardships of those they left behind. The body was sent to Ward's, the undertaker in Wallace, while a pit boss filled out a form entitled "First Notice of Death and Preliminary Application." Its questions asked if the deceased spoke English, was intoxicated when killed, if the tool involved in the accident was hand- or mechanically powered, if the death was self-inflicted. If a widow applied for compensation, a hearing was held by the Industrial Accident Board of the State of

Idaho. Case No. 3372 was a good example of what she could expect. On September 9, 1918, William H. Brusie, a thirty-seven-year-old miner working in the Hercules Mine, was killed in an explosion that charred his chest and blew off his head. His wife applied for relief. Although there were no children, she was pregnant when he died. Mrs. Brusie was entitled to 45 percent of William's weekly wages up to $12 a week for 400 weeks. Since Brusie made $5.25 a day and worked seven days a week, he made $36.75. Mrs. Brusie's $12 weekly maximum was too little to live on, and she left the Coeur d'Alenes to survive.

38 The world stock of gold from 1492 to 1850 was estimated from "Gold," *Microsoft Encarta Encyclopedia*, which priced gold at the 1990s average price of $370 per troy ounce.

39 "to miners, he was an undercover man." The prevalence of undercover operatives in the mining district was not just paranoia on the part of the miners. The most famous today is Charles Siringo, the "cowboy detective," who in 1891–92 posed as union secretary and whose testimony resulted in the arrest and conviction of eighteen union leaders. After more riots in 1898–99, agents filled the mines. The most successful was Edward L. Zimmerman, known as Operative 58A or Operative Z, who worked for the Spokane office of the Thiel Detective Agency, a competitor of Pinkerton's. Like Siringo, Zimmerman got himself elected union secretary and kept mine owners informed. By the turn of the century, surveillance was a daily fact of life affecting men's jobs. A set of Thiel instructions dated November 10, 1900, told agents to list all miners by belief and affiliation. The name of a "Union Man" would be followed by X, a "Dangerous Agitator and Union Man" by XX, and a "Dangerous Unemployed Union Man" by XXX. These lists resulted in firings and blacklistings. The instructions were reproduced in Luke, *100 Years of Mining*, p. 16.

40 The saga of "Stumpy" Wicks is in Wendell Brainard, *Golden History Tales: From Idaho's Coeur d'Alene Mining District*, pp. 19–20.

40 "While Frank . . . was learning that Westerners held a heightened, romantic notion of themselves." Paraphrased from Wallace Stegner, *The American West as Living Space*, p. 68.

40 The saga of Molly B'Damn is found in Brainard, *Golden History Tales*, pp. 7–8.

47 "Folks come easy, and they go easy." Owen Wister, *The Virginian*, p. 37.

48 "safety valve . . . fountain of youth in which America continually bathed." Turner's 1896 speech is quoted in Henry Nash Smith, *Virgin Land: The American West as Symbol and Myth*, p. 297.

48 According to the 1890 Census, the West's suicide rate stood at 121 deaths per million population, far surpassing the North Atlantic, the second-highest region, with a rate of 77.9. More people died in the West from alcoholism (99 per million) than anywhere else, followed by the North Atlantic with a rate of 65.3. In the West, 1,878 men and women per million descended into madness, second only to the North Atlantic, where the rate was 2,385.

48 "I instantly preferred . . . a true nobility." Wister, *The Virginian*, pp. 23–24.

49 "committed suicide . . . but was prevented from doing so." Quoted in Michael

Lesy, *Wisconsin Death Trip*. The pages are unnumbered, but Zweekbaum's tale is contained in the section titled "1901."

49 "The mother became ... driven mad by the "morbid state" of the frontier." Blackmar's account of the Smoky Pilgrims is quoted in Lesy, *Wisconsin Death Trip*, "Conclusion."

52 "I am not the man ... I would have to kill or be killed." Bat Masterson's letter is quoted in Time-Life Books and Paul Trachtman, *The Gunfighters*, p. 125.

Chapter 2: "When We Are Absent, One from Another"

General details on the histories of the Mud Cut Gang, Alice Evans, and Lillian Stevenson, as well as Frank's travels and his love affair with Alice, are contained in Pinkerton files.

59–60 "The Western marriage of gold and sex. . . . "The discussion of the attitude toward prostitutes in mining towns comes from several sources, especially from Bradley Smith, *The American Way of Sex*, p. 153.

63 "It was estimated that during this time . . . found more socially acceptable jobs." The discussion of turn-of-the-century prostitution was found on the History Channel's site on the World Wide Web, URL:www.historychannel.com.

63 "Many of these women became temporary prostitutes because of acquaintances and friends." Survey on causes of prostitution, from the collection of the Port Townsend Historical Museum, Port Townsend, Washington. Quoted from Dr. William W. Sanger, *The History of Prostitution: Its Extent, Causes, and Effects Throughout the World*, 1858. Sanger's work, one of the nineteenth century's most famous studies of prostitution, asked two thousand women the simple question: "What was the cause of your becoming a prostitute?" Their reasons included:

Destitution	525
Inclination	513
Seduced and abandoned	258
Drink and the desire to drink	181
Ill-treatment by parents, relatives, or husband	164
As an easy life	124
Bad company	84
Persuaded by prostitutes	71
Too idle to work	29
Violated (raped)	27
Seduced on board emigrant ships	16
Seduced in emigrant boardinghouses	8

A surprising number of women, nearly 41 percent, made such "free will" choices as "inclination," "an easy life," "persuaded by prostitutes," "too idle to work," and "bad company," suggesting that, notwithstanding the social stigma and fear of venereal disease, these respondents still saw opportunities in prostitution that were not offered to them in a more "respectable" life.

64–65 "bottles of White Lily Face Wash . . . for 'improving and relaxing the nerves and brain.' " All these patent medicines were offered for sale in the Sears mailorder catalog. *Sears, Roebuck & Co. Consumers Guide: Fall 1909*, pp. 379–382 and 401–4.

74 "Although they were suspects . . . they were never arrested and charged." At times, the Spokane police apparently adopted a live-and-let-live attitude that was rarely chronicled but still arose in hints and whispers. The most persistent and provocative of these was the rumor that Robert LeRoy Parker, the famous Butch Cassidy of the Wild Bunch, returned to the United States from exile in South America and, on December 23, 1910, took up permanent residence in Spokane. His new name was William T. Phillips, engineer and owner of the Phillips Manufacturing Company, and he stayed in town until he died of rectal cancer at the county poor farm on July 20, 1937, at the age of seventy-two. Spokane residents officially dismissed the claim, but the rumors were still circulating in 1977 with the publishing of Larry Pointer's book, *In Search of Butch Cassidy*. The author cited several sources: Cassidy's surprise visit to his sister in 1929; a 1937 letter from the head of the Wyoming Writers Project claiming that Cassidy was living in Spokane as William Phillips; a September 1937 obituary in a Wyoming newspaper announcing the death of the "real Butch Cassidy" in Spokane. In October 1938, Phillips's widow wrote that her husband was raised back east until 1879, when he headed west at age fourteen "owing to the dime novel influence" (Pointer, p. 11). After that, he "fell in" with Cassidy, she said. Pointer concluded: "Butch Cassidy was last known to have been in South America in February 1908; William T. Phillips first appeared three months later, apparently out of thin air. Interviews with those who had known Cassidy best revealed that those who had seen Phillips . . . believed him to be Butch Cassidy" (Pointer, p. 24).

Chapter 3: The Mud Cut

General details on the Mud Cut Robbery are contained in Pinkerton files, in coverage by the *Omaha World Herald* and *Omaha News*, and in court records of the trial of the Mud Cut Gang.

83 "so diabolically daring . . . revere its perpetrators." Kansas City Times, September 27, 1872.

83 "As for the old time Oklahoma outlaw . . . the cast-iron breed they were." Jon E. Lewis, *The Mammoth Book of the West*, p. 270.

83 "Inspector Thomas Byrnes . . . the self-made man." Byrnes's views of the criminals he pursued were first printed in Thomas Byrnes, *Professional Criminals of America, 1886* (New York: Chelsea House, 1969), and quoted in Charles E. Silberman, *Criminal Violence, Criminal Justice*, p. 34–35.

84 "all leaders should be exterminated. . . . my head nearly split with pain." Quoted in Edward Robb Ellis, *Echoes of a Distant Thunder*, p. 55.

84 "proletariat's artillery." American anarchists at the turn of the century saw dynamite in the same vein as the Winchester Model 1873, the "rifle that won the West"; it was an equalizer, allowing lone revolutionaries to fight back against the forces marshaled against them in ways not previously realized. "One man armed with a dynamite bomb is equal to one regiment of militia," warned the *Alarm*, the anarchist journal of Chicago. "Dynamite is the emancipator!" claimed the *Nemesis* of Baltimore. "In the hand of the enslaved it cries aloud: 'Justice or— annihilation!' " See J. Anthony Lukas, *Big Trouble*, p. 64.

85 "About an hour . . . train robbers are not fools." Charles Siringo, *A Cowboy Detective*, p. 506.

88 "equal to about $1.29 million in today's dollars." This and all later conversions to present-day, or inflation-adjusted, dollars are calculated by using a "Dollar Adjuster" developed by Professor Robert Sahr of the Oregon State University Political Science Department and included in the Resources section of the *Columbia Journalism Review*'s site on the World Wide Web, URL:http://www.cjr.org.

95 "By noon, editorials screamed . . . in this modern age!" Omaha World-Herald, May 23, 1909, and *Omaha Daily News*, May 23, 24, 25, 1909. The newspaper reports of the robbery, arrest, and trial—and especially of the evidence—were extremely haphazard and often inaccurate, a problem that affected accounts of the robbery and of Frank Grigware's role that appeared throughout the nation and Canada in 1910 and 1934, as well as the few contemporary articles and video reenactments. The descriptions that follow are a synthesis drawn as accurately as possible from various sources, including trial testimony and federal records.

96 "A mail clerk . . . to watch out for suspicious cars." Tommy R. Thompson, "The Great Omaha Train Robbery of 1909," *Nebraska History* 63(2):217 (summer 1982).

96–97 "do everything in its power to get the bandits." Omaha Daily News, May 23, 1909.

97 "considerable strides . . . engaged in the game." Omaha World-Herald, May 27, 1909.

97 "hundreds of callers . . . 'excited imaginations.' " Omaha World-Herald, May 25, 1909.

97 "he spotted a dark red car . . . on the night of the robbery." Omaha World-Herald, May 27, 1909.

97 "One of the party done all the talking . . . they were strangers to me." Statement of Henry Smith, barkeeper, South Omaha Stock Exchange, Omaha, Nebraska, May 25, 1909. *Mud Cut Robbery* file, Union Pacific archives, Omaha, Nebraska.

97 "considered quite tough . . . was connected to the Postal Department sometime ago." Union Pacific memo, *Mud Cut Robbery* file, Union Pacific archives.

98 "a stranger with 'dark complected hair . . . close watch was made.' " Union Pacific memo, *Mud Cut Robbery* file, Union Pacific archives.

98 "to keep on working . . . Pinkerton's shrewdest operatives." Omaha World-Herald, May 25, 1909.

99 "it was also becoming . . . Murder Central." Chicago was well on its way to such infamy by the late nineteenth century. According to early Justice Department statistics, Chicago's murder rate had quadrupled by 1885, outstripping the city's population growth. By 1893, one in eleven Chicago residents was arrested for some crime.

100 "The great myth of a pure Gaze . . . of the singular events that occurred." Michel Foucault, The Birth of the Clinic, pp. 114–115.

100 "After the murder of a bank teller . . . had named him 'The Eye.'" Time-Life Books and Paul Trachtman, The Gunfighters, p. 73.

100–101 "Operatives were methodical and scientific plodders . . . flew into a towering rage." The details of Pinkerton's character come from many sources, but the specific quotes are contained in Lukas, Big Trouble, p. 80–81.

101 "I shall not give up . . . knife to the hilt." Ibid., p. 78.

102 "It was kidnapping . . . but the ends justified the means." Ibid., p. 79.

102 "As did all vigilantes . . . into their mirror image." Richard Slotkin, The Fatal Environment, p. 136–37.

104 "the arrest of 'Old Bill' Miner . . . 'I guess it's all up with me now,' he said." James D. Horan and Howard Swiggett, The Pinkerton Story, p. 74.

105 "weave together the bits and pieces of crime." James D. Horan, The Pinkertons, p. 515.

105 "Is an inveterate tobacco chewer . . . can shoot equally good with right." Horan and Swiggett, The Pinkerton Story, p. 248.

106 "As soon as Cassidy entered . . . hideout with the native population." Time-Life Books and Paul Trachtman, The Gunfighters, p. 93.

106 "IBM's early punch-card technology." See Edwin Black, IBM and the Holocaust: The Strategic Alliance Between Nazi Germany and America's Most Powerful Corporation. Black alleges that IBM gave the Nazis the means to cross-index the names, addresses, genealogy charts, and bank accounts of citizens that made the Holocaust possible.

106 "I rule my office . . . I must have my own way of doing things." Horan, The Pinkertons, p. 516.

107 "Never has the private detective been used to such an extent . . . among workingmen." Quoted in Lukas, Big Trouble, p. 82.

107 "The lone detective was . . . 'treated as a piece of machinery.'" Quoted and paraphrased from Siringo in Slotkin, Gunfighter Nation, p. 221.

108 "The question might be asked . . . against a cyclone to stop its force." Charles Siringo, Two Evils Isms: Pinkertonism and Anarchism, ed. by Charles D. Peavy, pp. 4–5.

Chapter 4: The Sweatbox

General details of the investigation of Frank and the others come from daily newspaper coverage in the competing Omaha newspapers and from the Pinkerton files.

115 The story of Downer's arrest and his stop for a drink was related during an interview with one of the surviving policemen in the *Toronto Daily Star*, April 12, 1934.

116 "The Idaho Statesman, when reporting . . . 'close questioning' to determine guilt or innocence." Idaho Statesman, quoted in J. Anthony Lukas, *Big Trouble*, p. 59.

116–117 "In Beaufort, North Carolina . . . at more than one whipping." Quoted in Edward Robb Ellis, *Echoes of a Distant Thunder*, p. 106.

121 "They all 'looked guilty,' . . . signs that also indicate tuberculosis." Omaha World-Herald, May 29, 1909.

121 "He apparently did not smoke . . . an unnamed minority." Omaha Daily News, May 29, 1909.

125 Jack Golden's letter to Jim Grigware is quoted in the *Spokesman-Review*, November 10, 1909.

126 "a mistake that echoes down to contemporary tellings." A 1999 account of the robbery, included in the History Channel's "Big House" series about federal penitentiaries, portrayed the Mud Cut bandits as driving to and from the scene of the heist in a Model T Ford.

131 "The second visitor was the superintendent . . . 'upset him materially.' " Jack's near breakdown when viewing Frank Grigware's photo was recorded in Supt. E.E.P's report, "Denver, Wednesday, June 2nd, 1909," Pinkerton Archives.

134 "The Old Man 'smiled pleasantly . . . with no more warmth in him than a hangman's rope." Dashiell Hammett, *Red Harvest*, p. 170.

135–136 "Orchard had been placed . . . 'I am that McParland,' the old detective said." The first encounter between McParland and Harry Orchard is best described in Lukas, *Big Trouble*, pp. 174–75.

136 "You are to remain in the field until every cutthroat has paid with his life." Cleveland Moffett, "The Overthrow of the Molly Maguires: Stories from the Archives of the Pinkerton Detective Agency," *McClure's Magazine*, 1894, p. 91. World Wide Web URL:www.history.ohio-state.edu/projects/coal/mollymaguire/mollymaguires.htm.

Chapter 5: The Trial

General details of the Mud Cut trial can be found in court records, the coverage of the Omaha newspapers, and in follow-ups in 1934 by the *Toronto Daily Star*.

140–141 "Spokane detective Alexander MacDonald . . . Frank had never been in trouble before." Spokane Daily Chronicle, June 1, 3, 7, 1909.

141 "the James boys of the West." Omaha Daily News, June 3, 1909.

141 "the railroad 'never quits . . . going to be put away for keeps.' " Omaha World-Herald, June 13, 1909.

141 "I don't care to say . . . the left flank of an antique pack mule." *Spokesman-Review*, June 2, 1909.

144 "I know that my son has done nothing wrong. . . . There must be some terrible mistake." Spokesman-Review, June 4, 1909.

146–147 "One of the mail clerks, Fred Eastman . . . 'too much for our nerves.' " *Edmonton Journal*, April 14, 1934. The accounts of the trial suffer from the same malady as those of the investigation: the passage of time. Trial transcripts are not complete, the appellate court summary often stored by the court instead. The newspapers often give conflicting accounts. In this case, the testimony of Eastman and account of Niles are culled from interviews and recollections twenty-five years later.

149 " 'Miss Stevenson is rather a pretty woman' . . . read about the holdup in the Denver paper." *Spokesman-Review*, November 10, 1909.

149 "I heard them planning some job . . . in a Denver restaurant." Omaha World-Herald, June 5, 1949.

154 "practically the say of how the reward money shall be split." *Omaha World-Herald*, May 31, 1909.

156 "go to the limit . . . in the cases of Grigware and Golden." *Omaha World-Herald*, November 12, 1909.

156 "By then Charles Goss's term had expired. . . . [Howell] did his duty and won." Prosecutor Frank Howell, later a justice on the Nebraska Supreme Court, described his dilemma in an interview in the *Toronto Daily Star*, April 14, 1934.

Chapter 6: A Kind of Prophecy

The history of Leavenworth and details of its daily operation come from penitentiary files held in the National Archives in Washington, D.C., and Kansas City, Missouri, as well as in the archives of the U.S. Bureau of Prisons. This includes both files and the annual reports of Leavenworth penitentiary, 1901–10.

159 "Little is known about the early prison rail cars today." John Kobler, *Capone*, p. 365.

160 "They grazed in fields separated by crumbling stone fences." In 1867, the federal government passed a law abolishing open range, forcing farmers and ranchers to fence their land. They were paid 40 cents per rod, the equivalent of 16½ feet, to build and keep a 4½ foot high fence. Since 320 rods equaled one mile, a landowner could make $128 per mile of fence, confirmed by the U.S. Census Bureau, the equivalent of $1,325 in today's dollars.

164 "In the prison lived at least 887 inmates of all races." By Thanksgiving 1909, there were 504 white, 303 blacks, 68 Indians, 9 Mexicans, and 3 Asians (Chinese and Japanese). Immigrant prisoners were born in Austria, Canada, Denmark,

China, England, France, Germany, Greece, Hungary, Ireland, Italy, Japan, Mexico, New Zealand, the Philippines, Poland, Romania, Russia, Sweden, and Switzerland. The countries most represented in Leavenworth in 1909–10 were Italy with 32 native sons and Germany with 12. *Annual Report of the United States Penitentiary, Leavenworth, Kansas, for the fiscal year ending June 30, 1910.*

164 "most daring holdup in the West." Leavenworth Times, November. 20, 1909.

166 "Frank as 6768, Matthews as 6769, Jack as 6770, Fritz as 6771, and Dan as 6772." Leavenworth Annual Report, June 30, 1910. The next lifer to be admitted to Leavenworth arrived six days after Frank, on November 25, 1909; Robert Gilland, 6777, was convicted of murder.

167 "broader view of life . . . into this wicked world." "Report of Chaplain," *Leavenworth Annual Report June 30, 1910*, p. 43.

168–169 The stories of prisoners 3701, 4002, 5846, and 5657 are contained not in official documents but in the letter of Thomas Kating to President Woodrow Wilson, April 20, 1913, cited in Notes to the Prologue.

171 "the greatest reform . . . freedom at the earliest moment he was capable of returning to society." *Leavenworth Times*, February 25, 1897.

172 "McLaughry worried about credits and debits, not lofty ideals."A good example of McLaughry's parsimony can be seen in his worries about rising food costs. In 1903, when the Missouri River flooded and washed out his farm crops, he warned Washington that his food bill would be higher. It wasn't. The daily cost of subsistence for fiscal year 1903 was 11 cents per prisoner, compared to 10.7 cents per man in fiscal year 1904.

173 "Turn it on him, men! . . . turn it on him!" Kating's letter to Wilson, p. 19.

174–175: *"His accompanying paper. . . . 'The extremities of criminals are often deformed.'"* From Arthur MacDonald, "Statistics of Crime, Suicide, Insanity, and Other Forms of Abnormality," pages 1, 65, 67, & 72. MacDonald's report is found in *The Congressional Record*, 57th Congress, no. 11, v. 2, serial 4417.

175–176 "Such obsessive classification indicated another stream . . . observed, codified, and controlled." Paraphrased from the works of Michel Foucault, but most specifically from Michel Foucault, *Discipline and Punish: The Birth of the Prison*, trans. by Alan Sheridan.

176–178 Although mention of the William West mix-up is included in many sources, the encounter between West and the admissions clerk seems most fully documented in Eugene B. Block, *Fingerprinting*, p. 17–19.

179 "Many habitual criminals . . . in line with the law." Leavenworth Annual Report, June 30, 1906, p. 4–5.

Chapter 7: The Rules of the Game

The specifics of Frank's stay in Leavenworth were reconstructed from prison coverage in the *Leavenworth Times* as well as the prison files of Frank Grigware, Tom Kating, Arthur Hewitt, John Gideon, Bob Clark, and Theodore Murdock.

188 "start and stop new coin designs with disconcerting suddenness." The gold Indian head eagles that Murdock was charged with passing in Milwaukee were a good example of the confusion caused by federal policy. The coin's initial issue in 1907 did not carry the motto IN GOD WE TRUST on the back, a situation reversed in 1908. Instead of the ribs stamped on the edges of other coins then in circulation, put there to thwart counterfeiters, the 1907 gold eagle carried forty-six raised stars, meant to represent the existing states. As more states were admitted to the Union, more stars were added. It was easy for a counterfeiter to prosper in such conditions.

189 "He is capable of doing much good or much harm . . . if either stood in the way of his path to escape." Letter of Warden Robert W. McLaughry to Mrs. G. P. Black, June 29, 1908.

191 " 'a very shrewd and sharp villain' . . . he said, in refusing her request." Letter of Warden Robert W. McLaughry to Mrs. G. P. Black, June 24, 1908.

191 "Bob Clark had nearly been driven insane." Letter of Thomas Kating to President Woodrow Wilson, April 20, 1913.

191 "fired off a letter . . . 'the invention will not prove patentable.' " Letter of Warden Robert W. McLaughry to U.S. Attorney General George Wickersham, July 8, 1909.

191 "guessed he would not run anymore." Letter of Kating to President Wilson.

192–193 "A great deal depends upon the characters . . . do not tend to elevate." Letter of F. H. Tyree to R. V. LaDow, April 26, 1910.

194 "darkness, threat, ruin . . . frightful inscriptions." Francesco Milizia, *Principi di architettura civile* (Venezia, 1785), II, pp. 227–28.

195 "Countries notorious for the severity of punishments . . . were committed." Cesare Beccaria, *Dei delitti e delle pene*, quoted in Thomas Laqueur, "Festival of Punishment," *London Review of Books* 22:19 (October 5, 2000) p. 18.

198 "inmates dug railroad tunnels . . . surviving at most ten years." Paul W. Keve, *Prisons and the American Conscience: A History of U.S. Federal Corrections*, p. 21.

198 "I have seen men brought out . . . scraped off by someone else." James W. French, quoted in *Proceedings of the Annual Congress of the National Prison Association of the United States, 1897*, p. 211.

199–200 " 'Don't you dread to leave' ". . . . " 'Sell hogs, buy clothes,' " Lincoln Wolf exulted. Leavenworth Times, Dec. 21, 1909.

203 "He is a large, good-natured prisoner . . . may result in his escape." Letter of Robert W. McLaughry to George Wickersham, November 25, 1911.

203 "To Hewitt's mother he wrote that Arthur . . . associated with 'evil disposed prisoners.' " Letter of Robert W. McLaughry to Mrs. J. P. Hewitt, March 9, 1911.

204 "If you get a foot out of line . . . that is my orders from the warden." Kating's letter to President Wilson.

Chapter 8: The Clockwork Train

Accounts of the escape, the events leading up to it, and the hunt for the fugitives are contained in the reporting of newspapers in Leavenworth, Kansas City, and Topeka, as well as in Thomas Kating's letter to President Wilson, April 20, 1913.

210 "the finest penal institution in the United States." *St. Paul Pioneer Press*, May 8, 1910.

210 "one of the strongest prisons in the world." *Topeka Daily Capitol*, April 22, 1910.

212 "Evidence suggests that Hewitt was in the Hole at the same time as a man who'd stabbed a fellow prisoner." Kating's letter to President Wilson makes brief mention of a trusty killed by another prisoner during the same period in which, according to his own prison file, Arthur Hewitt was spending time in the Hole. Attempts to find the name of the prisoner were unsuccesful; in fact, records of prisoner deaths at that time are scanty, only obliquely referred to in the physician's section of the prison's annual report, and this only in statistical data concerning type of injury or death. Thus it is hard to determine the fate of the unidentified killer, but prison rules did stipulate that the punishment for injuring or killing a fellow prisoner was isolation in the Hole. There were no executions at Leavenworth until Carl Panzran's in the 1930s.

213 "They begged McLaughry to install a switch . . . that could derail all engines." Kating's letter to President Wilson.

218 "We have been waiting . . . will take the big engine." Murdock's note to Bob Clark was reproduced in *Leavenworth Times*, April 26, 1910.

219 "Mark Twain died, as truly as it can be said of any man, of a broken heart." *Topeka Daily Capitol*, April 22, 1910.

229 "With the almost certain fact . . . their escape seems impossible." *Leavenworth Times*, April 22, 1910.

230 "Confederates on the outside had succeeded in smuggling at least two revolvers." *Kansas City Star*, April 21, 1910.

230 "Newspapers said the escape's split timing . . . 'when the guards were not watching.' " *Leavenworth Times*, April 22, 1910.

231 "seized the very opportune moment . . . we have to take chances." *Topeka Daily Capitol*, April 22, 1910.

231 TAKE NO CHANCES . . . BAD MEN. *Paul Pioneer Press*, May 8, 1910.

233 "on the verge of nervous prostration." *Leavenworth Times*, April 23, 1910.

Chapter 9: A Face in the Crowd

The tale of Frank's escape across the prairie would come years after the fact, in 1934, when he gave an account of his fugitive years to the *Toronto Daily Star* and other newspapers. Another, more detailed, version was carried in *True Detective Magazine* (January 1935), and although the details themselves correspond with those found in the newspaper accounts, it appears that the writer may have taken some stylistic license with Frank's tale. Because of that, the *True Detective* account is quoted but not extensively, since the voice does not appear to be Grigware's own.

238 "a man who was simply 'escaping from work,' not prison." *Leavenworth Times*, April 26, 1910.

239 "Entirely Humanitarian in its Application." T. L. Gross, *Manacles of the World*, p. 147.

239 "This improved shackle has been repeatedly tried . . . to prevent the escape of desperate characters." Gross, *Manacles*, ibid.

239 "Inside of three days . . . the Oregon boot had begun to cut into our legs." This and all subsequent quotes by Thomas Kating on the prisoners' treatment after the escape attempt were taken from his twenty-page letter to President Woodrow Wilson, April 20, 1913.

239 "the boot was 'light weight' and . . . 'does not hurt him so long as he walks as he should do and behaves himself.' " McLaughry's quotes are taken from his letter to James A. Finch, Pardon Attorney, Department of Justice, July 2, 1910.

239–240 "he began to complain of vague symptoms . . . the end is inevitable." Dr. Yohe's comments on Murdock's deteriorating condition were made in a letter to Thomas W. Morgan, Warden, U.S. Penitentiary Leavenworth, October 21, 1913.

240–241 "His place of concealment was not far from the prison." Although Frank's written statement about his escape and fugitive years was carried in 1934 in several Canadian newspapers, only one source seemed to address the days immediately following the breakout. This was a statement printed in one of the true crime magazines then so popular: "The Holdup of the Overland Limited," by A. C. Andersen, Inspector of Detectives, Police Department, Omaha, Nebraska, as told to T. R. Porter and Col. G. C. Porter, *True Detective Magazine* (January 1935). Contained in Pinkertons file "Mud Cut Robbery."

243–244 "To me, homesteading is the solution . . . and a home of her own in the end." Elinore Pruitt Stewart, *Letters of a Woman Homesteader*, p. 214.

246 "It was thought that they were originally called 'hoe-boys.' " From the Website "What Is a Hobo?" URL: www.angelfire.com/or/fmoritz/hobo.htm.

246 "As late as twenty years ago . . . developed into the word 'hobo.' " William Pinkerton's speeches are included on the Pinkerton's Website, "History: Yeggmen, Holdup men, Sneak Thieves, and Forgers." URL: www.pinkertons.com.

246 *Little Red Card. A Treasury of Railroad Folklore: The Stories, Tall Tales, Traditions, Ballads, and Songs of the American Railroad Man*, ed. by B. A. Botkin and Alvin F. Harlow, p. 223.

247 "three types: hoboes, who worked and wandered; tramps, who dreamed and wandered; and bums, who drank and wandered." Botkin and Harlow *A Treasury of Railroad Folklore*, p. 222, footnote.

247 "The writer Jack London . . . residents were not generous in San Marcial." Jack London, *The Road* (New York: International Magazine Co. and Macmillan Co., 1907), p. 128.

248 *For Jeff Carr*, see Glen H. Mullin, *Adventures of a Scholar Tramp*, p. 286–87.

Chapter 10: The Wanted Man

The hunt for Frank Grigware was contained in a few newspapers and in Leavenworth files, but it is almost exclusively documented in the FBI files on the fugitive.

254 "The meetings engineered by the Socialists . . . [require] more caution than more vigorous efforts." Edward Robb Ellis, *Echoes of a Distant Thunder: Life in the United States, 1914–1918*, p. 435.

255 "securing from McLaughry 'all available data.' " Bureau of Investigation memo, Kansas City office, August 8, 1910.

256 "No one could figure out why . . . he fell in with bad company." Comments of Lucille Dean Grigware, wife of James Grigware, contained in Bureau memo of July 8, 1932.

258 "He has been quite successful there and is well thought of." Ibid.

258 "the small e being finished just below the line . . . the little additional slant given the small l.": Bureau letter, Spokane office to San Antonio office, May 1, 1915.

260 "Splain was the 'mastermind of this crowd.' " Bureau memo, September 5, 1914.

260 "he had 'no doubt that Splain and Grigware are corresponding.' " Bureau memo, April 1, 1914.

260 "pay a snitch the 'lowest practical compensation' to get close to Splain." Bureau memo, March 17, 1914.

262 "a girl who answered the description of Alice Evans . . . come out and mail a letter." Bureau memo, August 29, 1910.

263 Alice had once told him that Frank 'had a rich uncle in the lumber business' " Bureau memo, October 23–29, 1910.

263: "When a man is robbed . . . see if he made connection with the officers." Bureau memo, September 5, 1911.

263–264 "That day, he told his handlers . . . he will be killed before he goes back to the penitentiary." Bureau memo, September 6, 1911.

264: "The statement . . . a woman in a house of prostitution at Waco." Bureau memo, April 14, 1913.

264 "Agents found a Mrs. Alice Evans . . . a clerk in one of the big stores." Bureau memo, February 1915.

266 "War is the health of the State . . . coercing into obedience the minority." from "The State," an unfinished essay by Randolph Bourne. Excerpted in the Website, "Randolph Bourne—Quotations." URL: www.bigeye.com/rbquotes.htm.

266 "a new broom." Jack Cope, Prisoner # 72485, *1300 Metropolitan Avenue: A History of the United States Penitentiary at Leavenworth, Kansas*, p. 39.

267 "buy a tub full of ice cream." A. C. Andersen, "The Holdup of the Overland Limited," *True Detective Magazine*, January, 1935. Contained in Pinkertons' file "Mud Cut Robbery."

269 "barely possible Grigware may show up . . . necessary expenses incurred." Letter from R. E. Mason to A. V. Anderson, October 26, 1920, Grigware file, National Archives.

269 "Grigware was seen in Spokane . . . in the robes of a Catholic priest." Bureau memo, July 20, 1922.

270 "With the arrest was revealed a tragedy . . . seldom, if ever, seen." Unidentified newspaper, March 4, 1915, Pinkerton file "Grigware."

271 "He had a reputation of being a remarkably competent . . . a sensation in Carbondale." *Philadelphia Public Ledger*, May 24, 1921.

272 *WE ARE FRANK TO SAY. . . . O'BOYLE IS CAPABLE OF PULLING IT.* Cable of Harry Kegler, Chief of Carbondale Police, to Warden A. V. Anderson, U.S. Penitentiary Leavenworth, May 23, 1921. In "Mud Cut Robbery" file, Union Pacific archives.

274–275 "During the 'long hot summer' of that year . . . arson left more than a thousand black Chicagoans homeless." Samuel Walker, *Popular Justice: A History of American Criminal Justice*, pp. 164–65.

275–276 "In the Justice Department . . . a milestone of political and social control." Anthony Summers, *Official and Confidential: The Secret Life of J. Edgar Hoover*, p. 34.

276 "Now began . . . 'the sorriest episode in the history of our country.' " Judge Lawrence Brooks, quoted in Summers, *Official and Confidential*, p. 35.

276–277 "Wall Street Junkers . . . 'the gentry who are today wrapped up in the American flag.' " Quoted in Edward Robb Ellis, *Echoes of Distant Thunder: Life in the United States, 1914–1918*, p. 447.

277 "Emotion had replaced all reason . . . trampled under foot, submerged, forgotten," All quotes from Ellis, *Echoes of Distant Thunder*, p. 459.

277–278 "This investigation having been dormant for several years . . . any inkling of the present activity." Bureau memo, August 14, 1928.

Chapter 11: A Man of Substance

The outline of Frank's fugitive years comes primarily from the *Edmonton Journal, Toronto Daily Star*, and, to a certain extent, *True Detective Magazine.*

282 "the present opportunity would never occur again." Bill McKee and Georgeen Klassen, *Trail of Iron: The CPR and the Birth of the West, 1880–1930*, p. 139.

285 "That the U.S. are bound finally to absorb . . . 'everything that is in sight.' " Quoted in ibid., p. 14.

286 "A new consciousness . . . the taste of blood in the jungle." Howard Zinn, *The Twentieth Century: A People's History*, p. 3.

288 "the men 'work like horses, eat like hogs . . .' eating twenty seven breakfast sausages." Don Beers, *Jasper-Robson: A Taste of Heaven*, p. 210.

Chapter 12: The Net

The record of Frank's sojourn in Jasper is contained in the *Toronto Daily Star*, the *Edmonton Journal*, and *True Detective Magazine*, while the hunt for the fugitive and his discovery are chronicled in FBI files and the files of the Canadian National Archives in Ottawa.

308 "death by Depression." Pierre Berton, *The Great Depression: 1929–1939,* p. 209.

308 "A migrant worker in Cabri, Saskatchewan. . . . despair over the loss of his farm." Ibid, p. 210.

308 "The stories never focused. . . . People got leaner and more close-mouthed with each passing day." The plight of the middle class was captured best in "Broke at Fifty-Five," by Frank G. Moorhead, *Nation,* (May 13, 1931), pp. 528–30.

310 "Mackenzie King promises you conferences. . . . Which plan do you like best?" Quoted in Kenneth McNaught, *The Pelican History of Canada,* p. 247.

312 "The social violence that began in 1866 . . . to John Dillinger and Charles 'Pretty Boy' Floyd." This bloodline of outlaws was first delineated in Western historian Paul Wellman's *A Dynasty of Western Outlaws.* Its abbreviated form can be found in Jon E. Lewis, *The Mammoth Book of the West,* p. 289–293.

314 " 'I almost did it once,' he'd bragged. . . . 'starts to attack officer of the law.' " Robert Carter, "Boys Going Nowhere," *New Republic,* March 8, 1933, p. 92–95. Reprinted in *The Strenuous Decade: The Social and Intellectual record of the Nineteen-Thirties,* ed. by Daniel Aaron and Robert Bendiner, p. 50.

314 "We were rounded up . . . to keep them out of Atlanta." Carter, "Boys Going Nowhere," p. 51.

317 "Humbly recognizing the responsibilities . . . making each assignment a masterpiece." Quoted in Anthony Summers, *Official and Confidential: The Secret Life of J. Edgar Hoover,* p. 46.

317 "One agent remembered . . . 'our serious and hard-working instructors.' " William C. Sullivan with Bill Brown, *The Bureau: My Thirty Years in Hoover's FBI,* p. 17.

319 "It was an offense for which "the offender is seldom shot on the spot.' " Fred J. Cook, *The FBI Nobody Knows,* p. 188.

319 "rather superficial." Letter from Hoover to Seattle office, January 8, 1931.

320 "raging that revolutionaries be crushed under 'the iron heel of ruthlessness.' " Quoted in Pierre Berton, *The Dionne Years: A Thirties Melodrama,* p. 72.

320 "Emerson's dictum, that an institution was 'the lengthened shadow of one man.' " Summers, *Official and Confidential,* p. 50.

321 "his extended family in Michigan . . . considered Frank a 'family disgrace.' " Bureau letter, May 22, 1929.

321 "a search of the records. . . . in the Canadian Army, the fingerprints are not taken of soldiers." Bureau memo, Buffalo, N.Y., office, August 2, 1929.

322 "Paul Deford was a drinking man . . . 'it was to be greatly discounted that he had been told anything of the kind.' " Bureau memo, Detroit office, March 30, 1933.

324 "If it is not too much trouble . . . around Edmonton or is even there?" Letter of D. H. Dickason to RCMP, January 30, 1930.

Chapter 13: The Ends of Justice

The daily chronology of Frank's ordeal was covered most extensively by the Canadian newspapers, while the reaction of Hoover and his agents is contained in the FBI files. In addition, Frederick Griffin's *Variety Show* contains the newsman's impressions of Frank and an account of Griffin's experiences in America.

333 "When they had restored Mrs. Fahey . . . he had left it 24 years ago." *Spokesman-Review*, April 15, 1934.

336 'some of the most imaginative writings of Dickens or Victor Hugo." *Toronto Daily Star*, March 29, 1934.

337 "The lives of children are a bigger concern in Canada than profits." Quoted in Berton, *The Dionne Years*, p. 74.

337 "Weeping and holding her dazed husband . . . 'whither thou goest I will go.' " James D. Horan and Howard Swiggett, *The Pinkerton Story*, p. 78.

339 "The 'Faheys' have won the fullest sympathy. . . . a cultured, attractive woman of pleasing personality." *Edmonton Journal*, March 29, 1934.

347 "the experience, the quickened living, the freshness of interest." Griffin, *Variety Show*, p. vii.

348 "John Francis Grigware. . . ." The confusion about Frank's given name is indicative of other problems with details in Frank's story: record-keeping was often spotty, and at times even Frank seems confused, especially when remembering whether he was twenty or twenty-three when thrown into Leavenworth. Various accounts listed Frank's given name as Francis, Francis John, or Francis Frank Grigware, born in either 1886 or 1888 on February 27, in Rush Lake, Michigan, but Michigan birth records listed him as Francis John Grigware, born February 26, 1886. This would make him twenty when he left home in 1906, twenty-three when the Mud Cut Robbery occurred in 1909, nearly two months into his twenty-fourth year when he escaped in 1910, and a month into his forty-eighth year when picked up for trapping game in 1934.

351 "Prison records showed . . . and in that way at least partially atone." Pinkerton archives, "Mud Cut Robbery" file.

352 "I was never convinced . . . he was caught in bad company." *Toronto Daily Star*, April 11, 1934.

352 "I have known for twenty years that Grigware was in Canada." Goss's tale of his supposed knowledge of Frank's whereabouts was contained in his interview with Frederick Griffin, *Toronto Daily Star*, April 10, 1934.

353 "Shoemaker was an odd choice for an ally." The strange and contentious history of Francis Henry Shoemaker, which in its own way mirrors the contentious politics of the several midwestern populist parties during the Depression, can best be found in Frederick L. Johnson, "From Leavenworth to Congress: The Improbable Journey of Francis H. Shoemaker," *Minnesota History,* spring 1989 p. 166–177.

354 "Plenty of men . . . would not be tolerated in any other country in the world." *Edmonton Journal*, April 4, 1934.

354–355 The shouting match between Judge Munger and Frederick Griffin was narrated in Griffin's story from Omaha, *Toronto Daily Star*, April 10, 1934.

360 "one of the biggest mistakes I ever made. . . . attracting too much attention to himself." Anthony Summers, *Official and Confidential: The Secret Life of J. Edgar Hoover*, p. 70. Quoted from the Cummings Papers at the University of Virginia.

361 "I am glad Dillinger was taken dead. . . . The only good criminal is a dead criminal." Summers, *Official and Confidential*, p. 78.

Epilogue: "He Should Therefore Be Considered Dangerous"

The FBI surveillance of Grigware, and his relatives after 1934 is contained exclusively in FBI files.

364 "Until that pardon is issued . . . in his own good time." *Edmonton Journal*, May 14, 1934.

Bibliography

I. Publications

Andersen, A. C., as told to T. R. Porter and Col. G. C. Porter, "The Holdup of the Overland Limited," *True Detective Magazine*, January 1935.

Bagdikian, Ben H. *Caged: Eight Prisoners and Their Keepers*, New York: Harper & Row, 1976.

Beccaria, Cesare. *Dei delitti e delle pene*, quoted in Thomas Laqueur, "Festival of Punishment," *London Review of Books*, October. 5, 2000 (22:19).

Beers, Don. *Jasper-Robson: A Taste of Heaven*. Calgary, Alberta: Highline Publishing, 1996.

Berton, Pierre. *The Dionne Years: A Thirties Melodrama*. Toronto: Penguin Books Canada, 1991.

———*The Great Depression: 1929–1939*. Toronto: Penguin Books, 1990.

Block, Eugene B. *Fingerprinting: Magic Weapon Against Crime*. New York: David McKay Co., 1969.

Botkin, B. A., and Alvin F. Harlow, eds. *A Treasury of Railroad Folklore: The Stories, Tall Tales, Traditions, Ballads, and Songs of the American Railroad Man*. New York: Bonanza Books, 1953.

Brainard, Wendell. *Golden History Tales: From Idaho's Coeur d'Alene Mining District*. Wallace, Idaho: Crow's Printing, 1995.

Carter, Robert. "Boys Going Nowhere," *The New Republic*, March 8, 1933, pp. 92–95. Reprinted in Daniel Aaron, and Robert Bendiner, eds., *The Strenuous Decade: The Social and Intellectual Record of the Nineteen-Thirties*. Garden City, N.Y.: Anchor Books, 1970.

Cook, Fred J. *The FBI Nobody Knows*. New York: Macmillan Co., 1964.

Cope, Jack, Prisoner # 72485. *1300 Metropolitan Avenue: A History of the United States Penitentiary at Leavenworth, Kansas*. Washington, D.C.: U.S. Bureau of Prisons.

Crawford, William. *Report on the Penitentiaries of the United States*. Reissued Montclair, N.J.:Patterson Smith, 1969.

Earley, Pete. *The Hot House: Life Inside Leavenworth Prison*. New York: Bantam Books, 1992.

Ellis, Edward Robb. *Echoes of a Distant Thunder: Life in the United States, 1914–1918*. New York: Kodansha America, 1975.

Fahey, John. *The Inland Empire: Unfolding Years, 1879–1929*. Seattle, Wash.: University of Washington Press, 1986.

Faith, Nicholas. *The World the Railways Made*. New York: Carroll & Graf Publishers, 1990.

Foster, Harris. *The Look of the Old West*. New York: Viking Press, 1955.

Foucault, Michel. *The Birth of the Clinic: An Archaeology of Medical Perception*, trans. A. M. Sheridan Smith. New York: Pantheon Books, 1973.

———*Discipline and Punish: The Birth of the Prison*, trans. by Alan Sheridan. New York: Vintage Books, 1995.

Gaddis, Thomas E., and James O. Long. *Killer: A Journal of Murder*. New York: Macmillan Co., 1970.

di Gennaro, Giuseppe, projects director, United Nations Social Defense Research Institute. *Prison Architecture: An International Survey of Representative Closed Institutions & Analysis of Current Trends in Design*. London: The Architectural Press, 1975.

Graham, Hugh Davis, and Ted Robert Gurr, eds. *The History of Violence in America: Historical and Comparative Perspectives*. New York: Bantam Books, 1969.

Griffin, Frederick. *Variety Show: Twenty Years of Watching the News Parade*. Toronto: Macmillan Co. of Canada, 1936.

Gross, T. L. *Manacles of the World*. St. Louis, Mo.: self-published, 1997.

Hammett, Dashiell. *Red Harvest*. New York: Vintage Books, 1992, reprinted from 1929 ed. published by Alfred A. Knopf.

Horan, James D. *The Pinkertons: The Detective Dynasty That Made History*. New York: Crown Publishers, 1967.

———, and Howard Swiggett. *The Pinkerton Story*. New York: G. P. Putnam's Sons, 1951.

Hunt, Elvid. *History of Fort Leavenworth: 1827–1927*. Fort Leavenworth, Kans.: General Service Schools Press, 1926.

Johnson, Frederick L. "From Leavenworth to Congress: The Improbable Journey of Francis H. Shoemaker." *Minnesota History: The Quarterly of the Minnesota Historical Society* 51:5, (spring 1989), pp. 166–177.

Johnston, Norman. *The Human Cage: A Brief History of Prison Architecture*. New York: Walker and Co., 1973.

Keve, Paul W. *Prisons and the American Conscience: A History of U.S. Federal Corrections*. Carbondale, Ill.: Southern Illinois University Press, 1991.

Kibler, M. Alison. *Rank Ladies: Gender and Cultural Hierarchy in American Vaudeville*. Chapel Hill, N.C.: University of North Carolina Press, 1999.

Kobler, John. *Capone: The Life and World of Al Capone*. New York: G. P. Putnam's Sons, 1971.

Kooistra, Paul. *Criminals as Heroes: Structure, Power, and Identity*. Bowling Green, Ohio: Bowling Green State University Popular Press, 1989.

Kraenzel, Carl Frederick. *The Great Plains in Transition*. Norman, Okla.: University of Oklahoma Press, 1955.

LeGaye, E. S. "Rocky." *Gold . . . ABC's of Panning*. Deming, N. M.: Carson Enterprises, 1975.

Lesy, Michael. *Wisconsin Death Trip*. New York: Anchor Books, 1973.

Lewis, Jon E. *The Mammoth Book of the West*. New York: Carroll & Graf Publishers, 1996.

London, Jack. *The Road*. New York: International Magazine Co. & Macmillan Co., 1907.

Lukas, J. Anthony. *Big Trouble: A Murder in a Small Western Town Sets Off a Struggle for the Soul of America*. New York: Simon & Schuster, 1997.

Luke, Stella. *100 Years of Mining*. (Wallace, Idaho: self-published in cooperation with the Mining Museum of Wallace, 1998.

MacDonald, Arthur. "Statistics of Crime, Suicide, Insanity, and Other Forms of Abnormality," in *The Congressional Record*, 57th Congress, no. 11, v. 2, serial 4417.

Maclean, Norman. *Young Men and Fire*. Chicago: University of Chicago Press, 1992.

McKee, Bill, and Georgeen Klassen. *Trail of Iron: The CPR and the Birth of the West, 1880–1930*. Vancouver, B.C.: Douglas & McIntyre, 1983.

McNaught, Kenneth. *The Pelican History of Canada*. London: Penguin Books, 1969.

McPhee, John. *Rising from the Plains*. New York: Farrar, Straus & Giroux, 1986.

Milizia, Francesco. *Principi di architettura civile*. Venezia, 1785, II.

Moffett, Cleveland. "The Overthrow of the Molly Maguires: Stories from the Archives of the Pinkerton Detective Agency." *McClure's Magazine*, 1894, pp. 90–100.

Moorhead, Frank G. "Broke at Fifty-Five." *The Nation*, May 13, 1931, pp. 528–530.

Mullin, Glen H. *Adventures of a Scholar Tramp*. New York: Century Co., 1925.

Needham, Gordon. *Official Map and Handbook of the Coeur d'Alene Mines and Needham Family Memoirs*. Portland, Oreg.: 1888, reprinted 1988.

Pointer, Larry. *In Search of Butch Cassidy*. Norman, Okla.: University of Oklahoma Press, 1977.

Proceedings of the Annual Congress of the National Prison Association of the United States, 1895, 1897, 1902, 1903, 1904. Pittsburgh: Shaw Bros. On file at the American Prison Association, XXX, MD.

Roffman, Peter, and Jim Purdy. *The Hollywood Social Problem Film: Madness, Despair, and Politics from the Depression to the Fifties* (Bloomington, Ind.: Indiana University Press, 1981).

Rotman, Edgardo. "The Failure of Reform," in Norval Morris, and David J. Rothman, eds., *The Oxford History of the Prison: The Practice of Punishment in Western Society*. New York: Oxford University Press, 1998.

Sears, Roebuck & Co. Consumers Guide: Fall 1909. New York: Ventura Books, reprinted 1979.

Silberman, Charles E. *Criminal Violence, Criminal Justice*. New York: Vintage Books, 1978.

Siringo, Charles A. *A Cowboy Detective: A True Story of Twenty-two Years with a World-Famous Detective Agency*. Lincoln, Nebr.: University of Nebraska Press, 1988 (reprint of 1912 ed.).

———*Two Evil Isms: Pinkertonism and Anarchism*, ed. by Charles D. Peavy. Austin, Tex.: Steck-Vaughn Co., 1968 (reprint of 1915 ed.).

Sloane, Eric. *A Museum of Early American Tools*. New York: Ballantine Books, 1964.

Slotkin, Richard. *The Fatal Environment: The Myth of the Frontier in the Age of Industrialization, 1800–1890*. Norman, Okla.: University of Oklahoma Press, 1994.

———*Gunfighter Nation: The Myth of the Frontier in Twentieth-Century America*. New York: Atheneum Press, 1992.

———*Regeneration Through Violence: The Mythology of the American Frontier, 1600–1860*. Middletown, Conn.: Wesleyan University Press, 1973.

Smith, Bradley. *The American Way of Sex*. New York: Two Continents Publishing Co., 1978.

Smith, Henry Nash. *Virgin Land: The American West as Symbol and Myth*. New York: Vintage Books, 1950.

Stegner, Wallace. *The American West as Living Space*. Ann Arbor, Mich.: University of Michigan Press, 1987.

Stewart, Elinore Pruitt. *Letters of a Woman Homesteader*. Lincoln, Nebr.: University of Nebraska Press, 1914, (reprinted 1961).

Stover, John F. *American Railroads*. Chicago: University of Chicago Press, 1961.

Sullivan, William C., with Bill Brown. *The Bureau: My Thirty Years in Hoover's FBI*. New York: W. W. Norton & Co., 1979.

Summers, Anthony. *Official and Confidential: The Secret Life of J. Edgar Hoover*. New York: Pocket Books, 1994.

Tannahill, Reay. *Sex in History*. New York: Scarborough Books, 1982.

Thompson, Tommy R. "The Great Omaha Train Robbery of 1909," *Nebraska History: A Quarterly of the Nebraska State Historical Society* 66(2):216 (summer 1982).

Time-Life Books and Paul Trachtman. *The Gunfighters*. Alexandria, Va.: Time-Life Books, 1974.

Turner, Frederick Jackson. *The Frontier in American History*. New York: 1920.

Twain, Mark. *Roughing It*. New York: New American Library, 1980.

U.S. Bureau of Prisons. *Annual Report of the United States Penitentiary, Leavenworth, Kansas, for the fiscal year ending June 30, 1901*. Leavenworth, Kans.: Leavenworth Press, 1901.

———*Annual Report of the United States Penitentiary, Leavenworth, Kansas, for the fiscal year ending June 30, 1906*. Leavenworth, Kans.: Leavenworth Press, 1906.

———*Annual Report of the United States Penitentiary, Leavenworth, Kansas, for the fiscal year ending June 30, 1910*. Leavenworth, Kans.: Leavenworth Press, 1910.

———*Handbook of Correctional Institution Design and Construction*, 1949.

Walker, Samuel. *Popular Justice: A History of American Criminal Justice*. New York: Oxford University Press, 1980.

Wharton, Charles S. *The House of Whispering Hate*. Chicago: Madelaine Mendelsohn, 1932.

Wister, Owen. *The Virginian*. New York: Macmillan Co., 1902 (reprinted in Pocket Books edition, 1972).

Zinn, Howard. *The Twentieth Century: A People's History*. New York: Harper & Row, 1984.

II. Newspapers

A. In the United States
   Kansas City Star
   Kansas City Times
   Leavenworth Times
   New York Times
   Omaha Daily News
   Omaha World-Herald
   St. Paul Pioneer Press
   Spokane Daily Chronicle
   Spokesman-Review
   Topeka Daily Capitol
   Topeka State Journal
   Topeka State Ledger
B. In Canada
   Calgary Herald
   Edmonton Journal
   Toronto Daily Star

III. Government Sources, Archives, and Museums

Alberta Genealogical Society, Edmonton, Alberta
Alberta Family Histories Society, Calgary, Alberta
American Correctional Association, Lanham, Maryland
Federal Bureau of Investigation, Washington, D.C.
Jasper Historical Society, Jasper, Alberta, Canada
Kansas Historical Society, Topeka, Kansas
Leavenworth County Historical Society, Leavenworth, Kansas
Museum of Northern Idaho, Coeur d'Alene, Idaho
National Archives, College Park, Maryland
National Archives, Kansas City, Missouri
Pinkerton's, Inc., Archives, Westlake Village, California
Port Townsend Historical Museum, Port Townsend, Washington
Shosone City Museum, Wallace, Idaho
Shosone County Recorders Office, Wallace, Idaho
Tallgrass Prairie National Preserve, Strong City, Kansas

Union Pacific Archives, Omaha, Nebraska
U.S. Bureau of Prisons Archives, Washington, D.C.

IV. The World-Wide Web

Columbia Journalism Review, "Dollar Adjustor." URL: www.cjr.org.
History Channel. URL: www.historychannel.com.
Pinkerton's, "History: Yeggmen, Holdup men, Sneak Thieves and Forgers." URL:
    www.pinkertons.com.
"Randolph Bourne—Quotations." URL: www.bigeye.com/rbquotes.htm.
"What Is a Hobo?" URL: www.angelfire.com/or/fmoritz/hobo.htm.

V. Films and Videos

"The Big House," production of the History Channel.

Acknowledgments and Sources

T ACKLING A PROJECT like this—with its foot in three centuries and two nations—made me appreciate the legwork of both the operatives of the old Pinkerton's National Detective Agency and the agents of the U.S. Bureau of Investigation (later the FBI); it also gave me a better understanding of the miles Frank Grigware put behind him in his flight from those efficient minions of the law. America and Canada are huge nations, epic in scope and history, which we often forget in this age of instantaneous international communication. One feels insignificant beneath the endless sky of the prairie, the mountains that loom up suddenly on the landscape, the violent and hypnotic storms that sweep across the miles. Every American should take a journey like Frank's at least once: it puts us in touch with our past, and it's good to be humbled every once in a while.

This book would not have been possible without the help of some very knowledgeable people in many different walks of life. Leavenworth Penitentiary no longer stores its own historical records, but Robert Bennett, executive assistant to the warden, was helpful with suggestions on where to find such information. Pete Earley, author of *The Hot House*, one of the best books I've seen on contemporary prison life, and Paul Keve, author of *Prisons and the American Conscience*, an essential sourcebook on the history of American prisons, were both generous with tips and with their time. Pierre Berton, an author who's something of an institution in Canada, was helpful in locating information on journalist Frederick Griffin. In Jasper, Jack and Barbara Pugh and Phyllis Jeffrey were friendly and open with their memories of Jasper in another era; especially helpful was Dwain Wacko, owner of Jasper's Chaba Theatre, who not only provided information and photos of the Depression-era movie emporium but also gave excellent directions to Trapper's Creek, where Frank set his traps but found that he'd actually caught himself. For their aid in extremely specialized fields I'd like to thank: Frederick Johnson, for information and the use of his article on populist firebrand Francis Henry Shoemaker; magic-meister and escape artist Mike Carnevale, for information on the Oregon Boot; and my old friend and colleague Earl Swift, for helping me figure out the hidden secrets of several important maps.

Frank Grigware's family and relations were also generous in providing information and helping me figure out Frank's character. In the United States, there were many Grigwares who answered my questions about their fugitive ancestor, but most of all I'd like to thank Linda Hernandez and her family in Renton, Washington; Joseph Grigware of Littleton, Colorado, for the use of his reams of genealogical research; and Kay Werner, granddaughter of Frank's brother James, in Newport, Washington. I would especially like to thank Marie Paramteau, Frank Grigware's youngest daughter, and Marie's daughter, Joann Pavich, both in Grande Prairie, Alberta. Marie was reluctant to talk, but considering all that had been written about her father in the press, especially the American press, I can't say I blame her. What she did say, however, about her parents was both illuminating and invaluable. Perhaps this book can help salve some of the old wounds.

The vast majority of the information in this book, however, was found in archives throughout the United States and Canada, and I'd like to thank several archivists and librarians who smoothed my way. Most of all I'd like to thank Anne Diestel, archivist for the U.S. Bureau of Prisons, and Mark Corriston, head archivist at the National Archives, Central Plains region, Kansas City, Missouri; both provided information that proved to be the bedrock of Frank's saga. I'm also indebted to Alice Finns, director of publications for the American Correctional Association, Lanham, Maryland; Fred Romanski, Civilian Records archivist at the National Archives, College Park, Maryland; Glenda Cornforth, archivist at the Jasper Yellowhead Museum and Archives, Jasper, Alberta; Winnie Lichtenwalter at the Leavenworth Research Library, Leavenworth, Kansas; John Amonson, director of the Shosone City Museum in Wallace, Idaho; Don Snoddy, archivist for the Union Pacific Railroad in Omaha, Nebraska; Jane Adler, archivist for Pinkertons, Inc., in Venice, California; Norma Wolowyck, at the Alberta Genealogical Society; Adeline Northey, news librarian at the *Edmonton Journal*; and the news librarian I only know as Marian for the *Toronto Daily Star*. The kind people at the Leavenworth County Historical Society, the National Archives of Canada in Ottawa, Ontario, and the Freedom of Information section of the Federal Bureau of Investigation also have my thanks.

SPECIAL THANKS GOES to the staff of the Thurber House in Columbus, Ohio, where I was visiting writer in spring 2001 and where I put the final polish on this book. Trish, Laura, Elizabeth, Pam, Kyle, Michael, and Donn, were excellent housemates, and Chuck, Gloria, and Emily kept everything running smoothly. Although I was told to watch out for the resident ghost, I never saw him; perhaps that's just as well. I'd like to thank him for remaining peaceful during my visit and not stomping around on the stairs outside my little garret apartment.

AS ALWAYS, I'D like to thank my editor, Philip Turner, and my agent, Noah Lukeman, without whom this book would not have been possible. And, of course, I'd like to thank Kathy and Nick for enduring my moods during the long hours of writing.

Index

('n' indicates an endnote)